THE NATION-STATE IN QUESTION

THE NATION-STATE
IN QUESTION

Edited by
T. V. Paul, G. John Ikenberry,
and John A. Hall

PRINCETON UNIVERSITY PRESS   PRINCETON AND OXFORD

Copyright © 2003 by Princeton University Press
Published by Princeton University Press, 41 William Street,
Princeton, New Jersey 08540
In the United Kingdom: Princeton University Press, 3 Market Place,
Woodstock, Oxfordshire OX20 1SY
All Rights Reserved

Library of Congress Cataloging-in-Publication Data

The nation-state in question / edited by T. V. Paul, G. John Ikenberry,
and John A. Hall.
p.   cm.
Includes index.
ISBN 0-691-11508-7 (alk. paper) — ISBN 0-691-11509-5
(pbk. : alk. paper)
1. National state.   2. Nationalism.   3. Globalization.
I. Paul, T. V.   II. Ikenberry, G. John
III. Hall, John A., 1949–

JC311.N2766   2003
320.1 — dc21   2002193076

British Library Cataloging-in-Publication Data is available

This book has been composed in Sabon

Printed on acid-free paper. ∞

www.pupress.princeton.edu

Printed in the United States of America

1   3   5   7   9   10   8   6   4   2

10   9   8   7   6   5   4   3   2   1

Contents

Illustrations

FIGURES

TABLES

Preface

THIS VOLUME focuses on the condition of the nation-state in an era of rapid social change. Analysis is necessary given the conceptual confusion of recent years. Political scientists in the West became interested in the state in the 1970s, leading to powerful new work on revolutions, political economy, and international relations. This work had little impact on policy choices. Policymakers in the 1980s set about dismantling states, in part because they heeded more to economists than to political scientists, and in part because they listened to the voices of people in the former Soviet Union and elsewhere who had been oppressed by vicious and inefficient states. When this was linked to striking global economic change, the belief arose not just that the state should be dismantled but that it could not be reconstituted, that it had permanently lost its powers.

Times have now changed. In some areas of the world it is increasingly clear that life without a Hobbesian minimum is indeed "nasty, brutish, and short" — as in the chaos of Liberia and the Mafia control so obvious in postcommunist Belarus. Further, events in the Balkans remind us forcefully that state powers most certainly do exist, while the Asian response to the financial crisis seeks a modern state different from that of the Anglo-American variety. Accordingly, the time has come to reassess state-society relations, with reference to particular regions and to the nature of contemporary social understandings.

This volume brings together scholars working in a variety of international and comparative settings who seek to assess what states can now do, that is, to analyze the dimensions of state capacity in the contemporary era. In their respective chapters authors address the questions: what are the sources and forms of state power today? Are states retreating from their traditional functions/roles? If so, how? How are states coping with the challenges posed by globalization? Are they reactive, passive, or proactive in their responses? What determines the capacity of the state to respond and adapt? What inhibits state capacity to confront challenges? By assembling scholars from a variety of fields and regional specialties, we are able to offer an array of answers for a deeper analytic appreciation of state capacity as it is evolving today. The logic for this approach is that not all states are equal in their strength or institutional structures. We believe that a cross-regional and interdisciplinary exchange provides the highest intellectual dividends.

This book project is sponsored by the University of Montreal-McGill Research Group in International Security (REGIS) and the Christopher

Browne Center for International Politics at the University of Pennsylvania. A preliminary conference was held at the University of Pennsylvania in May 2000, followed by a second conference at McGill in November 2000. The papers were thoroughly revised in light of the discussions
and commentaries at these conferences. We are grateful for financial
support from the Security and Defence Forum, Fonds pour la Formation de Chercheurs et l'Aide a la Recherche (FCAR), and the Faculty of
Graduate Studies and Research at McGill University. Discussants at
both conferences — Thomas Callaghy, Atul Kohli, Baldev Nayar, Phil
Oxhorn, Alan Patten, Norrin Ripsman, Michael Smith, Charles Taylor,
and Robert Wade — did a great deal to improve our exchanges. Able
administrative and research assistance was provided by Bill Hogg and
Cori Sommefeldt (particularly through their help in the preparation of
the volume), Scott Silverstone, Pushkar, and Emilia Scognamiglio. We
greatly appreciate the unfailing support of our families.

THE NATION-STATE IN QUESTION

Nation-States in History

JOHN A. HALL

THE STATE — let alone the nation-state — was not at the center of attention of Western social scientists for the quarter century that followed the end of the Second World War. The defeated fascist powers seemed so close to nationalism and to statism that these forces received a bad name. The fact that victorious Western powers championed a postwar order organized around liberal ideas thereby set the intellectual agenda. From the 1970s, however, the state was "brought back in." One reason for this was that American scholars felt, for the first time, the impact of their own state — through conscription, the civil rights movement, the expanding welfare state, and government management of the economy. The return of Weberian concerns also owed a good deal to structuralist marxism: it is easy to give names of academics who moved from saying that the state was "relatively autonomous" to arguing that it was in fact wholly autonomous. The impact of scholars of this generation is still being felt, in the ongoing works of Theda Skocpol, Michael Mann, and Peter Evans. But just when it seemed that an intellectual battle had been won, putatively new circumstances arose that encouraged a reversion to societal, economistic modes of analysis — held to be superior to state-centered views. The collapse of state socialism, the Maastricht Treaty, and the freeing of financial markets suggested to many that the powers of the nation-state were under attack within a new world. The most sophisticated statements made much of a dual assault on the nation-state, from above in the form of global economic forces and from below in the form of various national or ethnic revivals.

Skepticism toward this view is now surfacing. Many hold the European Union to depend, as it always has, on the Franco-German condominium, that is, on the calculations of two major states. Equally, the power of the United States, in both economic and geopolitical terms, may well be best understood in wholly traditional terms. The terrorist attacks of 11 September 2001 put an end to to the talk of dismantling the state. Further, behind the post–Cold War spread of markets is a structure of rules and institutions that is sponsored and maintained — for better or worse — by American state power. At a more general level, there seems no reason to believe that the appeal of the nation-state has in any way diminished for those yet to experience its protection and comforts. If these are descriptive points, prescriptive considerations also come to mind. The ending of state socialism did indeed destroy a lousy — large but inefficient — form of the state, but Eastern and Central Europeans rapidly came to realize that statelessness was quite as awful a condition. What mattered was the construction of the right sort of states, that is, states that provided basic services while giving up command-administrative methods more generally. This consideration seemed to apply all the more strongly to Africa. How complacent of those in the West to imagine that "the state" was no longer needed! Perhaps a diminution of state power was possible for us, but state and nation building surely remained the key concern of the vast majority of humankind.

This volume was occasioned by these skeptical considerations — which the majority of chapters end up by endorsing. It should be stressed immediately, and very firmly, that this is not to say the contributors to this volume somehow think that the world "has not changed." Very much to the contrary, the volume as a whole charts varied responses in different issue areas and in different continents to changes in the social portfolio of late modernity. Insofar as a general view is present, it is best expressed by recalling the aristocrat in *The Leopard*, who proclaimed that it was necessary to do a great deal for everything to remain the same. The powers of the nation-state have varied, but this very variation has allowed them to survive. But that is a provisional view, and much remains to be said.

This introduction immediately highlights the theme of variation by charting and explaining changes in moods and in levels of intensity of feeling of the nation-state in the advanced world since about 1870. Attention to change is central to the analysis. It is quite as present when turning to the demise of state socialism, and to the situation of the nation-state in the South. Once this historical background has been sketched in, attention turns to underscoring the contributions made by the authors of this volume.

THE POLITICS OF MODERNITY

It may be as well to begin with, and to keep in mind, the most powerful and interesting claim made about the politics of modernity. Ernest Gellner insisted that the modern social contract comprised only two elements: a society would and *should* be seen as legitimate if it was industrialized and ruled by those co-cultural with the population as a whole.[1] It might seem that this amounts to a single force, for Gellner's claim was that nationalism derived from industrialism. In fact, Gellner draws a very useful distinction. In general, class conflict within ethnically homogeneous societies was held not to be likely to disrupt social formations. In contrast, conjoining social inequality with an "entropy-resistant" status category of one sort or another was and would likely remain genuine social dynamite. Gellner in fact had rather different emphases in his work on nationalism, but this claim — that ethnic stratification in combination with social mobilization had the power to change social relations — is one that has great force. Beyond this, it should be noted that Gellner's general view has a good deal to say about our possible politics. It cannot be highlighted enough that democracy and/or liberalism are not present as a third element of the modern social contract — even though Gellner's own substantive sociology after this initial statement focused more on the chances of extending liberty than on any other single issue. In this area Gellner liked to cite two chapters from John Stuart Mill's *Considerations on Representative Government*, first published in 1861, perhaps to underline the fact that his own troubling conclusions had an impeccable liberal pedigree. On the one hand, Mill had famously noted that representative government was not possible until the nationalities question had been solved.[2] Differently put, the conflict so dear to liberalism's heart had to be muted and seminar-addicted; that is, it had to take place within the background of consensual national homogeneity. On the other hand, Mill also insisted that the centralization of power for developmental purposes was wholly justified. It was very unlikely that "traditional" social actors would choose the benefits of sobriety and political economy: social engineering was needed in order to establish a new world. "The early difficulties in the way of spontaneous progress are so great," Mill noted, that "a ruler full of the spirit of improvement is warranted in the use of any expedients."[3] Liberal societies had been lucky, in Gellner's view, because their development took place so early; all that could be hoped for elsewhere was the possibility of liberalizing once industrialization had taken place.

Gellner himself had deeply divided feelings about all this — not surprisingly, for he was at once attuned to the inevitability and the attractions of nationalism while being equally a determined proponent of uni-

---

[1] Ernest Gellner, *Thought and Change* (London: Weidenfeld and Nicolson, 1964), chap. 2.

[2] John Stuart Mill, *Considerations on Representative Government*, in *Three Essays* (Oxford: Oxford University Press, 1975), chap. 16.

[3] Ibid., chap. 18.

versal liberal rationalism. Of course, he could not help but see things this way. He had been born in the genuinely multicultural world of German-Czech-Jewish interwar Prague, and he lived to see most of the Jews killed, the Germans expelled, and the secession of the rich majority from the Slovaks. He certainly hated the boredom of cleansed Prague in the 1990s, even though it fitted his model of nationalism as homogeneity, and he sought at a prescriptive level to find new ways in which several nations could live inside a single political shell. If this meant that Gellner was at one with his critics at the normative level, a considerable difference remained at the descriptive, sociological level. In stark, ideal-typical form, the counterargument to Gellner's socioeconomic general sociology insists that the character of social movements results overwhelmingly from the nature of the state with which they interact. There is a great deal of evidence to support this political sociology as it applies to working-class behavior.[4] Liberal states that allowed workers to struggle at the industrial level avoided creating politically conscious movements; in contrast, authoritarian and autocratic regimes so excluded workers as to give them no option but to take on the state. This general notion — that the barricades are so terrifying that reform is habitually more attractive than revolution — has large applications. The case against Gellner is that secession results more from the authoritarianism of empires than from the nature of nationalism. Liberalism before nationalism may allow for containment — that is, respect for historical liberties might allow multinational frames to exist. Voice might create loyalty and so rule out the attraction of exit.[5] Differently put, multinational entities rather than homogeneous nation-states may after all be possible. We have no wish to rule on this theoretical issue now, and we do not anyway believe — as will be seen in the emphasis to be given to international power politics — that it provides a sufficient explanatory frame. Nonetheless, it is worth noting immediately that none of the great multinational old regimes extant at the end of the nineteenth century was able to transform itself successfully. No traditional empire was able to move in a more liberal direction — which would in effect have meant becoming a constitutional monarchy. The subject that concerns us is accordingly that of rupture rather than continuity.

None of this is to suggest that we should uncritically romanticize democracy. Tocqueville long ago pointed out that majorities could in

---

[4] Michael Mann, *Sources of Social Power*. Volume Two: *The Rise of Classes and Nation-States, 1760–1910* (Cambridge: Cambridge University Press, 1993), chaps. 15, 17–19.

[5] Albert Hirschman, *Exit, Voice and Loyalty* (Cambridge: Harvard University Press, 1970).

theory be tyrannical. Whether he was correct or not about the United States, there can be no doubt that numerous instances exist—for instance, of Protestant hegemony in Northern Ireland from 1922 to 1969—in which democracy has been exercised freely and fairly, and at the expense of minorities. It is quite as relevant to note that the voice of the people in Ireland made it very difficult to establish constitutional accords capable of containing nationalism. In contrast, the absence of democracy in the Austrian Monarchy actually helped in moving toward a partial solution of the nationalities problem. The creation of Austro-Hungary in 1867 held the empire together by giving rights to the Magyars, a move that was possible only because an authoritarian ruler was prepared to abandon the minorities in the Hungarian half of the empire. It was much harder to devise a system of home rule for Ireland given Britain's parliamentary regime. If a move to home rule was made necessary by the wrecking tactics of Irish members of Parliament, political advantage could nonetheless be found by "playing the Orange Card." The powerful Protestant minority could not be ignored—indeed its salience brought Britain to the verge of civil war by 1914.[6] More generally, democratic participation is not always good in and of itself, despite the recent vogue for civil society and civic virtue. A contrast that makes the point is that between the very different postindependence fates of Malaya and Sri Lanka.[7] Social passivity in the former case was very much a part of the surprising creation and maintenance of a consociational regime that allowed Chinese and Malay to live together. Democratic participation in Sri Lanka was directed against Tamils, which is not altogether surprising given the size of state employment and of their share within it. As Tamils were geographically concentrated, exclusionary politics were possible—which then, of course, led to the countermovement violence that still continues. Equally relevant is the vibrant world of civil association in Weimar Germany. This autonomous and active group life led of course to violence in the streets. Individuals were caged within groups wholly bereft of any overarching sense of shared identity.[8]

This suggests an equally important corollary. Bluntly, democracy matters less than liberalism. Soft political rule tends to diminish social conflict for the reasons already given. Ralf Dahrendorf made essentially this point when arguing that the superimposition of different issues—of,

---

[6] Dominic Lieven, *Empire* (London: John Murray, 2000), 115.

[7] Donald L. Horowitz, "Incentives and Behavior in the Ethnic Politics of Sri Lanka and Malaysia," *Third World Quarterly* 10 (1986): 18–35.

[8] Sheri Berman, "Civil Society and the Collapse of the Weimar Republic," *World Politics* 49 (1997): 401–29.

say, a religious divide on top of a left-right division — increased the intensity of conflict.[9] Differently put, liberal regimes may achieve very great stability by diffusing various conflicts through society rather than concentrating them at the political center. Pure democratic participation will destabilize unless it is channeled through social institutions that tend to contain, manage, and regulate conflict. In this connection, a comment of Raymond Aron's offering an explanation of the disaster of Europe and modernity irresistibly comes to mind.[10] Aron blamed the debacle of the heartland of modernity on the stupidity of the old regime — whose duty he held to have been that of escorting the people into calm responsibility by the devolution of power. There is a type of truth to this: had such liberal devolution taken place, then democratic passions probably would have been civilized. But the point is in fact normative rather than descriptive and to that extent hides the truth from us. For imperial rule was — felt itself to be — fragile, based as it was on distrust of the people. Sterile, low-intensity rule was long preferred to the dangers of social mobilization. In this spirit, divide-and-rule politics were often practiced since the creation of rivalries allowed the state to gain autonomy by balancing on top of generalized hatreds. The legacy of this strategy was, as Tocqueville stressed, disastrous: a political opening was more likely to see the expression of resentments than cooperation in a common cause.[11]

These warning notes about the nature of democracy can be neatly summarized by noting Jack Snyder's recent work on nationalist violence and democratization.[12] The Balkan wars of the last years have demonstrated that democratization does not necessarily bring peace and prosperity, sweetness and light. However, the collapse of communism did not lead to violence in every instance, suggesting that attention be given to two variables. First, political leaders who imagine that a new world can only bring their downfall may well be tempted to play the nationalist card in order to stay in power: Slobodan Milosevic is such a figure — where, say, Vaclav Klaus clearly was not. Second, democracy may well lead to violence if it lacks the institutional framework that allows it to control its passions, that force it to reflect. Snyder stresses in this context that democratization clearly led to violence when news comes from a single authority. And all this is to say that in our own time a multina-

[9] Ralf Dahrendorf, *Class and Class Conflict in Industrial Society* (Stanford: Stanford University Press, 1959).

[10] Raymond Aron, "On Liberalization," *Government and Opposition* 14 (1979): 37–57.

[11] Alexis de Toqueville, *The Old Regime and the French Revolution* (New York: Anchor Books, 1955), 107.

[12] Jack Snyder, *From Voting to Violence* (New York: Norton, 2000).

tional state, even with the benefits of the purported lessons of the past, utterly failed to successfully transform itself.

LEARNING THAT LESS IS MORE

In the middle of the nineteenth century, Europe was at the pinnacle of its power, confident that it represented progress. The European balance of power depended on the interactions of Austro-Hungary, Wilhelmine Germany, Imperial Russia, Great Britain, and France. The fate of the Ottomans was very much part of the mental world of these great powers; the position of the United States came slowly to assume great significance, especially for Great Britain. If all this suggested ebbs and flows of power and influence, no indication was available as to what actually occurred. In fact, Europe in the twentieth century became the scene for a new, great Peloponnesian War—a conflict so visceral that it knocked Europe off the perch that it held briefly as the leader of the world. Mark Mazower's striking general account of Europe's twentieth century is entitled *Dark Continent*.[13] This must be the guiding sentiment when seeking to understand states within their historical context. What were the essential contours of this conflict?

The rivalry between these states was such that the most immediate structural element at work was that of the need to industrialize. An obvious consequence that troubled ruling elites was the emergence of working classes. In fact, a whole series of sectoral divisions among workers meant that no unitary class existed inside a particular state, let alone between them—at least when workers were left to themselves.[14] This was most clearly seen in the United States, where splits between respectable business unionism of the crafts contrasted with the radicalism of the International Workers of the World. Extreme repression of radicals combined with liberal treatment of the rest famously created a world in which workers began to consider themselves as middle class. Something of the same pattern had destroyed the Chartists in England, but the presence of some, albeit very limited, state interference ensured that class loyalty was created—that is, socialism was avoided but a labor party was created. In contrast, regime exclusion did create socialist class unity. Antisocialist laws in Wilhelmine Germany created a movement with political and industrial wings, formally wedded to revolutionary ideas but in fact made reformist by the speedy abolition of the laws in question. The radicalism of German workers seemed wholly

[13] Mark Mazower, *Dark Continent* (London: Allen Lane, 1998).
[14] Mann, *Sources of Social Power*, chaps. 17–19.

ridiculous and unnecessary to Max Weber, who argued that they would become a loyal part of the nation if accorded more substantial citizenship rights. The most interesting case was that of Imperial Russia.[15] Autocracy differed from authoritarianism in being at times even more suspicious of capitalism. The desire to be in control led to oscillating policies toward capitalism, which in itself helped radicalize the workers of Moscow and St. Petersburg. The fundamental factor at work, however, was regime policy. Militancy varied precisely in relation to state actions: reformists came to the fore as the result of the political opening of 1905, while revolutionaries triumphed inside the movement once concessions were abandoned. The end result of these policies was the creation of the only genuinely revolutionary working class in human history.

To consider industrialization only in terms of its impact on class would be a mistake. Every state sought an exactly similar set of industries in order to maintain its geopolitical independence, and this in turn led to economic tensions — as, for example, when the various steel industries sought to "dump" their excess product. The importance and character of imitative industrialization is captured in Gautam Sen's *The Military Origins of Industrialization and International Trade Rivalry* — not least as the author is unaware that he is speaking the language of Friedrich List rather than, as he imagines, Karl Marx.[16] Mentioning Germany as perhaps the first industrial late developer brings to attention three of the factors that do most to explain the nature of Europe's twentieth-century disaster.[17] Each factor can be seen as an extension of ideas suggested by Max Weber, namely, his views on nationalism, his role as a Fleet professor, and his views of the empire's conduct of its foreign affairs. And it should be said clearly that these factors were at work in all the countries involved. The "catch-up" economic and political policies of the end of the nineteenth century should not be seen completely as imitation of Great Britain. In the minds of contemporaries was the notion, best expressed by Tocqueville and List, that two great powers — Russia and the United States — would dominate the future. Differently put, British theorists and politicians felt that their lead might well be transient. To that end, policies seeking a Greater Britain by means of tighter links with the white dominions had enormous appeal.

[15] Timothy McDaniel, *Capitalism, Autocracy and Revolution in Russia* (Berkeley: University of California Press, 1988).

[16] Roman Szporluk, *Communism and Nationalism* (Oxford: Oxford University Press, 1988).

[17] A fourth factor, hard to pin down but of great importance, was the emergence of a purportedly scientific social Darwinist culture promoting both racialism and "the triumph of the fittest."

Developmental states characteristically felt weak when they ruled over a mass of different ethnic and national groupings. For one thing, Britain seemed to gain strength from its homogeneity, although this perception faded once home rule politics made it clear that Britain was in its way as composite a state as were other empires. Still, it is worth remembering that Max Weber's nickname in his closest circle was "Polish Max" on account of his obsessive belief that Polish workers on the East Elbian estates would weaken the German nation. For another, fiscal extraction was difficult when obeisance had to be paid to the historical liberties of particular regions—most notably, those of Hungary, used to such effect by the Magyars as to debilitate the monarchy's military arm. But the determination to copy the ethnic homogeneity of leading European powers had a further element to it, namely, that of seeking to strengthen the legitimacy of the state by playing the national card against socialism. Accordingly, nationalism comes to the fore at the end of the nineteenth century as much from above as from below. A distinction must be drawn, however, between integrating workers and immigrants, on the one hand, and nations, on the other. The former task proved relatively easy, although its full achievement in the United States was in fact much helped by participation in war. The integration of nations could be much harder. At best, peasants might be assimilated before much national awakening had taken place, as nearly happened to the Slovaks under Magyar rule. At worst, empires might contain distinct, culturally differentiated "historic nations"—notably those of Hungary and Poland. Little could be done to assimilate such peoples. The trickiest problem was posed by the newer, more invented nations, able to consolidate themselves thanks to their ability to control their own schooling system. Liberal treatment might produce a situation in which such nations, possessed of their historic rights, would consent to live under a larger political roof; illiberal treatment was likely to encourage secession.

Perhaps curiously, nationalism had not been enormously successful in the years before 1914. Geopolitical interference stood behind the cleansing of perhaps five million Muslims from the new Balkan nation-states.[18] This suggested of course that the stakes of any general conflict, should it occur, might well be very great indeed.[19] But as long as the balance of power remained in operation, nationalism had great difficulty in breaking the mold of state borders. A clear contrast can be drawn between the logic of the situations facing different empires.[20] Austro-Hungary

[18] Mark Mazower, *The Balkans* (London: Weidenfeld and Nicolson, 2000).
[19] David Kaiser, *Politics and War* (Cambridge: Harvard University Press, 1990), part 4.
[20] Lieven, *Empire*.

quite simply had no chance to become a modern nation-state: the dominant ethnicity was simply too small to serve as a *Staatsvolk*. What
evolved in consequence was a situation, in Count Taaffe's words, of
"bearable dissatisfaction."[21] If the Magyars were content, the Slavic nations within the Austrian half were not terribly treated, for all that they
hoped that the monarchy would move toward greater constitutionalism.
Demands were contained, however, by a clear awareness of geopolitical
realities. As early as 1848 the Slavs had realized that to become small
but unprotected nations was to risk annihilation should Germany or
Russia be drawn into a power vacuum. The situation in Russia was
much more complex. If the inclusion of the Poles, convinced that they
were more advanced than their masters, proved, then and later, to be
disastrous, there was realistic hope that assimilation might occur
throughout much of Central Asia. Almost everything depended upon
the Ukraine. Russians alone were a minority in the empire, but if they
combined their numbers with "the little Russians," then a majority of
sufficient size would be created to allow the formation of a nation-state.
As it happens, tsarist policy toward the Ukraine—a complete ban on
the teaching of Ukrainian—was probably mistaken.[22] For one thing,
Ukrainian could not be wiped out given the position that it had established in Austrian Galicia. For another, the Ukrainians regarded both
Poles and Germans as far worse enemies than Russians, and they would
almost certainly have been state loyal even had rights of national autonomy been granted. Finally it is worth noting that Great Britain was not
free from the pressures that faced Austro-Hungary and the Russian empire. There were in fact two British empires: the potentially Greater
Britain of the white races and the "backward peoples" who were merely
a burden.[23] Interestingly, Ireland was treated as a member of the latter
camp—with predictable results in the Curragh mutiny of 1914 and the
Easter Rising of 1916.

The second factor to be considered is best introduced by saying that
nationalism is an essentially labile force, able to connect with and
deeply influenced by the social forces of any particular historical moment. The reference to Max Weber as Fleet professor brings to attention
the crucial fact that nationalism was, in this period, linked to imperialism. There is a sense in which Weber himself should have known better.
At a conference in Vienna in 1907, his imperialist sentiments were attacked by the Austrian economist Eugen Bohm-Bawerk on the entirely
sensible grounds that Germany was becoming rich without colonies,

[21] Ibid., 191.
[22] Ibid., 278–81.
[23] John R. Seeley, *The Expansion of England* (London: Macmillan, 1885).

which were — as Adam Smith had stressed long ago — more of a millstone than an advantage. But it is often the case that what matters socially about economics are less the facts in and of themselves than what people believe to be the facts. In this case, imperial dreams had a considerable rationale. When Lord Roseberry admitted that the British Empire did not pay, he went on immediately to say that it was nonetheless absolutely necessary. If other states established protectionist policies, Britain would need imperial possessions in the future to secure not just its prosperity but its very food supply. More generally, an era of intense geopolitical competition made the idea of capitalist interdependence, of trading rather than heroism, seem very dangerous.[24] Germans tended to think of the British advocacy of Free Trade as hypocrisy given the presence of the Royal Navy: the abolition of the Corn Laws meant little, in other words, since geopolitical strength ensured that supplies could be brought from the outside. Had Weber seen the war plans being drawn up in the years before 1914 by Lords Esher and Fisher, his imperialist beliefs would have been underscored. For Britain's plan was indeed to blockade Germany so as to starve it into submission.[25]

The link between nationalism and imperialism deserves to be seen in the same light accorded to nationalism more generally — that is, as a factor creating tensions (which was likely to make war, should it occur, escalate to the extremes) without causing the onset of war. It is the third factor, the nature of foreign policy making inside imperial courts, to which attention must be given for an explanation of the breakdown of order that then allowed nationalism and imperialism to cause disaster. A preliminary, scene-setting point is simply that the late-nineteenth-century European great powers *were* engines of grandeur, whose leaders habitually wore military uniform. The difficulty that such rulers faced, however, was that making foreign policy was becoming ever more difficult. Jack Snyder has usefully suggested that foreign policy making tends to be rational when states are unitary.[26] Examples of such rational states include the rule of traditional monarchs, the collective domination of a revolutionary party so much in control of a late, late-developing society as to have no fear of popular pressure, and the checks and balances on foreign adventures provided by liberal systems. In contrast, late-developing societies — which combine authoritarianism with genuine pressures from a newly mobilized population — tend to lack the state

---

[24] Werner Sombart, *Handler und Helden* (Leipzig: Dunckler and Humbolt, 1915).

[25] Avner Offer, *The First World War: An Agrarian Interpretation* (Cambridge: Cambridge University Press, 1989).

[26] Jack Snyder, *Myths of Empire* (Ithaca: Cornell University Press, 1991). See also Mann, *Sources of Social Power*, chap. 21.

capacity necessary to calculate by means of realist principles. The contrast that needs to be made here is accordingly that between Bismarck and Kaiser Wilhelm II. The Iron Chancellor was the epitome of a rational realist calculator, in charge of every arm of the state and determined to weigh up and discriminate between different priorities. It was the essence of his policy that Germany should never allow itself to be placed in a situation where it would have to fight a war on two fronts—for such a conflict would assuredly be lost. In contrast, Kaiser Wilhelm did not regularly attend either the army or the naval councils, and he was addicted to symbols of grandeur rather than to genuine thought. More importantly, policy in the court over which he presided was often based on factions, and upon their access to key personalities. Accordingly, Tirpitz (and thereby some heavy industrialists, and even the Social Democrats) gained a *Weltpolitik*, while the more traditional officer corps gained endorsement of an Eastern policy. Such bandwagoning pleased everyone but had as its consequence Bismarck's nightmare, that is, the creation of enemies to the east and west. The feeling of encirclement that so terrified the political elite—and from which it sought to break out in 1914 by underwriting Austro-Hungary's harsh ultimatum to Serbia—was accordingly self-created. The epitome of authoritarian incapacity in the field of foreign affairs is evident in the fact that Chancellor Bethmann-Hollweg simply did not know that Germany's war plans involved invading Belgium—something that he knew would bring Britain into the war—until sometime in July 1914.

The First World War was not a Clausewitzian affair, in that statesmen lost control of policy making. Industry applied to war in part explains this, but still more important was the fact that a war of peoples needed justifications other than the merely dynastic or territorial. The chaos that resulted exhausted the European fabric. It was this factor that made the peace treaty disastrous. Differently put, the treaty was flawed less because it was harsh than because its rigors could not be sustained. Of course, the removal of both the United States and Russia from the international arena meant that balance-of-power politics was anyway likely to be hard to achieve. Further, the Wilsonian stress—amended of course by geopolitical interests—on national self-determination created exactly the unstable power vacuum in Central Europe that the Slav leaders had feared in 1848. The result of all this was thoroughly obvious. The lack of genuine geopolitical agreement encouraged the politics of economic autarchy. The failure to solve the security dilemma cemented the link between nationalism and imperialism.

To say that the way the war ended was disastrous is not for a moment to deny the birth of the two great revolutionary forces of twentieth-century Europe. One very particular development in the last tsarist years was the creation of an empire-saving intelligentsia. If the reaction to tsarist policies of forced assimilation was the creation of nationalist parties, the experience of those parties did a great deal to create — particularly among those of Jewish background — distrust of nationalizing practices sure to involve much ethnic cleansing. The first Bolshevik cadre was accordingly more than half non-Russian.[27] This development was of course not one to make the tsar feel happy: to the contrary, the empire that the Bolsheviks wished to save was to be universal and socialist rather than autocratic. So here was the creation, by military means, of a regime that offered an autarchic, socialist developmental model. Though it is unfashionable to say so, bolshevism and nazism did share key attributes — from the role of a single party emphasizing moral renewal to an obsession with economic autarchy. Still, Hitler's racism did make a difference. The Third Reich was certainly imperial in seeking *Lebensraum*, but it was not imperial in the habitual sense of contemplating ruling over multiple ethnicities. To the contrary, expulsion of aliens so as to allow resettlement by Aryans was the order of the day, making this regime historically novel and of course utterly repulsive.

There is a great deal to be said for remembering that these two revolutionary forces seemed to be the wave of the future in the interwar years, the two regimes capable of providing collective moral enthusiasm and prosperity in the face of the Depression. Only when we realize this can we make sense of the life work of John Maynard Keynes, desperately trying to salvage liberalism when the enlightened had written it off. Keynes's characteristic brilliance did enable him to predict the worm in the bud of the great revolutionary forces.[28] This had nothing to do with their ability to run their societies and economies: given the concentration of power, there was, Keynes unhappily acknowledged, every reason to believe that they could survive and prosper. But the concentration of power in the hands of sacralized leaders might well, Keynes believed, lead to geopolitical adventures. All that liberals could do was to wait for self-destruction to take place in this manner. Mercifully such proved to be the case, suggesting that in the long run the most rational way in which to conduct foreign policy is one that allows for checks and balances to prevent against disaster.[29]

The First World War ended badly despite the making of formal treaties. In contrast, the Second World War ended well without formal agree-

[27] Liliana Riga, "Identity and Empire: The Making of the Bolshevik Elite, 1880–1917" (McGill University, Ph.D. dissertation, 2000).

[28] Robert Skidelsky, *John Maynard Keynes*. Volume Three: *Fighting for Britain, 1937–46* (London: Macmillan, 2000).

[29] John A. Hall, *International Orders* (Oxford: Blackwell, 1996).

ments. What mattered most of all was consideration given to power politics, that is, the creation of a secure frame within which economic and social forces could then prosper. The central element of the structure was of course hinted at in Stalin's remark to Churchill to the effect that each side would — as was, Stalin stressed, historically normal — impose its own social system on the territories it held at the end of the war. Despite much sound and fury, that is precisely what happened: spheres of influence were established between two great superpowers, which very rapidly came to understand each other extremely well, not least because the presence of nuclear weapons forced them to be rational. Nationalism was ignored, stability achieved. This reliable, easily calculable system came to an end with the breakup of the Soviet Union, to which attention turns below. But let us consider here the transformations of the states at the heart of capitalism, most notably those in Europe.

There were two elements at work in the reconstitution of Europe.[30] Europeans themselves made a major contribution. Genuine learning had taken place in the sense that fascism was thoroughly discredited, beaten in its own chosen arena of military valor. More particularly, French bureaucrats, aware of the devastation caused by three wars with Germany within a single lifetime, effectively changed France's geopolitical calculation. If Germany could not be beaten militarily, it could perhaps be contained through love. The origin of what is now the European Union came from a decision by the two leading powers to give up their geopolitical autonomy, by establishing genuine interdependence in coal and steel — that is, in giving up the capacity to make their own weapons. This move was made possible by the second factor, the presence of American forces. Europeans of course did a great deal to pull Americans in, with Lord Ismay famously arguing that foreign policy should seek to keep the Americans in, the Russians out, and the Germans down. American presidents were in fact surprised that they were invited to establish an empire,[31] and for a long period they thought they might be able to escape from this commitment. But that never happened because Europeans realized that their security dilemma was solved by the presence of a modern Mamluk force. At times, there could be great resentments in this relationship — as when the United States, refusing to fund the Vietnam War and Great Society programs from taxes, ex-

---

[30] Charles Maier, "The Two Postwar Eras and the Conditions for Stability in Twentieth Century Western Europe," *American Historical Review* 86 (1981): 327–52; John Ruggie, "International Regimes, Transactions and Change," *International Organization* 36 (1982): 379–415.

[31] Geir Lundestad, "Empire by Invitation?" *Journal of Peace Research* 23 (1986): 263–77.

ported its inflation to its allies. But Europeans preferred to be mildly exploited and supine for the most basic of reasons: they did not trust each other.

It is important to characterize the European situation properly, as has Milward.[32] European states had sought, between 1870 and 1945, to be complete power containers, unitary and in possession of markets and secure sources of supply. The fact that this led to complete disaster produced humility—which is not to say for a moment that state power somehow lost its salience. Rather states discovered that doing less proved to give them more, that interdependence within a larger security frame allowed for prosperity and the spread of citizenship rights. Differently put, breaking the link between nationalism and imperialism enhanced rather than undermined state capacity. One needs to be a little careful at this point. For one thing, Europeans sometimes congratulate themselves rather too easily in regard to neonationalist movements. It is true that Spain represents a rare case of a state able to prosper while maintaining its multinational status. Further, the diminution of geopolitical conflict has allowed many states to be less unitary, more federal, and thoroughly interested in consociational deals. This is welcome, but in the scheme of things it stands as rather little compared to the brute facts of ethnic cleansing.[33] Liberalism in Europe, from the Atlantic to Ukraine, and including most of southeastern Europe, is made easier because great national homogeneity has been established, in largest part thanks to the actions of Hitler and Stalin. For another, suspicion needs to be shown—for all that one happens to like the policies in question— toward the view that European traditions of corporatism, through incorporating the working class within a "Keynesian world" designed to secure full employment, have been responsible for growth and stability.[34] To begin with, the mix of such policies was often incomplete. Germany had corporatism for labor but shunned Keynesian macroeconomic policies, while the reverse was true for Britain. More importantly, the ending of social contract policies in Britain did not lead, as was predicted, to any loss of social stability. To the contrary, the state found economic policy easier when it no longer had to provide beer and sandwiches for union leaders. While the continuing effect of rising prosperity for the majority cannot be ignored, it may well be the case that social stabil-

[32] Alan Milward, *The European Rescue of the Nation-State* (Berkeley: University of California Press, 1992). Cf. P. Gowan and P. Anderson, eds., *The Question of Europe* (London: Verso, 1997).

[33] Norman Naimark, *Fires of Hatred* (Cambridge: Harvard University Press, 2001); Michael Mann, "The Dark Side of Democracy," *New Left Review* 235 (1999): 18–45.

[34] Michael Smith, *Power, Norms and Inflation* (New York: Aldine de Gruyter, 1992).

ity — but not any increase in social justice — results from a measure of depoliticization.

A final word is in order about Europe in the years since the collapse of the Soviet Bloc. This fundamental change in geopolitical realities certainly played a part in key developments within the European Union, most notably that of binding Germany within Europe by avoiding any German economic hegemony through the Bundesbank. Still, continuities are more important than new developments. For one thing, this liberal democratic league has the capacity, not least given that one cannot be a member without respecting minority rights, to consolidate liberal democracies in Central Europe just as it did in Southern Europe a generation ago. For another, statist calculations remain at play: the Franco-German condominium survives, while French determination to balance Germany has led France virtually to rejoin the NATO command structure. Perhaps most important of all, there is no sign of fundamental change to the rules of the geopolitical game. The mere threat of withdrawal on the part of the United States has seen Europeans own up to the fact that they wish the American presence to continue, despite its varied imperfections. This is scarcely surprising given the lack of any common European foreign policy. Any European defense initiative will be subordinate rather than an alternative to NATO — whose commander-in-chief will remain American.[35]

THE DECLINE AND FALL OF THE SOCIALIST EMPIRE

Ideas and actions about the transformation of states have changed as the result of the collapse of the Soviet Union. Accordingly, attention must be given to what is genuinely a world historical event. As it happens, the analytic tools developed to this point do a great deal to help us understand what happened to a regime that was at once developmental, militarist, socialist, and imperial.

The period since 1989 has made crystal clear that the command-administrative developmental model was deeply flawed. Whatever the benefits of initial heavy industrialization and social modernization, there is now no doubt but that the absence of market mechanisms doomed Soviet-style economies to waste and inefficiency. There is as yet only anecdotal evidence to confirm that the way in which this led to an attempt to once again pull Russia up by its bootstraps had everything to do with the military. What mattered here was probably not the fact that

[35] G. John Ikenberry, *After Victory: Institutions, Strategic Restraint and the Rebuilding of Order after Major War* (Princeton: Princeton University Press, 2000).

Soviet defense spending was eating ever larger proportions of GDP. Rather, military leaders realized that their weapons capabilities were declining as the Soviet Union fell behind technologically. A high-technology, computer-literate society was necessary if communism was to survive. Once the power elite had made this calculation, the rule of Andropov and Gorbachev became possible.

There are two fundamental reasons that explain the failure to transform communist states. Socialism as a power system had sought to establish its own channels of control, thereby in effect continuing tsarism's distrust of independent civil society. When power was absolute, untrammeled by conscience, command-administrative methods had great force. Once softer political rule became necessary, it became obvious that force was linked to rigidity. One needs only to think of the attempt of workers in the failing shipyards of Gdansk to establish a trade union of their own, free from party interference. To seek such a union was to act politically, to put the rationale of the party-state in question. With hindsight, how astonishing it is that a whole regime was severely damaged by a strike! If the lack of flexibility caused problems, the inability to decompress—that is, the inability of socialism to emulate some authoritarian capitalism regimes in liberalizing from above—resulted from another facet of an atomized society, bereft of social institutions. Liberalization processes depend upon the striking of bargains, often in some roundtable negotiations. Gorbachev's difficulty was that there were no leaders of independent organizations, able to control their members, with whom he could negotiate.[36] In these circumstances, controlled decompression was impossible. Democratization took the place of liberalization.

This is not for a moment to deny the impact of Gorbachev's own policies, as is immediately evident once we think of the second factor that explains the failure of communism to transform itself. The reconstitution of the empire by 1921 and its expansion in 1939 and in the years from 1944 presented problems with which the tsars would have been all too familiar. Several systems of rule were again contained within a single political umbrella, with the greatest difficulties again coming from the inclusion of advanced Western nations whose consciousness was so advanced as to make assimilation impossible. The situation was in fact worse than it had been for the tsars: the Baltic states and Poland had tasted independence, the Czechs knew that socialism was taking away their industrial lead, while a united Ukraine, freed from fear of Poland and Germany, concentrated all its ire on

[36] Russell Bova, "Political Dynamics of the Post-Communist Transition," *World Politics* 44 (1991): 113–38.

Russia. But if the empire became an expensive burden, it is important to remember that the nationalities did less to cause breakdown of the Soviet bloc than to make sure that reconstitution would be impossible. Differently put, they occupied the space that *glasnost* created. But if some secessions were inevitable, the fact that there were so many had everything to do with Gorbachev. Ignorant of the nationalities question and loathe to stand for election himself while allowing elections among the nationalities, Gorbachev did at least attempt to create a large multinational frame. But he then unconsciously put into practice the lesson to be derived from Tocqueville that would ensure ultimate collapse. A political opening increases noise. Nerve is required to put up with new pressures, so that discontents take a normal form — from revolution to reform. The worst move in such circumstances is to step backward, to make the newly vocal fear and thereby to confirm them in their suspicion of the continuity of an old regime. The interventions in Georgia and Lithuania were accordingly utterly disastrous. Yeltsin was given the cards by means of which he was able to destroy the Soviet Union. The collapse of the socialist project has had an enormous but incalculable impact in the rest of the world. The Left, deprived of its model of development, thereby lost a great deal of its power. The situation in Russia is of course far from stable. For one thing, the standard problem of metropoles deprived of their imperial possessions — the search for a new national identity — haunts Russia in a particularly powerful form. It took Spain at least a century to reinvent itself after the loss of its empire, and there is a sense in which Britain has not yet managed this difficult task. Russia has scarcely begun to establish a nonimperial national identity for ethnic Russians. Until it does so, it cannot be at ease with itself. For another, foreign policy making is likely to be confused given the combination of popular mobilization and semi-authoritarianism. There are as yet few established liberal institutions, most notably in the media, which can provide information and critical reflection. The lack of such institutions has been apparent in Russian behavior in Chechnya. Still, any fears that might be entertained about Russian adventurism need to be set in the context of the collapse of Russian GDP (now roughly the size of that of Denmark) and of projections of a wholly unprecedented decline in population. Rarely has a great power fallen so far, so fast.

SPLENDORS AND MISERIES OF THE SOUTH

It only takes a moment to think of issues in the South that affect the transformation of states. It may be that socialist China can manage to transform itself, both because it placed *perestroika* before *glasnost* and because it has very largely become a nation-state. A great deal will surely depend, however, upon relations with Taiwan — currently one of the most troubling issues facing the world community. More generally, however, the North has washed its hands of the South, much of which could drop off the face of the globe without the purportedly global economy even noticing.[37] One wonders whether politics can in the longer run be so subject to a new form of international apartheid as is economics. The spread of weapons of mass destruction, especially to states with the fiscal advantages given by the possession of fossil fuel, must surely present future problems — despite America's much vaunted military revolution.[38] Moreover, in the post–September 11, 2001, era, fears have increased of the immense harm that terrorists, armed with weapons of mass destruction, can cause to advanced industrial societies.

It is beyond our powers to do more than note the salience of these issues. But the perspective that has been argued does suggest the usefulness of considering the situation of multinational regimes in the South. Given that development seeks in its very essence to copy the advanced, it behooves us to ask whether the South's twenty-first century will be as dark as that through which Europe has just passed. If there are obvious reasons to fear, there are — remarkably — reasons for optimism.

Some regimes in the developing world have managed multinationalism far better than did Europe. A general background condition was an initial realization in some quarters that imagination was needed so as to avoid disaster. It was precisely because African borders were absurd that it was essential, Julius Nyerere argued, to maintain them. Perhaps the most substantive achievement that resulted is that of the language repertoires of some African states and, above all, of India. David Laitin's analysis of the Indian situation suggests that a fully capable Indian citizen needs a language repertoire of three plus or minus one languages.[39] Two languages are needed to begin with because India has two official languages, English as well as Hindi, for Nehru's desire to produce a unitary and monoglot society was stymied by the desire of civil servants to maintain their cultural capital, the ability to function in English. A third language is that of one's provincial state. But one only needs two languages when one's provincial state is Hindi-speaking. In contrast, one needs four languages when one is in a minority in a non-

[37] John A. Hall, "Globalization and Nationalism," *Thesis Eleven* 63 (2000): 63–79.
[38] See T. V. Paul, "Great Equalizers or Agents of Chaos: Weapons of Mass Destruction and the Emerging International Order," in T. V. Paul and John A. Hall eds., *International Order and the Future of World Politics* (Cambridge: Cambridge University Press, 1999), chap. 18.
[39] David D. Laitin, *Language Repertoires and State Construction in Africa* (Cambridge: Cambridge University Press, 1992).

Hindi-speaking provincial state. India is the most important exception
to Gellner's generalization that homogeneity is a functional prerequisite
of modernity. This is a remarkable achievement, the creation of an Austro-Hungary that seems to work. And this linguistic arrangement could
be complemented by a varied collection of agreements, habitually consociational and regional, which have allowed ethnic groups to survive
within a single shell. The complex case of Malaya is a prime case in
point.[40]

Language is of course only one of the markers that can be used as the
basis on which to homogenize peoples into a single nation, and one can
always fear — though not, to this point, excessively — that religion could
again serve as the basis for terrible ethnic cleansing in India. It is worth
remembering in this context that the full impact of ethnic superstrati-
fication is felt during the process of modernization, which is by no
means complete in most of the world's polities. If hope has some descriptive base, the fact that there have been many failures of multinational federations — from Yugoslavia and the Soviet Union, to the Caribbean, sub-Saharan Africa, and British Central Africa — should make
us realize how very hard it is to make such arrangements work. Still
more obvious are the genocidal horrors of Kampuchea and Rwanda, in
which other peoples behave as did Europeans in the very recent past. It
is hard to imagine that such actions, now visible on our television
screens, will not have any effect on the condition of those who inhabit
the more comfortable zones of the world.

The economic gains that have been realized in the developing world
owe a great deal to the ability of elites to harness the power of the state
to mobilize resources, ward off rent seeking, and promote inward investment and outward trade. This is the story of the developmental
state, a model of state-led economic modernization pioneered by Japan
and emulating in varying ways across East Asia and beyond.[41] The distinction has been made by Ronald Dore between the "drifter states" of
Latin America and the "purposeful states" of East Asia whose political
economies can be traced to the legacies of Japanese imperialism, the
Pacific War, and the way the Cold War divided and mobilized the nations of Korea and China, thereby creating societal-wide motives to engage in economic modernization.[42] The so-called backward countries

---

[40] Horowitz, "Incentives and Behavior." See also Baldev R. Nayar and T. V. Paul, *India
in the World Order: Searching for Major Power Status* (Cambridge: Cambridge University
Press, 2002), chap. 4.

[41] M. Woo-Cumings, *The Developmental State* (Ithaca: Cornell University Press, 1999).

[42] Ronald P. Dore, "Reflections on Culture and Social Change," in Gary Gereffi and
Donald Wyman eds., *Manufacturing Miracles: Paths of Industrialization in Latin America
and East Asia* (Princeton: Princeton University Press, 1990).

that have lifted themselves up in the last quarter-century have been able to take advantage of state capacity that has given governments the necessary autonomy to pursue policies and channel investments into internationally competitive industries.[43] For countries in the developing world today, the goal is not participation in a globalized world where the state disappears in significance; it is to evolve a stable and capable state that can harness the energies and technologies of development.

THE CHAPTERS

The contribution of the chapters can now be set within the general context sketched. Of course reasons of space make it impossible to focus on every variation in nation-state strength. Accordingly, attention focuses on four areas, and in particular on key debates within each of them.

There is no better place to begin than that of the national question, for this foundational issue, for all that events have forced it to the fore, remains undertheorized in mainstream social science. There is a sense in which Bernard Yack and Brendan O'Leary converge on a set of issues. Nationalism at once gives great strength, while equally having the capacity to undermine state power. Yack's central contention is that nationalism is deeply written into our politics. If he resembles Gellner in saying that the nation-state is the essential political form of modernity, he ascribes its salience to the notion of popular sovereignty rather than to the needs of industry. O'Leary is well known for an interest in the management of ethnic conflict in Northern Ireland, but his consideration here of federalism is very much in the light of Gellner's insistence on the necessity of homogeneity within nation-states. In particular, O'Leary recognizes that pressures to social homogeneity make alternative arrangements very difficult to create and to sustain. The conclusion of his chapter is that a ruling people must be present if federal arrangements are to work, unless such arrangements are combined with consociational measures. Given that Europe, like Austro-Hungary, simply does not have enough Germans, the European Union would be well advised to retain all the consociational deals that reassure small states, as well as to find ways to give representation to such stateless nations as Catalonia and Scotland. Getting institutional design right in Europe is going to be very difficult indeed.

Anatoly Khazanov begins by noting that the Soviet Union was not in existence long enough to create a new Soviet people. Further, Soviet

---

[43] Peter Evans, *Embedded Autonomy: States and Industrial Transformation* (Princeton: Princeton University Press, 1995).

nationalities policies may have done something to encourage nationalism, at least in Central Asia, by creating administrative units that could
then be filled by putative nations. The Bolsheviks were of course continuing a tradition of empire, albeit supposedly under new and leftist
management. Khazanov points out that it is not possible to distinguish
ethnic Russian identity from imperial Russian identity. The loss of empire is always difficult for metropoles: it took Spain centuries before a
new identity was found, and Britain has not yet met the comment of
Dean Acheson to the effect that it had lost an empire and failed to find
a new role. In the Russian case the problems are very severe. Without
sense of nonimperial national identity, peace and prosperity in the region will be impossible.

   One striking benefit of Peter Baldwin's analysis of changing patterns
of state welfare provision lies in its starting point. The popular conception of the American state as weak and that of Sweden as strong in fact
inverts reality, at least in relation to key aspects of public health provision. More generally, Baldwin suggests that genuine multiculturalism —
that is, the presence of genuinely different cultures prone to different
dietary and health regimes — would indeed undermine powers hitherto
held to have characterized the nation-state. In fact, he suggests that formal and informal control in the United States is such that all that is on
offer is "multiculturalism lite" — that is, the presence of entirely superficial differences within a strong common cultural frame. This is an extremely striking demonstration of the continuing force of social homogenization by nation — and within the most powerful society that the
world has yet seen.

   Part 2 turns to the traditional area of state authority, that of national
security. T. V. Paul argues that realist elements of world politics are still
in the background, and he points to the remarkable role of the United
States — and its security protection function — in creating order today.
Even if war among the great powers is no longer a risk — which is itself
a controversial assumption — Paul shows that geopolitical competition
and security worries will not disappear. New forms of competition are
replacing old forms — today it is geo-economic and geo-technological
competition. There are also the new risks of biological and chemical
terrorism. The challenge of transnational terrorism was vividly presented in September 2001, and since then the United States has been
attempting to contain this asymmetric scourge with both traditional and
nontraditional means. Paul shows that behind the scenes, the United
States provides extended military protection and global hegemonic leadership. American power lurks in the background, but world politics is
still organized by and around concentrations of power. In this sense,
globalization is really a creature of a far-flung political order that,

through alliance partnerships and multilateral economic cooperation, provides a bulwark for markets and investment to thrive. The defeat of asymmetric challenges, especially posed by transnational terrorism, may be essential to sustain the American power, in both the military and economic arenas.

Jeffrey Herbst considers an entirely different matter under the broad rubric of security. He explores the plight of states in Africa and shows that the problem on this bleak continent is that states are not sufficiently evolved or capable. The problem is not enough state—or the absence of the right type of state—rather than a loss of the state. The dysfunctionality of states in Africa is at least partly explained by the absence of the sort of conflict that drove the state-building process in Europe. In Africa, the conflicts are primarily within states—manifest as bloody civil wars—and therefore differ sharply from the sort of inter-state dynamics that pushed forward political development within the West. At the same time, the wider international community continues to recognize the political boundaries of African states even when their governments have completely lost control of territory and borders. Again, this has stopped what in the West was an evolutionary process that shaped and reshaped the lines of the nation-state and served to produce politically viable nation-states. Africa is caught on a closed political pathway. It is not able to re-create the state-building history of Europe, but it has not been able to discover an alternative pathway toward the modern state. The chances of it being able to do so depend very much upon finding answers to the questions raised earlier by Brendan O'Leary.

Part 3 is concerned with the classic question of state autonomy. Francesco Duina considers the position of the powers of nation-states within the European Union and Mercosur. He shows that even when these common markets create pressures toward authority structures above national legislatures, the social reality that results is much more mixed and complicated than any bland suggestion that the nation-state is at risk allows. It is true that the legal systems of common markets deprive national legislatures of control in some areas related to trade and even in areas less related to the flow of physical goods, such as the environment. But Duina demonstrates that national legislatures continue to exercise control over broad aspects of services, labor, and capital even when this impinges on the functioning of the common market. The image that emerges is of an evolving and enduring division of labor between regional and national political entities. Political authority and decision making are not simply pushed upward to the supranational level; rather, they are evolving in multiple vertical and horizontal directions. The continuing debate within the European Union—including the decisions made recently in Nice—continue to give the major states of Europe great power. Duina's is a subtle argument because it shows that the pressures that are shaping the form and locale of political authority are not all flowing in one direction. National legislatures must adapt, but they will continue to be central players in regional political economic orders.

Christopher Hood looks at one critical aspect of state power that is arguably under pressure by globalization, namely, the ability to extract revenue from society. When capital is increasingly mobile, states are presumably less able to tax—either because the assets themselves are more difficult to identify and tax or because the threat of "exit" reduces the ability of states to impose the tax burden. Hood shows remarkably little evidence of these problems. The tax state is alive and well at the turn of the century. The extractive capacity of the wealthy Western democratic states actually grew during the twentieth century, and overall taxation grew as a proportion of GNP in the developed countries. Hood shows that while the information age poses possible threats to the tax state's extractive capacity, it also provides new opportunities. These potential tax strategies include creating tollbooths on the information superhighway and taxes on websites. If the state finds it difficult to monitor the virtual services that are performed on the internet, it can still tax the electricity that runs the infrastructure. In can also resort to old-fashioned tax strategies such as printing money and allowing inflation to indirectly reduce the fiscal burden of the state.

John Campbell deconstructs the fashionable notion of globalization in such a way as to demonstrate the continuing salience of divergence within capitalism. To begin with, he argues that economic globalization itself is oversold as a force. Campbell shows that the extent of economic globalization has been exaggerated, as have been its effects. There is no doubt that economic integration has intensified in recent decades, but it does not constitute the sharp shift in global economic relations that is widely believed. Moreover, what globalization theorists also miss is the ways in which states—institutions and economic actors—mediate and respond to global forces. The institutional structures of states, which vary widely across the developed and developing world, constitute a weight that itself helps shape the interaction of global economic forces and domestic response. Campbell shows that what has been missing in the debate on globalization is a proper specification of the tools and mechanisms by which governments and other actors grapple with global economic integration.

Rudy Sil critiques the universalist claims of globalization theory in a more particular way, by linking the evolution of the world economy with convergent patterns of industrial relations worldwide. The common view is that technological innovation and global competition are creating uniformly decentralized patterns of collective bargaining that erode the capacities of trade unions, labor ministries, and national employee associations. Sil looks at the experiences of so-called transitional late-industrializers and finds that the state continues to play a role as a focal point for the regulation of industrial relations. Institutional legacies and variable state capacities still are evident across the late-developing world. While many of these countries are in fact pursuing policies that are accommodating to business interests, this does not suggest a decline in the importance of the state as the critical guarantor of the pacts that inevitably must be negotiated among labor, business, and international actors. As states will continue to remain at the center of industrial relations in these transitional countries, so too will variation in systems of industrial relations remain the norm.

The final part of the book offers a neatly opposed pair of papers concerned with state capacity within parts of the world deeply affected by communism. The common view of the communist state is that it is large and not very efficient, manifest for example in the amount going to investment — for very poor returns. Hence, it was not surprising that the slogan of civil society came to have such resonance within this social world. But these chapters show how much the state is needed.

Grzegorz Ekiert demonstrates that the astonishing and totally unforeseen success of postcommunist Poland is best explained by reforms to its state structure. His focus is on the pattern and sequencing of state reforms in Poland. During the 1990s Poland was a leader within postcommunist Eastern Europe both in the reform of the state and in the pursuit of market reforms. Ekiert is interested in the relationship between the two reform movements, and he argues that it was precisely the ability to get the state reorganized along democratic and legal-rational lines that allowed the economic modernization process to succeed. In contrast, Minxin Pei shows how the reform of the Chinese state may be leading the country toward decentralized predation. The focus is on how the regime and economic transitions are eroding state capacity. Some decline in Chinese state capacity is to be expected — and welcomed — with the transition away from the Maoist-Leninist model. But it is state predation — the expropriation of wealth by the state from society to sustain itself in power — that has emerged in China rather than a more efficient and rule-based order. Ironically perhaps, it is the emergence of decentralized state predation that has been most evident in China and that is responsible for the decline in state capacity. The decentralization of power in China has not been accompanied by measures to monitor the compliance of state agents, and rising predation has been the result. Pei shows that state capacity depends on the rule of law. Decentralization of power might bring with it more democratic politics, but if it happens without enforceable laws and rules, the result is dysfunctional for the state and society. A legal-rational system of government may in the first instance limit the power of the state, but ultimately it provides the essential element for a capable state.

The volume concludes with a succinct analysis by John Ikenberry of the condition of the nation-state in the contemporary era. He echoes the general tone of various chapters to the effect that the capacities of states continue to evolve, declining in some areas but increasing more generally. He notes the consensus among the authors in this volume that states remain the dominant sociopolitical organization of modernity, not least as there are no competing social organizations in sight that possess equivalent powers and capacities. However, he argues that the definition of a strong state has changed: the bureaucratic and/or authoritarian variant has lost salience, to be replaced by one that is flexible and capable of effectively working with different societal groups. Ikenberry calls for assessing state capacity by desegregating the various dimensions of state power and authority. Much like modern corporations have adapted from the days of the East India Company, contemporary states are changing, but while doing so they remain powerful sociopolitical entities, calling our attention to sustained theoretical and empirical analysis, a task we undertake in the following pages.

Part 1

NATIONAL IDENTITIES

CHAPTER 1

Nationalism, Popular Sovereignty, and the Liberal Democratic State

BERNARD YACK

THE AGE OF liberal democracy is also the age of nationalism. Every great landmark in the rise and spread of the liberal democratic state — the Glorious Revolution in 1688, the North and South American wars of independence, the great French Revolution of 1789, the "springtime of peoples" in 1848, the collapse of European and colonial empires in the twentieth century — looms large in the history of nationalism as well. It should not be surprising, then, that the collapse of Soviet communism has led to a resurgence of nationalist politics as well as the extension of liberal democratic ideals and institutions. The pattern is familiar. It looks somewhat odd to us now only because the end of the Cold War, which has accompanied the collapse of Soviet communism, has also inspired intense new hopes for global integration, hopes that are challenged by the resurgence of nationalist politics.

What, if anything, connects nationalist politics to the spread of liberal democratic ideals and institutions? We need to answer that question in order to begin thinking about the extent to which nationalism and the nation-state will survive the challenge of globalist theory and practice. For globalism relies heavily on the hegemony of liberal democratic ideologies, as well as on processes of cultural and economic integration. If liberal democratic ideals and institutions promote nationalist politics in some way, then the globalist challenge to the nation-state may undermine itself in at least one important way.

Most answers to my question about the connection between nationalism and liberal democracy focus on the impact of democratization on the politics of community.[1] Democratize government, so the argument

---

[1] Of course, the reason that liberal democracy and nationalism shadow each other may be that they both share a deeper, common source, such as the processes of modernization that figure so largely in theorizing about nationalism. One problem with this reliance on modernization, in any of its various forms, to explain nationalism is that it almost always seems to come on the scene too late to account for the origin, as opposed to the persistence, of nationalist attitudes and behavior. But even if modernization lies behind both

goes, and you are bound to nationalize it. "Bring the people into political life," as Michael Walzer puts it, "and they arrive marching in tribal ranks and orders, carrying with them their own language, historical memories, customs, beliefs, and commitments."[2] From this point of view, nationalism and the politics of ethnic cleansing represent the "dark side of democracy."[3] In ethnically divided societies, democratization provides competing groups means and opportunities to mobilize against each other that they never had before. "In such conditions," Donald Horowitz notes, "democracy is more the problem than the answer to the problem" of ethnonationalist violence.[4]

Liberal democrats, however, have no difficulty in identifying a solution to this problem, even if it is often very hard to implement. If democratization opens the door to ethnonationalist violence, then that is just one more reason for liberal democrats to emphasize that democratic institutions must be balanced by liberal respect for limited government, diversity, and individual rights. Liberal democracy is a blend of two basic principles, principles that constrain as well as complement each other. One derives all legitimate political authority from some form of majority consent; the other limits the scope and means of governmental authority to make room for individual freedom and diverse forms of association. If the unrestrained application of the first principle tends to promote ethnonationalist violence, it can and should be constrained by an application of the second. From this point of view, which is widely shared, liberal democracy provides us with a solution to nationalist problems, even if it had a hand in creating them.

In this chapter I challenge this conclusion by arguing that the liberal half of the liberal democratic ideology, no less than its democratic half,[5] contributes to the rise and spread of nationalism. I argue, in particular,

---

nationalism and liberal democracy in some important way, that does not preclude the possibility of the kind of causal connections between the two social phenomena that I explore in this chapter.

[2] Michael Walzer, "The New Tribalism: Notes on a Difficult Problem," in Ronald Beiner, ed., *Theorizing Nationalism* (Albany: SUNY, 1998), 206.

[3] See Michael Mann, "The Dark Side of Democracy: The Modern Tradition of Ethnic and Political Cleansing," *New Left Review* 23 (1999): 18–45.

[4] Donald Horowitz, "Self-Determination: Politics, Philosophy, and Law," in Ian Shapiro and Will Kymlicka, eds., *Ethnicity and Group Rights*, Nomos 39 (New York: New York University Press, 1997), 451.

[5] Moreover, it is very easy to exaggerate the contribution that democratization makes to the rise and spread of nationalism. The premodern history of democracy does not support the general claim that when you give people the freedom to participate in politics, they will vigorously assert their national loyalties. And even in modern democracies, where this is more likely to happen, it is just as often the case that democratization leads to the discovery of national loyalties, rather than their release from political constraint.

that liberal principles have contributed more than their democratic counterparts to the delegitimation of given state boundaries so central to nationalist politics. More generally, I try to show that liberal politics rests on a familiar but rarely analyzed image of political community, one that tends to nationalize our understanding of politics and politicize our understanding of nationality.

The key to my argument is an analysis of popular sovereignty, a deeply ambiguous concept that is far too often treated as little more than a synonym for the rule of the people. Like Istvan Hont, I believe that "without a historically informed understanding of the theory of popular sovereignty, no clarification of the language of nation-states and nationalism is possible."[6] But, as Hont has argued as well, I believe that the nature of popular sovereignty's contribution to the rise and spread of nationalism has been badly misunderstood because of the failure to recognize its ambiguous role in liberal democratic politics.

THE PEOPLE'S TWO BODIES, OR LIBERALISM'S IMAGINED COMMUNITY

That popular sovereignty plays a crucial role in the rise and spread of nationalism is something of a commonplace in the scholarly literature. Hans Kohn, for example, proclaims that "nationalism is incoherent without popular sovereignty." And Hugh Seton-Watson claims that nationalism represents nothing more than "the application to national community of the Enlightenment doctrine of popular sovereignty."[7] Nevertheless, the failure to recognize the ambiguity of this central concept of liberal democratic politics — its reference to two complementary but very different ideological principles — has limited our understanding of its contribution to the rise and spread of nationalism.

The simpler and more familiar conception of popular sovereignty is the idea of democratic rule, the exercise of power by majorities. The people, in this conception, are the majority of ordinary or nonprivileged individuals whose endorsement is the ultimate source of legal authority in any democracy. The members of the people exercise their sovereignty by making laws, sitting on juries, taking turns in executive offices, or selecting the people who perform these official activities. This democratic conception of popular sovereignty is much the older of the two, going back at least to the republics of ancient Greece and Italy. Contem-

---

[6] Istvan Hont, "Permanent Crisis of a Divided Mankind: The Contemporary Crisis of the Nation-State in Historical Perspective," *Political Studies* (1994): 171.

[7] Hans Kohn, *The Idea of Nationalism* (New York: Macmillan, 1945), 3; Hugh Seton-Watson, *Nations and States* (London: Methuen, 1977), 445.

porary political rhetoric draws heavily on this older, democratic conception of the people as governmental sovereign. But it also draws on a newer conception of the people as "constituent," rather than "governmental" sovereign.[8] This new conception of popular sovereignty — which is most closely associated with Locke and Sieyès and was made popular by the English, American, and French Revolutions — invests in the people the final and unlimited power to establish or dissolve forms of government. But it denies to majorities, as it denies to any other individuals or groups of individuals, final and unlimited exercise of the governmental authority that the people creates. For this conception of popular sovereignty was designed to limit the authority of republican majorities as well as authoritarian monarchs. It is quite compatible with democratic forms of government, but it restrains the authority of democratic peoples — i.e., governmental majorities — by conjuring up an image of a larger and more inclusive people that precedes the establishment of even democratic forms of government and survives their dissolution.

This new conception of popular sovereignty certainly has many affinities with its older counterpart. It promotes a more egalitarian picture of political order since it eliminates the possibility that any individual or group of individuals can claim political authority as a proprietary right, as something that they can dispose of as they choose. And it can easily become the starting point for justifications for more democratic forms of government, by extending the principle of consent from the establishment and accountability of state authority to the election of officeholders and the approval of particular policies. But its major goal is the limitation, rather than the democratization, of governmental authority.[9]

---

[8] On the distinction between governmental and constituent sovereignty, see Samuel Beer, *To Make a Nation* (Cambridge: Cambridge University Press, 1993), 312–21; P. Pasquino, *Sieyes et l'invention de la constitution en France* (Paris: Odile Jacob, 1998). On the theory of constituent sovereignty, see Julian Franklin, *John Locke and the Theory of Sovereignty*; Hont, "Permanent Crisis," 201; Murray Forsyth, "Thomas Hobbes and the Constituent Power of the People," *Political Studies* 29 (1981): 191; O. Béaud, *La puissance de l'état* (Paris: PUF, 1994), 208–27.

[9] As Edmond Morgan notes (*Inventing the People* [New York: Norton, 1988], 60), although the new doctrine of popular sovereignty "encouraged greater popular participation, its purpose remained the same" as the ideologies it was designed to replace: "to persuade the many to submit to the few." Much of the history of the doctrine "can be read as a history of the successive efforts of different generations to bring the facts into closer conformity with the fiction, efforts that have gradually transformed the very structure of society" (ibid., 152). As a result, the modern notion of popular sovereignty is frequently attacked by supporters of participatory democracy in the name of an older, more direct understanding of the concept. See, for example, J. Mostov, *Power, Process, and Popular Sovereignty* (Philadelphia: Temple University Press, 1992).

No wonder, then, that de Maistre sneered that according to this new doctrine "the people is the sovereign that cannot exercise sovereignty."[10]

When liberal democrats celebrate the sovereignty of the people, they thus invoke two different conceptions of the people and its role in government. Like medieval kings, the liberal democratic people has "two bodies."[11] One is the collection of flesh-and-blood bodies that constitute majorities in any given state. The other is the community of all individuals subject to the same authority imagined as a single body that constitutes and deconstitutes structures of government. The latter is as mysterious a conception—if not more so—as the conception of the king's eternal body in medieval political theology.[12] Nonetheless, this image of the people as constituent sovereigns "is now accepted in all [liberal democratic] constitutional systems . . . it may even appear obvious."[13] The older idea of the people as the *plebs*, the mass of humble, ordinary citizens, as opposed to upper- and middle-class elites, certainly survives in modern politics. It is always available to fuel populist appeals against the advantages of the rich and powerful. And the idea of the people as *demos* certainly survives to sustain demands for greater democracy. But just as important, and even more widely relied upon in modern political life, is this new conception of the people that leads to allowing all of a territory's inhabitants to be spoken of as the collective source of the state's authority.

The fact that we have come to take for granted such a disembodied conception of community is one of the most remarkable, if little discussed, features of modern political life. Hegel, for one, complained that this conception of popular sovereignty turns the people into "a formless mass," an "indeterminate abstraction" that lacks every one of the institutional characteristics that allow us to identify real communities.[14] Al-

---

[10] Joseph de Maistre, "On the Origins of Sovereignty," in Richard Lebrun ed., *Against Rousseau* (Montreal: McGill-Queen's University Press, 1996), bk. 1, chap. 1.

[11] Morgan, *Inventing the People*, 83. Morgan is alluding to Ernst Kantorowicz's famous study of mediaeval political theology, *The King's Two Bodies* (Princeton: Princeton University Press, 1957).

[12] "A king, however dubious his divinity might seem, did not have to be imagined. He was a visible presence, wearing his crown and carrying his scepter. The people, on the other hand, are never visible as such. Before we ascribe sovereignty to the people we have to imagine there is such a thing, something we personify as though it were a single body." Morgan, *Inventing the People*, 153.

[13] Franklin, *John Locke and the Theory of Sovereignty*, 124. See also Hont, "Permanent Crisis," 201; Murray Forsyth, "Thomas Hobbes and the Constituent Power of the People," *Political Studies* 29 (1981): 191.

[14] "Opposed to the sovereignty of the monarch, the sovereignty of the people is one of the confused notions based on the wild idea of the 'people.' Taken without its monarch . . . the people is a formless mass and no longer a state. It lacks every one of those

though no democrat, Hegel had no difficulty with descriptions of the people as governmental sovereign, since they merely referred to rule by institutionally defined majorities. But the image of a prepolitical people that creates and disbands its own institutions seemed both illogical and politically dangerous to him. For it provides us no way of identifying the people's will apart from competing and unverifiable claims to have discovered or, perhaps, embody it. The lack of institutional definition in such a conception of the people makes it the perfect vehicle for irrational appeals to public passions, according to Hegel.[15]

In retrospect, one has to admit that Hegel has a point. For although this new conception of popular sovereignty was invented to justify liberal principles of limited government, it has spread far beyond its origins. Every regime today claims, in some way, to represent the deeper will of its people, whether or not it does so by means of democratic institutions. The Soviet regimes were the last holdouts, since they insisted that the Communist Party's special knowledge of history's "line of march" justified its political authority. Now postcommunist cabals join fascists and military juntas, no less than liberal democratic reformers, in legitimating their authority by appealing to the will of the prepolitical people that the state should represent. No doubt the rhetoric in each case is self-serving, but the spread of this notion of a preinstitutional people provides them with a new way of justifying their power — one that does not require a commitment to either democratic institutions or liberal restraints.[16]

THE NATION AND THE PEOPLE

The older, democratic understanding of popular sovereignty promotes the expression of nationalism by giving nations and their leaders the

---

determinate characteristics — sovereignty, government, judges, magistrates, class-divisions, etc. — [by which] a people cease to be that indeterminate abstraction which, when represented in a quite general way, as the 'people.'" Georg Wilhelm Friedrich Hegel, *Philosophy of Right* (Oxford: Oxford University Press, 1967), para. 279. On this passage, see Jacqueline Stevens, *Reproducing the State* (Princeton: Princeton University Press, 1999), 79–80.

[15] "The word most on its lips is the 'people'; but the special mark which it carries on its brow is the hatred of law." For law "is the shibboleth which marks out these false friends and comrades of what they call the 'people.'" Hegel, *Philosophy of Right*, preface, 6–7.

[16] I should note, however, that this more abstract notion of popular sovereignty continues to inspire radical democrats as well, at least to the extent that they are attracted to the idea that "the will of the people resists all representation." See P. Markell, "Making Affect Safe for Democracy: On Constitutional Patriotism," *Political Theory* 28 (2000): 50.

means and opportunities to mobilize their communities. The new understanding of popular sovereignty promotes the expression of nationalism in a more indirect way, by bringing our images of polity and nation much closer together than they had been in the past. But to see how and why this might happen, we need first to establish a clear distinction between the conception of the people associated with the new doctrine of popular sovereignty and the conception of national community with which it has become so entangled.

Disentangling these two conceptions of community, however, is extremely difficult, since we tend to use the words "nation" and "people" interchangeably, in both ordinary and scholarly language. Indeed, one sign of the impact that this new conception of the people has had on the growth of nationalism is the way in which contemporary scholars often incorporate this conception into their definitions of nationhood, as in Benedict Anderson's famous definition of the nation as a community "imagined as both inherently limited and sovereign."[17] Accordingly, I want to emphasize that my distinction between these two images of community is *conceptual*, rather than linguistic, in nature. When I describe one image of community as "the people" and the other as "the nation," I am not suggesting that this is how the terms are ordinarily used in English or in any other language with which I am familiar.[18] I am using these terms merely as reference points for two distinct ways of imagining community. The straining of ordinary language is worth the effort if it helps us capture something important about the way we think about community in modern political life.

With that caveat, here is how I propose to distinguish these two conceptions of community.[19] Both the people and the nation are, in Benedict Anderson's phrase, "imagined communities." That is to say, they derive their character as communities from the way in which distant individuals imagine their connections to each other, rather than from their di-

---

[17] Anderson, *Imagined Communities* (London: Verso, 1991), 6–7.

[18] In English the term nation tends to have more of a cultural connotation, the people more of a political connotation. In German it is the other way round, though, as Emmerich Francis points out, that is the result of a long evolution that reversed the use of the terms. See Francis, *Ethnos und Demos* (Berlin: Duncker und Humblot, 1965), 61.

[19] Needless to say, I present here a sketch of conclusions rather than an elaboration of the evidence that might support my distinction. This is especially true with regard to the definition of national community, a field of vast controversy that I deal with in "The Myth of the Civic Nation" and in the first three chapters of my forthcoming book, *Nation and Individual: Contingency, Choice, and Community in Modern Political Life*. With regard to the people, in contrast, there is a relative dearth of serious reflection. See Margaret Canovan, *Nationhood and Political Theory* (Northampton, MA: Edward Elgar), 16, for an interesting discussion of why this is so.

rect or indirect interaction with each other.[20] Nevertheless, they are based on two distinct ways of imagining the connections that bind us to each other.

National community, I suggest, is an image of community *over time*. What binds us into national communities is our images of a shared heritage that is passed, and altered, from one generation to another. National communities, as a result, are imagined as starting from some specific point of origin in the past and extending forward into an indefinite future. The people, in contrast, presents an image of community *over space*. It portrays all individuals within the given boundaries of a state as members of a community from which the state derives its legitimate authority. If national community provides a bridge across the chasm that separates one generation from another, the people offers a bridge over the chasm that separates individuals from each other in their efforts to shape and control the authority of the state.[21] The concept of the nation allows us to imagine the evolving community that precedes our existence and survives our death.[22] The concept of the people allows us to imagine the community that we share at any particular moment in dealing with the state's coercive authority.

As such, the people exists in a kind of eternal present. It never ages or dies. Nor does it change in character from one instance to another. The people invoked as the ultimate source of the Swedish state's legitimate authority is no different in character from the people invoked as the source of the legitimate authority of the Chinese or Canadian state. In

[20] Although I employ Benedict Anderson's expression (*Imagined Communities*, 1–3), I use it in a somewhat different manner from the way Anderson does. Anderson focuses on lack of familiarity, treating an imagined community as one in which its members have no direct interaction with each other. As I am using the concept, an imagined community is one whose existence is derived from its members' imagination of their connections, rather than through shared processes or interactions. The nation is an imagined community in both Anderson's and my sense because it is a community based on an imagined heritage shared by widely separated groups of individuals. But, as I am using the term, there can be large, impersonal communities that are based on shared interactions and procedures that are not imagined communities. When, for example, we speak of the urban or even the world community, we can be speaking about shared interdependence or interaction, rather than any kind of image of sharing a community. And there can be small communities that are based on imagined connections rather than on any direct interaction or interdependence.

[21] Accordingly, the people is conceived with reference to the state, in particular to the modern state that integrates all coercive authority within a territory in a single hierarchical structure. When scholars suggest that is "pointless to talk about nations apart from the state" (Eric Hobsbawm, *Nations and Nationalism since 1780* [Cambridge: Cambridge University Press, 1990], 9), they are conflating the nation with this image of the people.

[22] See Canovan, *Nationhood and Political Theory*, 22; Anderson, *Imagined Communities*, 9–12.

every case the people is the same: the whole body of a territory's inhabitants imagined as the final or sovereign judge of how the state's authority should be constructed and employed.[23]

National community may be strong or weak, rising or falling. The people, in contrast, is always in place, always available to be invoked in one's struggles with political authority or in one's competition for political power. For the people exists by right, rather than by custom or consciousness-raising. To assert or deny its existence is a matter of ideology rather than sociology.[24] It exists as long as one believes in a particular theory of political legitimacy. Those who deny its existence are guilty of an injustice rather than a misdescription. Perhaps that is why there is no common concept of "people-building" to parallel the familiar concept of "nation-building."[25] A nation needs time and effort to establish a legacy of memories and symbols salient enough to link one generation to another. Indeed, one cannot really be sure about the existence of a nation until one has given it sufficient time to grow — or collapse.[26] The people, in contrast, needs no nurturing. It is available as soon as individuals accept the principle of legitimacy that asserts its existence.

The nation is an old form of community, though new nations are

[23] The fact that French political tradition tends to follow Sieyès in calling this form of community "the nation," rather than Rousseau in calling it "the people," should not be allowed to confuse the distinction that I am making here. As Sieyès himself makes clear, "a political society, a people, a nation are synonymous terms." Emmanuel Joseph Sieyès, "Contre la ré-totale," in P. Pasquino, Sieyes et l'invention de la constitution en France, 175. In another place he insists that public authority "comes from the people, that is to say, the nation," adding that "these two terms ought to by synonymous." Emmanuel Jospeh Sieyès, Écrits Politiques (Paris: Editions des Archives Contemporaines, 1985), 200. The revolutionaries' preference for the term "nation" reflects the lingering negative associations of "the people" with the plebs or mob. See Elisabeth Fehrenbach, "Nation," in Handbuch der Politische-Soziale Grundbegriffe in Frankreich 1680–1782 (1986): 7, 83–84; Hont, "Permanent Crisis," 194, n. 50; and Greenfeld, Nationalism (Cambridge: Harvard University Press, 1992), 6–8. One consequence of this development is that French legal and political thought has long distinguished between national and popular sovereignty, even though by national sovereignty what is meant is the kind of indirect or constituent sovereignty associated with the new doctrine of popular sovereignty that I have been describing. See G. Bacot, Carré de Malberg et l'origine de la distinction entre souveraineté du peuple et souveraineté nationale (Paris: Editions du Centre National de la Recherche Scientifique, 1985).

[24] On this point, see Roger Scruton, "In Defence of the Nation," in The Philosopher on Dover Beach (Manchester: Carcanet, 1990), 301.

[25] Canovan (Nationhood and Political Theory, 107) notes this absence. Rogers Smith tries to correct for this absence in "Trust and Worth: The Politics of People-Building," the 1999 Charles E. Lindblom Lecture at Yale University.

[26] Robert Emerson, From Empire to Nation (Cambridge: Harvard University Press, 1960), 90.

constantly being born and old ones are dying off as different configurations of cultural symbols and historical memories gain or lose significance. The people, in contrast, is relatively new or modern; it was invented to solve certain problems of political legitimacy in the modern state. It draws, as we have seen, on older images of the people as the plebs or multitude of ordinary folks in any community, as well as images of the people as the demos or the ruling group within a community. But the people of popular sovereignty doctrine significantly alters both of these earlier images. It alters the image of the people as plebs by making *all* inhabitants of a governed territory members of the people, an invention that lowers the status of the nobility and raises the status of ordinary people in important ways.[27] And it alters the image of the people as demos or rulers by making the people the constituent sovereign that establishes government rather than the governing sovereign, as noted above.

Before turning to my argument about popular sovereignty's contribution to the rise of nationalism, I would like to emphasize an important ambiguity or inconsistency in this new conception of the people. The people is clearly imagined as a bounded community. But whence does it derive its boundaries? On the one hand, it seems like there is a simple and clear answer to the question. A people derives its boundaries from its state. It is sovereignty within the boundaries of its state's territories, and nothing more, that the people claim. If peoples are the communities to which states are accountable, then the boundary between one people and another will be the boundaries that distinguish the reach of one state's coercive authority from another's. On the other hand, if the people is imagined as *prior* to the state, as the community that authorizes the establishment of the state's authority and survives its dissolution, then its boundaries cannot be defined by the boundaries of particular states. An appeal to the people is an appeal beyond the constituted authority of state actors and institutions to the community that lends them their authority. And if the appeal to the people is an appeal beyond the state, why should we imagine peoples as limited by the contingent borders that a history of accident, force, and fraud has established for states?

The people, it seems, is imagined *both* as existing prior to the state and as defined by the borders of an already constituted state, or, if you prefer, as both a pre- and postpolitical community. In practice, the application of popular sovereignty doctrine usually takes for granted existing state boundaries and asks questions about the organization of legitimate authority within these boundaries. But by raising the prospect of a

---

[27] On this point, see especially Greenfeld, *Nationalism*, 6–8.

prepolitical community upon which the legitimacy of state authority depends, the new popular sovereignty doctrine raises questions about the prepolitical sources of community, questions that visions of national community are much better equipped to answer than visions of the sovereign people.

THE NATIONALIZATION OF POLITICAL COMMUNITY

The central argument of this chapter is that the doctrine of popular sovereignty contributes to the rise and spread of nationalism by introducing a new image of political community, an image that tends to nationalize political loyalties and politicize national loyalties. In making this argument I am assuming that, to put it in a nutshell, while the nation is a relatively old form of community, nationalism is relatively new.[28] In other words, I am assuming that while intergenerational communities based on imagined cultural heritage have been with us for a very long time, it is only in the last 250 years or so that the political self-assertion of national communities has become commonplace. There were nations long before nationalism,[29] as I am using the terms, because there were national communities long before the assertion of national sovereignty became anything like an empirical or moral norm. Explaining the rise and spread of nationalism, according to this way of thinking, requires that we ask why this particular form of communal loyalty has come to be so closely associated with political self-assertion. My argument about popular sovereignty is designed to provide part of the answer to that question.

Let me begin then with the nationalization of political community. Defenders of the new doctrine of popular sovereignty argue that monarchs and aristocrats usurp an inalienable right of the people when they claim the right to make unlimited and arbitrary use of the state's authority over persons and territory. But, as we have seen, they do not counter these claims to personal sovereignty by insisting that the people, rather than the monarch or aristocrats, possess this right to make unlimited and arbitrary use of the state's authority. Instead, they argue that whatever form government takes, it derives its authority from a territory's inhabitants, imagined as a collective body.

---

[28] This is my formula for a truce between the "modernist" and "primordialist" understandings of nationalism. I repeat that I am not suggesting that all or most nations are old; I mean only to suggest that the nation as a *form* of community is, unlike nationalism, relatively old.

[29] See John Armstrong, *Nations before Nationalism* (Chapel Hill: University of North Carolina Press, 1982).

Understood in this way, the people represents a new kind of political community. In earlier conceptions what binds the political community is sharing either subjection to a particular kind of political authority or the opportunity to take turns in exercising that authority.[30] But the people, as imagined by the defenders of popular sovereignty, represents neither the absolutist's community of subjects nor the republican's community of sharers in ruling. Instead, it is the community from which political authority arises and to which it reverts when that authority no longer serves its proper function. This new conception of political community "undercuts traditional notions of popular sovereignty as much as traditional notions of the princely state," for "it disqualifies "the actual flesh and blood commonality of the people no less than princes or aristocrats as the depository of rightful ultimate decision-making."[31] Since popular sovereignty, in this new conception, is indirect or mediated sovereignty, something other than the structure of political institutions or the exercise of ruling and being ruled must define the people who exercises it. For if the people precede the establishment and survive the dissolution of political authority, then they must share something beyond a relationship to that authority.

But what it is that common, prepolitical characteristic? As we have seen, the defenders of popular sovereignty have no consistent answer to this question. It is their lack of an answer that opens the door to the identification of political with national community, of the people with the nation. For the nation provides precisely what is lacking in the concept of the people: a sense of where to look for the prepolitical basis of political community. By encouraging us to think of political community as distinct from and prior to the establishment of political authority, the liberal conception of popular sovereignty thus brings our image of political community much closer to national community than it had been in the past.

The nationalization or culturalization of political community is, I am arguing here, an unintended consequence of the widespread acceptance of the liberal conception of popular sovereignty. Its defenders certainly did not intend to transform our image of political community in this way. They were attempting, instead, to solve the problem of legitimacy and limited government. But the way in which they solved this problem introduces a new one: the identification of political with cultural community. For to conjure up an image of the people as standing apart from

---

[30] The classic statement of the traditional, activist understanding of citizenship is found in Aristotle's *Politics* (1275a23), that the citizen is someone who shares in "ruling and adjudicating" and takes turns in ruling and being ruled.

[31] Hont, "Permanent Crisis," 184–85.

and prior to the establishment of political authority, one has to think of its members as sharing something more than political relationships. And the pre- or extrapolitical community that most resembles the form of the people is the kind of cultural community celebrated by nations. The problem is thus not just that the doctrine of popular sovereignty ignores the prepolitical foundations of political community. It is rather that commitment to this doctrine encourages us to look for those foundations in the places where national loyalties lurk. The new doctrine of popular sovereignty does not just lack means of resisting the nationalistic sentiments of the people it brings into politics. It positively invites the nationalization or culturalization of politics by the way in which it transforms our image of political community.

One can see this process taking place in seventeenth- and eighteenth-century Great Britain, the site where, most would agree, both the new doctrine of popular sovereignty was invented and nationalism first emerged. English or British nationalism has been frequently portrayed as a prime example of civic or political nationalism, as an expression of shared loyalty to political principles and institutions, rather than an expression of shared cultural loyalties — most emphatically by Liah Greenfeld in her recent book, *Nationalism: Five Roads to Modernity*.[32] The implausibility of this characterization becomes clear once one pays some attention to the way in which British patriots expressed themselves about those "garlic-eating" Catholics across the channel.[33] But what interests me here is how the assertion of particular cultural loyalties follows directly on the heels of the assertion of popular sovereignty, a development apparent in some of the very passages that Greenfeld cites to defend her claim that Anglo-American visions of nationhood lack the emphasis on "unique characteristics" celebrated by ethnic nationalists in Germany and other points eastward.[34]

When John Milton, for example, brags that it is their new and unprecedented civil liberties that give the English "the honor to precede other nations," he is certainly identifying the English community with a form of civil liberty rather than any kind of cultural heritage. But when he goes on to talk about why the English deserve these liberties, he makes it clear that he has a very different understanding of community in mind. "Consider what Nation," he asks Parliament, "it is whereof ye are the governours: a Nation not slow and dull, but of a quick, inge-

---

[32] I discuss the strengths and weaknesses of Greenfeld's argument in "Reconciling Nationalism and Liberalism," *Political Theory* 23 (1995): 175–80.

[33] See especially Linda Colley, *Britons: The Making of a Nation* (New Haven: Yale Univerisity Press, 1992).

[34] Greenfeld, *Nationalism*, 3–14, 76–77.

nious, and piercing, spirit, acute to invent, suttle and sinewy to discourse." These shared characteristics, this shared heritage, help Milton
explain why the English are the "nation chos'n before any other" to
receive from God his epoch-making revelation of liberty.[35] Indeed, the
very claim that England has "the honor to precede other Nations"
makes it absolutely clear that Milton does *not* view nationhood as nothing more than a container for popular sovereignty and civil liberties.
For it is precisely the achievement of these things that distinguishes England *among* the different nations.

One might complain that what is happening here is that two different
images of national community are being superimposed on each other:
one of the nation as a body of citizens and the other as a cultural community with unique historical characteristics. Nationalism, from this
point of view, involves "a sleight of hand" whereby one uses the same
word for the two different images of community without acknowledg-
ing their opposition.[36] But such a complaint misses the fact that both of
these images of community, the demos as a body of citizens and the
nation as a prepolitical cultural community, provide ways of representing a *third* image of community, the people of the new doctrine of
popular sovereignty. Each captures one aspect of that image of community — the demos its inclusiveness, the nation its prepolitical character —
while missing other aspects. It is not surprising, then, that they should
be asserted together. The people of the new popular sovereignty doctrine is an especially abstract image of community. It invites representation in more concrete images in order, so to speak, to give the body
politic a body. It would indeed involve a "sleight of hand" to represent
an institutionally defined body of citizens as a nation or unique cultural
community. But in order to represent the *pre-institutional* people of
popular sovereignty theory as a nation, all that one needs is imagination
and some cultural heritage of shared symbols and memories to call upon.

THE POLITICIZATION OF NATIONAL COMMUNITY

Let me turn now to the second half of my argument, the way in which
the new conception of popular sovereignty tends to politicize our image
of national community. This doctrine's vision of indirect sovereignty
tends to nationalize our image of political community by encouraging
us to look for the prepolitical and cultural roots that bind the people

[35] Quoted in ibid., 76–77. The quotations are mostly from Milton's most famous and
influential political essay, *Areopagitica*.
[36] This argument is presented most effectively by John Breuilly, *Nationalism and the
State* (Chicago: University of Chicago Press, 1994), 62, 390.

into a community. It politicizes our image of national community, in contrast, by introducing a stronger and more exclusive way of thinking about communal possession of territory.

Attachment to particular territories almost always plays an important role in assertions of national community. A nation, I would suggest, is best understood as an intergenerational community bound by an imagined heritage of cultural symbols and memories associated with a particular territory or territories. I deliberately use this rather weak expression, "associated with," to characterize the relationship between nations and territories in order to contrast it with the strong expressions of control or mastery connected to the assertion of sovereignty over territory. Sovereign control or mastery of territory is exclusive. If one community possesses it, another cannot. For the sovereign is whoever has the final say in the exercise or establishment of authority in a territory. Joint or divided sovereignty is either a metaphor or a contradiction in terms. But nations need not control or master territories to make them the basis of their community. Dwelling in or even remembering doing so is quite sufficient to generate the stories and symbols that constitute a national heritage. Indeed, a nation's strongest sentiments often center on territories that it neither dwells in nor controls: the homelands that earlier generations left behind.

As a result, the same territory can figure prominently in the stories that more than one nation tells about itself without necessarily inviting serious conflict. The really dangerous conflicts emerge when nations begin to measure their relationship to territory in terms of control or mastery. For then all the overlapping homelands or overlapping sites of past greatness turn into potential flashpoints in nationalist conflicts.[37] And that happens as soon as the new understanding of popular sovereignty introduces its new conception of communal mastery over territory. Of course, national foundation myths regularly refer to the granting of lands to nations and their progeny. But the new idea of popular sovereignty introduces a much stronger and more political sense of the communal control of territory, one that helps explain the politicization of national loyalties.

The new popular sovereignty doctrine teaches us to think of states as masters of territory and peoples as masters of states. Or to put it an-

---

[37] I add "sites of past greatness" to emphasize, with Istvan Bibo, that it is the memory of connection to territory, not just present dwelling, that leads to nationalist conflicts. The intermixing of peoples in the Balkans, Bibo suggests, might have been sorted out with far less violence if it were not for the fact that these peoples were sustained by tales of past greatness in the same territories. See Istvan Bibo, "The Distress of East European Small States," in *Democracy, Revolution, and Self-Determination* (New York: Columbia University Press, 1991), 22–23.

other way, it teaches us that states are the means that people establish in order to exercise their mastery over given territories. Such mastery, based as it is on the use of the state's singular structure of authority, is, by definition, exclusive. No more than one people can be master of a given territory, since the state, with its exclusive claim to authority, is the means by which it is exercised.

The assertion of this new kind of communal mastery of territory leaves little room for the vaguer and less exclusive connections to territory that have so long characterized national communities. For how can we continue to talk about a territory as our own when another community — moreover, a community that, as we have seen, almost inevitably expresses itself in national terms — claims exclusive mastery over it? Pride, fear, envy, or just a strong sense of justice and injustice makes anything less than such mastery seem dangerous or degrading to those who lack it. In this way, the dissemination of the new understanding of popular sovereignty politicizes national loyalties, as the leaders of one national group after another demand that they be, as the Québécois say, *maîtres chez nous*. Or, as Daniele Manin, leader of the ill-fated Venetian revolt in 1848, proclaims: "We do not ask Austria be humane and liberal in Italy . . . we ask her to get out. We have no concern with her humanity and liberalism; we wish to be masters in our own house."[38]

Of course, popular sovereignty doctrines insist that it is the people, the collective body of a territory's inhabitants, rather than a national community that should exercise such mastery. Nevertheless, these doctrines open the door to assertions of national sovereignty by justifying the right of peoples to disestablish and reconstruct the authority of the state. For when they arrive on the scene they find people living not only with the injustices that flow from absolutism, feudal privilege, and other abuses of authority within states, but with all of the injustices that come from the history of conquest, royal marriages, sales of territory, and just plain bad luck that defines the boundaries of states and empires. Some people, when they are introduced to the new doctrine of popular sovereignty, find themselves ruled from distant and alien capitals, from which they can expect little understanding or sympathy for distinctive local conditions. Others find themselves subject to the authority of imperial rulers who treat them as inferior races incapable of civilized forms of self-government. Still others find themselves conspicuous and dangerously exposed minorities within larger communities that share a sense of belonging to a national community. The establishment of legitimate and humane forms of government might ease many concerns about injustice for these groups of people. But it would be foolish or naïve to

[38] Quoted in Emerson, *From Empire to Nation*, 43.

say that it could erase all of the potential for injustice that is created by the history of force, fraud, and chance that has led to the current boundaries among states.

Defenders of popular sovereignty often proclaim that human beings are capable "of establishing good government from reflection and choice," rather than "destined to depend, for their political constitutions, on accident and force."[39] But why should exposed minorities, subordinated peoples, and those at the periphery of large, indifferent states simply accept state boundaries as given when they begin to think about how to establish legitimate structures of political authority with which to govern themselves? It is one thing when you tell the members of a group who form the great majority of a state's subjects—Englishmen, say—to take for granted the state's boundaries in their deliberations about what "the people" should do. It is quite another when you tell that to the members of the other groups I have just mentioned. To tell them that they must simply cast their lot with whatever group that history has served up to them seems manifestly unfair. Why should the dance of history that provided some people with communities in which they feel comfortable stop just when *they* get a turn to express themselves on the floor? One does not have to believe, with Herder and Mazzini, that nations are natural divisions of the human race in order to express impatience with such a demand. One need only share their perfectly reasonable insistence on the arbitrariness or artificiality of the historical divisions among states.[40]

Resignation to the contingencies of history does not at all fit with the rhetoric of popular sovereignty. Yet, in effect, that is what many liberal democratic theorists seem to demand from peoples uncomfortable with the shape of their communities: that they should accept whatever potential injustices history has served up to them with the boundaries of states so that we can all get on with the task of establishing liberal democratic forms of government. The fact that this advice almost invariably comes from people who are quite comfortable and unexposed within the given boundaries of states—people who, in effect, are happy with the partners they were given when the music stopped playing at the dance of history—makes it harder to accept than it would otherwise be.

Thus while popular sovereignty is not designed to help us determine

---

[39] Alexander Hamilton, John Jay, and James Madison, *The Federalist Papers*, no. 1.

[40] "Natural divisions, the spontaneous tendencies of the peoples will replace the arbitrary divisions sanctioned by bad governments. The countries of the People will rise, defined by the voice of the free, upon the ruins of the countries of Kings and privileged castes." Giuseppe Mazzini, *The Duties of Man* (London: Dent, 1907), 52.

the legitimacy of a particular community's control over a particular territory, it definitely opens the door to this question. And in doing so it raises a question that it cannot itself answer. Who belongs to "the people" in 1848 Venice, 1955 Algeria, or 1999 Quebec? Inhabitants of Venice, Algeria, or Quebec or all of the Austrians and Italians, French and Arabs, Anglophones and Francophones who share the boundaries of the larger states to which they belonged at the time? We cannot simply say to those who put forward competing claims to territory in the name of different peoples, "let the people decide," since it is precisely which "people" should be associated with which territory that is at issue. Does letting the people decide disputes like those surrounding demands for Quebecois independence require a referendum among all the citizens within the boundaries of the province of Quebec or among all the citizens within the boundaries ruled by the federal government of Canada? One cannot answer such questions without, in effect, taking sides on the issue that one wants to put before "the people."[41]

One needs to assume the existence of boundaries between peoples before one can exercise the principle of popular sovereignty. Therefore, one cannot use popular sovereignty to determine where the boundaries between peoples should lie. Popular sovereignty can help guide us in determining our political arrangements. It cannot help us decide how to determine the shape of our collective selves.[42] But by arguing that this collective self, the people, precedes and survives the state, it opens up the question of how to determine our collective selves and their control of states and territory. Where there is little concern or discomfort with the given boundaries of the state, this question will probably not surface. But where there is some controversy or discomfort, the inconsistency between these two ways of talking about self-determination is bound to come out. For while popular sovereignty rests on the assumption that the state is the creature of the people, to be dissolved and reconstituted as the people will, the people only gets the limits of its identity from the boundaries of the state according to the doctrine of popular sovereignty. It is little wonder, then, that those who are uncomfortable with the boundaries that history has delivered to them start looking to other visions of community as the source of state sovereignty. The new doctrine of popular sovereignty does not single out national communities and encourage them to take control of their own affairs.

[41] See Fredrick Whelan, "Democratic Theory and the Boundary Problem," in James Roland Pennock and John W. Chapman eds., Nomos XXV: Liberal Democracy (New York: NYU Press, 1983), 13; Canovan, Nationhood and Political Theory, 17–18.

[42] This ambiguity between collective self-determination and the determination of collective selves plagues most attempts to justify the right to national self-determination.

But it does justify the delegitimation of state boundaries without giving any useful guidance — other than resignation — to those who are dissatisfied with the way in which they currently divide up political and cultural communities.

CONCLUSION

I have tried in this chapter to show how a distinctly liberal conception of popular sovereignty contributes to the rise and spread of nationalism. This account of the relationship between nationalism and popular sovereignty raises some serious doubts about contemporary attempts to use liberal ideals and institutions to tame nationalist politics. For if that account is correct, then liberal politics is one of the sources of the politicization of cultural loyalties that makes nationalism such a powerful force in modern political life.

Nationalism threatens liberal ideals and institutions primarily by the way in which it connects political rights and privileges to relatively exclusive understandings of cultural community. As a result, promoters of distinctly liberal forms of nationalism have sought means of severing the nationalist connection between political and cultural community. They pursue this goal in two different ways: by trying to refocus national loyalties on purely political objects or by trying to refocus them on purely cultural objects. The first strategy, the one chosen by defenders of what I have elsewhere described as "the myth of the civic nation,"[43] aims at purifying national loyalties of the sense of cultural uniqueness that accompanies national life in most modern political communities.[44] The second strategy, in contrast, aims at purifying cultural particularism of the temptation to seek political power to which it

[43] Bernard Yack, "The Myth of the Civic Nation," in Ronald Beiner ed., *Theorizing Nationalism* (Albany: SUNY Press, 1998), 103–18.

[44] For example, see Michael Ignatieff, *Blood and Belonging* (New York: Farrar, Strauss & Giroux, 1993), 7–13. For similar arguments, see Bogdan Denitch's defense of civic nationalism in *Ethnic Nationalism: The Tragic Death of Yugoslavia* (Minneapolis: University of Minnesota Press, 1994); Liah Greenfeld's distinction between Anglo-American and continental European forms of nationalism in *Nationalism*; and Dominique Schnapper's defense of the idea of the civic nation, in which she attempts to prove that the "very notion of an ethnic nation is a contradiction in terms," in *La communauté des citoyens: sur l'idée moderne de la nation* (Paris: Gallimard, 1994), 24–30, 95, 178. Habermas's influential argument in favor of what he calls "constitutional patriotism" represents another version of this argument, though it relies on a distinction between patriotism and nationalism, rather than between civic and ethnic nationalism. See Jurgen Habermas, "Citizenship and National Identity," in Beiner ed., *Theorizing Citizenship* (Albany: SUNY Press, 1995), 255–82. See also Maurizio Viroli, *For Love of Country: An Essay on Patriotism and Nationalism* (Oxford: Oxford University Press, 1995).

has succumbed in the age of nationalism. In other words, while some liberal democrats seek to departicularize national loyalties, others seek to depoliticize them.

The argument that nationalism comes in distinctly political and cultural variants is an old one.[45] But it has become increasingly popular among liberal theorists as a means of preserving nationalism's enhancement of state capacity while, at the same time, neutralizing its threat to liberal democratic principles and practices. Where national community rests on shared political principles rather than some particular cultural heritage, so the argument goes, then reliance on national loyalties need not threaten social diversity and individual rights, as long, of course, as it is liberal democratic principles that we share. Conceived in this way, civic nationalism turns "national belonging [into] a form of rational attachment" that strengthens states without exposing them to the dangers associated with the cultural or ethnic nationalist's belief that "an individual's deepest attachments are inherited, not chosen."[46]

The argument that politics corrupts the intrinsically cultural bonds of national community is also old and familiar, stretching back at least to Herder's defense of cultural nationalism. It was popular among Austro-Hungarian pluralists like Otto Bauer and has been given new life in Yael Tamir's recent book, *Liberal Nationalism*. Rebecca West presents a particularly eloquent version of this argument in *Black Lamb, Grey Falcon*, her extraordinary account of her travels in Yugoslavia during the 1930s. It comes near the end of that long celebration of Yugoslavia's cultural diversity, when West finally reaches Kosovo and its shrines to Serbian nationalism. Deeply moved by the way in which some boys recite the legend of Serbian self-sacrifice here on Kosovo's "field of blackbirds," she is inspired to defend cultural nationalism against its critics.

> The little boys looked noble and devout as they recited. Here was the nationalism which the intellectuals of my age agreed to consider a vice and the origin of the world's misfortunes. I cannot imagine why. Every human being is of sublime value, because his experience, which must be in some measure unique, gives him a unique view of reality, and the sum of such views should go far to giving us the complete picture of reality, which the human race must attain if it is ever to comprehend its destiny. Therefore every human being must be encouraged to cultivate his consciousness to the fullest degree. It follows that every nation, being an association of human beings who have been drawn together by common experience, has also its

[45] See, for example, Friedrich Meinecke, *Cosmopolitanism and the National State* (Princeton: Princeton University Press, 1970); Hans Kohn, *The Idea of Nationalism* (New York: Macmillan, 1945), 329–30.

[46] Ignatieff, *Blood and Belonging*, 7–8.

own unique view of reality, which must contribute to our deliverance. There is not the smallest reason for confounding nationalism, which is the desire of a people to be itself, with imperialism, which is the desire of a people to prevent other peoples from being themselves. . . . Here certainly I could look without any reservation on the scene, on the two little boys darkening their brows in imitation of the heroes as they spoke the stern verse. . . . This was as unlikely to beget any ill as the wild roses and meadowsweets we had gathered by the road.[47]

After the terrible violence unleashed by the recent attempt to keep Kosovo Serbian, these words are, of course, weighed down with a terrible irony. Little boys "darkening their brows" in imitation of Serbian national heroes cannot help but suggest to us something considerably more sinister than the gathering of roadside flowers.[48] Nevertheless, West's argument is not at all unreasonable. How can we deny that there is great value in the diverse ways in which people have come to express themselves and hand those forms of expression down to their children? Would not a world in which we lost touch with these forms of expression be immeasurably poorer? Why not try to recover and protect the life-affirming creativity of cultural nationalism from the life-threatening temptations of political nationalism?

Such is the goal that Yael Tamir, among others, pursues in her attempt to purge nationalism of its illiberal tendencies. Nations, she declares, should be understood as communities that allow for shared and voluntary forms of cultural expression. Nationalism, she suggests, is the form that such expression takes, although it has unfortunately been confused with the pursuit and exercise of political power. She concludes that if we can return to the original cultural understanding of nations and nationalism, then we can truly reconcile nationalism and liberalism.[49] Others share this conclusion but speak instead of a return to "nations without nationalism" or "nations against states,"[50] since, like myself, they identify nationalism with the political self-assertion of nations.

[47] Rebecca West, *Black Lamb, Grey Falcon* (London: Penguin, 1988), 843. Like Tamir's, West's liberal cultural nationalism is inspired by Herder's cultural pluralism.

[48] A different, but equally terrible irony hung over the book at the time of its publication. For West published *Black Lamb, Grey Falcon* shortly after the Nazis invaded Yugoslavia and destroyed so many of the people and forms of life that she had so lovingly described. See her remarks in the book's preface.

[49] Yael Tamir, *Liberal Nationalism* (Princeton: Princeton University Press, 1993), 57–58. I discuss the strengths and weaknesses of Tamir's argument more generally in "Reconciling Liberalism and Nationalism," 170–75.

[50] Julia Kristeva, *Nations without Nationalism* (New York: Columbia University Press, 1993); Gidon Gottlieb, *Nations against States* (New York: Council on Foreign Relations, 1993).

The viability of these solutions to the problems that nationalism creates for the liberal democratic state depends on just what it is that has led to the politicization of national community in the modern world. If the political self-assertion of intergenerational communities is a passing phenomenon based on values and practices that we are ready to discard, then these may indeed be promising paths for liberal democrats to follow. If, instead, it has developed because of features of modern life and politics that we now hold dear and/or indispensable, then it is not.

In this chapter I have argued that the latter is true. For one important source of the politicization of national loyalties in the modern world seems to be an idea that most liberals continue to hold both dear and indispensable to a decent political order: the principle of popular sovereignty. Indeed, one of the many ironies of the process of globalization is that while it tends to diminish cultural differences, it also spreads a principle of political legitimacy that tends to politicize those differences that remain.

CHAPTER 2

What States Can Do with Nations: An Iron Law of Nationalism and Federation?

BRENDAN O'LEARY

A federal state requires for its formation two conditions. There must exist, in the first place, a body of countries . . . so closely connected by locality, by history, by race, or the like, as to be capable of bearing in the eyes of their inhabitants, an impress of common nationality . . . A second condition absolutely essential to the founding of a federal system is the existence of a very peculiar . . . sentiment . . . the inhabitants . . . must desire union, and must not desire unity.
— Albert Venn Dicey, *Introduction to the Study of the Law of the Constitution*

Providence has been pleased to give this one connected country to one united people — a people descended from the same ancestors, speaking the same language, professing the same religion, attached to the same principles of government, very similar in their manners and their customs, and who, by their joint counsels, arms and efforts, fighting side by side throughout a long and bloody war, have nobly established their general liberty and independence.
— Publius (John Jay) et al., *The Federalist Papers*

Federalism as such is no guarantee for ethnic harmony and accommodation in the absence of other factors.
— Rudolpho Stavenhagen, *Ethnic Conflicts and the Nation-State*

THIS BOOK, under the lucid guidance of its editors, asks: what can states do now?[1] The question is driven by the dismal science of political econ-

---

[1] This chapter adapts ideas presented in the fifth Ernest Gellner Memorial lecture. See Brendan O'Leary, "An Iron Law of Federations? A (Neo-Diceyian) Theory of the Necessity of a Federal *Staatsvolk*, and of Consociational Rescue," *Nations and Nationalism* 7 (2001): 273–96.

omy, the "new" public management, and the empirically casual but high-excitement field known as the sociology of "globalization." Within each of these fields, claims of varying rigor, intelligibility, and testability have been made about the

- declining potency of governments, public policy programs, and the tools of big government;
- diminishing autonomy of states and their officials to act on their own preferences as they are increasingly hemmed in by international and domestic social and economic agents, processes, and structures;
- reduced capacity of states to steer, manage, and regulate as they might wish, and once did;
- inevitability of "regional" — meaning confederal or federal — blocs of trading states replacing individuated units that are now deemed too small or too weak.

The literature across these fields advertises itself in the slogan "the death of the nation-state," though more circumspect scholars use more measured words: "crisis," "limits," "decline," and "erosion."[2]

An analogous debate has not arisen within the field of the political science and political sociology of national and ethnic conflict regulation.[3] The coming "death of the nation-state" seems a highly premature if not bizarre claim given that the number of member-states of the so-called United Nations has just significantly expanded. The proclaimed extinc-

[2] For specimens in this genre, which vary significantly in their philosophical and empirical qualities see, e.g., Jean-Marie Gueheno, *The End of the Nation-State*, trans. V. Elliott (London: University of Minnesota Press, 2000 [1993]); Kenichi Ohmae, *The End of the Nation-State: The Rise of Regional Economies* (London: Harper Collins, 1995); Mathew Horsman and Andrew Marshall, *After the Nation-State: Citizens, Tribalism and the New World Disorder* (London: Harper Collins, 1995); John Dunn, ed., *Contemporary Crisis of the Nation-State?* (Oxford: Basil Blackwell, 1995); Jurgen Habermas, "The European Nation-State — Its Achievements and Its Limits: On the Past and Future of Sovereignty and Citizenship," *Ratio Juris* 9(2) (1996); David Held, "The Decline of the Nation State," in S. Hall and M. Jacques, eds., *New Times: The Changing Face of Politics* (London: Lawrence and Wishart, 1990); and M. Kolinsky, "The Nation-State in Western Europe: Erosion from Above and from Below," in L. Tivey, ed., *The Nation-State* (Oxford: Martin Robertson, 1981). For one critical response, see Michael Mann, "Nation-States in Europe and Other Continents — Diversifying, Developing, Not Dying," *Daedalus* 122 (1993): 115–40.

[3] See inter alia Donald L. Horowitz, *Ethnic Groups in Conflict* (Berkeley: University of California Press, 1985); Arend Lijphart, *Democracy in Plural Societies: A Comparative Exploration* (New Haven: Yale University Press, 1977); John McGarry and Brendan O'Leary "Introduction: The Macro-Political Regulation of Ethnic Conflict," in J. McGarry and B. O'Leary, eds., *The Politics of Ethnic Conflict Regulation* (London: Routledge, 1993); Eric A. Nordlinger, *Conflict Regulation in Divided Societies*, vol. 29, Occasional Papers in International Affairs (Cambridge: Center for International Affairs, Harvard University, 1972).

tion of the nation-state came at the end of a century that saw the collapse of the empires that ruled the world in 1900, and that closed with the collapse of a new one built from the debris of that of the tsars.[4] So, in logic, one might have expected reflections on the death of empires and the triumph of nations—especially when we all uncertainly await China's evolution, wondering whether it has failed to solve its national questions, and whether it will repeat its old cycle of breakdown after unification.[5] The claim that nation-states are fading fast also seems highly provocative and indeed deeply insensitive when numerous nations without states strive to reverse what they generally and correctly see as a major disadvantage in their collective powers, including their power of self-determination and self-government.

In the field of national and ethnic conflict regulation there has always been some recognition of the limits of states, or of the capacity of politics more generally, as institutions or means for resolving or managing ethnic and national antagonisms. But the field has shared a common assumption that governments and states have significant capacities to shape, for good or ill, the destiny of national and ethnic relations. "Nationality" and "ethnicity" are not regarded as primordial brute facts that governments and states must take as givens. State officials can pursue strategies either to eliminate or to manage ethno-national differences.[6] When pursuing elimination they can execute genocide or ethnic expulsion; they can partition territories; or they can homogenize peoples through integration or assimilation programs. Governments can, in short, try to "right-size" their states, and to "right-people" them.[7] We all know that modern governments have immense and awful powers to kill in genocidal or democidal programs,[8] and that they expel huge numbers of people. Some even insist that nation-state and democracy building are refugee-creating processes.[9] Individual states and military alli-

---

[4] See Brendan O'Leary, "Introduction," in B. O'Leary, I. S. Lustick, and T. Callaghy eds., *Right-Sizing the State: The Politics of Moving Borders* (Oxford: Oxford University Press, 2001).

[5] See inter alia Thomas Heberer, *China and Its National Minorities: Autonomy or Assimilation?* (Armonk, NY: M. E. Sharpe, 1989).

[6] See McGarry and O'Leary, "Introduction."

[7] See Brendan O'Leary, "The Elements of Right-Sizing and Right-Peopling the State," in O'Leary, Lustick, and Callaghy eds., *Right-Sizing the State*.

[8] See Rudolph J. Rummel, *Death by Government* (London: Transaction Publishers, 1997).

[9] See, e.g., Aristide R. Zolberg, "The Formation of New States as a Refugee-Generating Process," *Annals of the American Academy of Political and Social Science* 467 (1983): 24–38; Michael Mann "The Dark Side of Democracy: The Modern Tradition of Ethnic and Political Cleansing," *New Left Review* 235 (1999): 18–45.

ances of states still consider partitions as possible means to eliminate troublesome ethno-national antagonisms. In pumping significant resources and coercive capacities into integrating or maintaining the right peoples, molding them into common citizenship, and in some cases blending them within full-scale assimilation projects, the OECD's states seem, prima facie, no different from the mostly newer states outside their privileged ranks. "Nationalising states," as Rogers Brubaker has called them, are everywhere.[10] In short, to eliminate national and ethnic differences that might become politically salient, states have exercised awesome powers and ambitions in the century just passed, and they have often done so on behalf of their dominant nation or ethnic group(s). Whatever is happening in political economy or in new public management, there is no death of the nation-state in this domain — though there has been a lot of premature dying in the war of nation against state, state against nation, and nation against nation.

Exterminations or eliminations have not always been successful, thankfully; and not all states or governments have been exterminist or eliminationist. Indeed, in the field of national and ethnic conflict regulation, major theoretical, empirical, and normative effort is devoted to demonstrating that states can, in many cases, be designed or run to steer, manage, and regulate multinational, polycultural, and multilingual societies[11] in tolerable, tolerant, and democratic ways.[12] An increasing repertoire of institutional "technologies" — that is, legal strategies, systems of rights-protection, and public policies — is being identified, and in some cases pioneered, to manage ethno-national differences. For example, the ability of political agents, through benign or malign choices, to design elec-

[10] Rogers Brubaker, *Nationalism Reframed: Nationhood and the National Question in the New Europe* (Cambridge: Cambridge University Press, 1996) (a good book vitiated by its epistemic philosophical prejudices, which led the author to deny the reality of nations). Influenced by realism and an adaptation of Gramscian Marxism, Ian Lustick has argued that states have and may continue to develop "hegemonic projects," which, if successful, will incorporate territories and their peoples. See his *Unsettled States, Disputed Lands: Britain and Ireland, France and Algeria, Israel and the West Bank-Gaza* (Ithaca: Cornell University Press, 1993), and the follow-up debates in O'Leary, Lustick, and Callaghy eds., *Right-Sizing the State.*

[11] See, e.g., David D. Laitin, "Language Choice and National Development: A Typology for Africa," *International Interactions* 6 (1979): 291–321; *Language Repertoires and State Construction in Africa* (Cambridge: Cambridge University Press, 1992); *Politics, Language and Thought: The Somali Experience* (Chicago: University of Chicago Press, 1977).

[12] Some go further and claim that polyethnic states are the norm in world history, one to which we shall inevitably return, e.g., William H. McNeill, *Polyethnicity and World History: National Unity in World History* (Toronto: University of Toronto Press, 1986).

toral systems that provoke, calm, or rechannel ethnic tensions is now appraised in a literature of increasing comparative sophistication.[13]

States and governments may of course seek to manage ethno-national differences through malign and hierarchical methods, through systems of control that organize the dominant group and that disorganize the dominated.[14] But what is normatively and empirically challenging is to ask whether there are limits to what states can do when seeking to manage ethno-national differences in a benign, liberal-democratic manner. That is how I have chosen to respond to the editors' question of what states can do now in my field. I take as my text Ernest Gellner's theory of nationalism, which, at least on a standard reading, suggests that in transit to modernity states must choose between nationalizing or homogenizing their constituent cultures, or face breakup, and that the subjects of states must choose between being assimilated or being cleansed.

THE PERSISTENCE OF POLYCULTURAL
AND MULTINATIONAL STATES

The starting point is a standard criticism of Gellner's theory of nationalism. Here is one attempt to summarize it. Gellner

> appeared to assume that the range of possibilities in modern times is bifurcated: there is a simple choice between nationalist homogenization through assimilation, and nationalist secessionism which produces another nationalist homogenization. . . . [But] modern political entities have . . . developed strategies . . . that *prima facie*, counteract the potency of nationalist homogenization . . . systems of control; arbitration; federation/autonomy; and consociation. The last three of these are compatible with liberal and egalitarian pluralist principles. Throughout modernity these methods have existed at various times, and in many parts of the world, and new versions of them are continually springing into being. . . . [T]he persistence of such strategies, and regimes based upon them, are empirical embarrassments for Gellner's theory. The equilibrium condition of one nation, one state, seems to be continually elusive.

I was the author of the words just quoted,[15] but my position was not unusual. Professor Alfred Stepan expressed very similar sentiments in

[13] See Ben Reilly and Andrew Reynolds, *Electoral Systems and Conflict in Divided Societies* (Washington, DC: National Academy Press, 1999).

[14] The pioneering article here is Ian S. Lustick, "Stability in Deeply Divided Societies: Consociationalism versus Control," *World Politics* 31 (1979): 325–44.

[15] Brendan O'Leary, "Gellner's Diagnoses of Nationalism: A Critical Overview *or* What

the same edited volume—his chapter is entitled "Modern Multinational Democracies: Transcending a Gellnerian Oxymoron."[16] Al Stepan and I are political scientists by trade. We have no quarrel with the evidence in favor of Gellner's theory: in the last two centuries the bleak testimony of genocides, ethnic expulsions, coercive assimilations, partitions, secessions, and territorial restructurings following imperial collapses has tempered the optimism of all but the most fanatical exponents of human progress. But Stepan and I, representing political scientists, had two responses to Gellner. The first was empirical: the persistence of liberal democratic polycultural or multinational states, federal and/or consociational in format, suggests blatant disconfirmation of Gellner's pessimism. The second was normative: we did not want to accept fundamental sociological limitations on state capacity and autonomy, particularly in constitutional statecraft, especially if these limitations suggested severe constraints on the institutional management of cultural and national differences consistent with liberal democratic values.

There is no doubt that Gellner held the views we ascribed to him. Here are four samples, one from *Nations and Nationalism*, two from *Conditions of Liberty* and one from *Nationalism*:

> Nowadays people can only live in units defined by a shared culture, and internally mobile and fluid. Genuine cultural pluralism ceases to be viable under current conditions.[17]

> [T]he new imperative of cultural homogeneity . . . is the very essence of nationalism . . . [F]or the first time in world history a High Culture . . . becomes the pervasive and operational culture of an entire society. . . . The state has not merely the monopoly of legitimate violence, but also of the accreditation of educational qualification. So the marriage of state and culture takes place, and we find ourselves in the Age of Nationalism.[18]

> At the beginning of the social transformation which brought about the new state of affairs, the world was full of political units of all sizes, often overlapping, and of cultural nuances. . . . Under the new social regime, this became increasingly uncomfortable. Men then had two options, if they were to diminish such discomfort: they could change their own culture, or

---

Is Living and What is Dead in Gellner's Philosophy of Nationalism?" in John A. Hall, ed., *The State of the Nation: Ernest Gellner and the Theory of Nationalism* (Cambridge: Cambridge University Press, 1998), 63–64.

[16] Alfred Stepan, "Modern Multinational Democracies: Transcending a Gellnerian Oxymoron," in Hall, ed., *The State of the Nation.*

[17] Ernest Gellner, *Nations and Nationalism* (Oxford: Basil Blackwell, 1983), 55.

[18] Ernest Gellner, *Conditions of Liberty: Civil Society and its Rivals* (London: Hamish Hamilton, 1994), 105–8.

they could change the nature of the political unit, either by changing its boundaries or by changing its cultural identifications.[19]

> In our age, many political systems which combine . . . cultural pluralism with a persisting inequality between cultures . . . are doomed, in virtue of their violation of the nationalist principle which, in past ages, could be violated with impunity.[20]

Gellner emphasized that nationalism is the primary principle of political legitimacy of modernity — along with affluence.[21] It is not the only principle, and it is not irresistible,[22] but his readers are left in no doubt of its potency. He was emphatic, especially in his posthumously published essay, *Nationalism*, that he would strongly have preferred matters to be otherwise. He did not welcome political instability, such as that engendered by the breakup of the federations of the Soviet Union, Yugoslavia, and Czechoslovakia. He entertained hopes that advanced industrialization might diminish national conflicts; that emerging global imperatives might prompt a new global division of competencies with supranational government to manage technological, ecological, and terrorist threats in conjunction with the cantonization of local and educational functions; and that the "defetishization" of land might be possible.[23] In brief, he was not against federalism, or other forms of polycultural and multinational government — or indeed the postnational government foreseen by some seers. If anything, he was strongly in favor of them. He was just skeptical about their prospects, and their likely robustness.

The arguments made by me, and by others, against Gellner may, however, have been incorrect, or at least premature. In what follows I argue that Gellner's implicit theses about the limited prospects for the reconciliation of nationalism with federalism were more powerful, and more consistent with the evidence, than they seemed — though he himself may not have done the research to demonstrate this. I will therefore extend Gellner's theory in a manner consistent with his own propositions, if not with his words. If the arguments are persuasive, then the criticisms leveled by me and others need to be rejected, or severely qualified. But they will also suggest that there is more room for constitutional statecraft than Gellner acknowledged.

To explain what follows, definitions of federalism, federal political systems, federation, and nationalism are required, together with a brief

---

[19] Ibid., 108.

[20] Ernest Gellner, *Nationalism* (London: Weidenfeld and Nicolson, 1997), 104.

[21] Ernest Gellner, *Thought and Change* (London: Weidenfeld and Nicolson, 1964).

[22] Gellner, *Nations and Nationalism*, 138.

[23] Gellner, *Nationalism*, 102–8.

résumé of how they have been jointly treated in practical political argument. Then I elaborate and explain a theory of why stable democratic federations require a *Staatsvolk*, a dominant people. Having done that, I present evidence in favor of the theory, together with some apparently awkward evidence. This apparently awkward evidence will then be explained or, if you prefer, explained away. Lastly, I turn to the political implications of the arguments, and the implications for this volume.

FEDERALISM, FEDERAL POLITICAL SYSTEMS, FEDERATIONS, AND NATIONALISM

Federalism is a normative political philosophy that recommends the use of federal principles, that is, combining joint action and self-government.[24] 'Federal political systems' is a descriptive catchall term for all political organizations that combine what Daniel Elazar called "shared rule and self-rule." Federal political systems, thus broadly construed, include federations, confederations, unions, federacies, associated states, condominiums, leagues, and cross-border functional authorities.[25] Federations, with which I will be particularly concerned here, are distinct federal political systems[26] and are best understood in their authentic — that is, representative — governmental forms.[27] In a genuinely democratic federation, there is a compound sovereign state, in which at least two governmental units, the federal and the regional, enjoy constitu-

[24] Preston King, *Federalism and Federation* (London: Croom Helm, 1982).

[25] Daniel Elazar, *Exploring Federalism* (Tuscaloosa: University of Alabama, 1987).

[26] Ronald L. Watts, "Federalism," in V. Bogdanor, ed., *The Blackwell Encyclopaedia of Political Institutions* (Oxford: Basil Blackwell, 1987), and "Federalism, Federal Political Systems, and Federations," *Annual Review of Political Science* 1 (1998): 117–37.

[27] The Soviet Union, Yugoslavia, and Czechoslovakia were not democratic federations. Citizens' "choices" of representatives in all governmental tiers were fictional until the late 1980s. When their choices became more democratic, the relevant states disintegrated largely mostly around the territorial units of the previously sham federations. The "federal republics" offered opportunity-structures for old and new political elites as the communist systems opened. The fact that the republics had titular nationalities, mostly substantive, made this prospect even more likely. Their experience offers additional confirmation of the generalization that "the dissolution of authoritarian structures cannot possibly save a supranational entity; instead it initially destroys it and helps to create new national entities that then need to be laboriously democratized." Cf. Alfred Pfabigan, "The Political Feasibility of the Austro-Marxist Proposal for the Solution of the Nationality Problem of the Danubian Monarchy," in U. Ra'anan, M. Mesner, K. Armes, and K. Martin, eds., *State and Nation in Multi-Ethnic Societies: The Breakup of Multi-National States* (Manchester: Manchester University Press, 1991), 63. What might have happened had the centers of these federations been democratized first must remain a matter for speculation. The argument developed here suggests that the Soviet and Yugoslav cases would have required consociational federations to have had any prospects of endurance.

tionally separate competencies—although they may also have concurrent powers. Both the federal and the regional governments are empowered to deal directly with the citizens, and the relevant citizens directly elect (at least some components of) the federal and regional governments. In a federation the federal government usually cannot unilaterally alter the horizontal division of powers—constitutional change affecting competencies requires the consent of both levels of government. Therefore federation automatically implies a codified and written constitution and normally is accompanied at the federal level by a supreme court, charged with umpiring differences between the governmental tiers,[28] and by a bicameral legislature—in which the federal as opposed to the popular chamber may disproportionally represent, that is, overrepresent, the smallest regions. Elazar rightly emphasized the "covenantal" character of federations; that is, the authority of each government derives from the constitution, not another government.

Having defined the "F-words," let us turn to nationalism. Nationalism is a political philosophy that holds that the nation "should be collectively and freely institutionally expressed, and ruled by its co-nationals."[29] This definition is similar to Gellner's, who held that nationalism is "primarily a political principle, which holds that the political and the national unit should be congruent."[30] Nothing in either definition makes nationalism automatically incompatible with federalism, or federal political systems, or federation. Collective and free institutional expression of more than one nation may, in principle, be possible within a federation. The federation may be organized to make the regional political units and the national units "congruent." Being "ruled by co-nationals" may appear to be breached somewhat in a federation when the federal level of government involves joint rule by the representatives of more than one nation, but providing the relevant nations have assented to this arrangement, no fundamental denial of the principle of national self-determination is involved. Moreover, if we acknowledge that dual or even multiple nationalities are possible, then federations, in

---

[28] The judicial constructions of the relevant supreme court may radically affect the nature of the federation and the distribution of effective competencies. Despite an avowedly centralized federal constitution, the Canadian provinces are more powerful and the federal government is weaker than in any other federation, while the Australian federal government has become much more powerful and state powers have waned, despite operating a constitution designed to create a weak federal government. In both cases these outcomes are the result of judicial decision-making. Cf. Leslie Zines, *Constitutional Change in the Commonwealth* (Cambridge: Cambridge University Press, 1991), 79 and chap. 7 passim.

[29] Brendan O'Leary, "On the Nature of Nationalism: A Critical Appraisal of Ernest Gellner's Writings on Nationalism," *British Journal of Political Science* 27 (1997): 191.

[30] Gellner, *Nations and Nationalism*, 1.

principle, provide effective ways of giving these different identities opportunities for collective and free institutional expression. These definitions therefore permit federalism and nationalism to be compatible political philosophies. They avoid shutting off empirical research on the
relation between nationalism and federation. They do not axiomatically
deny the possibility of dual or multinational federations, and they avoid
any obvious commitments on the nature or status of nations.

NATIONALISM AND FEDERALISM IN PRACTICAL
POLITICAL DESIGN AND ARGUMENT

Three clear positions can be identified on the relationships between federalism and nationalism in the literature of state theory and practical
politics in the last two centuries. The first holds that nationalism and
federalism are mutually exclusive. The exemplary illustration of this
viewpoint is that of the French Jacobins, who believed that federalism
was part of the counterrevolution, thoroughly hostile to the necessity of
linguistic homogenization, a roadblock in the path of authentic, indivisible, monistic popular sovereignty. In his report to the Committee of
Public Safety of January 1794, Barère declared that "Federalism and
superstition speak low Breton; emigration and hatred of the Republic
speak German; the counterrevolution speaks Italian, and fanaticism
speaks Basque."[31] On one reading of Gellner's work, the Jacobins were
the nationalist state-builders par excellence. They sought cultural assimilation; they were determined to make peasants into Frenchmen; and
therefore they were deeply hostile to all forms of accommodation that
inhibited this goal, including federalism.

In partial agreement with the Jacobins, many nineteenth-century federalists, notably Joseph Proudon and Carlo Cattaneo, were resolutely
hostile to nation-state nationalism,[32] and many twentieth-century federalists, notably within the European movement, reciprocated the Jacobin
view that nationalism and federalism are mutually exclusive.[33] Such federalists have been, and are, resolutely antinationalist, associating nationalism with ethnic exclusiveness, chauvinism, racism, and parochially

[31] Michel de Certaus, Julia Dominique, and Jacques Revel, *Une Politique de la Langue.
La Révolution Française et les patois: L'eenquête de Grégoire* (Paris: Gallimard, 1975),
295, cited in Rogers Brubaker, *Nationalism Reframed*, 7.

[32] Luigi Vittoria Majocchi, "Nationalism and Federalism in 19th Century Europe," in
Andrea Bosco, ed., *The Federal Idea: The History of Federalism from Enlightenment to
1945* (London: Lothian Press, 1991), 162.

[33] Andrea Bosco, ed., *The Federal Idea: the History of Federalism since 1945* (London:
Lothian Foundation Press, 1992), vol. 2, Part 3.

particularistic sentiments. For them federalism belongs to an entirely different cooperative philosophy, one that offers a nonnationalist logic of legitimacy, and an antidote to nationalism rather than a close relative. This viewpoint was most clearly articulated by Pierre Trudeau — educated at the LSE by Elie Kedourie, Gellner's counterpoint — before he became Canadian prime minister. In an article entitled "Federalism, Nationalism and Reason," Trudeau squarely associated federalism and functionalism with reason, nationalism with the emotions.[34] Thinkers like Trudeau regard federalism as the denial of and solution to nationalism, though occasionally they adopt the view that federalism must be built upon the success of nationalism, which it then transcends in Hegelian fashion.[35] In effect they echo Einstein's reported remark that nationalism is the measles of mankind.

The second perspective, by contrast, holds that nationalism and federalism, properly understood, are synonymous. This was the thesis of the Austro-Marxists, Karl Renner and Otto Bauer, in the last days of the Habsburg empire.[36] Lenin, Stalin, and their colleagues in the course of Soviet state-building pressed their arguments, in a suitably bowdlerized format, into service. In this conception, nationalism and federalism were to be harnessed, at least for the task of building Soviet socialism. In the authoritative words of Walker Connor, Lenin's second commandment on the management of nationalism was strategically Machiavellian: "Following the assumption of power, terminate the fact — if not necessarily the fiction — of a right to secession, and begin the lengthy process of assimilation via the dialectical route of territorial autonomy for all compact national groups."[37] Marxist-Leninists were, of course, formal cosmopolitans, committed to a global political order, but pending the world revolution, they maintained that federal arrangements, "national in form, socialist in content," were the optimal institutional path to global communism.

The third perspective unites those who think that federalism and nationalism can intersect, and be mutually compatible, but who sensibly believe that not all nationalisms are compatible with all federalisms. But this agreement masks an important difference, one between what I shall

---

[34] Pierre Elliot Trudeau, *Federalism and the French Canadians* (Toronto: University of Toronto Press, 1968).

[35] Majocchi, "Nationalism and Federalism," 161.

[36] See, e.g., Otto Bauer, *Die Nationalitätenfrage und die Sozialdemokratie* (Vienna: Wiener Volksbuchhandlung, 1907); Theodor Hanf, "Reducing Conflict through Cultural Autonomy: Karl Renner's Contribution," in Ra'anan et al., eds., *State and Nation in Multi-Ethnic Societies; and Alfred Pfabigan, "Political Feasibility."*

[37] See Walker Connor, *The National Question in Marxist-Leninist Theory and Strategy* (Princeton: Princeton University Press, 1984), 38.

call national or mononational federalists, and multinational or multi-ethnic federalists. National federalists are exemplified by the first exponents of federation in its modern form, for whom its prime function was "to unite people living in different political units, who nevertheless shared a common language and culture."[38] The earliest federalists in what became the Netherlands, in the German-speaking Swiss lands, in what became the United States, and in what became the second German Reich, were national federalists. They maintained that only an autonomous federal government could perform certain necessary functions that confederations or alliances found difficult to perform, especially a unified defense and external relations policy.[39] They often advocated federation as a stepping stone toward a more centralized unitary state.

The United States may serve as the paradigm case of national federalism, which has been imitated by its Latin American counterparts in Mexico, Brazil, Venezuela, and Argentina. The U.S. federation shows "little coincidence between ethnic groups and state boundaries,"[40] with one major exception: most of its original and subsequent states had white Anglo-Saxon Protestant majorities. Federation preceded the great expansion in the internal ethnic diversity in the United States, and new states were generally created only when they had WASP or assimilated white demographic and electoral majorities.[41] English-speaking whites were the creators of every American state, "writing its Constitution, establishing its laws, ignoring the previously settled American Indians, refusing to grant any [autonomy] rights to blacks, and making only slight concessions to French and Spanish speakers in a few states."[42] National federalism was part and parcel of American nation-building,[43] aiding the homogenization of white settlers and immigrants in the famous melting pot of Anglo conformity,[44] and was evident in the writing

---

[38] See Murray Forsyth, ed., *Federalism and Nationalism* (Leicester: Leicester University Press, 1989), 4.

[39] William H. Riker, *Federalism: Origin, Operation, Significance* (Boston: Little, Brown, 1964).

[40] Nathan Glazer, *Ethnic Dilemmas, 1964–82* (Cambridge: Harvard University Press, 1983), 276.

[41] There were some exceptions to this pattern, as Glazer points out. Moreover, a fully correct description of the U.S. constitutional form enumerates it as consisting of 50 states, 2 federacies, 3 associated states, 3 local home rule territories, 3 unincorporated territories, and 130 Native American domestic dependent nations. Cf. Ronald L Watts, *Comparing Federal Systems in the 1990s* (Kingston, Ontario: Institute of Intergovernmental Relations, Queen's University, 1996), 10.

[42] Glazer, "Federalism and Ethnicity," 284.

[43] Samuel H. Beer, *To Make a Nation: The Rediscovery of American Federalism* (Cambridge: Belknap Press, Harvard University, 1993).

[44] See Milton M. Gordon, *Assimilation in American Life: The Role of Race, Religion and National Origins* (New York: Oxford University Press, 1964).

of *The Federalist Papers*. National federalism poses no problem for Gellnerian theory. Indeed, it confirms it, because national federalists aim to make the sovereign polity congruent with one national culture.

Multinational or multiethnic federalists, by contrast, may pose a significant challenge to Gellnerian theory if they prove successful in their political endeavors. They advocate federation "to unite people who seek the advantages of membership of a common political unit, but differ markedly in descent, language and culture." They seek to express, institutionalize, and protect at least two national or ethnic cultures, often on a permanent basis. Any greater union or homogenization, if envisaged at all, is postponed for the future. They explicitly reject the strongly integrationist and/or assimilationist objectives of national federalists. They believe that dual or multiple national loyalties are possible, and indeed desirable. Some of them make quite remarkable claims for federalism. Political scientist Klaus von Beyme, referring to Western democracies, argued in 1985 that "Canada is the only country in which federalism did not prove capable of solving . . . ethnic conflict."[45] Multinational federalists have been influential in the development of federations in the former British Empire, notably in Canada, the Caribbean, Nigeria, South Africa, India, Pakistan, and Malaysia. They influenced Austro-Marxists and Marxist-Leninists and have had an enduring impact in the postcommunist development of the Russian Federation, Ethiopia, and the rump Yugoslavia. The recent democratic reconstructions of Spain and Belgium also bear their imprint. The most ambitious multinational federalists of our day are those who wish to develop the European Union from its currently largely confederal form into an explicit federation, into a "Europe of the nation-states and a Europe of the citizens," as the German foreign minister recently urged at Berlin's Humboldt University.[46]

Multinational federalists have two ways of arguing that national and ethnic conflict regulation can work to harmonize nationalism and federalism. The first is an argument from congruence. If the provincial borders of the components of the federation match the boundaries between the relevant national, ethnic, religious, or linguistic communities, that is, if there is a "federal society" congruent with the federating institutions, then federation may be an effective harmonizing device. That is precisely because it makes an ethnically heterogeneous political society less heterogeneous through the creation of more homogeneous subunits. Of the seven large-scale genuine federations in durable Western democracies, three significantly achieve this effect for some culturally distinct

---

[45] Klaus Von Beyme, *Political Parties in Western Democracies*, trans. E. Martin (Aldershot: Gower, 1985), 121.

[46] Joschka Fischer, "Apologies to the UK, but 'Federal' Is the Only Way," *The Independent*, London, May 16, 2000, 4.

communities: those of Belgium, Canada, and Switzerland. The federations of Australia, Austria, Germany, and the United States do not achieve this effect and are not organized to do so, and in consequence this possibility in federal engineering cannot be used to explain the relative ethno-national tranquillity of Australia, postwar Austria and Germany, and the postbellum United States (in which past genocides, the overwhelming of the indigenous populations, and/or integration/assimilation are more important in explaining ethno-national stability). In Belgium, Canada, and Switzerland, the success of federation in conflict regulation, such as it is, has not been the result of comprehensive territorial design. Rather it has been based largely upon the historic geographical segregation of the relevant communities. Postindependence India, especially after Nehru conceded reorganization of internal state borders along largely linguistic boundaries, is an example of deliberate democratic engineering to match certain ascriptive criteria with internal political borders.[47] Postcommunist Russia and Ethiopia may prove to be others.

Plainly this defense of federation as a way of managing nations — to each nation let a province be given — cannot satisfy those communities that are so dispersed, or small in numbers, that they cannot control federal units or provinces, such as Quebec Anglophones, Flemish speakers in Wallonia, Francophones in Flanders, and blacks in the United States; or small and scattered indigenous peoples in Australia, India, and North America. Indeed one reason federation proved insufficient as a conflict-regulating device as Yugoslavia democratized was that there was insufficient geographical clustering of the relevant ethnic communities in relation to their existing provincial borders. However, federal engineering to achieve something approximating the formula "one nation, one province" does look like a prima facie challenge to the tacit Gellnerian notion that in modern times the equilibrium condition is one sovereign state, one culture (or nation). If we treat broadly the "political unit" in Gellner's definition, to encompass regional or provincial units in a federation, then his theory can accommodate such arrangements, but at the significant concession of recognizing that such federal systems are compatible with dual and possibly multiple nationalities.

There is a second and more subtle way in which multinational or ethno-federalists may argue that nationalism and federalism can be harmonized, though it is rarely explicitly defended, because it is really a

---

[47] See inter alia Balveer Arora and Douglas V. Verney, *Multiple Identities in a Single State: Indian Federalism in Comparative Perspective* (New Delhi: Konark Publishers, 1995); Paul R. Brass, *The Politics of India since Independence* (New Delhi: Cambridge University Press, 1991).

strategy to defeat national self-determination. It has been eloquently defended by Donald Horowitz.[48] He suggests that federations can and should be partly designed to prevent ethnic minorities from becoming local provincial majorities. The thinking here recommends weakening potentially competing ethno-nationalisms: federalism's territorial merits are said to lie in the fact that it can be used as an instrument to prevent local majoritarianism (which has the attendant risks of local tyranny or secessionist incentives). Designing the provincial borders of the federated units on this argument should be executed on "balance of power" principles — proliferating, where possible, the points of power away from one focal center, encouraging intraethnic conflict, and creating incentives for interethnic cooperation (by designing provinces without majorities), and for alignments based on nonethnic interests. This logic is extremely interesting, but empirical support for Horowitz's argument so far seems confined to the rather uninspiring case of postbellum Nigeria. In most existing federations, to redraw regional borders deliberately to achieve these results would probably require the services of military dictators or one-party states. Already mobilized ethno-national groups do not take kindly to efforts to disorganize them through the redrawing of internal political boundaries. Belgium may, however, become an interesting exception to this skepticism: the Brussels region, created in the new federation, is neither overtly Flemish nor Wallonian, and perhaps its heterogeneity will stabilize international relations in Belgium, because without Brussels Flanders will not secede, and there is at present little prospect of Brussels obliging Flanders.

Multinational and multiethnic federations have, of course, been developed for a variety of reasons, not just as means to harmonize nationalism and federalism. They have often evolved out of multiethnic colonies — to bind together the coalition opposing the imperial power (e.g., in the West Indies and Tanzania). They may have been promoted by the colonial power in an attempt to sustain a reformed imperial system but subsequently developed a dynamic of their own, as has been true of Canada, India, and indeed South Africa. A history of common colonial or conquest government usually creates elites (soldiers, bureaucrats, and capitalists) with an interest in sustaining the postcolonial territory in one political unit, as has sometimes been true of Indonesia, which has recently been recanvassed as a candidate for an authentic federation.[49] Large federations can often be sold economically — they promise a larger single market, a single currency, economies of scale, reductions in trans-

---

[48] Horowitz, *Ethnic Groups in Conflict*, chaps. 14 and 15.
[49] See Benedict Anderson, *The Spectre of Comparisons: Nationalism, Southeast Asia and the World* (London: Verso, 1998).

actions' costs, and fiscal equalization. Such instrumental discourses are the common coinage of Euro-federalists. Federations can also be marketed as geopolitically wise, offering greater security and protection than small states; indeed, William Riker rather prematurely assumed that this was the basis for the formation of all federations.[50] Lastly, federations can be advertised as necessary routes to superpower status, a foreground note in the enthusiasms of some Euro-federalists. But the fact that multinational or multiethnic federations may be overdetermined in their origins does not affect our central question: can the state-holders of multinational federations successfully and stably reconcile nationalism and federalism in liberal democratic ways?

The answer at first glance looks like "yes and no." There are federal successes and failures. Even some positive "yes" answers, however, would be enough to counteract the pessimism induced by Gellnerian theory. But let us first do a Cook's tour of the failures, which pose no problems for Gellnerian theory. Multinational or multiethnic federations have either broken down or failed to remain democratic, throughout the communist and the postcolonial world. The federations of Latin America — Mexico, Venezuela, Argentina, and Brazil — are either national federalisms or have yet to prove themselves durably democratic. The federations of the Soviet Union, Yugoslavia, and Czechoslovakia broke down during or immediately after their respective democratizations. In the postcolonial world, multinational or multiethnic federations failed, or failed to be successfully established, in the Caribbean, notably in the West Indies Federation. Even the miniature federation of St. Kitts-Nevis faced the prospect of secession by referendum by the smaller island of Nevis.[51] Multinational or multiethnic federations have failed in sub-Saharan Africa — in Francophone West and Equatorial Africa, British East Africa (Kenya, Uganda, and Tanganyika), in British Central Africa (Northern and Southern Rhodesia and Nyasaland) — or have failed to remain durably democratic — in Nigeria and Tanzania — or have yet to be established as durable authentic democracies — in South Africa. The Mali and the Ethiopian federations in independent Africa have experienced breakups; while the Cameroons has experienced forced unitarism after a federal beginning. The Arab world knows only one surviving federation, the United Arab Emirates, which does not score highly on democratic attributes. In Asia there have been obvious federative failures, in Indochina, Burma, and Pakistan, and of the union of Malaya followed by the secession of Singapore. Durably

---

[50] Riker, *Federalism*.

[51] Ralph R. Premdas, *Secession and Self-Determination in the Caribbean: Nevis and Tobago* (St. Augustine, Trinidad: University of the West Indies, 1998).

democratic federations have been rare—consider the history of Pakistan. In short, new multinational federations appear to have a poor track record as conflict-regulating devices, even where they allow a degree of minority self-government. They have broken down, or failed to be durably democratic, throughout Asia, Africa, and the Caribbean. India stands out as the major exception in Asia.

These failures in federation have had multiple causes, according to their analysts.[52] In some cases minorities were outnumbered at the federal level of government; in others, notably Malaya, the relevant minority was not welcome at the federal level of government—Lee Kuan Yew's courting of the Malay Chinese helped break the Malay federation. In both scenarios the resulting frustrations, combined with an already defined boundary, and the significant institutional resources flowing from control of their own province provided considerable incentives to attempt secession. Breaks from federations may, of course, invite harsh responses from the rest of the federation: the disintegration of the Nigerian and American federations were halted through millions of deaths. India, the most successful postcolonial, multiethnic federation, has so far faced down vigorous secessionist movements on its frontiers, especially in Kashmir and Punjab. The threat of secession in multinational or multiethnic federations is such that the late Eric Nordlinger consciously excluded federalism from his list of desirable conflict-regulating practices.[53] The recent emergent principle of international law that permits the disintegration of federations along the lines of their existing regional units is in some people's eyes likely to strengthen the belief that federation should not be considered a desirable form of multinational or multiethnic accommodation.[54] Integrationist nation-builders in Africa, Asia, and the Caribbean have distrusted federalism precisely because it provides secessionist opportunities. The kleptocratic Mobutu only offered federalism as a model for Zaire as his power-base collapsed. Tunku Abdul Rahman only offered federation with Singapore because he shared Lee Kuan Yew's fears of a communist takeover. Postcolonial state-builders' antipathy to federalism is now matched among the intellectuals of Eastern Europe, who regard it as a recipe for secession, given the Czechoslovakian, Yugoslavian, and Soviet experiences.

[52] See Thomas M. Franck, "Why Federations Fail," in *Why Federations Fail: An Inquiry into the Requisites for Successful Federalism* (New York: New York University Press, 1968); Ursula K. Hicks *Federalism, Failure and Success: A Comparative Study* (London: Macmillan, 1978); Elazar, *Exploring Federalism*, 240–44.

[53] Nordlinger, *Conflict Regulation in Divided Societies*.

[54] Donald Horowitz, "Self-Determination: Politics, Philosophy and Law," in Margaret Moore, ed., *National Self-Determination and Secession* (Oxford: Oxford University Press, 1998).

Two final generalizing statements must be added to this quick global survey of multinational or multiethnic federal failures. The first is that federations appear to have been especially fragile in bi-ethnic, bi-national, or bi-regional states. In 1982 Maurice Vile could not find a single case of a surviving federation based upon dyadic or triadic structures.[55] Pakistan's western and eastern divorce has been the biggest example of the instability of dualistic federations. Czechoslovakia is a more recent case. Whither Serbia and Montenegro, the last two units in Yugoslavia? Belgium may seem like a subsequently emergent exception to Vile's rule, but technically it is a four-unit federation, and it is of rather recent vintage. St. Kitts-Nevis may seem another, but, as already indicated, Nevis has been tempted to go. The second generalization is that failures have occurred largely in developing or poor countries, where most theorists of democratization would predict great difficulty in obtaining stable democratic regimes of whatever hue. This suggests that India, and the multinational democratic federations in the advanced industrial world, are the apparently anomalous successes that Gellnerian theory needs to be able to explain, or else stand overtly falsified.

A THEORY OF THE NECESSITY OF A FEDERAL *STAATSVOLK*

The theory that I wish to advance and explore is that *a stable democratic majoritarian federation,[56] be it national federal or multinational, must have a* Staatsvolk, *a national or ethnic people, who are demographically and electorally dominant* — though not necessarily an absolute majority of the population — and who must be the co-founders of the federation. This is a theory consistent with liberal nationalism, national federalism as I presented that idea earlier, and with Ernest Gellner's theory of nationalism. It is inconsistent with liberal cosmopolitan and radical multiculturalists' hopes, and with the more optimistic be-

---

[55] Maurice Vile, "Federation and Confederation: The Experience of the United States and the British Commonwealth," in D. Rea, ed., *Political Co-operation in Divided Societies* (Dublin: Gill and Macmillan, 1982).

[56] By a majoritarian federation I mean a nonconsociational one — this makes sure that the argument rests on clear antonyms. The federation is intended, at the federal level, to enable at least one branch of the federal government to have a clear federation-wide mandate based on some notion of a popular majority of the people established through a winner-take-all electoral formula of some kind. Normally both a president and a congressional house of representatives embody these notions, but so may a premier-cabinet. A majoritarian federation does not follow the principle of ethnic proportionality as a rule in its representative, bureaucratic, electoral, and judicial institutions; it does not officially recognize ethnic community as opposed to territorial autonomy; and it does not permit veto-rights to belong to ethnic groups — as opposed to territorial governments.

liefs of some federalists, though, as I shall argue, it does not require entirely bleak conclusions to be drawn about the prospects for constitutional statecraft and state management in multinational or multiethnic federations that lack a Staatsvolk. Let us call the theory the Dicey-O'Leary theory, as nice a compound pun as one could have.

The theory states a necessary condition of stability in a liberal democratic majoritarian federation, but not a sufficient one. Its logic rests on simple micro foundations. In liberal democratic systems the population-share of an ethno-national group can be taken as a reasonable proxy for its *potential* electoral power, if its members were fully mobilized en bloc — admittedly a rare occurrence. The underlying idea is therefore simple: in a majoritarian federation, an ethno-national group with a decisive majority of the federal population has no reason to fear federation. It has the ability simply to dominate the rest of the federation through its numbers, or to be generous — because it does not feel threatened. A Staatsvolk, a people who own the state, and who could control it on their own through simple democratic numbers, is a prime candidate to lead a federation — whether the federation is a national federation or a multinational federation, to be what the Russians called the titular nationality. The theory may also give a clue as to why multiple-unit federations appear at first glance to be more stable than binary or triadic federations. A Staatsvolk may be more willing to have its own national territory divided up into multiple regions, states, or provinces, knowing that it is not likely to be coerced by minority peoples at the federal level. The theory also implies that if there is no Staatsvolk, then majoritarian federalism, of whatever internal territorial configuration, will not be enough to sustain stability — a point to which I shall return.

Table 2.1 provides data that appear to confirm the Dicey-O'Leary theory. It lists the twenty-three currently democratic federations in the world — the data were collected before the coup in Pakistan —and it lists the share of the federation's population that I have classified as belonging to the relevant (or potential) Staatsvolk. I have arranged the data in descending order of the proportionate size of the relevant Staatsvolk. Let us take 50 percent as our initial threshold for the existence of a Staatsvolk, a plausible threshold for democratic majoritarian assessment. The data suggest that all the federations that have been durably democratic for more than thirty years have, prima facie, a Staatsvolk that is significantly over 50 percent of the relevant state's population: Australia (95), Austria (93), Germany (93), India (80) if its Staatsvolk is considered to be religious, the United States (74), Canada (67), if its Staatsvolk is considered to be Anglophones, Switzerland (64), and Malaysia (62). The African federations have not been durably democratic, but on this measure the Comoros Islands and South Africa have

TABLE 2.1
Size of the Actual or Potential Staatsvolk in Current Democratic Federations

Federation Name	Staatsvolk Name	% of Population
Comoros Islands [1980 ethnicity]	Comorian	97
Commonwealth of Australia [1986 ethnicity]	White Australians	95
St. Kitts and Nevis [1991 ethnicity]	Blacks	95
Federal Republic of Yugoslavia [1991 ethnicity]	Serbs	93
Federal Republic of Austria [1991 national origin]	Austrians	93
Federal Republic of Germany [1990 ethnicity]	Germans	93
Russian Federation [1984 ethnicity]	Russians	85
Argentine Republic [1986 ethnicity]	Whites	85
India (1)[a] [1991 religion]	Hindus	80
United States of America [1994 racial]	White Americans	74
Kingdom of Spain[b] [1980 ethno-lingual]	Spaniards	72
Canada [1991 linguistic]	Anglophones	67
Venezuela [1993 ethnicity]	Mestizo	67
South Africa (1)[c] [1994 ethnicity]	Blacks	65
Switzerland [1990 linguistic]	Swiss Germans	64
Malaysia [1990 ethnicity]	Malays	62
United Mexican States [1990 ethnicity]	Mestizo	60
Kingdom of Belgium [1976 linguistic]	Flemings	59
South Africa (2)[c] [1994 ethnicity]	Blacks (excl. half Zulus)	54
Brazil [1990 ethnicity]	Whites	54
Republic of Pakistan[d] [1991 linguistic]	Punjabis	48
Micronesia [1980 ethnicity]	Trukese	41
Republic of India (2)[a] [1981 linguistic]	Hindi speakers	39.7
Ethiopia [1983 ethnicity]	Amhara	38
Federal Republic of Nigeria [1983 ethnicity]	Yoruba	21.3

Sources: United Nations; *Britannica Year Book*; Edmonston; CIA.

[a]India has two obvious candidates for the title of Staatsvolk, Hindus, who constitute approximately 80 percent of its population, and Hindi speakers, who constitute just less than 40 percent.

[b]Spain's status as a federation is controversial (Arend Lijphart does not think it is a federation, Juan Linz and Al Stepan believe it is).

[c]South Africa's blacks can be considered a potentially homogenous category, though it is politically incorrect to say so. Since Zulus are politically differentiated between Zulu nationalists and South African nationalists, the new black Staatsvolk, excluding half of Zulus, can be estimated at 65 percent. If Zulus are considered an entirely separate group and all other blacks are regarded as the new Staatsvolk, then the latter compose about 54 percent of the population.

[d]Pakistan's recent coup makes it currently undemocratic.

reasonable prospects. By contrast, neither Ethiopia nor Nigeria has a Staatsvolk, so the theory suggests that they are not likely to survive long if they are run as majoritarian democratic federations. The Russian Federation may not prove durably democratic, but it has a Staatsvolk; so in the Dicey-O'Leary theory it has the necessary condition for survival. As for the other Asian cases, the table suggests that Pakistan should be on the threshold of crisis, and that India would be too if an attempt were made to construct a Staatsvolk out of Hindi speakers. Of Micronesia I cannot speak because I am wholly ignorant. Likewise, I have little confidence in interpreting the Latin American data, but at first glance they appear to suggest that Mexico and Brazil are closer to the threshold of the necessary condition than might be expected, though their status as durable democracies is far from confirmed.[57] The data in table 2.1 even suggest that Switzerland and Belgium have a Staatsvolk each, though doubtless this may raise eyebrows.

This attempt to test for the existence of a Staatsvolk based on these data may seem very crude, and the data-set (n = 23) may seem small, even if it is exhaustive of current democratic federations. Nevertheless the data are highly suggestive; there are no immediately anomalous cases. The federations without a Staatsvolk are of recent vintage and are not obviously democratically stable. The data in short appear to confirm Gellnerian theory on the political impact of nationalism. Naturally they cannot prove causation: the stability of the durably democratic federations may have other causes, possibly mutually independent in each case, but it is suggestive that the data satisfy the necessary condition of the Dicey-O'Leary theory.

But more sophistication may be demanded before jumping to conclusions. I have been taxed by some of my co-contributors with the question of whether the Staatsvolk is objective or real. How exactly should we determine whether a group is a candidate for the title of Staatsvolk? Without subscribing to constructivist epistemological views, or social constructivism in general or particular, I want to emphasize that the notion of a Staatsvolk is a concept that is intended to capture what real people think, sense, or imagine about a dominant group in a state, and which describes what may or may not be present as a result of political

---

[57] Francisco Panizza observes that the nonmestizo minority in Mexico both is ethnically very heterogeneous and shares a common Catholic culture with the rest of the population. Mestizo dominance is therefore much greater than the raw figures for the Staatsvolk suggest. In Brazil race is not as a deep a cleavage as it might appear—blacks are dispersed throughout the country, and racial, ethnic, and cultural mixing are significant, despite notable differentials in advantages between nonblacks and blacks. Though Brazil's federalism has some consociational devices, these are intended to accommodate regional-territorial rather than ethno-national differences.

construction in various states, namely, it is something that can be forged through political strategies and alliances. Plainly, I am suggesting that so-called primordial elements will normally be the foundations of efforts to construct a Staatsvolk—race, language, and common religion—though I do not insist on this. These elements are also easy to find relatively reliable and testable data on, and it is relatively easy to gain knowledge about their salience within the relevant states. All this argument and the data are possible to accept without subscribing to any particular theories of race, religiosity, or linguistics. All that my test so far does, in other words, is to check whether one of these elements—chosen on the basis of reading about the federation's history—has the possibility of having formed or has the potential to form the basis of a federal Staatsvolk.

It might also be suggested that investigation should focus more deeply on the durably democratic and formally multinational or multiethnic federations that might be considered to constitute the strongest challenges to Gellnerian theory, that is, India, Canada, Switzerland, and Belgium. If the primary division in India is linguistic rather than religious, then India may appear to lack a Staatsvolk.[58] If Anglophones are considered too heterogeneous a category, it might be suggested that Canada's real Staatsvolk is those of British and Irish descent—which would take the size of its Staatsvolk down, closer to the threshold of the necessary condition. If Swiss historic divisions were fundamentally religious rather than linguistic, then Helvetica too might appear to lack a definite Staatsvolk. The sheer size of the Francophone minority in Belgium and the country's long traditions of dualism might also lead us to pause before deciding if Belgium has a Staatsvolk.

I have no quarrel with the deeper investigation of cases to see whether my n-case argument is false in the particulars. But what I would like to suggest here is that what we may perhaps need most of all is not just an index of the largest group, however defined, but a measure of the relative weight of groups according to any particular specific ascriptive criterion. So let me rephrase the Dicey-O'Leary theory in this way: In a stable democratic majoritarian federation the politically effective number of cultural groups must be less than 2 on the index of the effective number of ethnic groups, ENENg (defined as the reciprocal of the Herfindahl-Hirschman concentration index of ethno-national groups).

[58] If one accepts that the dominant cleavage is linguistic, then it is interesting to note that India's linguistic arrangements have been seen as both highly federal and highly consociational in character. For various discussions, see David D. Laitin, "Language Policy and Political Strategy in India," *Policy Sciences* 22 (1989): 415–36; Arend. Lijphart, "The Puzzle of Indian Democracy: A Consociational Interpretation," *American Political Science Review* 90 (1996): 258–68.

Let me demystify this wordy mouthful. Specialists in the field of electoral analysis and party systems will immediately recognize the index as an application of a measure developed by Albert Hirschman in economics, and extended to political science by Rein Taagepera and his colleagues, who were interested in finding an objective and tractable way of measuring the effective number of parties in a party system, and in whether or not one party or bloc of parties was dominant.[59] Let me illustrate it through an example. How might we respond to the question: how many ethno-national groups are there in Belgium? One would expect to be told that there are two big groups, Flemings and Walloons, with a smaller number of other groups, notably Germans, and recent migrants, all of whom might self-identify in these categories, especially if obliged to do so by a census. But does that mean that for politically important purposes that bear on the stability of the state, Belgium has two, or two and an eighth, or two and a sixteenth ethno-national groups? The Herfindahl-Hirschman concentration index is designed to provide an objective way of measuring the effective number of components in a system. It does so in a way that stops analysts from following their intuitive (though often sensible) prejudices about what should count as a big or a small and negligible component.

The Herfindahl-Hirschman index (HHi) runs from 0 to 1. Applied to ethno-national groups it has the following logic. In a perfectly homogeneous nation-state, in which one ethno-national group has a 100 percent of the population, HHi = 1. If the state has an extremely poly-ethnic character in which every ethno-national group is vanishingly small, that is, each person is an ethno-national group, then HHi tends toward 0. The measurement method used for the index allows each group's share of the population to "determine its own weight," so its share is multiplied by its own share. In Belgium let us agree that the most salient definition of ethno-national groups is linguistic. In 1976 Flemings made up 59 percent of the population, Walloons 39.3 percent, and Germans 0.64 percent.[60] Of the total population, Flemings therefore had a fractional share of 0.59, Walloons 0.393, and Germans 0.0064.

[59] See Albert O. Hirschman, *National Power and the Structure of Foreign Trade* (Berkeley: University of California Press, 1945); M. Laakso and Rein Taagepera, "Effective Number of Parties: A Measure with Applications to West Europe," *Comparative Political Studies* 12 (1979); 3–27; Rein Taagepera and Matthew Soberg Shugart, *Seats and Votes: The Effects and Determinants of Electoral Systems* (New Haven: Yale University Press, 1989), chap. 8.

[60] Jan Erik Lane and Svante O. Ersson, *Politics and Society in Western Europe* (London: Pinter, 1990), appendix. The authors provide data on no other linguistic groups in Belgium. Their source is M. Stephens, *Linguistic Minorities in Western Europe* (Llandysul: Gomer Press, 1976).

Using the HHi index, the weighted share of Flemings is determined by its own weight, by multiplying 0.59 by 0.59 = 0.348. Correspondingly, the share of Walloons is 0.393 × 0.393 = 0.153 The share of Germans is $(0.0064)^2 = 0.00004096$. So, without imposing any arbitrary cutoff points, the political importance of the Belgian Germans is going to be discounted by this measure, which will conform to all but the most ardent Germanophiles' intuitions. The result of adding up the weighted values of all components is our Herfindahl-Hirschman concentration index:

$$HHi = \Sigma \, p^2_i$$

where p_i is the fractional share of the i-th ethno-national group and Σ stands for summation over all components. In the Belgian case, in 1976 the HHi was therefore 0.501 when we reduce to three decimal places. What we shall call the effective number of ethno-national groups (ENENg) is defined as the reciprocal of the HHi index:

$$ENENg = 1/HHi = 1/ \, \Sigma \, p^2_i$$

Given our Belgian data, the ENENg = 1/0.501 = 1.996, or 2 if we round off. The somewhat elaborate procedure adopted to calculate the effective number of ethno-national groups in Belgium conforms to our intuitions about this case — there are two effective ethno-national groups.

The merits of the HHi and ENENg indices are straightforward. HHi provides an index that runs from 0 to 1, and ENENg provides a measure of the effective number of ethno-national groups in a system that makes political and intuitive sense. ENENg turned out to be 2 using 1976 Belgian linguistic data. It is easy to see that a state divided into four equally sized ethno-national groups would have an ENENg of 4. These examples, of course, are neat cases, chosen to be helpful. But imagine that the demographic shares in Belgium shifted, say to the following proportions: 51 percent Flemings, 42 percent Walloons, 5 percent Germans, 1 percent British migrants, and 1 percent Italian migrants. Then the new Belgian HHi would be 0.439, and the new ENENg would be 2.28. The latter indicator, again, would conform with most people's intuitions about the effective number of ethno-national groups in the state — two big groups and a smaller third group, or a third clustering of smaller groups. These measures therefore provide means for potentially objective studies of the relationships between ethno-national groups and political systems. They also alert us to the importance of the

TABLE 2.2
Effective Number of Ethno-National Groups in Democratic Federations

Federation Name	Staatsvolk	SV % of Population	HHi Index	ENENg Index
Comoros Islands	Comorian	97	0.94	1.06
Commonwealth of Australia	Whites	95	0.91	1.1
St. Kitts and Nevis	Blacks	95	0.9	1.11
Federal Republic of Yugoslavia	Serbs	93	0.89	1.12
Federal Republic of Austria	Austrians	93	0.87	1.14
Federal Republic of Germany	Germans	93	0.87	1.15
Russian Federation	Russians	85	0.73	1.38
Argentine Republic	Whites	85	0.75	1.34
India (1)[a]	Hindus	80	0.66	1.52
United States of America	Whites	74	0.57	1.74
Kingdom of Spain[b]	Spaniards	72	0.56	1.8
Canada	Anglophones	67	0.51	1.96
Venezuela	Mestizo	67	0.5	1.99
South Africa (1)[a]	Blacks	65	0.46	2.18
Switzerland	Swiss Germans	64	0.45	2.22
Malaysia	Malays	62	0.48	2.10
United Mexican States	Mestizo	60	0.46	2.18
Kingdom of Belgium	Flemings	59	0.51	1.99
South Africa (2)[a]	Blacks (excl. half Zulus)	54	0.36	2.74
Brazil	Whites	54	0.45	2.24
Republic of Pakistan[a]	Punjabis	48	0.29	3.47
Micronesia	Trukese	41	0.26	3.91
Republic of India (2)[a]	Hindi speakers	39.7	0.19	5.19
Ethiopia	Amhara	38	0.28	3.58
Federal Republic of Nigeria	Yoruba	21.3	0.14	6.91

[a]As in table 2.1.

size of second, third, and other groups in the population, not simply the largest group.

Table 2.2 presents the HHi and ENENg scores for the current democratic federations in the world, in the same order as the federations in table 2.1, namely, according to the largest proportionate share held by the relevant (or potential) Staatsvolk. As is readily apparent, there is a close relationship between the size of the Staatsvolk and the HHi and

ENENg scores. All the federations with ENENg scores of less than 1.9 are, in fact, majoritarian federations, with the possible exception of India. By contrast, the bulk of the federations with ENENg scores of 1.9 and above have often been classified as nonmajoritarian federations because they have additional nonfederal power-sharing or consociational features, or else they have had such institutions recommended to stabilize them. Consociational arrangements, clarified and theorized by Arend Lijphart, involve four features: cross-community executive power-sharing, proportional representation of groups throughout the state sector, ethnic autonomy in culture (especially in religion or language), and formal or informal minority-veto rights.[61] All of the durably democratic multinational federations previously identified as potentially problematic for Gellnerian theory, namely, Canada, Switzerland, Belgium, and India, have ENENg scores of 1.9 or more. But the first three of these have relatively undisputed consociational histories,[62] and Lijphart has recently claimed that India had effective consociational traits during its most stable period under Nehru.[63] All this suggests that the Dicey-O'Leary theory should have a corollary — where there is no Staatsvolk, or where the Staatsvolk's position is precarious, a stable federation requires (at least some) consociational rather than majoritarian institutions if it is to survive, though of course its survival is by no means guaranteed. The microfoundations of this theory are straightforward: where no group has a clear majority, a balance of power among ethno-national groups is likely to exist, and such a balance of power is conducive to consociational settlements — though it is of course also conducive to warfare and secessionism. The corollary has both strong predictive and prescriptive power: Malaysia, South Africa with autonomous Zulu organization, Pakistan, India (with regard to its linguistic cleavages), Ethiopia, and Nigeria may not endure as democratic federations without some consociational devices. In India consociational add-ons have been most apparent in the development of ethnic autonomy in culture: the granting of provincial or, to coin a phrase, Landervolk status to major non-Hindi-speaking peoples.

[61] Lijphart, *Democracy in Plural Societies*.

[62] See Arend Lijphart, ed., *Conflict and Coexistence in Belgium: The Dynamics of a Culturally Divided Society*, Research Series, no 46 (Berkeley: Institute of International Studies University of California, 1981); Sid Noel, "Canadian Responses to Ethnic Conflict: Consociationalism, Federalism and Control," in J. McGarry and B. O'Leary, eds., *The Politics of Ethnic Conflict-Regulation: Case Studies of Protracted Ethnic Conflicts.* (London: Routledge, 1993); and Jurg Steiner, "Power-Sharing: Another Swiss Export Product?" in J. Montville ed., *Conflict and Peacemaking in Multiethnic Societies* (Lexington, MA: Lexington Books, 1989).

[63] Lijphart, "The Puzzle of Indian Democracy."

CONCLUSIONS AND IMPLICATIONS

If the arguments developed here are correct, then the Dicey-O'Leary theory seems, thus far, unfalsified: a majoritarian democratic federation requires a Staatsvolk, a demographically, electorally, and culturally dominant nation. This lends weight to Ernest Gellner's theory about the power of nationalism. It also suggests, in the spirit of addressing the core question of this volume, an important sociopolitical limit on what states can do. They cannot design and run successful majoritarian democratic and stable federations without having, or building, a Staatsvolk. But the theory has an important corollary, which leaves room for political initiative and statecraft. The absence or near absence of a Staatsvolk does not preclude democratic federation, but a democratic federation without a clear or secure Staatsvolk must adopt (some) consociational practices if it is to survive. This suggests that we are entitled to have greater optimism than Gellner allowed about statecraft in the management of multinational and multiethnic units.

Perhaps I should emphasize, for those who remain skeptical of the positivist cast of this chapter, or who dislike monocausal emphases, that federations can be destabilized for other reasons than the lack of a Staatsvolk, and that multinational federations may be destabilized for reasons that have nothing to do with the absence of consociational practices. What the theory and its corollary state are necessary conditions for stability in democratic federations. There may be other necessary conditions for stable federations — for example, voluntary beginnings, a favorable external environment, and appropriate matches between peoples and territories — but these causal arguments have not been defended or evaluated here. This is an initial statement: I plan to do more detailed research on the agenda suggested.

However, if the arguments sketched are broadly correct, then they have powerful practical political implications for what states can do with regard to reengineering or reinventing their institutional and constitutional formats. Those who want to federalize the United Kingdom have nothing to fear: the United Kingdom has a Staatsvolk, the English. They could live with either a majoritarian or an explicitly multinational democratic federation.

The implications are especially strong for Euro-federalists who wish to convert the European Union from a confederation into a federation. The European Union lacks a Staatsvolk. Its largest ethno-national people, the Germans of Germany, compose just over a fifth of its current population, about the same proportionate share as the Yoruba and Hausa have each in Nigeria. The European Union's ENENg score is at present 7.23, higher than Nigeria's 6.69, and it will go higher on the accession of the Poles, Hungarians and Ernest Gellner's Czechs. In the Dicey-O'Leary theory, to put it bluntly and insensitively, there are just not enough Germans for the European Union to function effectively as a majoritarian federation. This would still be true even if we, causing mutual outrage, were to treat Austrian, Dutch, and Swedish people as honorary Germans! The theory suggests, by implication, that calls to have a fully fledged European federation, with the classic bicameral arrangements of the United States, or to have a directly elected and powerful EU president, all to address the so-called democratic deficit in the European Union, may be a recipe for institutional disaster *unless* such calls are accompanied by strong commitments to consociational governance devices. Consociational governance implies mechanisms to ensure the inclusive and effective representation of all the nationalities of the European Union in its core executive institutions, proportionate representation of its nationalities in its public bureaucracies and legal institutions, national autonomy in all cultural matters deemed of profound cultural significance (e.g., language, religion, education), and last, but not least, national vetoes to protect national communities from being out-voted through majoritarian rules. In short, many of the current consociational and confederal features of the EU, which some federalists want to weaken or temper in their pursuit of formal federation, are in fact required to ensure its prospects as a multinational democratic federation.

This is not a Euro-skeptical or Euro-phobic argument. The European Union has been correctly defended as a forum that has resolved the security and ethno-territorial disputes between France and Germany; that has facilitated the possible and actual resolution of British-Irish and Italian-Austrian border and minority questions; that is a means through which Irish nationalists, Tyrolese Germans and Austrians, and Spanish and French Basques can be interlinked with their co-nationals and co-ethnics in transfrontier and functional cross-border programs and institutions; and that may encourage its multinational member-states to permit a fuller flourishing of internal regional autonomy. All this is true, though the European Union's therapeutic powers should not be exaggerated, as they standardly are. But one of the European Union's greatest current dangers may stem from its ardent majoritarian federalists. Given that many see the European Union as the exemplary illustration of the death of the nation-state or of its transcendence, the full irony of my argument should be apparent. Only a European Union constructed from secure nation-states cooperating within either a confederal or consociational federal format has reasonable prospects of development and maintenance as a democratic political system. It is, of course, possible that the Dicey-O'Leary law is wrong, but, if so, then a majoritarian federal democratic European Union will genuinely be unique.

CHAPTER 3

A State without a Nation? Russia after Empire

ANATOLY M. KHAZANOV

THE NOTION of civic versus ethnic nationalism apparently goes back to Hans Kohn,[1] who opposed "Western" nationalism (rational, democratic, based on statehood and citizenship) with "Eastern" nationalism (irrational, undemocratic, based on ethnicity and culture). This notion has been further developed by a number of scholars,[2] however it has also met with criticism.[3] In fact, ethnic and civic nationalisms differ mainly in their degree of inclusion; in other respects they have much more in common than is sometimes assumed. All civic nations have a cultural (and, in most cases, linguistic) core and a historical narrative linked with the dominant ethnocultural groups, which in most cases constitute a majority and are, or were, instrumental in creating the national identity.[4] As numerous examples from the past and present have proven, civic nationalism by itself does not eliminate cultural discrimination and oppression. Membership in a civic nation is never unconditional, although it is supposed to be voluntary. Usually it implies more than a common citizenship and a common statehood; it also requires the acceptance of shared cultural characteristics, norms, symbols, and myths, as well as a common past and an even more common present and future.

This is the theory; in practice things often look different. One may wonder whether the civic Canadian nation that supposedly embraces both Anglophones and Francophones is a reality or a failed project. Or whether one may speak of a Belgian civic nation. Or whether the civic Spanish nation that supposedly includes not only Castillians and An-

[1] See Hans Kohn, *Prelude to Nation States: The French and German Experience, 1789–1815* (Princeton: Van Nostrand, 1967); Hans Kohn, *The Ideas of Nationalism* (New York: Collier Books, 1944).

[2] For example, R. Brubaker, *Citizenship and Nationhood in France and Germany* (Cambridge: Harvard University Press, 1992); L. Greenfield, *Nationalism: Five Roads to Modernity* (Cambridge: Harvard University Press, 1992).

[3] B. Yack, "The Myth of Civic Union," in R. Beiner, ed., *Theorizing Nationalism* (Albany: SUNY Press, 1998), 103–18.

[4] A. M. Khazanov, "Ethnic Nationalism in the Russian Federation," *Daedalus*, 126 (1997): 121–42.

dalusians, but also Galicians, Catalans, and Basques, really exists. In the not too distant past, many people were confident in the existence of a civic Czechoslovak nation, and a civic Yugoslav nation. The validity of these claims is hardly worthy of discussion today.

The difficulties that the notion of civic nationalism encounters resulted, on the one hand, in attempts at finding some commonalities in other suggested notions, like political nationalism, territorial nationalism, or even "banal nationalism"; the latter defined as an identity to be found in the embodied habits of social life.[5] On the other hand, some scholars want to substitute another vague notion, patriotism, for civic nationalism.[6]

Apparently it is worthwhile to divorce conceptually ethnocultural identities, citizenship — which regulates the relations between the individual and the state and, in democracies, is based on legal equality of rights and duties — and civic nationhood, which implies more than simple membership in a political community and is connected with the acceptance and interiorization of common values, norms, rituals, and symbols that exceed the formal pledge of allegiance and are linked with a notion of *patria*. Consciously or not, the American notion of multiculturalism and the proliferation of hyphenated ethnic groups may reflect these differences.

This brings me to the concept of the nation-state, which due to its prevalence in the contemporary discourse is to a large extent responsible for the confusion of citizenship with civic nationhood. Actually, the very dichotomy of ethnic versus civic nationalism is based on the illusion of the universality of the nation-state. Historically, nationalisms have envisioned a world consisting of states that were uniform within but sharply distinct from what lay beyond their borders. It turns out, however, that the world as a whole may be becoming less diverse, while individual states are becoming more ethnically heterogeneous than has been perceived or designed. There is a certain terminological and even conceptual confusion in the social sciences. Many alleged nation-states are simultaneously characterized as multiethnic states, states with plural or multicultural societies, and so on. In fact, in addition to stateless nations, there are states without nations, that is, states that in the modern sense lack any nations at all. At best, these might be characterized as "nation-states to be," but only if one wants to demonstrate a good

---

[5] M. Bilig, *Banal Nationalism* (London: Sage Publishing, 1995), 8.

[6] See W. Connor, *Ethnonationalism: The Quest for Understanding* (Princeton: Princeton University Press, 1994), 196ff. Cf. the concept of constitutional patriotism developed by Jürgen Habermas, "Citizenship and the National Identity: Some Reflections on the Future of Europe," *Praxis International* 12 (1992): 1–19.

deal of optimism. At the same time, some of the states are already multinational rather than multiethnic, since the process of nation building is ongoing. Kurds and Palestinians in the Middle East; Sikhs, Bengali, and Assamese in India; Tamils in Sri Lanka; Ache in Indonesia; Uighur and Tibetans in China; Amhara and Oromo in Ethiopia; and many others are already nations. There is no reason to follow the French tradition, which goes back to Durkheim and Mauss and does not grant nation status to entities that do not enjoy political independence.[7] However, where ethnic groups develop into nationalities or nations, with literary languages, cultural institutions, mass media, occupationally differentiated social structures, specific economic interests, and political elites or counterelites, there is less room for unifying integration than in premodern and early modern societies. Multiethnic, and especially multinational, societies with particularistic identities increase the necessity for and simultaneously the danger of an activist state. The striving of a state for homogenization, however, is rife with the potential for conflict. In a broader sense, all kinds of nationalizing projects are at present less successful than in the past, even in cases where linguistic assimilation or accommodation has made progress. Pursuing nationalizing projects in countries where nationalities and nations are somewhat territorialized is an even more difficult endeavor. The belated, in comparison with other countries, disintegration of the Soviet Union has brought to the fore the question of to what extent Russia may be considered a nation-state, and different political forces are trying to address it in different ways. I will start with the nationalists.

Contemporary Russian nationalism, one of the most influential ideological and political forces in the country, consists of several trends and varieties. Still, most of them share some remarkably similar characteristics connected with the Manichaeian-type worldview. The only thing that prevents me from stating that Russian nationalism is nowadays turning away from the West is that its mainstream was always anti-Western. There is nothing new in this respect.

Postcommunist development in Europe is perceived in Russia as an advancement of Western Europe into the eastern part of the continent.[8] Poland, Hungary, the Czech Republic, and even more tacitly the Baltic countries are already considered Western European, or at least West European countries-to-be. Even countries like Romania and Slovakia are considered to belong to Western Europe, if not by their actual status then by their cultural affiliation and destiny. One may be rather sur-

---

[7] See, for example, D. Schnapper, *La communauté des citoyens* (Paris: Gallimard, 1994).

[8] I. G. Yakovenko, *Rossiiskoe gosudarstvo: Natsional'nye interesy, granitsy, perspektivy* (Novosibirsk: Sibirskii khronograf, 1999).

prised by how little room the former communist countries are occu-
pying in the thought and concepts of Russian nationalists and in the
minds of ordinary Russians. In this respect, there is a kind of consensus
in the country that, like it or not, the Soviet external empire has irreversibly disintegrated. Regrets are much more of a geopolitical than a cultural order, though even the former are rather muted. Gorbachev is
blamed for allowing the former clients to go their own ways, and even
more for not insisting that they should pay an adequate price for their
freedom.[9]

Does the sense of isolation and alienation from the West that may be
observed in Russia indicate that the country really turns to Eurasia —
whatever that vague term may imply? One should be cautious in this
respect, since the speculative constructs of some ideologists of contemporary Russian nationalism often do not correspond with the attitudes
and feelings of ordinary nationalists, and even less with the general public. While the ideologists talk and write about the Eurasian character of
Russian civilization, about the historical symbiosis of the Slavic and
Turkic peoples, and even about the alliance between Orthodox Christianity and Islam in their struggle against secularist Western ideologies,
in everyday life their followers demonstrate hostility toward the peoples
of the Caucasus and Central Asia, and toward "Asians" in general.
Likewise, a negative attitude toward Islam has become widespread in
Russia.[10]

For some time, the so-called Eurasianism was popular only among a
small but vocal segment of the Russian nationalists. While some "Eurasianists" insist on the historical and cultural unity of all peoples of the
former Soviet Union, others assign to Russia the role of the main strong-
hold of continental Eurasian civilization against the Atlantic one.[11] In
any case, the history of "Eurasianism" proves its "crisis ideology" character. It is hardly accidental that the first splash of eurasianist thought
had followed the collapse of the Russian Empire, and the second one
followed the disintegration of the Soviet Empire. Before the revolution,
very few Russian thinkers proclaimed the Eurasian character of the
Russian Empire; the majority conceived of it as a European state. The

[9] A. I. Utkin, *Rossiia i Zapad: Istoriia tsivilizatsii* (Moscow: Gardariki, 2000). Vladimir
Putin criticizes the withdrawal of Soviet troops from Eastern Europe and complains about
Russia's loss of her position in Europe in N. Gevorkyan, N. Timakova, and A. Koles-
nikov, trans. C. A. Fitzpatrick, *First Person: An Astonishingly Frank Self-Portrait by
Russia's President Vladimir Putin* (New York: Public Affairs, 2000), 72–74.

[10] A. Malashenko, *Islamskoe vozrozhdenie v sovremennoi Rossii* (Moscow: Carnegie
Endowment for International Peace, 1998), 187ff.

[11] A. Dugin, *Osnovy geopolitiki: Geopoliticheskoe budushchee Rosii* (Moscow: Ark-
togeia, 1997).

Eurasian school of thought first emerged in some Russian émigré circles in the 1920s. It was an attempt at suggesting an ideology for the restoration of the Russian Empire in another garment. In fact, this ideology was not very original and borrowed generously from different sources: the Russian messianic religious philosophy, the pessimistic criticism of Western capitalist civilization (Danilevsky, Spengler), and even fascism. This mish-mash was seasoned with a romanticized historical mythology. Thus, the early Eurasianists insisted on almost eternal enmity and antagonism between the continental Eurasian and Western Atlantic civilizations. They argued that for ecological and cultural-historical reasons, all peoples from the Hinggans to the Carpathians shared the same destiny and should have a common statehood. They also claimed that autocratic rule in Russia, which, incidentally, they praised, was a Mongol contribution to Russian development.[12]

Very soon, some Eurasianists discovered that many of their attitudes and goals, namely, the rejection of the capitalist West and especially the restoration of the empire, were not so different from the Soviet communist ones. The result of this discovery was far from glorious. Some Eurasianists became agents of the Soviet secret police.[13] Others became disillusioned with the ideology or with its practical applications.

Only since the 1970s have some ideas of the Eurasianists, especially the thesis about the cultural and political symbiosis of the Eastern Slavs and the Turko-Mongol nomads, been revived, though for a time in a somewhat less extreme form, by their epigonus, the Soviet historian Lev Gumilev.[14] It is true that Gumilev was a maverick in Soviet academia, whose unprofessional treatment of many historical problems was matched only by his unbridled fantasy. However, during the *perestroika* period, and especially after the collapse of the Soviet Union, neo-Eurasianism had been reborn and once again come into demand. Even the commu-

---

[12] For recent reprints of the most important publications by the eurasianists, see I. A. Isaev, ed., *Puti Evrazii* (Moscow: Russkaia kniga, 1992); L. I. Novikova and I. N. Sizemskaia, eds., *Mir Rossii—Evraziia* (Moscow: Vysshaia shkola, 1995); N. I. Tolstoi, ed., *Russkii uzel evraziistva* (Moscow: Belovodie, 1997). On ideology of Eurasianism, see V. Tsimbursky, "Dve Evrazii: omonimiia kak kliuch k ideologii evraziistva," *Acta Eurasica* 1–2 (4–5): 6–31.

[13] Later, when their usefulness expired, they were imprisoned in the Soviet Union, but this is already another story—see F. Ashnin and V. Alpatov, "Evraziistovo v zerkale OGPU-NKVD-KGB," *Vestnik Evrazii*, 2 (3): (1996) 5–18.

[14] L. Gumilev, *Poiski vymyshlennogo tsarstva* (Moscow: Izdatel'stvo vostochnoi literatury, 1970); cf. L. Gumilev, *Drevniaia Rus' i Velikaia Step'* (Moscow: Mysl', 1989). On Gumilev, see Y. M. Brudny, *Reinventing Russia: Nationalism and the Soviet State, 1953–1991* (Cambridge: Harvard University Press, 1998), 186–89; V. A. Shnirelman and S. Panarin, "Lev Nikolaevich Gumilev: osnovatel' etnologii?" *Acta Eurasica* N3 (10, 2000): 5–37.

nists, in the vain attempt to preserve the Soviet Union, began to exploit some of its speculations.[15]

Still, its influence on contemporary Russian nationalism should by no means be overestimated. Sometimes one might get the impression that Eurasianism attracted more attention in the West than in its own country. In Russia, it remains the domain of a narrow circle of ideologists and quite often is disjunct from the practical demands of Russian nationalists. Eurasianism is inseparably linked with a nostalgia for the lost empire and the vain dream of reversing the course of history. As such, it is a nationalist ideology with a strong imperial accretion. In a way, it is an inconsistent attempt somehow to overcome a narrow ethnic Russian nationalism, or rather to make it more attractive to non-Russian peoples.

At the moment, however, neo-Eeurasianism has ceased to be a marginal ideological movement and has acquired a certain respectability in the eyes of many in the Russian political mainstream.[16] Its principled anti-Westernism and its political schemes, however unrealistic they may seem to an objective observer (e.g., Russia's proposed alliance against the United States with China and India, or even with Iran, Iraq, and Libya), correspond well with the mood of those who cannot reconcile themselves to the country's loss of superpower status. The main ideologist of the Eurasianists, Alexandr Dugin, has become an advisor on geopolitics to the speaker of the Russian parliament and a leader of the new political movement "Eurasia." Dugin boasts that he has many followers in the military brass and among the president's associates.[17] Putin himself sometimes refers to Russia as a Eurasian country.

Still, neo-Eurasianism, because of its ambiguity and intellectual pretentiousness, does not have a sufficiently strong appeal to either Russians or non-Russians.[18] This brings me to other trends in contemporary

[15] See, for example, I. A. Isaev, "Evraziistovo: Mif ili traditsiia," *Kommunist* 12 (1991).

[16] For example, the recent statements by Vitaly Tretiakov, a former editor-in-chief of the influential daily *Nezavisimaia gazeta*, that the United States is a great and inevitable evil whose expansion threatens the whole world; and by Alexandr Dugin, a leader of the neo-Eurasianists, who insists that Russia must militarize her economy in order to oppose the *Pax Americana* (quoted in *Russkii zhurnal*, June 7, 2001 — www.russ.ru) bear a remarkable similarity to each other. Putin's turn to the West after September 11, 2001, has not been welcomed by many in the ruling elite and, especially by the nationalists.

[17] See his interview in *Russian marshrut*, June 3, 2001 — www.arctogaia.com/public/granizu/html.

[18] It is true that, at present, Gumilev's writings are rather popular among the intelligentsia of the Turkic-speaking peoples of the former Soviet Union, but only because he often idealized their ancestors. It is also true that the president of Kazakhstan, Nursultan Nazarbaev, advocates the formation of a Eurasian Union. But his vision of this union as a primarily economic organization is a far cry from the dreams of the Russian neo-Eurasianists.

Russian nationalism. One historical circumstance that has made a strong impact on all its varieties is that the Russian state, in all of its history, was never a nation-state; and even at present nation-state building in the country is more of a project than an accomplishment. Just as in the past, at present Russia in historical, ethnic, and cultural respects is more, and at the same time less, than the Russian state. I have to begin not with history, but with philology and linguistics.

The fact is that there are two different nouns in Russian, and consequently two different adjectives, for the country and for the people. The nouns are *Rus'* (an archaic word that nowadays is used mainly in a poetic, elevated fashion) and *Rossia* — Russia in English. Correspondingly, there are two different adjectives, *russkii* and *rossiiskii*. The first adjective is also used as a noun to designate ethnic Russians as a people. In English, both adjectives are translated as Russian or Russians.[19]

At present, *russkii* is an ethnic definition, while *rossiiskii* is mainly a political and territorial, and only potentially a civic definition. The word *rossiiskii* was first introduced in 1718 by Feofan Prokopovich, an associate of Peter the Great. At that time, and much later as well, it was used mainly in the official lexicon, and aimed at designating all subjects of the Russian Empire, nothing more. Thus, it had a strictly political meaning and, in fact, was rarely used at all. I may be wrong, but I could not find even one case when, in the prerevolutionary period, the word *rossiiskii* was applied to the non-Russian populations of the Caucasus, not to mention Central Asia. In the official lexicon, the former were usually identified as Armenian, or Georgian, or Muslim, or as other subjects of the Russian Empire, that was all. At the turn of the century, only a few liberals occasionally used the word *rossiiskii*.

In the Soviet period, the word *rossiiskii* was used either interchangeably with the word *russkii*, or, in some cases, as pertaining to the Russian Soviet Federative Socialist Republic, for example, to its territory, resources, administration, and so forth. Inasmuch as the Soviet concept of nation was based on the primordialist approach and ascriptive ethnic identity, there was no place in it for a civic nation. It is true that the Soviets initiated a much more ambitious project: the creation of a single Soviet people. However, this supranational community was called Soviet, not Russian, although it implied a linguistic and cultural Russification.

[19] To avoid confusion, the leading Russian anthropologist, Valery Tishkov, even suggests spelling the Russian state in English as "Rossia," and its citizens, without regard to their nationality (in ethnic terms) as "Rossians" (*Rossiyane*), but I assume that the introduction of linguistic neologisms into another language is beyond his control. See Valery Tishkov, *Ethnicity, Nationalism, and Conflict in and after the Soviet Union: The Mind Aflame* (London: Sage, 1997).

Thus, the very idea of a civic Russian nation is basically a new phenomenon. It began to be propagated by liberal-minded people in Russia only in the late perestroika period, and for political reasons it was taken up by Yeltsin. At that time, Yeltsin was fighting with Gorbachev for Russia's sovereignty, and in order to undermine his position Gorbachev tried to instigate the non-Russian Autonomous Republics against the central authorities of the Russian Federation. In turn, Yeltsin made a proposal to their leaderships that he would later prefer to forget: "Take as much sovereignty as you can swallow." Russia's declaration on state sovereignty of June 12, 1990, was announced on behalf of the "multi-national people of Russia," in other words, Russia was conceived of not as a nation-state, but as a state of many nations.

In any case, by the end of the Soviet period, ethnonational issues pertaining to Russia proper occupied only a secondary position in the programs of the Russian democratic movement.[20] Perhaps the most remarkable and unusual moment in the disintegration of the Soviet Union as an empire was that Russia played a decisive role in this process. Just at that time, those who were more or less acquainted with the Western theory of nation began to talk about a multiethnic and civic Russian nation. In the New Speak of the Russian democrats, the archaic and rarely used noun *rossiiane*, a derivative of *rossiiskii*, had acquired a new and different meaning. First, it implied not only citizenship, but also common interests, values, cultural characteristics, history, and fate that the Russian and non-Russian citizens of the federation supposedly shared, as well as the bright future that they would share together. On a more implicit level, it also suggested that all citizens of the Russian Federation, irrespective of their ethnicity, are or should become its patriots, although the word "patriotism" was not popular in democratic circles. At that time, many democratic-minded intellectuals made mention of it in another context. They liked to quote Samuel Johnson's famous dictum about patriotism as the last refuge of the scoundrel. I must remind that in the late 1980s and early 1990s, the Russian liberals considered the Russian nationalists, along with the communists, to be their enemies. Only during the 1995–96 election campaigns did some parties of liberal orientation begin to stress their patriotism and allegiance to the Russian nation. Their first and clumsy attempts were unsuccessful, however, and did not deliver more votes to the liberals. When Russia's Choice, the party of Egor Gaidar and Anatoly Chubais, decided to use the image of Peter the Great as its emblem in the 1995 parliamentary election, they met with much ridicule from democratic-

[20] O. Yu. Malinova, *Liberalism v politicheskom spektre Rossii* (Moscow: Pamiatniki istoricheskoi mysli, 1998), 134–35.

minded people. These pointed out that the despotic ruler was hardly fitting as a symbol of progress for a party that insisted on the priority of universal human rights; just as Peter's main achievements, the extension of the Russian Empire and the conquest of the Baltics, could in no way be associated with a party that welcomed the dissolution of the Soviet Union and the independence of the Baltic republics.

It is not enough to construct identities. To be successful, these identities have to be accepted. In this respect, the stories of failure are much more numerous than success stories. It soon became evident that there was no consensus in the country with regard to the civic Russian nation. Post-Soviet Russia remains not only a multiethnic, but to some extent a multinational state, which retains the principle of ethno-territorial autonomies inherited from the Soviet Union. Many members of non-Russian nationalities are suspicious of attempts at imposing upon them any common identity with ethnic Russians, with the exception of citizenship. The idea of common destiny is also contested. Many opinion polls and surveys indicate that among members of territorialized non-Russian nationalities, loyalty to their own nationality, republic, or small homeland is stronger than loyalty to the Russian Federation in general.[21] On the political and cultural levels, the negation of the idea of a civic Russian nation is most clearly expressed by non-Russian political elites and nationalist-minded intellectuals. If the concept of civic nation implies, at least in theory, ethnically neutral policies and the equality of all citizens everywhere in the territory of the nation-state, then this is precisely what they want to avoid. They insist that members of indigenous nationalities should have the right of preferential treatment in their titular republics.

A civic nation implies something more than citizenry. It should have some shared political, historical, and cultural symbols and myths acceptable to the multiethnic majority. Historical myths are never politically neutral. They are used as a means of manipulating public/ethnic/national opinion and attitudes by various movements and social strata, or by the state itself. Historical mythology tends to sacralize specific ideological concepts, thus imposing them upon a society. It is almost surprising that even after living in the same state for centuries, members of Russia's different nationalities have so few uncontested common identities, so few common sentiments, myths, and symbols indispensable for linking individuals into a nation. Russian history lacks a George Washington or Abraham Lincoln as symbols of civic nationhood acceptable to all, without regard to their ethnic background. Moreover, at the moment, all citizens of the Russian Federation, even the ethnic Rus-

[21] Khazanov, "Ethnic Nationalism," 135–36.

sians, lack undisputed Bolivars, Garibaldis, Kosuths, Ataturks, Ghandis, and Ben Gurions. Since the October Revolution and its heroes, including Lenin and Stalin among others, have become somewhat desecrated and discredited, the collective memory, common history, and civic national tradition have become shattered and contested in the country. Putin's partial rehabilitation and reappropriation of Soviet symbolism can hardly improve this situation. Members of different nationalities in Russia have quite different attitudes to the past; they develop ethnic counternarratives and create their own ethnocentric mythologies.[22] The past has become even more contested than the present; or, as the Russians now joke, the future is more predictable than the past.

One may read in the history textbooks used in Russian-language schools that the conquest of the Kazan' Khanate in the mid-sixteenth century was a great achievement of the expanding Russian state, beneficial to all of its ethnic groups, including the Tatars. But in Tatarstan, in the post-Soviet period, the day when Kazan' fell began to be commemorated as the greatest tragedy in the history of the Tatar people, and who knows, perhaps we are witnessing the emergence of another Kosovo myth. In the official Russian historiography the Mongol invasion and the consequent Golden Horde period are labeled as "the three-hundred-year Tatar yoke." However, the president of Tatarstan, Mintemir Shaimiev, claims that without the Golden Horde there would be no Great Russia, since only due to the patronage of the Golden Horde's khans were the Moscow princes capable of uniting the other Russian princedoms. The day of the Battle of the Kulikovo Field, in 1380, when the Russian Prince Dmitry Donskoi defeated the troops of the Golden Horde, has since 1995 been officially commemorated in Russia as the "Day of victory of the Russian warriors over the Mongol-Tatars." In 2001, however, the Council of Muftis of Russia issued a protest, pointing out that the celebration of this event does not contribute to the national unity of the country.[23]

Ermak, a Cossack who led the Russian conquest of West Siberia in the sixteenth century, is considered a hero by the Russians and a cruel conquistador by the indigenous peoples of West Siberia and Kazakhstan.[24] All Russian children know that General Yermolov was a hero of the 1812 Patriotic War. In the Northern Caucasus, nobody cares about this war. There, children are told that General Yermolov was a bloody

---

[22] K. Aimermakher and G. Bordiugov, eds., *Natsional'nye istorii v sovetskom i post-sovetskikh gosudarstavakh* (Moscow: AIPO-XX, 1999).

[23] *Nezavisimaia gazeta*, June 19, 2001.

[24] Yu. Zuev and A. Kadyrbaev, "Pokhod Ermaka v Sibir': tiurkskie motivy v russkoi teme," *Acta Eurasica* N3 (10) 2000: 38–60.

colonizer of the Caucasus. During the perestroika period a special police detail stood guard twenty-four hours a day at the monument built
to him in the city of Grozny, the Chechen capital, to protect it from
vandalism. It was removed to Central Russia after the disintegration of
the Soviet Union. The real hero of many North Caucasian peoples (especially in Daghestan and Chechnia) is Imam Shamil, their leader in the
Caucasian War with Russia. However, contemporary Russian historiography is still ambiguous in its treatment of him (in postwar Soviet
historiography, Shamil was branded a "reactionary" and even a "paid
agent of Turkey and England"). The official Russian historiography
holds that the Kabardinians had voluntarily joined the Russian state
already in the sixteenth century. The revisionist Kabardinian historians
claim that union with Russia happened only in the nineteenth century
and was in no way voluntary. They pay much more attention to the
ethnic cleansing in the Northwest Caucasus that happened in the aftermath of the Caucasian War, when most of the members of the Adyge
peoples were forced to leave for Turkey; but this event is largely ignored
in Russian history texts. Likewise, the trauma of Stalin's deportations is
still very much alive and occupies a central place in the historiographies
of the "punished peoples." However, most of the history textbooks in
Russian high schools either do not mention these events at all or, at
best, treat them in only one or two paragraphs; moreover, this treatment is sometimes quite ambiguous.

The contest is not limited to history only. In many non-Russian parts
of the country, one is now witnessing the popularity of *nats-art* (from
the Russian word *natsional'nost'*, nationality in English), a post-Soviet
variety of home-art or *Heimatkunst* aimed at reanimation or construction of ethnic "historical memories."[25] Striving for nativism and authenticity, along with a desire to oppose the dominant culture, sometimes
acquire very specific forms. Some Mari, Udmurt, Yakut, Chuvash, and
other nationalists are now advocating the rejection of Orthodox Christianity as a religion imposed by the Russian colonizers and the return to
old pagan beliefs that at present seem to be an essentially intellectual
construct.[26] Above all other things, a religious specificity in this context
should indicate an ethnic specificity.

These trends have not remained unnoticed by the Kremlin. However,

[25] S. M. Chervonnaia, *Vse nashi bogi s nami i za nas: Etnicheskaia identichnost' i etnicheskaia mobilizatsiia v sovremennom iskusstve narodov Rossii* (Moscow: TsIMO,
1999).

[26] V.A. Schnirelman, *Neoiazychestovo i natsionalism: Vostochno—evropeiskii areal*
(Moscow: Institut etnologii i antropologii RAN, 1998), 20ff; V. Filippov, "Chuvashi: poi-
ski uteriannogo Boga," in V. P., Filippov ed., *Buntuiushchaia etnichnost'* (Moscow: Tsentr
Tsivilizatsionnykh i regional'nykh issledovanii, 1999), 8–31.

so far the Russian leadership has not found an effective means to coun-
terbalance them. On the contrary, Yeltsin's decree restoring the old
Russian two-headed eagle, which was later confirmed by Putin and the
Russian Parliament, was met with widespread resentment in the non-
Russian parts of the country because historically it had been associated
with the Orthodox faith and with Russian imperialism and colonialism.
It does not inspire feelings of a shared identity but rather serves as a
divisive symbol.

Even a common citizenship is under dispute, and some republican
leaders insisted that priority should be given to republican citizenship
over federal. Things have gone so far that the Russian government's
decision to remove the notorious *piatyi punkt* (fifth point), the clause in
internal passports that fixed ethnic identity and virtually made it ascriptive, is resented and even resisted in some non-Russian republics. It is
perceived there as another attempt at Russification or as a desire to
deny non-Russians privileged status in their homelands. Interestingly,
Russian nationalists also resent this decision, though for wholly different reasons.

But this is only one side of the coin. The other is that the concept of a
civic nation is not appealing to many ethnic Russians as well. It seems
that nationalism as a postimperial syndrome is quite different in stable
and prosperous countries from those that experience political uncer-
tainty and economic hardships. The Russians have still not overcome
the crisis of identity caused by the disintegration of the Soviet Union.
Many still perceive this as secessions from Russia. Characteristically, the
former Soviet republics are called the "near abroad" in the Russian
official and public lexicon, in opposition to the "real" abroad, namely,
the rest of the world. According to a poll taken by the Moscow Human-
itarian Academy in 2000, 61 percent of Russians wanted to live in a
single state with the Ukrainians and Belorussians, and 38 percent of
them favored the restoration of a unitary state of the kind that existed
in pre-1917 Russia.[27] At one time many Russians were afraid that even
some parts of the Russian Federation might also be taken away from
them. In the early 1990s one could witness the almost paranoid mood
in the country. Many people were convinced that Russia was in danger
of immediate disintegration. Even in 1994, 12 to 15 percent of ethnic
Russians considered the disintegration of their country to be quite likely.
In addition, the growth of ethnic nationalism among the non-Russian
peoples of the former Soviet Union and of the Russian Federation resulted in a Russian backlash. In the late 1980s and early 1990s only
Russian nationalists used the bugaboo of Russophobia; nowadays al-

[27] *Russia Today*, January 4, 2001.

most all political movements use it.[28] In 1993 some opinion polls indicated that one-third of Russian respondents believed that non-Russians were responsible for the country's social troubles, and 54 percent of them thought that non-Russians enjoyed an excessive influence in the country. Remarkably, the two groups especially strongly affected by xenophobia are the young people and the bureaucracy.[29]

Thus, the ideological space in Russia became open to only one variety of nationalism: ethnic nationalism. At present, the Russians are seeking out a new base for their identity as a nationality and a nation; hence the ongoing debate about the character of the Russian Federation and about the status of ethnic minorities there. Curiously enough, however, even the problem of an ethnic Russian nation is far from being solved. Who is an ethnic Russian remains a matter of heated debate. Many still argue that ethnic affiliation is hereditary and is defined by blood or genes. Among other things, ambiguity is reflected in the new terminology in the Russian official and public lexicon, which stresses the difference between genuine Russians and Russophones—acculturated members of other nationalities who have Russian as their first or even only language. This distinction is the direct consequence of the Soviet practice of ascriptive and hereditary ethnic identity.

However, the Orthodox Church and clerico-nationalists are propagating an even more restrictive concept of Russianness. They argue that only an Orthodox Christian can be a true Russian. Russians are the chosen people; Russians and the Orthodox faith are inseparable, insisted the late metropolitan of St. Petersburg and Ladoga, Ioann,[30] who has numerous followers. Orthodoxy has become a visible and fashionable symbol of the Russian identity even to a large number of nonpractitioners,[31] and Russian dignitaries, including Yeltsin, Luzhkov, and Putin, among others, hurried to demonstrate publicly their new allegiance to it. However, the polyconfessional character of contemporary Russian society is a fait accompli. Any attempts to impose upon it a Russian Orthodox monopoly and to discriminate against or limit the activities of other religions and denominations are detrimental to the prospects of the formation of a civic nation in the country.[32]

---

[28] L. Gudkov, "Antisemitizm v postsovetskoi Rossii," in G. Vitkovskaia and A. Malashenko, eds., *Neterpimost' v Rossii: Starye i novye fobii* (Moscow: Carnegie Endowment for International Peace, 1999), 44–98.

[29] Gudkov, "Antisemitizm", 55, 56.

[30] Ioann, Metropolitan of St. Petersburg and Ladoga, *Odolenie smuty* (St. Petersburg: Tsarskoe Delo, 1996), 9, 18.

[31] S. Filiatov and R. Lunkin, "Konets 90-kh: Vozrozhdenie religioznoi neterpimosti," in Vitkovskaia and Malashenko, eds., *Neterpimost' v Rossii*, 136–50.

[32] S. Filiatov, "Gosudarstvenno-tserkovnye otnosheniia v Rossii pered demokrati-

A more circumspect trend in Russian nationalism is advocating a more inclusive approach to the problem: the gradual assimilation of the members of non-Russian nationalities into the ethnic Russian nation. However, it does not provide a clear answer to the question of how to achieve this goal. Apparently, it pins its hopes on voluntary assimilation, but this seems dubious at the moment, at any rate with regard to territorialized nationalities in the Russian Federation.

Perhaps the most remarkable moment in the ongoing debate between various kinds of Russian nationalists is their intellectual poverty. Their debate does not contain anything new. The ideas and approaches under discussion go back to prerevolutionary times. This is despite the fact that one of the main concerns of prerevolutionary Russian nationalists had been the preservation of the empire, while the post-Soviet nationalists had to experience its dissolution.

One of the main features of Russian nationalism is that since the nineteenth century it has always acquired, and still acquires, illiberal, anti-Western, and authoritarian characteristics (I am writing now not about individuals, but about political movements, although there is little difference in this respect). Nationalism has many facets and varieties. It may be a political movement, or an ideology, or just a sentiment, or all of these together. Whatever one may have thought, nationalism does not necessarily belong to either the left or the right of the political spectrum. It is compatible with different political systems, from totalitarianism to democracy; and with different ideologies, from fascism and communism to conservatism, liberalism, and even social democracy. However, different varieties of nationalism are always connected with specific historical and political circumstances.

We used to think that nationalism strives for the congruence of political, linguistic, and ethno-cultural borders.[33] This was never the aim of Russian nationalism. In the prerevolutionary Russian context, nationalism was always aimed at preserving and extending the Russian Empire and at maintaining the dominant position of ethnic Russians in the empire. If these aims were provided with any ideological justification at all, then references were usually made to Orthodoxy as the only true Christian faith, to the messianic mission of the Russian people, and to similar arguments that have once again become popular in the country. Thus, this kind of nationalism might be called imperial nationalism. However, it was also quite contradictory.

---

cheskim vyzovom," in M. B. Olcott and A. Malashenko eds., *Religiia i gosudarstvo v sovremennoi Rossii* (Moscow: Carnegie Endowment for International Peace, 1997), 67–83.

[33] E. Gellner, *Nations and Nationalism* (Oxford: Basil Blackwell, 1983).

With regard to the non-Russian subjects of the empire, only two options were discussed: either their assimilation into the Russian people, or their subjugated minority status. However, even assimilation was a matter of debate: who might be allowed to assimilate and who should be prevented from it? In any case, the Russian nationalists considered linguistic and even cultural assimilation insufficient. To them and even to the majority of the general public, the sine qua non of assimilation was conversion to Orthodoxy. The Russian literature is abundant with characters of non-Russian ancestry who refer to their profession of the Orthodox faith in order to prove their Russianness. Even the last Romanovs and their ruling elite were increasingly trying to legitimize the existing order by identifying autocracy with the Orthodox Russian people at the expense of the imperial transnational identities and pretentions.[34] All this made Russian nationalism exclusive.

Thus, in the Russian political and ideological space, the boundaries between nationalism and other movements were quite different from those in many other European countries. It was possible to be simultaneously a nationalist and a liberal in England because there were clear geographic and other distinctions between England, or even Great Britain, and the British Empire. In Russia this was much more difficult because to the Russian nationalists, the territorially contiguous Russian Empire and Russia itself were at once single and indivisible. "Every place in Asia where an Urus [a nineteenth-century Turkic name for a Russian] has settled immediately becomes the Russian land," jubilantly stated Feodor Dostoevsky.[35] Ethnic Russia to them extended to the entire empire, but at the same time they denied its non-Russian subjects civic equality and strongly opposed the very idea of their administrative or even cultural autonomy.

After the suppression of the 1905 revolution, a large part of the main liberal party in the country, the Kadet (Constitutional-Democratic) Party, began to move toward statism with regard to the nationalities question.[36] Some of its influential members, such as P. Struve, S. Bulgakov, and N. Berdiaev, also began to claim that Russians were a Staatsvolk and that the Russian Empire was their national state. But they continued to insist on granting the non-Russians equal civil rights with the Russians, and this made them ideological and political oppo-

[34] M. von Hagen, "The Russian Empire," in K. Barkey and M. von Hagen, eds., *After the Empire: Multiethnic Societies and Nation-Building* (Boulder: Westview Press, 1997), 63.

[35] F. Dostoevsky, *Dnevnik pisatelia, in Polnoe sobranie sochinenii,* 27 (Leningrad: Nauka, 1984), 38.

[36] On the evolution of the Kadets' views on this question, see V. V. Shelokhaev, *Liberal'naia model' pereustroistva Rossii* (Moscow: ROSSPEN, 1996), 71ff.

nents of the nationalists.[37] Other liberals, like P. Miliukov, who wanted to transform the Russian Empire into a multiethnic nation-state in which ethnic Russians would not occupy a politically privileged position, were considered by the nationalists to be their archenemies.[38] Incidentally, Miliukov was known to sometimes use the word *rossiiskii* as opposed to *russkii*, and called for substituting *rossiisskii* state patriotism for the Great Russian ethnic variety.

The history of the Second International has proved that it was possible to be simultaneously a socialist and a nationalist. In Russia, this was possible only for members of ethnic minorities. There were Polish, Georgian, Jewish, Latvian, and other socialist parties with strong nationalist agendas; however, there was no Russian (*russkaia*) socialist party.

In tacit or overt forms, Russian nationalism continued to exist in Soviet times and remained empirecentric. One of its remarkable characteristics was the identification of Russia, not with the Russian Soviet Federative Socialist Republic, a pseudo-federative monster without many of the attributes of statehood possessed by other Soviet republics, but with the whole Soviet Union.[39] However, I will skip over the Soviet period and turn directly to the post-Soviet one. In spite of some differences, there are remarkable similarities between prerevolutionary and post-Soviet Russian nationalisms. Indeed, Russian nationalism remains antimodernist, anti-Western, antidemocratic, illiberal, authoritarian, and offensive, although nowadays sometimes in a defensive disguise. Steady screams on the threat to the Russian people from numerous external and internal enemies have become commonplace.

During the last few years I have devoted a lot of time to reading the growing number of Russian nationalist publications that are sold in millions of copies in the country.[40] I must say that it is not very exciting

---

[37] D. A. Kotsiubinsky, *Russkii natsionalizm v nachale XX stoletiia* (Moscow: ROSS-PEN, 2001).

[38] T. R. Weeks, *Nation and State in Late Imperial Russia: Nationalism and Russification on the Western Frontier, 1863–1914* (DeKalb: Northern Illinois University Press, 1996), 24ff.

[39] A. M. Khazanov, *After the USSR: Ethnicity, Nationalism, and Politics in the Commonwealth of Independent States* (Madison: The University of Wisconsin Press, 1995), 87ff.

[40] There is no possibility or reason to make more than a few selective references to these publications, especially since all of them are very repetitive (for good surveys, see V. Tishkov and M. Olcott, "From Ethnos to Demos: The Quest for Russia's Identity," in Anders Aslund and M. Olcott, eds., *Russia after Communism* (Washington, DC: Carnegie Endowment for International Peace, 1999), 61–90; A. Verkhovsky, E. Mikhailovskaya, and V. Pribylovsky, *Natsionalizm i ksenofobiia v rossiiskom obshchesteve* (Moscow: Panorama, 1998); A. Verkhovsky, A. Papp, and V. Pribylovsky, *Politicheskii ekstremizm v Rossii* (Moscow: Panorama, 1996); V. Likhachev, *Natsism v Rossii* (Moscow: Tsentr "Panorama," 2002).

reading. To a large extent, all nationalist ideologies are based on myth-ologies, and the Russian nationalist mythology, just like any other for that matter, pretends to be a self-evident truth that does not require proof. Favorite phrases of the Russian nationalists are: "It is evident," "It is well known." But there is an additional circumstance that makes the writings of Russian nationalists so boring: They are extremely ver-bose, bombastic, monotonous, declarative, and simply very bad, stylis-tically speaking.

This should not be surprising if one takes into account that many of the ideologists and proponents of Russian nationalism can most gener-ously be characterized as *lumpen-intelligentsia*: poorly educated and professionally incompetent people who became unnecessary and ex-pendable with the political change in the country and the transition to a market economy. To satisfy my curiosity, I inquired as to what some of these people were doing during the Soviet period. The results were quite beguiling. In the recent past, many of them were instructors of Marx-ism-Leninism, or of the so-called scientific communism. Others were *Komsomol'* or Communist Party functionaries, or KGB officers, or oc-cupied in other such "noble" professions. Now, the Sauls have become Pauls, or, perhaps more accurately, the Pauls have become Sauls.

There are also quite a lot of poets, writers, and journalists among the ideologists of Russian nationalism. Two or three are good or were good; the rest are very bad. In the Soviet Union they were protected from competition, patronized and fed, and fed quite well, by the Soviet gov-ernment for their loyalty to the regime. Nowadays they cannot compete and want to protect themselves by any means possible. Some years ago, one of them, the poet Sorokin, made a remarkable statement: "I admit that Joseph Brodsky's poems are as good as mine." (This is a very bold statement indeed, to compare oneself with a Nobel Prize winner and the greatest contemporary Russian poet.) But then he added: "However, I am Russian, and Brodsky is not. He does not have the right to write in Russian."[41]

Although at present the Russian nationalist movement, which self-characterized as "national-patriotic," is politically fragmented and con-sists of many parties and groups that are often competing with each other, it is not difficult to summarize the common characteristics of their mythology and political program. Let me start with mythology. It is almost disappointing in its lack of almost any new and original traits.

[41] Brodsky has become a symbol of Westernism in Russian culture and, thus, one of the most hated personalities by the nationalist lumpen-intelligentsia. One of their editions celebrated his death in the following words: "The Russian culture has become more clean. . . . The death of the crazy American Jew is irrelevant to our people." Another echoed: "The Russians reject the alien poetry of this Russophone poet." On these and other similar statements, see *Russkaia mysl'*, February 1, 2001.

In many respects, the contemporary Russian mythology repeats the myths of Soviet historiography and propaganda or goes back to pre-revolutionary nationalist myths.

In accordance with this mythology, we are now witnessing a clash of civilizations, a global struggle between the materialistic, individualistic, consumerist, cosmopolitan, corrupt, morally polluted, and decadent West led by the United States and the collectivist, idealistic, spiritually and morally superior Eurasia led by Russia. Russia is more than a country and a state, it is a civilization in which high spiritual qualities prevail over materialistic factors. Russians are the chosen people, who have a self-sacrificing mission to enlighten and save humankind. This claim goes back to the Russian religious philosophers, to Soloviev, Berdiaev, Fedorov, and others, and even to the "Russian idea" formulated by Dostoevsky in the 1870s and 1880s.[42]

Likewise, the Russian Empire was unique: it was the most humane in the history of the world. All peoples enjoyed peaceful coexistence and equality within her borders. Non-Russians joined it voluntarily. Russia never conquered and subjugated them, but if it did conquer them it was only for their own good, to protect them from external and internal enemies. This is a direct continuation of Soviet mythology; the pre-revolutionary Russian nationalists were more honest in this respect.[43]

So, what or who prevents Russia from fulfilling her messianic mission? Of course, the West, and at present the United States in particular. Russia has always been a besieged fortress, surrounded by enemies to the east and the west. For many centuries, the West has wanted to force Russia to her knees. The collapse of the Soviet Union is the result of this plot. Nowadays, the United States wants to break up Russia, to turn her into a source of raw materials.[44] And so on and so on. Conspiracy theory and the clarion call of Russophobia have become an indispensable part of contemporary Russian nationalist mythology.

It goes without saying that the majority of Russian nationalists are

---

[42] The "Russian idea" has many variations in quite different historical periods. See Tim McDaniel, *The Agony of the Russian Idea* (Princeton: Princeton University Press, 1996). Still, all of them share some common characteristics. The most important is the belief in Russia's uniqueness (the concept of Moscow as the Third Rome is but one of its components) and in its specific destiny in world history.

[43] Myths about the uniqueness of the Russian Empire, in which Russians and non-Russians allegedly enjoyed almost equal rights and the Russian nationalism, if it existed at all, was weak, are still rather popular among many Russian scholars and politicians and are even propagated by some semi-official publications (see, for example, V. A. Mikhailov, *Natsional'naia politika*, 46ff).

[44] See, for example, S. Kara-Murza, *Evrotsentrism: Skrytaia ideologiia perestroiki*, (Moscow: SIMS, 1996), 133; P. V. Chernov, *Rossiia: Etnogeopoliticheskie osnovy gosudarstvennosti* (Moscow: Vostochnaia literatura, 1999), 193; and many others.

virulently anti-Semitic. In this respect, they are also following prerevolutionary tradition. Jews have become the symbols and bearers of Westernism, rationalism, intellectualism, liberalism, democratic values, and individual achievements based on meritocracy that the Russian nationalists reject at hand.[45] The Jew is a transcendental image of the enemy. Yu. Beliaev, a leader of the ultranationalist National Republican Party, claims that, to him, every enemy of Russia is a Jew.[46] In other words, anti-Semitism is connected with their negative attitudes toward modernization and globalization.[47] People of Jewish origin, who are fairly numerous among the Russian democrats, are accused of Russophobia. The obsession with the alleged, eternal Jewish/Zionist/Judeo-Masonic conspiracy against Russia and the Russian people is a common topic in the writings of Russian nationalists. No wonder that the Protocols of the Elders of Zion, a prerevolutionary Russian fabrication,[48] is published in contemporary Russia by the thousands of copies, sometimes with the blessing of the high hierarchy of the Russian Orthodox Church, and many nationalist intellectuals and clerics insist on its authenticity. Another popular edition in this circle is *Mein Kampf*. Jews are considered to be the instigators and directors of all Russia's enemies, be they popes, international financial capital, NATO, the United States, or any other.[49] In the same fold, although rather incongruously, the Jews are accused of organizing the Bolshevik revolution in order to seize power and exterminate the Russian people, as well as the defeat of communism.[50] Judaism is not spared either. The Russian nationalists characterize it as a religion without any positive meaning, which has waged a stubborn war against Christianity for two thousand years.[51]

However, at the moment, negative attitudes toward natives of the Caucasus are, especially in practical terms, perhaps even stronger than anti-Semitism.[52] These are fueled by their ongoing migration to regions

[45] See, for example, I. P. Shafarevich, *Russkii narod na perelome tysiacheletii* (Moscow: Russkaia ideia, 2000), 295, 299.

[46] *Russkaia pravda* N2 (1994).

[47] Gudkov, "Antisemitizm."

[48] C. D. De Michelis, "Les 'Protocoles des sages de Sion.' Philolgie et histoire," *Cahiers du Monde Russe* 38, N3 (1997): 263–306.

[49] See, for example, A. P. Barkashev, *Azbuka russkogo natsionalista* (Moscow: Slovo-1, 1994), 7ff; G. Klimov, *Protokoly sovetskikh mudretsov* (Moscow: Astrasem', 1995); O. Arin, *Rossiia v strategicheskom kapkane* (Moscow: Flinta, 1997); Chernov, *Rossiia*, 3.

[50] Yu. Petukhov, *Tret'ia mirovaia voina* (Moscow: Metagalaktika, 2000), 254ff.

[51] Ioann, *Odolenie smuty*, 148. Curiously, some of those extreme Russian nationalists, although small in number, who turned away from Orthodox Christianity to neopaganism, consider the former a Jewish faith that corrupts the Russian spirit.

[52] V. N. Ivanov and L. V. Kozina, *Sotsiologiia mezhnatsional'nykh otnoshenii v tsifrakh* (Moscow: RITs ISPI RAN, 1996), 136–37.

of predominantly Russian population and are aggravated by their better adjustment to market reforms, different stereotypes of public behavior, clannishness, and perceived or real involvement in organized crime.[53] Contrary to anti-Semitism, Caucasophobia is encouraged in part by the Russian political and administrative elites and by the mass media, which have coined a new and bizarre term: "persons of Caucasian nationality."

There are two almost eternal Russian questions: *Kto vinovat?* (who is to blame) and *Chto delat'?* (what is to be done). The mythology of Russian nationalism provides an answer to the first question; its political program answers the second one. The extreme and sometimes overtly fascist organizations,[54] such as Russian National Unity, which by some estimates has up to 200,000 people under its influence,[55] or the skinhead movement, want to establish a system of apartheid and a corporate unitary state in Russia.[56] Other radical nationalist associations (e.g., the Union of the Russian People, the Russian Monarchist Union, the Union of the Archangel Mikhail) demand the strictest limitation of the political, civic, and economic rights of non-Russians. They insist that the power in Russia should belong to ethnic Russians as the state-forming people, while non-Russians may be represented in the institutions of politics, culture, science, and so forth only in proportion to their percentage of the country's overall population.

The program of the Russian nationalist mainstream is more moderate, but hardly appealing to non-Russians and democratically minded Russians as well. Russia should become the state of the Russian people, and the Orthodox faith should be proclaimed the state religion. Russia is single and indivisible and should become a unitary state, in which ethnic minorities will at best enjoy cultural autonomy, but no political or territorial autonomy whatsoever.

The Russian people must reject democracy and economic liberalism for the sake of a new and organic political and social order based on the so-called *sobornost'*. It is very difficult to translate this word, because even in Russian it has many different and vague meanings. The old Russian word *sobor*, which until recently was only rarely used, meant an assembly, whether ecclesiastical or lay. In the current nationalist parlance, *sobornost'* implies communitarian mentality and simultaneously

[53] A. Malashenko, "Ksenofobiia v postsovestskom obshchestve," in Vitkovskaia and A. Malashenko, eds., *Neterpimost' v Rossii*, 12–14.

[54] On these, see S. D. Shenfield, *Russian Fascism: Traditions, Tendencies, Movements* (Armonk, NY: M. E. Sharpe, 2001).

[55] V. Tishkov, "Kontseptual'naia evolutsiia natsional'noi politiki v Rossii," in V. Mikhailov, ed., *Natsional'naia politika Rossii: istoriia i sovremennost* (Moscow: Russkii mir, 1997), 238.

[56] Barkashev, *Azbuka russkogo*.

an alleged ethnic unity in which the interests of the Russian people as a whole should prevail over those of individuals. *Sobornost'* is allegedly based on the spirit of self-sacrifice and stresses the priority of the national community. In the lexicon of Russian nationalism, *sobornost'* also acquires a similarity with some concepts of fascist corporatism.

The purport and reason for the very existence of the Russian nation is a strong and mighty state (*derzhava*). The state, and by no means civil society, is the bearer, protector, and guarantor of national interests. The most immediate and urgent goal of the Russian people is the restoration of the mighty Russian state in its historical borders (in practical terms, the restoration of the Russian Empire, or, at least, the integration of the territories with predominantly Slavic populations). Since the West in general, and the United States in particular, strive to prevent Russia from achieving this goal, Russian foreign policy should become anti-Western and anti-American. In all, the political program of Russian nationalism is not only antidemocratic and illiberal, it is also revanchist.

Now, the final question: what role is the nationalist factor now playing in Russia's political life? Some observers point out that it is hardly likely that radical nationalists, especially neofascists, will come to power in the country in the near future. I tend to agree with them. One may even suspect that the Russian authorities sometimes use them as a scarecrow for the West and for domestic liberals. However, there is a danger of a different order. As Valery Tishkov points out: "There is no doubt that fascism *à la Russe* has transformed itself from a marginal political tendency of the late 1980s into a real political phenomenon of today."[57] One may also agree with his other statement, that the most serious obstacle to establishing civic nationalism or all-Russian patriotism is not so much the nationalism of non-Russians, but that of the Russians.[58]

First, some power structures and their officials are becoming increasingly receptive to the nationalist agenda. It is no secret in the country that extreme nationalist Russian organizations have many sympathizers in the Ministry of the Interior, in the judiciary, and in some regional administrations,[59] not to mention in the secret services. In direct violation of Russian law, the procurator's office and judicial bodies are sabotaging all attempts to prosecute those who are instigating and propagating ethnic and national hatred and even committing hate-related crimes. Second, and perhaps more important, other political

---

[57] V. Tishkov, *Ethnicity, Nationalism and Conflict in and after the Soviet Union: The Mind Aflame* (London: Sage Publications, 1997), 237.

[58] Ibid., 643; Tishkov and M. Olcott, "From Ethnos to Demos," 84.

[59] Some of the regional governors, like the former governor of the Krasnodar Territory, Nikolai Kondratenko, or the newly elected governor of Kursk Province, Alexandr Mikhailov, are overtly anti-Semitic.

movements are becoming increasingly receptive to nationalist programs and slogans. Nationalism in the country has become fashionable, and most of the political movements and parties are striving to advertise themselves as adequate defenders of national interests. The "national-patriotic" ideological formulas, rhetorics, and attitudes are spreading across the political spectrum and are being accepted by many mainstream politicians.[60]

The main Western, especially West European, patterns of ideological and political orientation — conservatism, liberalism, and social democracy — are still not applicable to Russia. Instead I would single out four major forces of the Russian political spectrum: nationalists, communists, what is called in Russian political parlance "the party (or parties) of power," and those democrats and liberals who, at the moment, are in opposition to the government or, at any rate, are not in the government (parties such as the Yabloko of Yavlinsky and, with some reservations, the Union of Right Forces of Gaidar, Chubais, and Nemtsov). It may be revealing to trace the extent to which these forces are becoming receptive to nationalist ideology.

One of the peculiar and intriguing elements of contemporary Russian political life is that it lacks a strong social-democratic movement. There are only a few tiny groups of social-democratic orientation, and this in a country with a very strong socialist tradition! There are several reasons for this state of affairs, but here I can only dwell upon one of them. While in many East Central European countries the communists are gravitating toward social democracy, their Russian counterparts are not. Instead, they are gravitating toward nationalism. It is true that at the moment there are several ideological trends in the Russian Communist Party, including a traditional or internationalist one.[61] But most conspicuous by far is the nationalist trend.

Let me summarize the main points of some books by Gennady Ziuganov, the leader of the Russian communists.[62] Russia is a unique, continental, Slavic, Orthodox civilization. At the same time, Russia is the legitimate successor to the empire of Jenghiz Khan. Russia continued

---

[60] Alexander Verkhovsky, "Ultra-Nationalists in Russia at the Onset of Putin's Rule," *Nationalities Papers* 28 (2000): 709, 719–20.

[61] J. B. Urban and V. D. Solovei, *Russia's Communists at the Crossroads* (Boulder: Westview Press, 1997).

[62] See, for example, G. A. Ziuganov, *Derzhava*, 2d ed. (Moscow: Informpechat', 1994); G. A. Ziuganov, ed., *Sovremennaia russkaia ideia i gosudarstvo* (Moscow: RAU Corporation, 1995); G. A. Ziuganov, *Rossiia — rodina moia: Ideologiia gosudarstvennogo patriotizma* (Moscow: Informpechat', 1996); G. A. Ziuganov, *Geografiia pobedy, Osnovy rossiiskoi politiki* (Moscow, 1997). Ziuganov, who evidently has a team of ghost writers, is a very prolific author indeed.

Jenghiz Khan's mission of uniting the Eurasian geopolitical space (Ziuganov is an assiduous student of the Eurasianists). The main achievement of the Soviet period was that the Russian state became even stronger; the main deficiency was that the Russianness of the Soviet Union was played down. Stalin understood this and wanted to strengthen the Russian character of the Soviet Union, but unfortunately he died too early.

Many Marxist ideas and doctrines contradict the Russian mentality and need revision. Thus, at present the struggle of states is substituted for the class struggle. Russia was always and still is opposed by the predatory Western civilization, which is negatively affected by Judaism.[63] The current goal of the West is to destroy Russia and Russians once and for all. There are too many non-Russians in science, culture, mass media, and the state structure. This proves that Yeltsin's leadership was pro-Western and thus anti-Russian.

I think that this is enough to create a clear picture of the contemporary ideological trend of the Russian communists. Whatever one calls them, they have ceased to be Marxists. We are now witnessing a merger of radical right-wing extremism with renascent anticapitalist populism on the conservative nationalist agenda.

Let me now turn to the party of power. Statism was always an important ideological factor in Russia. Its current nationalist accretion seems almost natural. One should keep in mind that a significant part of the Soviet/Russian establishment, including the party, the military, and the secret service, had been indoctrinated with ideas of Russian nationalism even before the perestroika period.[64] Many of these people remain in power today. In the new situation, they are additionally attracted to nationalism because it can provide them with a new legitimation of power. To other members of the Russian political elite, nationalism has become a matter of expedience. A number of Russian scholars notice the growing neo-*nomenklatura* nationalism. Already in 1994, Leokadia Drobizheva, currently the director of the Institute of Sociology of the Russian Academy of Sciences, warned that some politicians who were responsible for the elaboration of the nationalities policy in Russia had begun to repeat what in the past might have been heard only from the

---

[63] The Communist Party is the only major political party in Russia that sometimes does not disdain the deliberately provocative anti-Semitism (Malashenko, "Ksenofobia v postsovestskom," 11). General Albert Makashev, one of its influential members who has a seat in the State Duma, publicly claimed: "We will be anti-Semites and we must win" (*Itogi*, March 2, 1999).

[64] V. D. Solovei, "Russkii natsionalizm i vlast' v epokhu Gorbacheva," in P. Goble and G. Bordiukov, eds., *Mezhnatsional'nye otnosheniia v Rossii i SNG* (Moscow: ITs AIRO-XX, 1994), 58ff.

leaders of Pamiat' and other ultranationalist organizations.[65] The sense of alienation from and principal difference with the West is again becoming strong in the country. Thus, the author of a textbook recommended by the Ministry of Higher Education insists: "We will never become a Western people (at any rate, we will not become one in the foreseeable future)."[66]

Since 1994 *derzhavnichestvo*, statism, has almost become its official ideology, just like a little later its demonstrative anti-Americanism. For various reasons anti-Americanism is growing in the country, despite President Putin's recent rapprochment with the United States.[67] Many Russians cannot forgive the United States for winning the Cold War and, most especially, the consequences of defeat, which they consider a national humiliation. There are still many influential people in the Russian leadership who consider the United States and NATO to be the forces that prevent Russia from reestablishing her hegemony in East Central Europe and even within the Commonwealth of Independent States.

Actually, the Russian political elite is trying to sit on two chairs simultaneously, but not very successfully. In principle, the propagated state patriotism and allegiance to the strong and mighty state can be ethnically neutral. In Russia they are not. In some respects, the propagated ideology of *derzhavnichestvo* is a more circumspect nationalism, but it is still ethnic Russian nationalism. Remarkably, the name "Russian Federation" has been almost dropped from the official lexicon.

When the incomplete break with the Soviet past is accompanied by a growing desire to associate with the Russian imperial past and its symbolism, which non-Russians in the country completely reject, policy cannot be ethnically blind. When the state provides one of the many denominations in the country with the de facto status of state religion, policy cannot be ethnically neutral. When the new law on Freedom of Conscience and Religious Affiliations promulgates that Orthodoxy is an inseparable part of the all-Russia historical, spiritual, and cultural legacy, this law cannot be neutral with regard to non-Russian and non-Orthodox citizens of the country.

In Russia, all ideas of *derzhavnichestvo* imply two assumptions. First, the interests of non-Russian nationalities should coincide with the interests of ethnic Russians. Second, the Russians have special responsibili-

---

[65] L. M. Drobizheva, "Etnisizm i problemy natsional'noi politiki," in T. I. Zaslavskaia and L. A. Arutiunian, eds., *Kuda idet Rossiia? Al'ternativy obshchestvennogo razvitiia, I.* (Moscow: Interpaks, 1994), 189.

[66] Utkin, *Rossia i Zapad*, 426.

[67] Verkhovsky, "Ultra-Nationalists," 719.

ties for the preservation and strengthening of the state and are acting in the interests of all Russia's people. To pursue this line of argumentation to its logical end, one would have to claim that the one hundred thousand victims of the Chechen wars were slaughtered for their own sake.

For several years, Yeltsin's leadership was striving, although without great success, to work out a new "national idea" for the country that should allegedly define the nation's identity and inspire its citizens with a sense of direction. This elusive search has already become a national joke. However, it has revealed not only a deeply rooted authoritarian mentality, but also a specific vision of the post-Soviet Russian state. In a society that is already somewhat pluralistic, such an ideology can be promoted and disseminated only by the state and inevitably would be a statist ideology with strong nationalist and antiliberal accretions. However, everything indicates that the new leadership in Russia is not going to abandon this endeavor. The policy of authoritarian centralism that President Putin is imposing upon the country is, to a large extent, influenced by many concepts of Russian nationalism. The claim to Russia's uniqueness is now officially confirmed by the words of the old/new anthem: "You are unique in the world, one of a kind."

And what about the liberals? They also contributed to the growth of pro-empire sentiments, because in their struggle with the communists and their negative attitude toward the Soviet period they began to appeal to the idealized prerevolutionary past. What is more important, however, is that at present even the liberals have different attitudes to ethnic nationalism in the country. There are still staunch liberals and Westernizers who disdain all forms of nationalism, especially the Russian variety; but there are also growing numbers of other, so-called liberal statists or liberal imperialists, who are ready to make concessions to Russian nationalists. A few years ago, many of these supported the first Chechen war, and many more now support the second. Some are doing this because of their own conviction; others, because they want to exonerate themselves from charges of nonpatriotism.

To sum up, at the moment Russia lacks a consensus with regard to the concept of nation, and common identifications are very weak in the country. In these conditions of social and political fragmentation, nationalism has become a very important factor in the country's development, and, unfortunately, it could not be otherwise.

CONCLUSION

The stability and even the maintenance of democratic order poses a serious problem in many multiethnic and multinational states, which need a different design from more or less homogenous nation-states. Every ethnic group and nationality in such states should be convinced that their treatment by the government and by other nationalities is just and fair. I doubt that there is a universal solution to this problem applicable to all countries and situations. Many concepts seem much more attractive on paper than in reality. Thus, the Russian example hardly supports O'Leary's suggestion (see chapter 2 in this volume) that a stable democratic federation must have a Staatsvolk along with *Lander Volk*. The alleged exclusive rights of ethnic Russians as the Staatsvolk and the corresponding principle "Russia single and indivisible" is just what the Russian nationalists were advocating and are still advocating. Its practical applications have recently resulted in the two bloody Chechen wars with detrimental consequences for the still fragile Russian democracy and ethnic relations in the country.

There is a great difference between purely territorial and ethno-territorial federations, which is somewhat obscured by O'Leary. The very question of who belongs to the Staatsvolk and who does not is dangerous in the Russian context, just like the haphazard and inconsistent attempts to speed civic nation building. If the Russian Federation becomes a nationalizing state, it will have to resort to compulsory measures incompatible with genuine democratic order.

It seems that, at the moment, the country is facing two options. The first is the continuation of the current situation characterized by an uneasy cohabitation of different ethnic groups and minority nations with each other and, especially, with the dominant one, and their constant competition for power and resources on the local levels. The second option is an honest admission that the past, whether real or mythologized, is a dangerous divide in Russia, and that the best that can be done in this respect is simply to draw the line. The allegiance of all her citizens can be better achieved not on the notion of historical continuity, but on their mutual interest in developing liberal and democratic order, and on their joint membership in a secular political community willing to accommodate and compromise. Citizenship with corresponding rights and obligations, but not a membership in any particular nation, should provide ethnic minorities with a sense of security in a plural state and to some extent mitigate the excessive effect of ethnic identities. To achieve this goal, one should not even exclude specific constitutional arrangements of affirmative and consociational order, since trust is sometimes more important than an abstract principle of individual equality, which not infrequently results, in practice, in ethnic inequality. To put it bluntly, to buy may be better than to fight. After all, the asymmetrical character of the Russian Federation affirmed in her constitution has already implied a certain deviation from this principle.

At the moment, this is only a project, since Russia is still at a cross-roads. Nevertheless, I hope that Yack (see chapter 1 in this volume) is too pessimistic in his prediction that attempts at severing the connection between political and cultural loyalties are doomed. This is proven by many cases in which political loyalties to the state and its constitutional order take the upper hand over ethnic ones.

Only time will tell which choice will eventually prevail in Russia. What is clear, however, is that they are intrinsically linked with a more general choice between authoritarianism and democracy that the country still has to make.

CHAPTER 4

The Return of the Coercive State:
Behavioral Control in Multicultural Society

PETER BALDWIN

WHETHER ONE thinks of presocial humans as noble savages or mere barbarians, once they join in community with one another under the auspices of a state, they are made to adopt behaviors they once shunned. The nature of their constraints, however, have varied over the course of history, as it has among nations. One of the most notable shifts, described by Norbert Elias and Michel Foucault, has been from formal to informal control.[1] Sketched with a thumbnail, the early modern state imposed control formally on its inhabitants, from without, and with a hard hand. It set strict controls on certain behaviors and threatened draconian punishments for their violation. But beyond these clear boundaries it left its subjects largely alone. The modern state, in contrast, enlists its subjects, now elevated to the status of citizens, as participants in their own governance. In the process, it shifts the locus of control internally. Although state and civil society, public and private, are now clearly distinguished from each other, in fact the two are more inter-permeated than ever before. Citizens govern themselves, not just in terms of suffrage and political control, but also in terms of their own moral, instinctual, and emotional economy, limiting their actions before the fact and moderating their impulses. Thus the harshness of the early modern state is rendered unnecessary. The modern state no longer instructs, commands, and punishes. It educates, informs, persuades, and discourages.[2]

[1] From the now massive literature: Colin Jones and Roy Porter, eds., *Reassessing Foucault: Power, Medicine and the Body* (London: Routledge, 1994); Graham Burchell et al., eds., *The Foucault Effect: Studies in Governmentality* (Chicago: University of Chicago Press, 1991); Johan Goudsblom, "Zivilisation, Ansteckungsangst und Hygiene: Betrachtungen über ein Aspekt des europäischen Zivilisationsprozesses," in Peter Gleichmann et al., eds., *Materialen zu Norbert Elias' Zivilisationstheorie* (Frankfurt: Suhrkamp, 1977); Nikolas Rose, *Governing the Soul: The Shaping of the Private Self* (London: Free Association Press, 1990).

[2] Patrick Nützi, *Rechtsfragen verhaltenslenkender staatlicher Information: Strukturen-Zulässigkeit-Haftung, illustriert an den Beispielen AIDS und Listeriose* (Bern: Stämpfl, 1995), chap. 1.

Elias paid attention to differences between France and Germany. Foucault was locked into a more exclusively Francocentric mode. Generally speaking, however, the assumption was that all Western nations have passed from formal external control to informal internal regulation. One caveat to this presumption of a common path of evolution concerns the political inflections of statutory control. Thus, the connection between the development of democracy and citizens' participation in their own governance has encouraged the argument that more autocratic political systems would undergo this shift later, if at all, and that they would retain vestiges of the early modern state's formal control for longer. A well-known variant of this idea is the argument put forth by Erwin Ackerknecht in the realm of public health policy.[3] Ackerknecht distinguished between quarantinism and sanitationism, policies that he associated with autocracy and liberalism, respectively. Quarantinism was the armamentarium of traditional public health policies applied to ward off the plague during the Middle Ages: quarantines, isolation of the afflicted, disinfections and destructions of infective goods and possessions, and, generally, an approach that subordinated the personal liberty and autonomy of the ill and potentially diseased to the good of the community. Sanitationism, in contrast, sought to clean up the environment in hopes of avoiding disease, understood as something produced by noxious surroundings. It was thus a tactic that spared commercial interests and their desire for unfettered trade the imposition of quarantines, but also citizens the violation of their liberties, harmonizing thereby the interests of individual and community.

Hygienic behavior was part of the self-control and policing that was expected of the democratic citizen. Without it, a sanitationist approach to public health would not work. Sneezing and suffrage were linked. Citizens who failed to cover their mouth when coughing, expectorated in public, could not distinguish the functions of their water closet from their sink, or exposed their smallpox-stricken children in public were unlikely to be entrusted with the right of political self-governance. The French Revolution made it an explicit requirement of membership in the polity that citizens conduct themselves so as to remain healthy. While the state was now widely recognized as having a certain duty to support the health of its members, they in turn had obligations to their community in not acting so as to destroy the common property that

---

[3] Erwin H. Ackerknecht, "Anticontagionism between 1821 and 1867," *Bulletin of the History of Medicine* 22 (September–October 1948); Erwin H. Ackerknecht, *Medicine at the Paris Hospital 1794–1848* (Baltimore: Johns Hopkins University Press, 1967), 156–57; Henry E. Sigerist, *Civilization and Disease* (Chicago: University of Chicago Press, 1944), 91.

was their weal.[4] These trends, begun in the spirit of the Enlightenment, continued into the hyperpopulism of the totalitarian regimes. The Nazi slogan in such matters was "Your health does not belong to you."[5] With the development of bacteriology, and thus an improved understanding of the precise routes along which microbiological entities peregrinated via personal conduct, hygienically acceptable behavior was made scientifically more explicit and emphasized. The cult of hygiene, the fixation on anal, digital, and oral propriety that has become an unconsciously accepted element of childrearing, is part of a campaign of learned behavior stretching back at least to the first use of the fork. But it took off into all-encompassing proportions during the late nineteenth century.[6] The lessons of the laboratory, a recognition of the ability of unseeable microorganisms to spread disease, were translated into a strict code of personal hygiene and conduct. This led to the minimization of physical contact, an avoidance of common objects, an end to the indiscriminate discharge of bodily fluids, the shaving of men's beards, the shortening of women's hemlines, and untold other behavioral changes that we now regard as second nature.

Today, we have come full circle. Consider the German advertisements for Häckle Feucht, the moist toilet paper that is sold as a means of eroticizing the rear end. A clean derriere is a desirable derriere. The ultimate sanitary taboo, oral-anal contact, the first behavior every baby's parents vehemently discourages, has now reentered the realm of the hygienically and aesthetically possible. Along with the role switching (each partner both penetrating and being penetrated) that distinguishes modern North American and European homosexual practices from earlier varieties and from the Mediterranean and southern approaches, anal sex has been an integral part of the claim made for gay male eroticism, that it allows an appreciation of the potential mutuality of pleasure, both giving and receiving as no other couples — whether lesbian or straight — could.[7] Thus, it is more egalitarian and democratic than other forms of sex. (Though straights have increasingly sought the

[4] Dora B. Weiner, *The Citizen-Patient in Revolutionary and Imperial Paris* (Baltimore: Johns Hopkins University Press, 1993).

[5] Michael Burleigh and Wolfgang Wippermann, *The Racial State: Germany 1933–1945* (Cambridge: Cambridge University Press, 1991), 290.

[6] Nancy Tomes, *The Gospel of Germs: Men, Women and the Microbe in American Life* (Cambridge: Harvard University Press, 1998), chaps. 4–6; Pierre Darmon, *L'homme et les microbes, XVIIe–XXe siècle* (Paris: Fayard, 1999); Joseph A. Amato, *Dust: A History of the Small and Invisible* (Berkeley: University of California Press, 2000), chap. 6.

[7] Guy Hocquenghem, *Homosexual Desire* (Durham: Duke University Press, 1993), chap. 4; Daniel Mendelsohn, *The Elusive Embrace: Desire and the Riddle of Identity* (New York, 1999), 73–74; Peter M. Davies et al., *Sex, Gay Men and AIDS* (London: Falmer Press, 1993), 127–29.

same experience, with strap-ons no longer an item only for lesbians).[8] Anilingual sex became a major public health issue in the premonitory epidemics of intestinal ailments (amebiasis, giardiasis) among First World gays. Diseases otherwise encountered mainly in the unsewered areas of the developing world now sprang from the increasingly popular practice of rimming during the 1970s and 1980s. With the AIDS crisis, the sexual rediscovery of the anus became a political as well as public health issue as the dangers of fisting (possibly the only sexual practice invented in the last several centuries — showing once again, as though proof were required, just how cruel is the law of diminishing returns) were widely recognized.[9] Among lesbians, the HIV threat encouraged the use of dental dams for anilingual sex, at least as an excuse, though such behavior is not in fact especially risky.[10] As the German advertisements show, such hygienic completing of the bodily loop from mouth to anus has now been extended and suburbanized among the heterosexual population. It leads us, as it were, one small step back toward the corporeally polymorphous perversity that the civilizing process, reinforced by the bacteriological revolution, had put out of court. The return of the anus as a *salonfähig* orifice at the end of the twentieth century represents, in that sense, both a slight reversal and a higher stage of the civilizing process, a lapse premised on the highest possible standards of hygiene being otherwise observed.

MULTICULTURALISM LITE?

Excepting this Ackerknechtian public health inflection, which drew parallels between formal control and autocratic political systems, today, when all Western nations are assumed to be liberal, bourgeois, capitalist democracies, the idea of the shift from formal to informal regulation is generally thought to play little role, all nations having already undergone it. And yet the question of multiculturalism, however fraught with ambiguity, imprecision, and ideological posturing it may be, raises the issue once again. It does, that is, unless we are willing to argue that the cultures that coincide and cohabit in the increasingly balkanized major

---

[8] Michael Warner, *The Trouble with Normal: Sex, Politics and the Ethics of Queer Life* (Cambridge: Harvard University Press, 1999), 38.

[9] Gayle S. Rubin, "Elegy for the Valley of the Kings: AIDS and the Leather Community in San Francisco, 1981–1996," in Martin P. Levine et al., eds., *In Changing Times: Gay Men and Lesbians Encounter HIV/AIDS* (Chicago: University of Chicago Press, 1997), 103, 111; John-Manuel Andriote, *Victory Deferred: How AIDS Changed Gay Life in America* (Chicago: University of Chicago Press, 1999), 23.

[10] Robin Gorna, *Vamps, Virgins and Victims: How Can Women Fight AIDS?* (London: Cassell Academic Press, 1996), 338–39, 350–51, 354, 357, 365, 369.

metropolitan areas of the Western world are all ones that agree on the unspoken rules of informal control and behavior modification. That this is an unlikely proposition is implicit in the very concept of multiculturalism. If the informal rules of behavior that increasingly obviate the need for formal statutory control have been internalized by all citizens of multicultural societies, then the very concept of multiculturalism is gutted of its substance. What remains is a sanitized, superficial, folkloric sham exoticism, the multiculturalism of brightly colored sartorial accessories, moderately spicy cuisine, boppily banal world Muzak, and the ritual agreement that all religions have the right to celebrate Christmas, each with its own ceremonial inflections, but all at the same time.

If, in contrast, multiculturalism is to be taken seriously, then the possibility of real differences, with practical implications for urban life and the consequent reality of attendant conflict, must be faced. What does globalization, with its mass peregrinations and the resulting fragmentation of monocultural nation-states, imply for the nature of the state and its control apparatus and functions? If multiculturalism is not just veiled Enlightenment universalism, decked out with the trappings of easily digestible disparities — what Stanley Fish calls boutique multiculturalism — but something that implies real differences among contestatory ethnic and cultural groups, it raises once again the necessity of formal, external statutory intervention.[11] What happens when it's santeria and not just sangria? Multiculturalism claims to celebrate diversity and tolerance. Perhaps, instead and ironically, it necessitates statutory controls that contradict the general drift of social development over the past several centuries. Perhaps multiculturalism means returning to the impositions of the early modern and authoritarian state.

In the multicultural capitals of the industrialized world, real conflicts are fought out daily. In Los Angeles, Sikhs are forbidden to wear ceremonial daggers to school in a polity where gun ownership is considered a civil right. In France, Muslims are not allowed to cover their heads in school in a society where hats, in the form of haute couture, are otherwise sacred. In the United States, Muslim women are arrested for wearing veils under laws intended to prevent the Ku Klux Klan from appearing publicly in full regalia. Indochinese parents are charged with abuse when they minister to their fevered children with the ancient practice of moxibustion by pressing heated coins against their skin. So are Mexicans when they discipline their offspring by using the smoke from hot chili peppers to scorch the sinuses and eyes. Immigrant girls' clitorises are amputated, four thousand times annually in Paris alone.[12] Some cultures allow the murder of a wife in the heat of jealous rage. Others regard this as reprehensible and actionable lack of self-control.

When both views coexist, a more precise accounting of what is acceptable is required. A transsexual's desire to have his penis reconstructed as a vagina is considered legitimate medical mutilation. A woman's intent to be reinfibulated postpartum is not. One person's blood sport is another's Chicken McNuggets. In addition to the massive attempts at mind control exercised by both the tobacco interests and their enemies, nonsmoking enforcement is among the most drastic of direct statutory incursions, forbidding behavior that a decade or so ago was socially acceptable. Given that smoking is inversely proportional to socioeconomic status, it is perhaps the most overt, though wholly unacknowledged, act of class behavioral imposition since the antispitting campaigns of the late nineteenth century. When Clarence Thomas sought to entertain Anita Hill with pubic hairs on Coke cans, references to Long Dong Silver, allusions to cinematic bestiality, discussion of genital size, and the like, Orlando Patterson defended him against his "neopuritan" detractors for simply having pursued a "down-home style of courting." His habits were those of rural black males and thus offensive to the ethos of the white, and now increasingly feminized, upper middle-class urban establishment of which he had in the meantime become part.[13] When the Hmong, formerly of the Cambodian, now the Californian, hinterland, abduct child brides as part of their marriage ceremonies—committing rape, both statutory and otherwise, in the eyes of the community where they now live—they too are guilty of a "down-home style of courting."

Religion provides an even stronger example of what is at stake here. The Rushdie affair reminded us that theology is still a life-and-death issue in some cultures, ones that now dwell among us in the West and especially in Europe.[14] The ironic agnosticism with which the vast majority of Western intellectuals supported their fellow traveler against the strictures of the mullahs demonstrated once again that theological toleration is possible only once religion is no longer meaningful. Including, apparently, Salman Rushdie himself, no one—outside, of course, of the camp of believing Muslims—took his challenge seriously or was willing

---

[12] Catherine L. Annas, "Irreversible Error: The Power and Prejudice of Female Genital Mutilation," in Jonathan M. Mann et al., eds., *Health and Human Rights* (New York: Routledge, 1999), 340–44.

[13] Orlando Patterson, "Race, Gender and Liberal Fallacies," *New York Times*, October 20, 1991, 15.

[14] Michael S. Teitelbaum and Jay Winter, *A Question of Numbers: High Migration, Low Fertility, and the Politics of National Identity* (New York: Hill & Wang, 1998), 55.

to allow it consequences. As Walter Lippman once pointed out, liberalism's belief in the power of reason and free inquiry fails before those opinions that refuse to submit to the test of reason and free inquiry (a lesson accepted by the present German republic in its prohibition of both extreme left and right). So too a secular and nominally tolerant society cannot find room for a religion that makes absolute claims to truth. Only by gutting itself of its most essential characteristics can religion be multiacculturated. The only domestic religion taken seriously in Europe today is Scientology, with Saint Travolta as its martyr. Indeed, so earnestly do Europeans take the gospel according to Hubbard that they seek to define it as not a religion, precisely so that it may be persecuted. Just as Chicago gangsters were once brought low by the tax authorities, so too in the era of alleged theological toleration, religion is to be persecuted by the fiscus. But what, really, is the difference between Monsiegneur Leclerc, more Catholic than the pope, and Scientology, other than two millennia of elapsed time and the corresponding institutional accretion? In contrast, religion retains more meaning in the United States. Kansas parents find that they have to take it seriously, at least if they educate their children in public schools. In cases such as these, multiculturalism tests the boundaries of peaceful coexistence.

Proceeding from the sublime to the subterranean, consider mass transit.[15] In most nations, access to subways is restricted by some sort of physical barrier, with a ticket or token the price of admission. Once inside, the rider is spared official interference. The control is formal and at the perimeter of the system. But in Germany, Austria, Switzerland, and Scandinavia, the honor system reigns. No physical barriers prevent anyone from boarding, but there are irregular inspections and checks performed by plainclothes personnel, who masquerade as fellow travelers until the doors are shut. Then they suddenly morph into representatives of authority, flashing papers and rounding up miscreants. No one who has experienced this honor system in full regalia forgets either the heart-pounding, adrenalin-pumping shock as just another commuter turns, like something out of *Invasion of the Body Snatchers*, into an official, or the pervasive sense of smug satisfaction exuding from ticket holders as scofflaws get their just deserts: an unnerving feel of the steel within the velvet of informal control.

Why such a difference in the control of mass transit? There are obvious economic issues involved, it being no coincidence that the least labor-intensive approaches are found in those nations with the highest labor costs (although this depends on the mechanization of the physical

---

[15] See also Peter Baldwin, "Riding the Subways of Gemeinschaft," *Acta Sociologica* 41 (1998): 378.

barriers as well as the frequency of surprise checks). But there is more
to it than this. Clearly northern Europe assumes that the citizen's duty
to not be a free rider (of the most literal sort) can be taken for granted;
a mass transit superego is at work here on which other nations cannot
rely. Controls are internalized in a way that other societies, more heterogeneous or more in thrall to a Mediterranean notion of the citizen
resisting authority, cannot take for granted. Admittedly, there are exceptions to this neat rule. The Tokyo subway system, presumably serving a
population as homogeneous as, say, Stockholm's, works on physical-
access principles. Conversely, the Los Angeles subway, such as it is, is
used by what is arguably the most heterogeneous population in the
Western world and works on the honor system.[16] For the first anomaly, I
have no good answer. For the second, we should presumably look to the
limited nature of the system, an Angeleno on the subway being an unusual creature indeed.

But the assumptions once taken for granted no longer hold. The Paris
and London subways have suffered from sufficient violations of their
physical access that they have taken to spotchecks within the system as
well, thus eliminating the sense of insouciant unconcern that used to
characterize these systems once travelers had made it past the barriers.
Conversely, some of the north European systems have been subject to
massive violations of the honor system, with a possible breaking point
in the offing. In Berlin, one of the most ethnically and socially heterogeneous cities in the region, the closest the northern continent has to a
world-class metropolis, there are major problems with *Schwarzfahrer*.
They give false identities and thus cause fines to be levied on innocents,
usually friends or family of the culprits, whose names and addresses
they know offhand and whose identity they therefore assume when
caught. A system based on largely informal processes of control is thus
spilling over, in an era when presupposed commonalties are breaking
down, into the victimization of innocent bystanders.[17]

HETEROGENEITY AND CONTROL

Marx famously anticipated a withering away of the state once the inherent contradictions of capitalist society had given way to postrevolution-
ary harmony, as though private property were the source of all antagonism. Obviously, our desires to act in ways that others experience as

[16] *Los Angeles Times*, March 18, 2000, B1.

[17] Peter Baldwin, "State and Citizenship in the Age of Globalization," in Peter Kos-
lowski and Andreas Føllesdal, eds., *Restructuring the Welfare State: Theory and Reform
of Social Policy* (Berlin: Springer Verlag Press, 1997), 115.

antisocial are myriad beyond this narrow realm. Controls that curtail our behavior must be imposed for society to function. Self-denial is the basis not only of civilization, but of basic social order. The advice in nineteenth-century etiquette books that young female railway passengers hold pins between their lips whenever the train passed through tunnels, lest they be subject to stolen kisses (indeed the very concept of a stolen kiss is now actionable behavior and not at all romantic) and the ubiquity of the habit in Victorian novels of locking the bedroom door upon retiring for the night bespeak an emotional and sexual economy with much lower thresholds of stimulus resistance than in our own day. Modern society sees itself as sexually less strict. Yet our threshold of male arousal, or at least action in response to arousal, has been vastly elevated compared to what it was even a century ago. We police ourselves, and can be insouciant with respect to sex, only on the mutual agreement that we will not act on stimuli that our predecessors would have found unbearably provocative. (Asian tourists eagerly photographing seminude female sunbathers in Scandinavian parks and the unabashed gawking of Turkish men at similar scenes in Germany, while the local males resist tumescence as efficiently as hardbaked nudists, testify to the uncomfortable coexistence of different arousal thresholds.)

But the point, phrased here in erotic terms, has a broader significance as well. Would there even be a state if we were all middle-class, prudently abstemious, healthy, moderately drinking types who bought life insurance, saved for a rainy day, educated our children, always used condoms, drove only when sober, always covered our mouths when coughing, refrained from painting our houses bright primary colors or parking jalopies in the front yard? The state would scarcely need to intervene at all, or perhaps only in situations where ignorance of the risks incurred was the issue—to ensure workplace safety, for example. We would avoid the risks we could sidestep and voluntarily insure and redistribute the costs of those we could foresee, but not personally control, a form of what has been called "prudentialism."[18] With the right habits of prudence, the state might indeed wither away.

The rule of thumb would seem to be that informal control is most reliable and formal control least necessary in societies that are homogeneous—socially, ethnically, religiously. There, unspoken rules can be taken for granted and informal means of persuasion exert their influence. Where most share the same religion, clerics and their authority can be enlisted to obtain certain behaviors without requiring the force

[18] Nikolas Rose, "Governing 'Advanced' Liberal Democracies," in Andrew Barry et al., eds., *Foucault and Political Reason: Liberalism, Neo-Liberalism and Rationalities of Government* (Chicago: University of Chicago Press, 1996), 58.

of law, as it was in Sweden and Prussia early in the nineteenth century to bring about childhood inoculation and then vaccination against smallpox. Alcohol use can be regulated through outright prohibition and other limitations on consumption, but equally through attempts to encourage the habits of abstemious peoples, like Jews and Italians, among more hard-drinking cultures.[19] But what is meant by homogeneity? Perhaps it is true that the British state of the nineteenth century did not need to be as extensive or interventionist as its Continental counterparts because it governed a linguistically and geographically homogenous society.[20] Where, however, does that leave Sweden and other uniform societies where the state flourished and multiplied? Also, how to explain the allegedly residual American state with this argument? Difficulties lurk beneath the surface of homogeneity.

Wide dissemination of the ethos of prudence that would, in theory, have obviated the need for a great deal of formal statutory control was hampered during the last century by class-based differences in behavior and conduct. Today, the obstacles are more likely to rest on ethnic and national differences. There remain, however, wide-ranging overlaps between these categories, whether the congruence of race and socioeconomic status in the American urban underclass or the coincidence of poverty and ethnic otherness (combined with the nervousness that principled rootlessness evokes in the bourgeois soul) that make Roma and Sinti universally despised and persecuted across Europe. Moreover, contemporary multiculturalism deals not only with existing ethnic and cultural groups, brought into proximity through the era's mass peregrinations. It also celebrates difference to the point of spawning a veritable Noah's ark of multiplicity. The increasing specialization and balkanization of sexual identity, with gays of a hundred different stripes lurking behind an only apparently communal identity, is the most obvious example. As French conservatives have put it, it is a gigantic melting pot of copulations and populations.[21]

Class distinctions were paramount during the nineteenth century. One of the motives behind the formalized social insurance system pioneered by Bismarckian Germany was the belief that workers could not be relied on to save for old age and illness (both for lack of disposable income as well as for negligent habits of thrift and delayal of gratification). Just as workers were paid weekly, that being taken as their

---

[19] Mariana Valverde, *Diseases of the Will: Alcohol and the Dilemmas of Freedom* (Cambridge: Cambridge University Press, 1998), 101, 115.

[20] Pat Thane, "Government and Society in England and Wales, 1750–1914," in F.M.L. Thompson, ed., *The Cambridge Social History of Britain 1750–1950*, vol. 3 (Cambridge: Cambridge University Press, 1990), 2.

[21] Nicolas Mauriac, *Le mal entendu: Le sida et les médias* (Paris: Plon, 1990), 95.

horizon of prudence, while white-collar employees received their salaries every month, so too social insurance institutionalized an assumption of class-based differences in self-abnegation, long-term planning, and allocation of gratification. Ignoring for the moment the compensation via the employer's contribution and state subventions, compulsory social insurance required workers to redistribute risks and their costs over their lifetimes in a way that could — given habits which, alas, were not thought present — just as well have been accomplished voluntarily.

Conversely, the long tradition of working-class mutual aid in Britain helps explain why the state felt less pressure to intervene in such matters here, though it was very active, and in some respects more so than in Germany, in other areas. Similarly, the relatively better pay, ample housing, and higher standard of living enjoyed by nineteenth-century American workers, not to mention their integration into the political system, their widespread belief in improving circumstances through mobility and education, and their chance of advancement as subsequent waves of immigrants took the worst jobs, help account for the lack of perceived need in the United States for the state to intervene into areas that seemed to be functioning, if not well, then at least better than in Germany.[22] Of course, there is another element to this story, since the relative retardation of welfare policies in France was not due to workers being better off than in Germany or more autonomously prudent. The state and its initiatives, or lack of same, played a role. Nonetheless, the difference here related to the delayedly industrialized nature of the country, with a much larger percentage of the population still under the wing of more traditional means of security, petty bourgeois property ownership. House ownership played a role here, too, with Germany being notable for its many citizens who remained (even today) lifelong renters and the subsequent inability of workers to rely on one of the few traditional forms of security that has survived into the industrialized world even, and in many respects especially, in the Anglo-American nations. The traditional American approach to welfare was to ensure that the economic system functioned, providing a level playing field. It was less to tinker with the rules of the game.[23] This was possible only on the assumption that workers could and would play in the same way as the middle classes, an assumption that the Germans did not yet find plausible during the nineteenth century.

But how social fragmentation and heterogeneity influences state inter-

[22] Stein Rokkan, *State Formation, Nation-Building, and Mass Politics in Europe* (Oxford: Oxford University Press, 1999), 291.

[23] Daniel T. Rodgers, *Atlantic Crossings: Social Politics in a Progressive Age* (Cambridge: Harvard University Press, 1998), 498.

ventions goes beyond class to touch on more basic differences among social groups. Take public health controls imposed to curb the spread of syphilis during the nineteenth century.[24] The unique approach pursued first in Sweden during the early part of the century and subsequently also in Germany (after 1927) and France (in the 1960s) did not regulate prostitutes. Instead it imposed the controls familiar from the regulationist systems on all citizens. It required them to be inspected on occasion, to submit to medical treatment (such as it was) if infected, and to follow certain behavioral prescriptions to prevent transmission. The reasons for this — at the time — unique policy trajectory were several. Most importantly, Sweden was simply not sufficiently urbanized to focus on a still nonexistent class of metropolitan prostitutes. In addition, in Sweden (and also in Russia and elsewhere on the European periphery), people believed that syphilis was not a sexually transmitted disease as such. Rather, it was passed along through the quotidian interactions of domestic life.[25] The habits in question were common among peasants: shared use and negligent cleanliness of every conceivable household implement, spitting in or licking the eye to remove sties, polymorphous sleeping arrangements (including the indiscriminate bunking of travelers with the family), and earthy child-minding practices (sucking babies' penises to calm them, licking clean their runny noses, chewing their food for them). Thanks to such behavior, syphilis found other avenues of transmission than merely the sexual.

To see syphilis as a venereally transmitted disease, in other words, was possible only assuming that daily interactions did not involve the sort of mucous membrane contact and exchanges of bodily fluids that were common well into the nineteenth century among poor country folk. The nonsexual dissemination of VD has long been considered a sign of primitive customs and low cultural development. It indicates that the basic hygienic habits of urban middle-class life (the sanitized interface we present to each other, except — although increasingly even there, depilated, deodorized, belatexed — in sex) have not yet been achieved. Sex is the primary means of syphilitic transmission only in civilized, or at least hygienic, societies. Sexually transmitted diseases were thus created as a separate and stigmatized class of illness not only because people felt sex was a sin. Equally, it heralded the triumph of personal hygiene that eventually left venereal contact as their predominant mode of transmission.

---

[24] A story told in Peter Baldwin, *Contagion and the State in Europe, 1830–1930* (Cambridge: Cambridge University Press, 1999), chap. 5.

[25] Roger Davidson, *Dangerous Liaisons: A Social History of Venereal Disease in Twentieth-Century Scotland* (Amsterdam: Rodopi, 2000), 8.

The Swedish approach to VD control shifted attention from prostitutes and their clients to the population as a whole, which was assumed to be susceptible to the disease regardless of its sexual habits. In the European metropolitan core, where hygienic habits already excluded nonsexual transmission, prostitutes and their policing occupied the prophylactic foreground. Thus early nineteenth-century Sweden, a nation that is often regarded as highly homogenous in other respects, posited certain aspects of its legislation — one that imposed the sort of formal external control that we would expect in a multiplicious polity — on the premise that society was in fact heterogeneous, at least in matters of hygiene.[26]

HETEROGENEITY FROM ABROAD

When we turn from social heterogeneity by class or, as in the case of peasant proclivities, social group to ethnic and national divergence, the question of immigration immediately presents itself. Here, the U.S. experience is of greatest interest. In public health, the American approach has largely been motivated by immigration and the consequent possibilities of epidemic disease. All nations have had to deal with the public health implications of acculturation. In all, rural denizens with sanitary habits encouraged by wide open spaces have been transformed into urban dwellers, entangled in much denser webs of interconnectedness — microbiological, olfactory, and otherwise — and eventually into citizens with middle-class habits of contact avoidance, abstemiousness, pleasure delayal, foresight, and prudence. But not all have had to deal with the same problems also in terms of immigration. In Europe, fears, phobias, and revulsions attached themselves to the lower classes in big cities (although of course there were national inflections to such class identities, the case of the Irish in England being the most obvious). Where class was here the focus, in the United States, such concerns were also diffracted through the lens of foreignness. To immigrants in the classic sense came, of course, the issue of slaves and the black underclass that is its modern result, institutionalizing a permanent sense of epidemiological otherness.[27]

Despite its reputation for a liberalist, laissez-faire approach to statu-

---

[26] Assumptions of homogeneity: Henrik Stenius, "The Good Life Is a Life of Conformity: The Impact of the Lutheran Tradition on Nordic Political Culture," in Øystein Sørensen and Bo Stråth eds., *The Cultural Construction of Norden* (Oslo: Scandinavian University Press, 1997), 161.

[27] David McBride, *From TB to AIDS: Epidemics among Urban Blacks since 1900* (Albany: SUNY Press, 1991).

tory intervention, the United States has, in public health terms, long been one of the most openly and drastically intervening of states. American authorities, though more those at the local and state level (perhaps not surprising in so vast and geographically fragmented a polity), have been as eager as most European to interpose their powers to assure the well-being of the community. In the nineteenth century, interventions in the United States to assure the public's health were broad, drastic, compelling, compulsive, and sometimes even effective.[28] As Hermann Biggs, of the New York City Department of Health, put it at the turn of the century, defending his attempt to fight tuberculosis among the tenement immigrants of lower Manhattan by requiring behavioral change, removing children and institutionalizing the sick in families that refused to cooperate: "The government of the United States is democratic, but the sanitary measures adopted are sometimes autocratic, and the functions performed by sanitary authorities paternal in character."[29]

If there is anything to Ackerknecht's claim of an elective affinity between autocracy and quarantinism, then the United States was among the most autocratic of nations. The Americans kept the quarantinist tradition alive longer and more vigorously than most other nations, well into the twentieth century. They imposed attempts to block or cut chains of transmission long after such tactics had fallen out of favor in Europe. In 1879, for example, with yellow fever reported in Memphis, orders were issued to inspect all trains leaving infected places, cleansing and fumigating them, to transfer all passengers and baggage to new trains after five miles and all freight at a distance of fifty, and to heat all mail bags to 250 degrees.[30] During an 1888 epidemic in Jacksonville, other cities quarantined against that municipality and often each other; suspicious trains were not allowed to pass through uninfected cities, much less discharge passengers; the Texas health officer detained and disinfected every person and train traveling from east of the Mississippi River; health attests were demanded of travelers; every house in Jacksonville was fumigated, all infected bedding and clothing boiled and other materials bought and burned by the federal authorities. During the 1890s railway passengers were forcibly taken to fever camps, and,

[28] William J. Novak, *The People's Welfare: Law and Regulation in Nineteenth-Century America* (Chapel Hill: University of North Carolina Press, 1996), chap. 6 and passim; William R. Brock, *Investigation and Responsibility: Public Responsibility in the United States, 1865–1900* (Cambridge: Cambridge University Press, 1984); Rodgers, *Atlantic Crossings*, 80–81.

[29] Sheila M. Rothman, *Living in the Shadow of Death: Tuberculosis and the Social Experience of Illness in American History* (Baltimore: Johns Hopkins University Press, 1994), 188.

[30] Brock, *Investigation and Responsibility*, 144.

in so-called shotgun quarantines, trains from infected areas were not allowed to stop in as yet healthy ones.[31] Federal regulations required detention of passengers and fumigation of freight in trains from infected yellow fever zones.[32] In 1888 detention camps were first established, in this case between Georgia and Florida. Those seeking to travel north were held for a period sufficient to show that they were not infected, a system, it was hoped, that would end the informal and spontaneous practice of shotgun quarantines.[33]

During the 1892 cholera epidemic, mail of passengers on ships quarantined in the New York City harbor was disinfected with steam.[34] At the end of the Spanish-American War in 1899, to prevent the import of yellow fever with the returning troops, massive feats of quarantinism were performed. They included the inspection of more than thirty thousand soldiers, the detention of ten thousand simultaneously at one quarantine station, and the desinfection of eighteen thousand tons of baggage. In 1900 the entire Chinatown of San Francisco was quarantined, roped off with a police guard, when plague appeared.[35] Indeed, even today, the victims of communicable disease are formally forbidden to travel between states without permission from the health officer at their destination. Those suffering from the classic contagious ailments, such as plague, cholera, and yellow fever, are required to apply for a federal permit for interstate travel.[36] Well into the twentieth century, lepers had to have permission from the surgeon general as well.[37]

When the Foreign Quarantine Service was transferred to the Centers for Disease Control in 1967, it was one of the oldest and most prestigious units of the Public Health Service. Its personnel and esprit de corps (including its uniforms, designed and often redesigned by a man

[31] Margaret Humphreys, *Yellow Fever and the South* (New Brunswick: Rutgers University Press, 1992), 121–22, 138.

[32] Jo Ann Carrigan, "Yellow Fever: Scourge of the South," in Todd L. Savitt and James Harvey Young, eds., *Disease and Distinctiveness in the American South* (Knoxville: University of Tennessee Press, 1988), 68.

[33] Ralph Chester Williams, *The United States Public Health Service, 1798–1950* (Washington, DC: Commissioned Officers Association of the United States Public Health Service, 1951), 82–83.

[34] Howard Markel, *Quarantine: East European Jewish Immigrants and the New York City Epidemics of 1892* (Baltimore: Johns Hopkins University Press, 1997), 110.

[35] Williams, *The United States Public Health Service*, 86, 90–91, 121–22; Nayan Shah, *Contagious Divides: Epidemics and Race in San Francisco's Chinatown* (Berkeley: University of California Press, 2001).

[36] Christopher H. Foreman, Jr., *Plagues, Products, and Politics: Emergent Public Health Hazards and National Policymaking* (Washington, DC: Brookings Institution Press, 1994), 61.

[37] Robert D. Leigh, *Federal Health Administration in the United States* (New York: Harper & Brothers, 1927), 320–21.

in Washington whose full-time job this was) added much to the increasing prowess of the institution in Atlanta. At this time, the Quarantine Service still fulfilled such venerable (if technologically updated) functions as checking X-rays and vaccination certificates of arriving ship passengers, passing through the aisles of airplanes to inspect passengers' eyes for signs of jaundice, and administering some two hundred thousand smallpox vaccinations annually to border crossers from Mexico. Indeed so traditional did the approach to quarantinist activities at the frontier remain during this period that in 1966 the Weir committee, investigating such matters, recommended making the Mexican border as open as the Canadian. Smallpox vaccination at the point of entry, it observed, invoking the sort of logic (substituting steam for jet locomotion) that had been pursued a century earlier, was too late to be effective. One could not simultaneously permit international traffic and build a wall impenetrable to communicable disease. At the same time, intergalactic quarantine was put in place. Worrying both about exporting earthly microorganisms into space and extraterrestrial creatures back home, the National Aeronautics and Space Administration isolated the returning lunar astronauts for twenty-one days.[38] Though rarely used, quarantine of a very old fashioned sort, including the posting of warning placards and the swearing in of quarantine guards, remained on the books in several states until well into the 1960s. Also possible was the isolation of the communicably ill in hospitals, or as the law of Washington state quaintly put it as late as 1962, a "pest house."[39]

The American quarantinism was largely prompted by the problems raised by immigration and the perceived uncouth habits of newcomers. During the 1840s Lemuel Shattuck reported to the Boston City Council on the deleterious effect of recent immigrants' unsanitary habits. He advocated statutory intervention.[40] The fact that most immigrants came from rural areas added difficulties, since their customs and behavior were hard to reconcile with the sanitary necessities of dense urban conurbations.[41] Once Robert Koch had discovered the tubercle bacillus in

[38] Elizabeth W. Etheridge, *Sentinel for Health: A History of the Centers for Disease Control* (Berkeley: University of California Press, 1992), 157–58, 178–79, 184–86.

[39] Frank P. Grad, *Public Health Law Manual: A Handbook on the Legal Aspects of Public Health Administration and Enforcement* (New York: American Public Health Association, 1970), 47–48.

[40] Barbara Gutmann Rosencrantz, *Public Health and the State: Changing Views in Massachusetts, 1842–1936* (Cambridge: Harvard University Press, 1972), 19–20, 30; Suellen Hoy, *Chasing Dirt: The American Pursuit of Cleanliness* (New York: Oxford University Press, 1995), 24–27.

[41] John Duffy, *A History of Public Health in New York City, 1625–1866* (New York: Russell Sage Foundation, 1968), 192–93.

1882, tuberculosis became seen not just as a contagious disease, but as one that struck especially the poor and immigrants.[42] As of 1891 aliens were not permitted entry if afflicted with a dangerous, contagious disease. In 1892 New York City began inspecting immigrants bacteriologically for the cholera vibrio.[43] In 1911 all arriving travelers from Italy to New York were bacteriologically inspected for cholera, thus being spared the five-day detention period otherwise imposed.[44] In Europe, such bacteriological inspections of travelers' excrement had been mostly dismissed as impracticable (though they were practiced in Egypt). From the American point of view, insalubrious European immigrants presented the same sort of epidemiological threat that Europeans saw in Muslim pilgrims, journeying to Mecca from all over the globe, afterwards to carry disease back home.[45]

An inability, as it was seen, to rely on the individual sanitary habits of rural and poor foreigners encouraged a granting of more powers to the state in a polity that in other respects looked askance at such percolation upward from civil society. The public had to step in where private initiative did not suffice, and that was above all among immigrants.[46] Milwaukee's strict approach to smallpox in the late nineteenth century included vaccinating schoolchildren, placarding infected residences, and isolating the ill in a city hospital. Though later overturned after riots, it was adopted largely in response to fears of recent immigrants, above all Germans and Poles. They had arrived nonimmune and remained so since they refused vaccination (which they regarded as an autocratic imposition of precisely the sort they had left their old country to avoid).[47]

For diphtheria, drastic measures were also imposed. In the 1890s New York City required children with sore throats and their families and other contacts to undergo throat cultures, quarantined those with positive results, and required two negative outcomes twenty-four hours apart before they could be released. By the early years of the following

[42] Rothman, *Living in the Shadow of Death*, 181.

[43] John Duffy, *The Sanitarians: A History of American Public Health* (Urbana: University of Illinois Press, 1990), 194.

[44] Williams, *The United States Public Health Service*, 88.

[45] *Conférence sanitaire internationale de Paris*, 7 Février–3 Avril 1894 (Paris: Impr. Nationale, 1894), 100, 283–84; *Journal Officiel*, 1911, Chambre, Doc., Annexe 1218, 1062; *Proceedings of the International Sanitary Conference Provided for by Joint Resolution of the Senate and House of Representatives in the Early Part of 1881* (Washington, DC: Government Printing Office, 1881), 76–77; Paul Weindling, *International Health Organisations and Movements, 1918–1939* (Cambridge: Cambridge University Press, 1995), 5.

[46] Rosencrantz, *Public Health and the State*, 31–32.

[47] Judith Walzer Leavitt, *The Healthiest City: Milwaukee and the Politics of Health Reform* (Princeton: Princeton University Press, 1982), 89–90; Duffy, *History of Public Health in New York City*, 447.

century, preschool immunization was compulsory. In contrast, the British did not take decisive action and suffered much higher incidence rates.[48] In 1893 diphtheria also served as the springboard for the first mass use of bacteriological examination in New York City when Hermann Biggs pointed out that such testing to identify actual cases (half of those tested in the diphtheria hospital had not actually had the disease) was cheaper than disinfecting and quarantining the homes of all suspected patients. Spearheaded in New York, bacteriological testing became an important new tool in America's arsenal of public health.[49] TB provides yet another example of this robustly quarantinist approach. Robert Koch, who is often portrayed, by both contemporaries and subsequent scholars, as the incarnation of a Prussian tradition of bacteriologically inspired public health that imposed strict interventions on the individual to protect the community, was astonished to discover that New York City, where TB sufferers were compulsorily reported to the authorities, took a harder line than his native state.[50] Indeed, Koch wrote to Biggs in 1901 that, to persuade his fellow Prussians to accept making TB obligatorily notifiable, he wished to cite the example of the Americans, who, though freedom-loving, nonetheless accepted such limitations on their liberties for a higher good.[51] Conversely, in Britain reporting of tuberculosis was resisted as leading to ostracization and concealment of disease. The Medical Office of Health of Birkenhead warned that Britons would not tolerate being overruled in the way that the burghers of New York (not a metropolis accustomed to playing the foil to liberty) had to endure.[52]

Prompted not just by fears of immigrant others, but by the localization of the disease in marginal groups of transients and vagrants, American TB policies were notable for their harsh interventions. Most drastically, this included the use of compulsory incarceration, even into the

[48] Lawrence C. Kleinman, "To End an Epidemic: Lessons from the History of Diphtheria," New England Journal of Medicine 326 (1991): 774–75.

[49] Duffy, The Sanitarians, 195.

[50] On Koch's autocratic leanings: H. Oidtmann, "Beschwerdeschrift gegen den Geh.-Rath Dr. Koch, den Verfechter der Impfschutzlehre—aus dem Jahre 1889," Der Impfgegner 8 (January 1890); Richard Evans, Death in Hamburg: Society and Politics in the Cholera Years, 1830–1910 (Oxford: Clarendon Press, 1987); John Andrew Mendelsohn, "Cultures of Bacteriology: Formation and Transformation of a Science in France and Germany, 1870–1914" (Ph.D. dissertation, Princeton University, 1996). On Koch and NYC: Daniel M. Fox, "From TB to AIDS: Value Conflicts in Reporting Disease," Hastings Center Report 16 (December 1986), suppl.: 12.

[51] Sheila M. Rothman, "Seek and Hide: Public Health Departments and Persons with Tuberculosis, 1890–1940," Journal of Law, Medicine and Ethics 21 (1993): 292.

[52] John M. Eyler, Sir Arthur Newsholme and State Medicine, 1885–1935 (Cambridge: Cambridge University Press, 1997), 150.

post–World War II period, the antibiotic era, when this might have seemed outmoded.[53] From the 1980s, Directly Observed Therapy, the requirement that antibiotics to cure TB be taken in front of a public health authority to ensure the complete course of a treatment regimen (thus to prevent the development of resistant strains), has increasingly been imposed on transient and homeless patients. It is, of course, an outright admission that the informal assumption that patients properly take their medicine simply does not hold with certain marginal groups. Since multidrug-resistant TB has recently spread among liminal social groups, where informal behavioral prescriptions are weak, noncompliant patients in New York can now be detained throughout the course of their treatment and not just, as before 1993, for the first few weeks.[54]

Coinciding with the balkanization of multiculturalism and the corresponding discount on the value of informal behavioral control, a general shift has taken place in the value attached by courts to the inviolability of civil rights. From the 1970s on, these have been gradually hollowed out in favor of the community's prerogatives. Public health has benefited — if that is the right word — from this in that the authorities have been granted greater powers, in part through use of the criminal code, to detain and isolate those whose epidemiological status poses threats to society.[55] Renée and Jean Dubos once argued that measures to prevent the spread of TB did not require legal compulsion because they had "acquired the compelling strength of common sense."[56] Common sense, no one should be surprised to discover, is less common now than it was during the 1950s.

If we trace such divergences in public health trajectories up into the AIDS era, a sense may be had of the continuing influence of choices made in favor of more or less formal statutory interventions to bring about behavioral change to limit the spread of epidemic disease. One main dispute in HIV prophylaxis has been whether a traditionally quarantinist approach to transmissible illness should be used in this case too. Should we require reporting of the ill, prescribe the behavior of the infected, isolate recalcitrants, and impose other harsh strictures on bodily autonomy and individual liberty? (This is commonly called the

[53] Barron H. Lerner, *Contagion and Confinement: Controlling Tuberculosis along the Skid Road* (Baltimore: Johns Hopkins University Press, 1998).

[54] Foreman, *Plagues, Products, and Politics*, 63.

[55] Edward P. Richards, "The Jurisprudence of Prevention: The Right of Societal Self-Defense against Dangerous Individuals," *Hastings Constitutional Law Quarterly* 16 (1989).

[56] Renée Dubos and Jean Dubos, *The White Plague: Tuberculosis, Man, and Society* (Berkeley: University of California Press, 1952), quoted in George J. Annas, "The Impact of Health Policies on Human Rights: AIDS and TB Control," in Jonathan M. Mann et al., eds. *Health and Human Rights* (New York: Routledge, 1999), 43.

contain-and-control strategy.) Or, should the tactics that were first developed around 1900 in Britain against syphilis be used? The British assumed that sexual disease, spread in circumstances of intimacy beyond the state's ken and associated with sin and stigma, could not be cudgeled with heavy sticks. It required the enlightened tools of public education, easily available treatment, and encouragement of voluntary behavioral change to avoid transmissive conduct (what has been called the inclusion-and-cooperation strategy).[57]

A significant literature claims that eventually all industrialized nations adopted the second of these approaches. But, in fact, the divergence of public health tactics even in the face of the recent challenge of AIDS has been marked. Nations like Britain adopted a liberal approach out of old habit. Others, like France, followed suit by default, suffering from their traditional inability to be decisive in such matters. Still others, like Germany, did so for fear of repeating their tainted fascist past. Two nations not often lumped together, Sweden and the United States, adopted the most traditional strategies. Both used tactics rejected elsewhere: widespread testing of large groups of the population, in the United States including the military, immigrants, and some civil servants; potential quarantine of recalcitrant seropositives; and prescriptions, especially in Sweden, of nontransmissive behavior on pain of punishment in default.

Sweden, while now thought of as a homogenous nation where one might expect broad sway for informal controls to achieve much the same ends, in fact implemented more or less verbatim the policies implemented around 1918 for syphilis. These, in turn, derived from policies that had been first developed a century earlier, when the customs and habits of country folk had been seen as the problem. Though an enlightened and user-friendly welfare state, Sweden had also spawned some of the most aggressive eugenic sterilization policies during the interwar years. Among the nonfascist nations, Sweden and the United States had shared the greatest enthusiasm for sterilization and eugenics and were also the polities that remained most consistently quarantinist and least enamored of environmental reform as the response to public health problems.[58] In applying strict formal controls to the HIV epidemic, the Swedes demonstrated, as one observer has put it, that their

[57] The terms are from David L. Kirp and Ronald Bayer, eds., *AIDS in the Industrialized Democracies* (New Brunswick: Rutgers University Press, 1992).

[58] Gunnar Broberg and Mattias Tydén, *Oönskade i folkhemmet: Rashygien och sterilisering i Sverige* (Stockholm: Gidlunds, 1991); Maija Runcis, *Steriliseringar i folkhemmet* (Stockholm: Ordfront, 1998); Maciej Zaremba, *De rena och de andra: Om tvångssteriliseringar, rashygien och arvsynd* (np: Bokförlager DN, 1999); Gunnar Broberg and Nils Roll-Hansen, eds., *Eugenics and the Welfare State* (East Lansing: Michigan State University Press, 1996).

society did not trust its people to make rational decisions to protect their own health or others'.[59] Informal control was not, in other words, sufficient. The United States, too, was led along the policy path it had developed earlier when faced with the prospect of turning its huddled masses into sanitarily circumspect burghers.

THE POLITICS OF THE TECHNICAL FIX

Of course, politics can be found vermicillating under almost any rock one has the stomach to turn over. A society's overall political culture is reflected, often in unexpected ways, in the most basic assumptions its members take for granted. Whether a society seeks to prevent or cure, to tackle problems before or after the fact, is a political decision. One can seek to avoid calamity or redistribute its effects post facto: require lightening rods on houses or engage in barnraisings after the fires; insist on vaccination or isolate the sick; allow contraception or abortions; flouridate the water or foot the dentist's bills; eat healthily or install defibrillators in public places; pasteurize milk or treat consumptives; provide night schools or spend money on the dole; enhance workplace safety or distribute disability pensions; circumcise or treat cervical cancer; place condoms in all hotel rooms or give penicillin postcoitally.

Prevention is, as millions of samplers attest, worth more than its weight in cure. The highest medicine, F. de Chaumont wrote a century ago, is that which prevents the use of medicine, the best surgery that which prevents the loss of a limb.[60] But political logic is not always on this side. First, prevention requires a faith in human ability to intervene and tinker with nature. Smug anachronism sustains us when we contemplate the picturesque prescientific misunderstandings of the past in such matters. Yet, we need look no further than the controversy over gene-altered crops currently fought out across the Atlantic to get a sense of the stakes at issue. A century from now, as our cloned great-great grandchildren ingest their plasticene radiated goop with a hearty *Mahlzeit*, the European preference for carrots as-our-ancestors-knew-them will seem as quaint as the fear of lightening rods does now.

Second, prevention requires spending resources to discover the proper techniques. Though it may be cheaper in the long run, prevention often requires investment in the hope of a future payoff that is politically hard to justify. Safety lighting in airplanes costs well into seven figures per life

---

[59] Jeffrey Weeks, "Post-Modern AIDS?" in Tessa Boffin and Sunil Gupta, eds., *Ecstatic Antibodies: Resisting the AIDS Mythology* (London: Rivers Oran Publishers, 1990), 137.

[60] "Médecine publique ou préventive," *Annales d'hygiène publique et de médecine légale*, 3/5 (1881): 257–58.

saved; billions are sunk in pharmaceutical research. Finally, prevention often requires a modification (whether voluntary and consensual or compulsory and etched in law) of behavior. In multicultural societies, with few mutually agreed upon norms of conduct and fewer means of informal persuasion, this is increasingly difficult. So why do some political systems prefer prevention to cure?

Politics, not technology, made American car manufacturers the first widely to install passive restraint systems (airbags and especially seatbelts that embrace the passenger willy-nilly as the door is closed and ignition turned). Europeans, at least to the north, could rely on widespread compliance with compulsory seatbelt laws. For Americans, in contrast, this became one of those inexplicably neuralgenic issues where matters of deep-seated political culture are raised in a specific and technical context. Another example is compulsory helmet laws for motorcyclists, which some claim violate the inherent right of free citizens to feel the wind in their hair and leave their brains in a splat on the macadam. With seatbelts, a technical fix avoided major disputes over civil liberties. That Germans continue to insist on the right to drive as fast as they please on the highway as a basic right of citizenship, *freie Fahrt für mündige Bürger*, is as bizarrely peculiar as the American insistence on the right of citizens to bear arms. Part of the German fixation on the civil right to put pedal to the metal is due to their faith that the system of car inspections, the strict TÜV, means that their machines are safe at high speeds. A technical fix sidesteps an ideological battle. In the United States, where rusted, brakeless hulks ply the freeways as a matter of course, draconian automotive inspections (along with higher gas prices) would question the entire premise of the transportation system. In the absence of more extensive mass transit, cars are a matter of peregrinative democracy. Their cost cannot be put beyond reach of the working poor: therefore speed limits are required to make the system work. In Germany, where even today driving remains reserved for the better-off, the safari element — the treating of it as a sport and not merely a means of getting from point A to B — continues to be more palpable (German singles ads often use cars as an erotic lure). In both cases, political choices inform even the most mundane technical matters. The Americans value low taxes and individual mobility for all more than speed for the elite owners of well-slung cars; the Germans have made a choice the other way around. In the most general sense of the alternative between politics and technology, the choice by those nations with a meaningful defense strategy in favor of high-tech warfare is not just a matter of fielding the best technology most likely to be victorious. It is a policy equally motivated by hopes of avoiding the casualties attendant on old fashioned ground combat and thereby minimizing the politically costly sacrifices demanded of a citizenry that is increasingly imbued with the ethos of individualistic hedonism.

Political values informing apparently technical matters can also be observed in the choice between cure and prevention in public health. The unexpected return of infectious diseases has led to a marked national division of labor that reflects basic political ideologies. Spending on basic research is heavily concentrated in certain nations; the rest freeload on an inherent public good. The Americans have poured by far the most resources into finding a biomedical solution to the AIDS epidemic (a problem that, while it affected the United States disproportionately for the first few years, has now become an epic disaster for large swaths of the developing world). In 1993, for example, the United States provided some 90 percent of global governmental funding on AIDS research. The French were the next-largest funders of research. Nonetheless, their spending was only 3 percent (2 percent in 1997) of the American, but even this modest sum was a third more than the British, the nearest competitor, and thrice that of Germany.[61] In the 1980s American AIDS research, measured in monetary terms and per inhabitant, was one hundred times that of the British, ten times that of the Swedes.[62] Indeed, Swedish research efforts were largely underwritten by U.S. funds; during the mid-1980s the American government was providing Swedish researchers with more resources than their own.[63] The bulk of American federal spending on AIDS has gone to basic biomedical research, vaccine development, clinical trials, and epidemiological surveillance. Much less has been spent on public health education and prevention programs.[64]

One understands that the Americans would follow this course. U.S. research has dominated the biological sciences in the postwar period, and the nation has a legacy of believing in the technological mastery of nature.[65] But why have the French also pursued this policy trajectory?

---

[61] Jonathan M. Mann and Daniel J. M. Tarantola, eds., *AIDS in the World II* (New York: Oxford University Press, 1996), 203; Claude Évin and Bruno Durieux, *La lutte contre le sida en France* (Paris: La Documentation francaise, 1992), 23; Michael Balter, "Europe: AIDS Research on a Budget," *Science* 280 (June 1998): 1856.

[62] *Hansard*, January 13, 1989, vol. 144, col. 1147; *Riksdagens protokoll*, Bihang, 1985/86, Socialutskottets betänkande 1985/86:15, 10.

[63] *Riksdagens protokoll*, 1985/86, Bihang, Prop 171, 19–20; 1987/88, Bihang, Prop 79, 42; 1986/87:109, April 23, 1987, 140. This, of course, implied that the quality of Swedish research was up to snuff, but that the Swedish government saw no reason to fund it.

[64] Philip R. Lee and Peter S. Arno, "AIDS and Health Policy," in John Griggs, ed., *AIDS: Public Policy Dimensions* (New York: United Hospital Fund, 1987), 10; William Winkenwerder et al., "Federal Spending for Illness Caused by the Human Immunodeficiency Virus," *New England Journal of Medicine* 320 (1989): 1599, 1603.

[65] Stephen P. Strickland, *Politics, Science and Dread Disease* (Cambridge: Harvard Uni-

The French are usually said to have a historical penchant for a more environmentalist approach to medicine. Their Pasteurian variant of bacteriology has been described as especially environmentalist, if that is not a contradiction in terms. French physicians are reputed to be more concerned with the immunological response of patients to disease, their ability to ward it off, than with its microbiological causes. They are fixated on the terrain, the social and environmental context of disease.[66] Why should a nation with a medical approach supposedly so different from the technologically enamored U.S., with its Enlightenment belief in humanity's ability to tame nature, seek such solutions? Partly, of course, the French share the Enlightenment faith in humanity's ability to control nature. Whether they like it or not, they are closer to Americans in such respects than to Germans or even the British. In public opinion surveys, scientific research on medical issues appears as a key part of republican political ideology.[67] The French are, after all, the premier pill swallowers of the world. The impotence of the Greens in France and the willing embrace of nuclear power are also elements in this basic worldview.

Indeed, one aspect of the French enthusiasm for biomedical research has been their competition with the Americans in matters of scientific prowess and prestige, a tension demonstrated with unfortunate aplomb in the Montagnier-Gallo dispute over what eventually came to be known as the HIV. Since the end of the Second World War, the French have been fighting a rearguard action to preserve what is left of their preeminence as the foremost representative of the Enlightenment, and they have been battling, above all, with the American moloch. Yet French culture, to the extent that anyone pays any attention at all, leaves its mark primarily in increasingly obscure and impenetrable fields of the humanities and the softer social sciences, in philosophy of a certain bent, in history and sociology, in literary studies — and mainly, at that, in the eyes of its archenemy. How bitter that prophets like Braudel, Foucault, and Derrida have been more famous and certainly earlier known in the land of the foe than at home.

While the French may have conquered, and are still accorded the rit-

---

versity Press, 1972); Victoria A. Harden, *Inventing the NIH: Federal Biomedical Research Policy, 1887–1937* (Baltimore: Johns Hopkins University Press, 1986).

[66] Mendelsohn, "Cultures of Bacteriology," 234–63, chap. 8; Lynn Payer, *Medicine and Culture: Varieties of Treatment in the United States, England, West Germany and France* (New York: Owlet, 1988), 61–62; Jamie L. Feldman, *Plague Doctors: Responding to the AIDS Epidemic in France and America* (Westport, CT: Bergin & Garvey, 1995), 101–6.

[67] Bruno Jobert, "Mobilisation politique et système de santé en France," in Jobert and Monika Steffen, eds., *Les politiques de santé en France et en Allemagne* (Paris: Observatoire Européen de la Protection Sociale, 1994), 74.

uals of cultural cringe in, the university comp-lit departments of West Coast America, they have lost the battles that matter. In the physical and biological sciences their star has been fading, and fast. The 2000 faculty of Stanford, a small university on the outskirts of San Francisco, boasts more Nobel prizes (nine in the real sciences) than all living prize-winners of France, the proud inheritor of the tradition of Descartes and Pasteur (seven). So when the French found themselves on the cutting edge of the research to identify the cause of AIDS, the potential victory was one to be savored. Luc Montagnier may have had the ethical upper hand in the question of HIV priority. But other cases, like the Minister of Social Affairs' rush to publicize the "successes" in treatment with cyclosporine after only a week of experimentation, testified to the French ambition to preserve their national and scientific prestige in the face of American competition.[68] When Rock Hudson went to Paris in vain hopes of staving off death with HPA-23, it had been a long time (perhaps not since rabid Russians came seeking salvation at Pasteur's lab) since anyone with a choice had journeyed very far for the prospect of medical treatment in France.

Scientific prestige, national glory, and basic political assumptions were thus all at stake here. Both the United States and France had political and ideological motives for emphasizing a biomedical solution, for adopting a technical rather than a social angle to the problem. Both nations were among those hardest hit in the industrialized world. At the most general level, a cure would be a classic Enlightenment victory, showing that nature could be tamed and providing a public good of universal benefit to humanity.[69] Whatever one may think of such rhetoric, it certainly has separated the French and Americans from, say, the Swedes or the Germans, who were apparently not prepared to do the work of humanity, but only of themselves. Beyond such universalist posturing, a biomedical approach interested these nations because it allowed them, if successful, to sidestep certain problems. In France, emphasizing biomedical research of interest to all humanity, rather than social science investigations promising to target efforts more effectively at home, allowed the French to gloss over the traditional and persistent weaknesses of their public health system.[70] Also influential has been the French cultural prejudice against regarding sexuality as anything but an individual, personal, and private choice, and the consequent political

[68] Monika Steffen, "AIDS Policies in France," in Virginia Berridge and Philip Strong, eds., *AIDS and Contemporary History* (Cambridge: Cambridge University Press, 1993), 248.

[69] *Le Monde*, January 11, 1989, 17.

[70] Of the sort painfully laid bare in Aquilino Morelle, *La défaite de la santé publique* (Paris: Flammarion, 1996).

illegitimacy of groups based on sexual identity — gays above all — of the sort that have played such a large role in the Anglo-Saxon, Dutch, and Scandinavian realms.[71] Biomedicine and the technological fix promised an ability to sidestep such ticklish issues.[72]

The Americans, in turn, sought a biomedical solution in hopes that this might (assuming that, unlike AZT, it would prove cheaper than caring for the stricken) undercut the urgency of dealing with their persistent problems of insurance coverage and its all-too-glaring gaps. Pouring greater resources into medical research than any other nation has been an American tradition since the 1930s. Besides the universalist goal of pursuing public goods, there were also political payoffs. Voting for research funding was one of the few ways that American politicians could demonstrate their support for health, since other avenues of largesse, like health insurance for all, were blocked. "Medical research," as Melvin Laird, then a member of Congress, put it in 1960, "is the best kind of health insurance" the American people could have.[73]

All nations stood to gain, of course, from a cure, but not all nations were willing to throw resources in its direction. For countries with effective and universal health care systems, the epidemic did not really present itself as a political problem. So long as all citizens were entitled to whatever care was possible, and so long as the disease did not assume overly threatening proportions, a new illness was only another blip on the political radar. For such systems there was no political advantage to spending funds on biomedical research rather than (to put matters most starkly) building hospices to ensure terminal care for the stricken. Indeed, there was no benefit to doing anything at all so long as insurance coverage met needs. (Even in France, the annual budget for indemnifying infected hemophiliacs was many times that for research; in the United States, the proportions were reversed.[74]) For the United States, with its persistent problem of insurance coverage, where the disease struck precisely the uninsured as well as newly articulate and politically surprisingly adroit sexual minorities, AIDS was much less easily

---

[71] One of the themes of Frédéric Martel, *Le rose et le noir: Les homosexuels en France depuis 1968* (Paris: Seuil, 1996). Also Monika Steffen, "Les modèles nationaux d'adaptation aux défis d'une épidémie," *Revue française de sociologie* 41 (2000): 24.

[72] Michael Pollak and Marie-Ange Schiltz, "Les homosexuels français face au sida: Modifications des pratiques sexuelles et émergence de nouvelles valeurs," *Anthropologie et sociétés* 15 (1991): 54.

[73] Strickland, *Politics, Science, and Dread Disease*, 213; Harden, *Inventing the NIH*, 182.

[74] David Kirp, "The Politics of Blood: Hemophilia Activism in the AIDS Crisis," in Eric A. Feldman and Ronald Bayer, eds., *Blood Feuds: AIDS, Blood and the Politics of Medical Disaster* (New York: Oxford University Press, 1999), 312.

digestible. More generally, a biomedical approach was most consistent
with the values of a polymorphous democracy and especially one increasingly fraught with the problems of multiculturalism, its social, cultural, and sexual balkanization, and the consequent inability to rely
either on the persuasive cohesion of traditional European ethnic homogeneity or even on the classic assimilationist ethos of Americanization.
Seeking biomedically to cure a disease of great social stigma, one spread
initially and, in the West, still primarily through behaviors and lifestyles
widely regarded as immoral, was the socially and politically most hands-
off approach. It was the solution that involved least intervention into
civil society and its mutually antagonistic proclivities. Large and heterogeneous polities, like America, have most at stake in technical, and thus
politically and morally neutral, solutions.[75]

An AIDS cure held out the prospect of sidestepping the traditional
elements of disease prevention that violated the rights of individual citizens for the sake of the community's well-being.[76] Yet, it also promised
people the continued enjoyment of the very practices that helped trans-
mit disease. Curing was the most technologically enamored solution, of
course, but it was also completely amoral in its disregard of the religious or ethical objections to the behavior associated with transmission,
in its studied unconcern for cultural objections to the lifestyles of infec-
tion. Cure or prevent AIDS and it was back to business as usual at the
bathhouse or the shooting gallery. The hope of enlisting illness for the
purpose of social regeneration, held by many across the political spectrum, would vanish.

The technological fix had gotten Guilbert de Préval expelled from the
medical faculty of the University of Paris in 1772 for claiming to have
discovered a means of preventing syphilis and thus, in the eyes of his
detractors, giving libertinage free rein.[77] Such an approach had sent
moralist observers of syphilis into frenzies of self-righteousness ever
since. A cure, they worried, would lead to a spiritual syphilization more
pernicious than the merely corporeal version.[78] During this latest epidemic, such attitudes reemerged undaunted. A crash program for an
AIDS vaccine, the neoconservative journalist Norman Podhoretz thun-
dered like some west-side Jehova, meant that in the name of compas-

[75] Matti Hayry and Heta Hayry, "AIDS and a Small North European Country: A Study
in Applied Ethics," International Journal of Applied Philosophy 3 (1987): 59.

[76] Bundestag, Drucksache 10/4071, October 23, 1985.

[77] Erica-Marie Benabou, La prostitution et la police des mœurs au XVIIIe siècle (Paris:
Librarie Academique Perrin, 1987), 426; Norman E. Himes, Medical History of Contraception (New York: Gamut Press, 1970), chap. 8; Jacques Donzelot, The Policing of Families (Baltimore: Johns Hopkins University Press, 1979), 172.

[78] Ed. Jeanselme, Traité de la syphilis (Paris: Doin, 1931), vol. 1, 378.

sion researchers were giving "social sanction to what can only be described as brutish degradation." They would allow gays "to resume buggering each other by the hundreds with complete medical impunity."[79] Such reasoning made social conservatives, joined by those gay observers who thought that the hedonism of homosexual culture was in large measure to blame for the epidemic, ambiguous about the virtues of condoms: holding out the hope of sidestepping disease, they also allowed promiscuity.[80] Curing the disease also undercut the position of nominally left-wing radicals who insisted that, since AIDS had social causes, without changing society as a whole, the epidemic could not adequately be addressed. "Without institutional change, the virus wins." A cure would solve the problem "while allowing the distribution of power and health to remain the same."[81]

A biomedical approach thus promised to spare the United States vexing political choices: by intervening in nature, the need for social solutions could be sidestepped. The behavioral change that could not be assumed to come about through informal processes of social influence and whose strict enforcement via rules and laws, though often tried, contradicted native political instincts could be avoided altogether via the technical fix. The biomedically proactive approach sought to head off problems that would otherwise raise political dilemmas that were most conveniently left alone.

Different societies place the locus of control in different places, with the spectrum running from formal laws regulating behavior to informal prescriptions of conduct imbibed from our lactating mothers and nowhere spelled out. What societies take for granted reveals what can be assumed as informal control; conversely, what is chiseled in legal paragraphs indicates where the state's turf begins. A society that spells out and enforces a good samaritan law is one that does not trust the basic goodwill of its citizens. When there was talk of prosecuting the paparazzi who blithely photographed the dying Princess Diana, there was

[79] Michael L. Closen et al., *AIDS: Cases and Materials* (Houston: John Marshall Publishing Company, 1989), 182; *Congressional Record* (House) 131 (October 1, 1985): 25521.

[80] Bundestag, *Verhandlungen* 11/71, April 14, 1988, 4810C; Virginie Linhart, "Le silence de l'église," in Pierre Favre, ed., *Sida et politique: Les premiers affrontements (1981–1987)* (Paris: L'Harmattan, 1992), 128; Deborah Lupton, *Moral Threats and Dangerous Desires: AIDS in the News Media* (London: Taylor & Francis, 1994), 74–75; Gabriel Rotello, *Sexual Ecology: AIDS and the Destiny of Gay Men* (New York: Penguin, 1997), 10–13.

[81] Stephanie C. Kane, *AIDS Alibis: Sex, Drugs and Crime in the Americas* (Philadelphia: Temple University Press, 1998), 33. Similar sentiments: Nancy Krieger, "Introduction," in Nancy Krieger and Glen Margo, eds., *AIDS: The Politics of Survival* (Amityville, NY: Baywood Publishing Company, 1994), ix.

wide surprise that in many nations, first-aid obligations exist in principle and on the books. While the general tide of social development has
been away from formal state control and toward informal societal regulation of behavior, multiculturalism—as an element of the increasing
ethnic and social fragmentation of recent decades—may be helping
slow or even reverse this trend. Campaigns against drugs and alcohol
are becoming more formalized in the legal code and fought with heavy
statutory intervention. Tobacco smoking is now treated in the world's
allegedly most liberalist societies—America's granola belt: Madison,
Cambridge, Santa Monica, Berkeley, et al.—as it was in absolutist Prussia, with formal prohibitions in public, and sometimes in private too.
Sexual behavior is becoming increasingly regulated, especially in the
workplace. The penal systems of advanced democracies have recently
shifted in a notably harsh and punitive direction.[82]

One of the most regulated societies in the world is the small, posh
town of San Marino, in the mountains overlooking Los Angeles. Here,
residents are forbidden to leave their garbage cans out, park their cars
in the driveway for more than two days, or store anything other than an
automobile in the garage. They are not allowed to play with remote
control toy cars, rest bicycles against trees in parks, spit on sidewalks,
keep air conditioners in public view, install chain link fences, let their
lawns die, or indulge in recreational activities in their front yards. Those
who trim trees badly can be required to attend pruning classes.[83] True,
in central Europe rules regulate the color you can paint your house, the
noise you cannot make during nap time or on Sundays, and the evening
hours after which you may not flush the toilet or take a bath (cases of
illness mercifully excepted) in apartment buildings. Yet San Marino's is
micromanagement on a heroic scale, one that appears to reflect a basic
and deep-seated distrust of modern procedures of child-rearing and fundamental tenets of civility and politeness. Why?

San Marino's thirteen thousand residents have paid an average of
$650,000, almost thrice the Southern California mean, for their house.
How many are likely to act in an offensive manner? The town's rules
appear to be aimed at keeping monied riffraff out. They regulate a culturally fragmented society, where upper-middle-class wealth and status
do not necessarily guarantee polite behavior. San Marino, it seems, seeks
to generalize and enforce the behavior of the white elite that is now
being dispossessed by well-upholstered Asians (one-third of the current
population), at least insofar as the strictures of zoning can enforce it.

---

[82] David Garland, *The Culture of Control: Crime and Social Order in Contemporary
Society* (Oxford: Oxford University Press, 2001).

[83] *Los Angeles Times*, December 1, 1998, B1.

Every Southern Californian estate owner remembers the case during the 1980s of the Arab heir who, having purchased a large spread on Sunset Boulevard in Beverley Hills, garishly colored the house. To add injury to insult, he then painted in the pubic hair on his pseudo-Grecian statues. Mysteriously, and after much controversy with his neighbors, his house burned down in a still unsolved case of arson, and the lot remains unbuilt to this day. In multicultural circumstances, the absence of a pubic-hair paragraph in the local zoning code — an eventuality inexplicably overlooked by the municipal founding fathers — meant that his neighbors felt forced to resort to the post facto informal control of the house lynching they undertook. Multiculturalism, ironically, is teaching us to appreciate Lenin's famous insight, one that has somehow always sounded better in German than English translation: *Vertrauen is gut, Kontrolle ist besser.*

Part 2

STATE SECURITY

CHAPTER 5

States, Security Function, and the New Global Forces

T. V. PAUL

IN THIS CHAPTER, I explore the impact of globalization on one of the fundamental functions of nation-states — national security. Contrary to the polar positions of the proponents and the opponents of globalization, I argue that national security remains a core function of the nation-state, but the extent of security behavior varies depending on the particular situations of states. Largely under the influence of systemic changes propelled by the end of the Cold War, especially the resurgence of the American hegemonic power, rapid technological innovations in both the civilian and military spheres, and the emergence of transnational terrorism, the nature of security competition has altered somewhat, but it is premature to bury the nation-state or its role as the key provider of security.

I critique the contention that, because war created nation-states, the waning of major wars could result in citizens losing their identities based on citizenship and their loyalties to the state. I argue that geopolitical competition is unlikely simply to become an issue of the past, even though increasingly other forms of competition — geo-economic, geo-technological, and asymmetric — may occur, and these may sometimes compensate for active military rivalries for a period of time. Systemic forces are still at work, and over time the rise of new major powers and the decline of the present ones will affect the contours of world politics and state behavior. The chapter also briefly looks at the United States and its role as the security provider in this new era. I argue that the United States is likely to increase its role as a national-security state. The United States will face both hard and soft challenges to its security, given its extant position as the hegemonic power, and because of this, it is bound to be involved in asymmetric conflicts with weaker, dissatisfied regional states and substate terrorist groups and large-scale competition with other great powers, especially China. Although war in the great power system is unlikely in the near term, war preparation is likely to be actively present in it because of the fear that

losing out in the technological revolution for new arms may create opportunities and willingness for the great power that gains an advantage
in the competition to dominate others. States, especially major powers,
will choose allies and partners on the basis of congruence of interests in
the security sphere. The increasing unilateralism of the United States
and pressures emanating from the desire of other key states for multi-
polarity will result in the continuation of soft challenges, including technological competitions involving the United States and other developed
states, especially those in Europe. Since September 2001, the struggle
against the common terrorist enemy has unified major powers, but this
may prove to be temporary at best, as greater geopolitical challenges
reemerge in the international system over the long haul.

In the following pages, I explore the impact of globalization on the
state, especially the United States, as the national-security provider. I
make several interrelated arguments. First, globalization, despite its
wide sweep, is to a certain extent, although not exclusively, the "Americanization" of economic, political, and cultural ideas and practices. Second, globalization by no means has ended power competition among
the major powers. Limited peace caused by the decline and subsequent
domination of one or another major power is not a precursor to lasting
or perpetual peace. Efforts to convert hegemony into empire are unlikely to succeed; while benign policies might produce benign results,
these may not last indefinitely. Third, the relative-gains problem does
exist even when multiple global channels and networks link countries.
As long as nations gain economic benefits fairly uniformly, competition
is likely to remain limited, or even muted, but once large-scale inequalities creep in, states that lose out may resort to challenge by means
other than exerting voice from within or even "exit" if they are capable
of doing so. Fourth, hegemony, by its very nature, creates counterpres-
sures on those who are most affected by it. Those who can mobilize
against the hegemon may well do so, often through asymmetrical means
and strategies. Attempts by the hegemonic state to adjust to its decline
by extending its reach may also produce challenge and opposition. As
long as the hegemonic state is in a dominant position and can offer
collective goods to others, be they security or market access, large-scale
disturbances are unlikely to occur. However, in order for the hegemon
to prolong its power position, it has to innovate constantly and ward off
potential threats from weaker actors. Such innovation forces others to
catch up through arms races or asymmetric strategies that limit the extent
of the hegemon's innovative edge. Continued dominance by a single actor
creates insecurities for subordinate states, and these may manifest themselves in actions that appear "rogue," while the hegemon may make
responses that are "hyper" or are based on "technological fixes." Chal-

lengers can devise strategies based on asymmetric means, including terrorism, in an effort to weaken the power of the hegemonic actor.

CONTENDING VIEWS ON GLOBALIZATION AND THE STATE

Globalization enthusiasts have argued that "hard geopolitics" has become obsolete, partly due to the lethality of new weapons and partly because states are now more interested in wealth acquisition through economic liberalization and trade.[1] To them, war-making is no longer the state's primary focus, given the dramatic decline of interstate wars since the end of the Cold War in 1991. In the larger international arena, great-power competition is conducted through "soft geopolitics," with less emphasis on overt competition, arms buildup, or crisis activity.[2] To some, nontraditional issues such as terrorism, organized crime, drug trafficking, ethnic conflicts, exploding population growth, environmental degradation, and mass poverty have emerged as the key security threats. Competing notions of "human security" have begun to make inroads into official thinking in various countries, "suggesting that security be viewed as emerging from the conditions of daily life—food, shelter, employment, health, public safety—rather than flowing downward from a country's foreign relations and military strength."[3] For instance, James Rosenau contends that the nation-state has weakened as a result

[1] Different versions of the globalization thesis exist in the literature. Extreme proponents like Ohmae contend that under the irreversible influence of modern information technology, genuinely borderless economies are emerging, affecting values and behavior of citizens around the world. Kenichi Ohmae, *The End of the Nation State* (New York: Free Press, 1995), vii. More nuanced versions of this theme are presented by James N. Rosenau, "New Dimensions of Security: The Interaction of Globalizing and Localizing Dynamics," *Security Dialogue* 25 (1994): 255–81; Tony Spybey, *Globalization and World Society* (Cambridge: Polity Press, 1996); Hans-Henrik Holm and George Sorensen, *Whose World Order? Uneven Globalization and the End of the Cold War* (Boulder: Westview Press, 1995); David Held et al., *Global Transformations: Politics, Economics and Culture* (Stanford: Stanford University Press, 1999).

[2] Mann, although not a proponent himself, summarizes the position of the globalists in this respect: "Post-nuclearism undermines state sovereignty and 'hard geopolitics,' since mass mobilization warfare underpinned much of modern state expansion yet it is now irrational." Michael Mann, "Has Globalization Ended the Rise and Rise of the Nation-State?" in T. V. Paul and John A. Hall, eds., *International Order and the Future of World Politics* (Cambridge: Cambridge University Press, 1999), 238. See also James H. Mittelman, *The Globalization Syndrome: Transformation and Resistance* (Princeton: Princeton University Press, 2000), 6; Anthony Giddens, *The Consequences of Modernity* (Cambridge: Polity Press, 1990), 64.

[3] Jessica Mathews, "Power Shift," *Foreign Affairs* 76 (January/February 1997): 51; See also Victor D. Cha, "Globalization and the Study of International Security," *Journal of Peace Research* 37 (2000): 391–403.

of global social forces. To him, in political, social, and economic realms, fragmentation has occurred, and as a result the connection between territoriality and the state is decreasing. Political authority is relocated "upward toward supranational entities, sideward toward transnational organizations and social movements, and downwards toward subnational groups and communities. . . . These shifting tendencies . . . are diminishing the competence and effectiveness of states and rendering their borders more porous and less meaningful."[4] The salience of internal issues, in turn, has decreased the importance of the state as the national-security provider, whereas security has traditionally been the core function of the nation-state, endowing it with legitimacy and societal power.[5]

From the perspective of globalists, nations cannot afford to engage in large-scale warfare any longer, chiefly due to deepened economic interdependence and multilayered interactions among states and among transnational actors such as business corporations. More and more businesses are moving away from multinational to transnational levels of operation, that is, producing components in different countries worldwide and assembling them in others. Such production methods have made individual subsidiaries "practically unable to produce anything if cut off from the rest of the company. In many developed countries, businesses integrated transnationally now account for one-third to one-half of the industry's output."[6] War under these circumstances would mean high economic costs for all states concerned, and therefore it is only rational for interdependent states to forgo armed conflict as a mechanism to resolve interstate disputes.

Furthermore, as more and more countries choose democratic governance, the argument goes, the liberalizing elites deliberately undermine the power of their militaries and thereby decrease the role of the national security elite and its concerns in state policies. As the liberalizing elites seek foreign capital and investment as well as regional free-trade arrangements, they need to cut defense spending, reduce the size of the armed forces, and conclude regional cooperative security arrangements.[7]

---

[4] Roseanau, "New Dimensions of Security," 258.

[5] K. J. Holsti, *The State, War, and the State of War* (Cambridge: Cambridge University Press, 1996).

[6] Peter F. Drucker, "The Global Economy and the Nation-State," *Foreign Affairs* 76 (September–October 1997): 170–71; see also Mark W. Zacher, "The Decaying Pillars of the Westphalian Temple: Implications for International Order and Governance," in James N. Rosenau and Ernst-Otto Czempiel, eds., *Governance without Government: Order and Change in World Politics* (Cambridge: Cambridge University Press, 1992), 60.

[7] Etel Solingen, *Regional Orders at Century's Dawn* (Princeton: Princeton University Press, 1998), 46.

Such reductions are also necessary in order to gain capital and investment from international financial institutions and market access to powerful economies such as that of the United States.[8] Moreover, according to liberals, democracies rarely fight each other, and the widespread democratization of countries has reduced the propensity of states to use force against one another. Democracies deliberately play down military threats since they are reassured by the benign intentions of their democratic counterparts. There are both institutional-structural and normative reasons for the restraint that democracies show toward one another. Democratic institutions constrain states as they make it harder to respond militarily to other democracies in times of crises. Democracies also externalize their domestic political norms of tolerance and compromise in their foreign relations.[9]

More importantly, some believe that as threats decrease, the security function of the state declines, and, as a result, the attachment of citizens to their state declines as well. Nation-states, founded on the principle of protection to the citizenry as its core function, have trouble developing an alternative to war as a source of loyalty, which is often shown as the ultimate willingness of the citizen to sacrifice his or her life for the defense of the country.[10] The decline in the traditional national-security function of the state may also result in the weakening of states as divisive forces within step up their struggle over the basic principles of domestic order.[11]

However, the liberal and globalist views have not gone unchallenged. Indeed, the proponents of neorealism have argued that the security function of the state has increased and that the new global forces that are supposedly undermining states and their functions in the security arena are exaggerated. To them, with the end of the Cold War, the glue that held the international system together, the bipolar structure, has disintegrated, and this will eventually force countries to seek autonomous military capabilities. It is only a matter of time, in this view, that formerly

[8] The tension between the modern forces of globalization and the traditional forces of territory, culture, and glory is captured in Thomas Friedman, *The Lexus and the Olive Tree* (New York: Farrar Starus & Giroux, 1999).

[9] Michael Doyle, "Liberalism and World Politics," *American Political Science Review* 80 (December 1986): 1151–69; Bruce Russett, *Grasping the Democratic Peace* (Princeton: Princeton University Press, 1993); Steve Chan, "In Search of Democratic Peace: Problems and Promises, " *Mershon International Studies Review* 41 (1997): 59–85.

[10] Ronnie D. Lipschutz, *After Authority: War, Peace, and Global Politics in the 21st Century* (Albany: State University of New York Press, 2000), 5. A more modest version of this argument can be seen in Michael C. Desch, "War and Strong States, Peace and Weak States?" *International Organization* 50 (Spring 1996): 237–68.

[11] Daniel Deudney and G. John Ikenberry, "After the Long War," *Foreign Policy* 94 (Spring 1994): 21–35.

dependent countries, such as Japan and Germany, will seek greater international roles by acquiring the military wherewithal, including nuclear weapons, commensurate with their economic prowess.[12] Some neoclassical realists also argue that security competition does not change from age to age and that "bad times return." For instance, Colin Gray, paraphrasing Clausewitz, argues that "war is a chameleon—able to adapt to new circumstances effortlessly."[13]

Contrary to these polar positions, I argue that as we begin the twenty-first century, the picture in respect to the state's security function is a mixed one. Neither the optimism of the globalists nor the pessimism of the proponents of military security-first approaches is fully warranted. Similar predictions in the past of the demise of the nation-state, as well as the decline of the state's security function—in the face of the advent of nuclear weapons and growing economic interdependence—have been short lived.[14] Following brief episodes of interstate cooperation, states bounced back as national-security actors as the empirical reality of their independent role in security and security competition began to set in. Yet the manner in which states conduct military competition and war has changed in our times, a point that neorealists and neoclassical realists fail adequately to take into account. Especially noteworthy in this connection is the virtual absence of warfare among the major powers and among the established democracies.[15] Noticeable changes are also visible in the functions, attitudes, and threat assessments of the militaries across the world.[16]

[12] Kenneth N. Waltz, "The Emerging Structure of International Politics," *International Security* 18 (Fall 1993): 66; Waltz, "Globalization and American Power," *The National Interest* (Spring 2000): 46–56. See also John J. Mearsheimer, "Back to the Future: Instability in Europe after the Cold War," *International Security* 15 (Summer 1990): 5–56; Christopher Layne, "The Unipolar Illusion: Why New Great Powers Will Rise," *International Security* 17 (Spring 1993): 5–51.

[13] Colin Gray, "Clausewitz Rules, OK? The Future Is the Past—with GPS," *Review of International Studies* 25 (December 1999): 169. See also Gray, *Modern Strategy* (Oxford: Oxford University Press, 1999), 9–11, 362–64.

[14] John H. Herz, "The Territorial State Revisited: Reflections on the Future of the Nation State," in James N. Rosenau, ed., *International Politics and Foreign Policy: A Reader in Research and Theory* (New York: The Free Press, 1969), 76–77; See also Herz, "Rise and Demise of the Territorial State," *World Politics* 9 (1957): 473; Klaus Knorr, *On the Uses of Military Power in the Nuclear Age* (Princeton: Princeton University Press, 1966); Robert O. Keohane and Joseph S. Nye Jr., "Power and Interdependence Revisited," *International Organization* 41 (Autumn 1987): 727.

[15] For interesting arguments on this topic, see Raimo Vayrynen, *The Waning of Major War* (forthcoming).

[16] Moskos calls the new situation a "postmodern military paradigm." Charles C. Moskos, "Toward a Postmodern Military: The United States as a Paradigm," in Charles C. Moskos, John Allen Williams, and David R. Segal, eds., *The Postmodern Military: Armed Forces after the Cold War* (New York: Oxford University Press, 2000), 15.

My argument is that variations exist in the realm of security and state responses to challenges posed by globalization, but they are uneven and not so profound as globalists argue, and not so trivial as realists characterize them. I contend that to explain the variations we need to look at the political, economic, and security contexts of different states. These contexts cut across both domestic and international levels. To a great extent, the distribution of power determines systemic- and subsystemic-level variations, while domestic-level factors revolve around state strength and the political characteristics of the states concerned. Variations also exist in the behavior of middle and small powers that have great-power protection or whose regions have developed institutions to manage or contain interstate conflict. In the post–September 11, 2001, context, these variations have become pronounced, with transnational terrorism emerging as a major security challenge to the United States and its allies.

The argument is that great-power conflict has subsided since the end of the Cold War, but the system leaders are conducting their competition through technological innovations in armaments, of both offensive and defensive varieties, and creation of new balance-of-power alignments. The United States, Russia, and China have been engaging in new forms of arms races, this time focusing more on information warfare and "usable" mini nuclear weapons. The United States and China have increased their arms spending at the beginning of the new century. Moreover, the "end of history" is not in sight with respect to a fundamental characteristic of the modern international system, namely, power transitions resulting from the rise and fall of great powers. In fact, the international system is notorious for its lack of nonviolent mechanisms to integrate rising economic and military powers or provide them with leadership roles without conflict.[17]

On a global scale, there has been no substantial relinquishing of armed forces by states despite the fact that some states have scaled down the size of their armed forces. Only two small states, Haiti and Panama, have abandoned their armed forces and adopted the Costa Rica model. Moreover, many trading states in the world are big spenders on defense, belying the argument that the national security state has all but vanished in the face of the forces of globalization and economic liberalization.[18] Furthermore, the contention that the increasing transactions

---

[17] On this, see Kalevi J. Holsti, *Peace and War: Armed Conflicts and International Order 1648–1989* (Cambridge: Cambridge University Press, 1991), 339; Ronald L. Tammen et al., *Power Transitions: Strategies for the 21st Century* (New York: Chatham House, 2000).

[18] The twenty-five big defense-spending nations include several trading as well as Western liberal states. The U.S. defense expenditure of $305.4 billion (in 2000) was higher than the spending of all other twenty-four Western states combined. For these statistics, see *Fact Sheet* (Washington, DC: Center for Defense Information, February 7, 2000).

among nonstate actors and their assumption of the means of violence have fundamentally reduced the state's monopoly over force is not accurate. Historically, nonstate actors played significant roles along with states. As Bull contends, in eighteenth- and nineteenth-century Europe, states also co-existed and shared the stage with chartered companies, revolutionary and counterrevolutionary political parties, and national liberation movements.[19]

It is, however, wrong to argue that no change has occurred in the realm of the state's security functions as we enter the twenty-first century. Despite bleak predictions by neorealists and neoclassical realists, there is no strong evidence to suggest that, now that the Cold War is over, countries are rushing to acquire arms or adopt offensive military postures. In fact, during 1989–1998, world military expenditures declined by one-third (to $745 billion in 1998) on an average of 4.5 percent per year. However, since 1998 they have been on an upswing, and by 2000 they had reached $798 billion.[20] Some nuclear or nuclear-threshold states, such as South Africa, Argentina, Brazil, Ukraine, Kazakhstan, and Belarus, gave up their nuclear programs and aspirations, while several other technologically capable states are maintaining their nonnuclear policies.[21] Especially important is the fact that Germany and Japan, two potential great powers, are maintaining their nonnuclear commitments. India and Pakistan, two states that declared themselves nuclear in 1998, already had their weapons developed in the 1980s, while Israel, the third undeclared nuclear state, had developed its nuclear weapons capability in the 1970s. The programs of aspirants such as Iraq, Iran, and North Korea predate the end of the Cold War.

Changes have also occurred in the nature of warfare as a result of the increasing salience of internal as well as asymmetric wars over interstate warfare. Militaries, especially in the developed world, are increasingly focusing on the need to reduce casualties, especially of their own fighting forces and the enemy's civilian population. Because military actions in civil wars are more protective or peacekeeping in nature, there is all the more reason to focus on reducing casualties. However, this new

---

[19] Hedley Bull, "The State's Positive Role in World Affairs," *Daedalus* 108 (Fall 1979): 112.

[20] The decrease was most prominently manifest in Central and Eastern Europe, especially Russia, and this was due to continued economic constraints experienced by these states. Stockholm International Peace Research Institute, *SIPRI Year Book, 1998* (Oxford: Oxford University Press, 1999), 269–70. See also *SIPRI Yearbook, 2001*, 224–25. The immediate cause of the decline can be attributed to the end of the Cold War. However, in the aftermath of somewhat similar systemic events such as World War I and II, countries reduced arms spending, only to increase when new threats emerged.

[21] T. V. Paul, *Power versus Prudence: Why Nations Forgo Nuclear Weapons* (Montreal: McGill-Queen's University Press, 2000).

style of warfare has not reduced the collateral effects on civilian populations in terms of "displacement, deprivation through sanctions, exposure and famine."[22] Moreover, the United States and its allies increasingly have been using economic sanctions as a tool to achieve objectives that they have failed to obtain through war.[23] These sanctions, in instances like Iraq, have had effects somewhat similar to slow carpet bombings, in terms of their devastating impact on the target state's economy and well-being of the population.

The responses of states to global social changes have not been uniform throughout the world. In some regions, states continue to pay more attention to the traditional national-security function than in others. Despite incremental changes in regions like Latin America, the security function of states has not significantly declined in regions such as East and South Asia, Africa, the Persian Gulf, and the Middle East. In fact, in some of these regions, the security function has increased even among economically liberalizing states (e.g., India) and among those that have made regional security arrangements (e.g., Indonesia), especially in the area of domestic security. Although the European Union has made defense cuts in the wake of the collapse of the Warsaw Pact, the key European states—Britain, France,, and Germany—are in the process of strengthening their security ties through other means, such as the creation of the European Security and Defense Policy (ESDP) and a rapid reaction force. These states, after participating in the U.S.-led military operations in Kosovo in 1999, have concluded that they need to develop more autonomous defense capabilities in order to decrease their overdependence on the United States. Some EU members also harbor an interest in the creation of a version of a United States of Europe, and autonomous security behavior and capability are viewed as reinforcing that potentially unified entity. In East Asia, while China has increased defense spending, Taiwan has been on a weapons-buying spree, and both the Koreas have hiked their spending on defense. Japan, despite its four decades of a nonmilitary focus, has changed course somewhat, with spending increases, participation in overseas peacekeeping operations, and redefining of self-defense force functions, and of late has given indications that it may amend Article 9 of its Constitution, which forbids the militarization of Japan.[24] However, it has also strengthened

---

[22] John Leech, "War without Death: The Silent Strategies," *Strategic Review* 28 (Spring 2000): 20.

[23] On the value of sanctions as a tool of statecraft, see Jean-Marc F. Blanchard and Norrin M. Ripsman, "Asking the Right Question: When Do Economic Sanctions Work Best?" *Security Studies* 9 (Autumn 1999–Winter 2000): 219–53.

[24] According to one analysis, with a defense budget of $35 billion (in 1999), "Japan's defense spending exceeds that of both Russia and China. Tokyo has the second largest navy in Asia—behind the United States—a substantial standing army, and its technology

alliance ties with the United States, thereby ensuring that Tokyo's pursuit of security is not unilateral.

What explains the variations in state responses in the area of security in the face of changing global forces? Can we locate key explanations by focusing on international and regional factors or domestic political and economic forces? The international factors include the end of the Cold War, changes in balance-of-power politics involving major powers, the rise of transnational terrorism, especially since September 2001, and technological revolutions that are occurring in the instruments of warfare. At the domestic level, does the continuing hold of the military in power and the "holy cow" nature of national security (or what Tilly calls the "protection racket") have something to do with the continuation of the security focus of states?[25] The answer to these questions lies in the specific situations of the state, as the influence of such factors varies across different states with different contexts. Confronting asymmetric threats, such as terrorism, has become crucial, as these challenges are unlikely to wane in the foreseeable future.

The situations of the different states can be illustrated by placing them in the following broad categories. The particular context of a state, arising from systemic and subsystemic factors, has a great deal to do with explaining their national-security behavior in the post-Cold War era.

1. *Major powers.* Under this broad category, we need to look at the United States as the status quo power, Russia as the declining power, and China as the rising power. These states, despite holding leadership positions in global and regional institutions, are the least constrained by the norms of state behavior that downgrade national security. Global social and economic forces have made only a limited dent in the primacy they accord to the national-security state. Despite the apparent lack of overt hostility, the major powers are engaged in continuing competition over arms innovation, technology and spheres of influence.

The major powers are by definition national-security states; they are prone to engage in military behavior/competition beyond their regions that gives them leadership roles internationally. They tend to possess global power projection capabilities and are in the forefront of technological innovations that would facilitate the creation of such forces. Major powers acquire military capabilities not only for security reasons,

---

is second to few. The military option is Japan's for the taking, should it choose." "Asia's Future Centers on China and Japan's," *Stratfor.com, Global Intelligence Update*, December 22, 1999.

[25] Charles Tilly, "Warmaking and State Making as Organized Crime," in Peter B. Evans, Dietrich Rueschemeyer, and Theda Skocpol, eds., *Bringing the State Back In* (Cambridge: Cambridge University Press, 1985), 171.

that is, defense of the homeland and allies, but also for purposes such as maintaining structural, compellent, and deterrent power against other great powers and smaller adversaries, in whose affairs they wish to intervene. Among the major powers, security behavior varies depending on whether they are status quo, declining, or rising powers. In the post–Cold War international system, the United States has emerged as the status quo power, Russia as the declining power, and China as the rising power in terms of their overall power attributes and dispositions. These structural situations have affected their approach toward security and the acquisition and maintenance of military power capabilities.

2. *States that are heavily involved in regional organizations.* Members of the European Union, which have already established a pluralistic security community, are one example. Others include ASEAN and Mercosur member states that have been forming nascent security communities. The states in these regions have entered or are entering into security-interdependent relationships and have helped to avoid warfare among themselves for several decades. These states attempt to minimize the possibility of security competition while devising benign strategies vis-à-vis one another. Their military planning and preparations are largely based on most-probable threat assessments as opposed to worst-case assumptions. The protection provided by the United States has helped many of these states, especially in Europe, to pay less attention to national security. This aspect, however, could change over time, especially if the United States reduces its commitment to Europe.

3. *Regional states, which are engaged in enduring rivalries with one another and with the great powers.* There are two types of states in this category. First are states under some security protection of the United States (e.g., South Korea, Taiwan, and Israel). The second category consists of those states that enjoy no credible security protection from outside and are often targets of economic or military sanctions by the United States. India, Pakistan, North Korea, Iran, Iraq, and Syria are prime examples of the latter category of states. Some of these states seek regional hegemony and some face great-power intervention in their internal affairs. These states live in regional environments characterized by protracted conflicts and enduring rivalries. By definition, protracted conflicts are long-standing and are driven by intractable issues such as territory, ideology, or identity, and conflict relationships among protagonists spill over into most spheres of interstate interactions. They are also the targets of arms merchants, as they often buy advanced weaponry. These states may be weak in terms of their capacity to influence their societies as they hold minimum "infrastructural power," although they may have strong "despotic power" in terms of the strength of their armed forces in their regional environments. They are thus strong in

some attributes of state capacity, but weak in others relating to societal capacity. Their military planning and preparations are based on worst-case assumptions as opposed to most-probable threat assessments.

4. *Very weak and failed states.* Mostly in Africa, these states have failed to create state structures sufficient to provide security or economic protection to their citizens. Many such states are beset with problems of internal conflict driven by ethnic rivalries and political and economic inefficiencies. The state institutions often lack legitimacy, and state laws receive little compliance from citizens. The capacity of states to protect citizens from predators is also minimal.[26] However, over time some such states have created military institutions and have increased their external conflict behavior. African states such as Congo, Nigeria and Uganda fall under this category.

Category 1 and 3 states are the most concerned about the current and future revolutions in military affairs (RMAs), especially developments in information warfare and national defense and theater defense systems. Their concerns, however, vary depending on whether they are allies or adversaries of the leading global power, the United States.

The remaining section of the chapter will discuss the responses of the United States in the security arena in reaction to the forces of globalization. In that context, the positions of China, Russia, and some key smaller challengers to the U.S. hegemony will also be discussed. The U.S. case is important, as globalization is heavily shaped and influenced by the United States through its policies in international institutions and U.S.-based multinational corporations that are the engines of much of globalized economic activity. Globalization, if indeed a force that affects all states, should have had its most powerful impact on the U.S. national-security behavior. The effect seems perverse or limited on U.S. security policy. However, if we include the rise of transnational terrorism as a result of the ill effects of globalization, the U.S. has been affected in a profound way since September 2001. It is therefore imperative to explain why the United States is behaving in the security arena the way it does.

RESPONSE BY THE UNITED STATES

Of all the states in today's international system, the United States is probably the major beneficiary of economic globalization, as American-

---

[26] On such states, see Mohammed Ayoob, *The Third World Security Predicament: State Making, Regional Conflict and the International System* (Boulder: Lynne Rienner, 1995); Amitav Acharya," Beyond Anarchy: Third World Instability and International Order after the Cold War," in Stephanie G. Neuman, ed., *International Relations Theory and the Third World* (New York: St. Martin's Press, 1998), 159–211.

based multinational corporations have been its main engine. The United States is the winner of the Cold War, and there is a sense in many quarters of the U.S. establishment of the arrival of the unipolar moment. The new global social forces that globalists talk about should have had significant impact on this state. Yet the United States has been most prominent in the development of information warfare and missile-based defense systems. Its defense budget of nearly $343 billion (in 2002) is almost 40 percent of the world's total military expenditures, and higher than the combined budgets of the 24 other leading defense spenders, including Russia, China, and Japan. The national security function of the American state has shown no substantial decline from the Cold War days.[27] Since the September 2001 terrorist strikes, the national-security function of the United States has increased dramatically, with defense spending poised to increase in a big way. According to the five-year budget forecast by the Bush administration, the defense budget for fiscal year 2007 will reach $401.1 billion from $324.9 billion in fiscal 2001.[28] The reasons that have been presented for this phenomenon relate to both the international and domestic levels.

For instance, Donald Snow argues that the culprit lies in domestic factors. To him, the chief reasons for the high defense spending are "the inherent conservatism of military planners and practitioners" whose planning is based on worst-case assumptions; "the intellectual and physical attachment to the Cold War," especially with respect to the vested interests developed as a result of the "virtually stationary adversary"; and the "lack of urgency in making military adjustments."[29] The domestic imperatives for high defense maintenance are also often attributed to partisan politics at both presidential and congressional levels. But do these domestic factors exclusively account for the persistence of high U.S. spending?

I argue that domestic variables are important as proximate factors, but they arise from a larger systemic and structural context. The domestic consensus on military spending and technological innovation is the result of deeply embedded geopolitical factors and challenges to American hegemony that the U.S. elite perceives from its vantage point. Although the United States is not involved in any major military conflicts

<hr />

[27] This does not mean that the overall size of the U.S. armed forces has not been reduced from the Cold War days. In fact, it has shrunk by 40 percent or so from the Cold War peak in the 1980s. Ann R. Markusen and Sean S. Costigan, "The Military Industrial Challenge," in Markusen and Costigan, eds., *Arming the Future: A Defense Industry for the 21st Century* (New York: Council on Foreign Relations Press, 1999), 12.

[28] www.dtic.mil/comptrollers/fy 2003 budget/FY03GBpdf.pdf.

[29] Donald M. Snow, *The Shape of the Future*, 3 Edition (Armonk, NY: M. E. Sharpe, 1999), 96–97; see also William Greider, *Fortress America: The American Military and the Consequences of Peace* (New York: Public Affairs, 1998), xiv–xvii.

with other major powers at the dawn of the twenty-first century, the very fact that it is the global hegemonic power puts tremendous pressure on the American elite to maintain strong armed forces in the decades to come. Even though the "demands of war" have declined, the "demands for peace," as perceived by the elite, require a high level of military preparedness. The bottom line is that the U.S. elite wants to prolong the American hegemony as long as it can. The unprecedented economic prosperity of the 1990s occurred in the backdrop of no serious armed conflict involving the major powers. The U.S. consensus is not to allow any large or small power or combination of powers to challenge its dominance and, in order to achieve this, it ought to maintain its edge over others in military technology and the preparedness of its armed forces.[30] The United States especially wants to defeat the asymmetric terrorist challenge because, if it continues uncontained, it can weaken American primacy.

The American hegemony is built around both military and economic power, but often globalists ignore the military dimensions of American power. This is partly because military power stays in the background and it is often hard to pinpoint its impact on economic, political, and social forces.[31] The U.S. Navy and overseas-based forces continue to provide extended deterrence to allies and mount threats of intervention against smaller regional adversaries, including terrorists and their sponsoring states, and rising powers such as China. The navy controls the waters of all the strategically vital oceans and thus helps to keep the trade routes open for shipping. Allies who would contribute men and money to its military efforts, if called for, also strengthen its support base overseas. The United States has also relied on regionalism and regional arrangements for both economic and political/strategic purposes.[32] Much of the global economic interactions among the Western states and their allies is occurring in the backdrop of this order built around Amer-

---

[30] The U.S. strategic planning under the Clinton administration had increasingly focused on a "preventive defense" strategy. See Ashton B. Carter and William J. Perry, *Preventive Defense: A New Security Strategy for America* (Washington, DC: Brookings Institution Press, 1999), 14–18.

[31] According to some, the United States has more or less succeeded in achieving the three objectives that it had laid out in the early 1990s: maintain the post–Cold War global balance of power, ensure American technological and military superiority, and create an economic climate favorable to its own interests. Thus, the United States has not withdrawn from global balance of power "in the free market utopia. On the contrary, U.S. hegemony and sovereignty have been strengthened in spectacular fashion." Noelle Burgi and Philip S. Golub, "Has Globalization Really Made Nations Redundant?" *Le Monde Diplomatique* (April 2000).

[32] Mittelman, *The Globalization Syndrome*, 131.

ican power, be it in Europe, East Asia, the Middle East, the Persian Gulf, or Latin America.

The United States has been the chief beneficiary of the post–World War II international order, and in the post–Cold War era it has strengthened its primacy in both economic and military terms. The American decision-making elite, knowing that the unipolar moment is a passing phase, is attempting to establish and reinforce the rules of the game by creating and supporting a set of international institutions, regimes, and norms that would guarantee the nonarrival of a challenger in the foreseeable future. It sees the spread of nuclear, biological, and chemical (NBC) weapons and their delivery systems to dissatisfied regional states and subnational actors as undermining U.S. hegemony and its capacity to intervene in the affairs of regional states. These capabilities in the hands of minor actors could act as "great equalizers" under certain circumstances. However, if proper countermeasures are taken, which include balancing and bandwagoning of regional states and the creation of prohibitory regimes and norms, the United States believes it can remain the dominant actor in the international system for decades to come. Sanctions and technology denials are other means to keep recalcitrant states in their place, and they are cheaper alternatives to war, although their impact could be quite devastating on a target state (e.g., Iraq since 1991 and Serbia 1994–2000).

The favorable developments associated with RMAs are especially critical to the U.S. perceptions of continuation of its hegemony. These revolutions are occurring in the spheres of information warfare, electronic warfare, precision guidance, remote guidance and control, and improvements in munitions, target identifications, and command, control, and communication.[33] The U.S. defense planners have discussed the challenges and opportunities posed by RMA technologies. For instance, the Joint Vision 2010 Report, prepared by former Chairman of the Joint Chiefs of Staff John Shalikashvili, and the 1997 Quadrennial Defense Review, prepared under Defense Secretary William Cohen, have called upon the U.S. military to achieve "dominant battlefield knowledge," "full dimensional protection," "dominant maneuver," and "precision-strike ability for long-distance" in the first decade of the twenty-first century. They called for the U.S. to gain superiority in information technologies in areas of computers and electronic robotics; advanced

---

[33] Lawrence Freedman, "The Revolution in Strategic Affairs," *Adelphi Paper* 318 (London: International Institute of Strategic Studies, 1998), 21; Colin S. Gray, "Nuclear Weapons and the Revolution in Military Affairs," in T. V. Paul, Richard J. Harknett, and James Wirtz, eds., *The Absolute Weapon Revisited: Nuclear Arms and the Emerging International Order* (Ann Arbor: University of Michigan Press, 1998), 99–134.

munitions; ultramodern sensors; lighter, fuel-efficient and stealth vehicles, ships, and rockets, allowing rapid deployment capabilities; and
space-based weapons and directed energy beams.[34] The 2001 Quadrennial Defense Review reiterated these goals while adding the need for
developing capabilities and strategies to confront asymmetric challenges, especially terrorism.[35] The successful RMA applications will enable the U.S. commanders to lift the "fog of war." These are most visible in terms of traditional functions, such as intelligence gathering,
surveillance, battlefield reconnaissance, and transfer of data and their
expeditious communications to subordinates, and the use of precision
force with maximum accuracy and devastating effect. As Admiral
Owens states, "Together, these create the three conditions for combat
victory: dominant battle-space knowledge, near perfect mission assign-
ments and immediate/complete battle-space assessment."[36]

At the systemic level, the declining great power, Russia, and the rising
great power, China, both challenge U.S. primacy, although the Russian
challenge is a limited one. However, their challenge is no longer the
high-level zero-sum and frontal military threats that existed during the
Cold War era. Further, a group of regional powers often branded as
"rogue states" has emerged as challengers to the U.S.-led order, especially in the area of weapons of mass destruction. Soft challenges are
prevalent even among allies such as Germany and Canada, especially on
questions of nuclear first use, national missile defenses, and the expansion of NATO. The United States seems especially worried that weaker
powers would mount "asymmetric challenges" through new tactics and
strategies, and by obtaining weapons of mass destruction and long-
range delivery systems, including ballistic missiles. Even in the area of
RMA technologies, it fears that weaker adversaries could adopt countermeasures in order to "exploit the U.S. military's dependence on large
bases, ships and other vulnerable assets, when projecting power overseas, as well as Americans' aversion to suffering casualties."[37] Further,
the United States suspects that anti-U.S. coalitions will develop among
weaker states with the intention, at best, of extracting concessions from
the West.

[34] Michael O'Hanlon, *Technological Change and the Future of Warfare* (Washington,
DC: Brookings Institution Press, 2000), 2–3.

[35] www.defenselink.mil/pubs/qdr2001.pdf.

[36] Admiral Bill Owens, *Lifting the Fog of War* (New York: Farrar Straus Giroux, 2000),
99–100.

[37] O'Hanlon, *Technological Change*, 2–3. The interesting historical parallel is the Ro-
man Empire, whose hegemony was challenged and eventually ended by smaller actors.
Michael Mann, *The Sources of Social Power*, vol. 1 (Cambridge: Cambridge University
Press, 1986), 298.

The U.S. economic dominance is another factor that drives its security behavior. As nations become relatively wealthier in comparison with others, they, just as individuals, wish to keep their prosperity secure from encroachments by external actors, especially if that wealth is a function of the hegemony arising from dominance in military, technological, and normative dimensions. The dominance also results from the fact that the hegemon provides security to allies who in turn support the hegemon's key economic and security goals.

Domestically, the main source of lack of policy change has been the partisan pork-barrel politics and "holy cow" nature of national security among the contending parties. This is clear from debates among the two presidential candidates in the 2000 elections. Both George Bush and Albert Gore wanted to increase defense spending in order to ward off the threats arising from the so-called "rogue states" and dissatisfied great powers, China and Russia. They advocated increased spending on national missile defense (NMD) and theater missile defense (TMD) systems even when it is clear to many defense analysts and scientists that such systems are neither cost-effective nor foolproof.[38] But these competing positions come out of a systemic context with which the American political elite is attempting to grapple. The victory of Republican George Bush in the 2000 elections increased the pace of military spending and technological innovation by the United States. Deployment of missile defense emerged as a core national security objective of the Bush administration, even though such deployment would undermine the 1972 Anti-Ballistic Missile (ABM) Treaty. Since September 2001 the Bush administration has been focusing national attention on the war against terrorism and on new homeland security plans and programs, as well as stepping up spending on defense. All this adds up to the increasing role of the American state as the key national-security provider.

In other words, unlike the assertion by globalization enthusiasts, the national-security function of the American state has not declined substantially, and it is unlikely to decline as long as Washington wishes to remain the global hegemon and as long as its economic and security interests span the world. The competition for new and better weapon systems and higher allocation for developing cutting-edge technologies are also functions of the U.S. desire to reduce casualties in war and obtain its political and military goals expeditiously if war occurs. Edward Luttwak terms this imperative as arising from "post-heroic warfare," which according to him has replaced the grand style of wars

---

[38] On this, see James J. Wirtz, Jeffrey A. Larsen, and John Warner, eds., *Rockets' Red Glare: Missile Defenses and the Future of World Politics* (Boulder: Westview Press, 2001).

fought for Napoleanic-type majestic military visions.[39] This is the most prominent change in the way the security business is conducted. Democracy, mass media, and technology all contributed to the demand for weaponry that would minimize, if not eliminate, casualties.

The continued economic prosperity due to globalization is likely to put pressure on augmenting U.S. military strength. Globalization is a source of insecurity for the United States, as potential challengers gain technology and wealth generated by spreading global economic forces. Improvements in the defense realm by potential adversaries such as China would demand further building up of the American military. An appreciation of the challenges that the hegemonic state faces requires a look at the main sources, that is, other major powers, both declining and rising.

Major Power Challenges to American Hegemony

The key challenges to American hegemony are likely to come from China and Russia and anti–status quo states/actors in the developing world. China has emerged as the test case of how a national-security state and globalized economic power can go hand in hand. In fact, China has simultaneously adopted both a trading-state strategy and a high-pitched national-security state strategy aimed at making it a leading global power of the twenty-first century. One of the key aims of China to pursue a trading-state strategy has been to enhance its power and status in the international system as a major power. Thus, Chinese foreign and security policies in this era of new global social forces are largely driven by traditional realist concerns of power, prestige, and territorial security.

China has also increasingly been playing the role of a selective supporter of regional and global institutions, and the norms and principles embedded in them, to the extent that these contribute to China's rise as a full-fledged major power. Sinologists have noticed the evolution of China during the 1980s as both a "system-exploiting great power" and a "system-maintaining great power," willing to join and utilize international institutions to further its power goals. The change in China's position on international organizations coincided with "the dramatic rise of China's international standing in the hegemonic world order, and its sui generis status as a 'poor global power' can be explained by the change in China's national role conception from a revolutionary system-

---

[39] Edward N. Luttwak, "Toward Post-Heroic Warfare," *Foreign Affairs* 74 (May/June 1995): 109–22.

transforming actor to a neo-realist system-maintaining status quo actor."[40] Becoming a full-fledged global power remains a core national objective of China. Chinese policymakers justify their goal of great-power status in order to "prevent the historical humiliations suffered at the hands of Western and Japanese imperialism."[41]

Although the People's Liberation Army (PLA) has reduced its size since 1997, it is still aiming at a "lean, combined and highly efficient army." China's military modernization is increasingly focusing on a ten-year plan to refurbish its nuclear forces in order "to make them more accurate, easier to launch and far less vulnerable to attack than they are today. And it is hoping to use high technology to offset its outmoded conventional forces." What China seeks is an arsenal big enough to deter but not so expensive as the Soviet forces that led to Moscow's economic bankruptcy.[42]

The challenge that Russia poses to U.S. hegemony has declined since the days of the Cold War, although it remains the most potent power that can decimate the United States in a nuclear attack. This Russian capability itself provides the United States the incentive to modernize and establish technological superiority in weaponry. The foreign and domestic policies of Mikhail Gorbachev and Boris Yeltsin were largely failures, and as a result Russia has emerged as a weak state in "infra-structural power" and somewhat in terms of "despotic power." Some call it a "messy state."[43] Yet Yeltsin's successor, Vladimir Putin, initially resurrected security as a plank on which to gain popular support and to build strength as a major-power nation. Putin's brutal war in Chechnya and his regime's military doctrine—which gives considerable promi-nence to nuclear first-use—indicate the revival of a national-security state, despite daunting economic and political constraints in doing so. As Khazanov argues in this volume, renewal of nationalism, increased reliance on nuclear strike force, and a strategic alliance with China are central to Putin's plans for enhanced international standing, while lim-ited accommodations with the West could be pursued through arms-

[40] Samuel S. Kim, "China's International Organizational Behavior," in Thomas W. Rob-inson and David Shambaugh eds., *Chinese Foreign Policy: Theory and Practice* (Oxford: Clarendon Press, 1994), 401–34. See also Mel Gurttov and Byong-Moo Hwang, *China's Security: The New Roles of the Military* (Boulder: Lynne Rienner, 1998); Allen S. Whiting, "Chinese Nationalism and Foreign Policy after Deng," *China Quarterly* 142 (June 1995): 295–316.

[41] Paul H. Goodwin, "Force and Diplomacy: China Prepares for the Twenty-First Cen-tury," in Samuel S. Kim, ed. *China and the World*, 4th edition (Boulder: Westview Press, 1998), 171.

[42] *New York Times*, March 15, 1999.

[43] Thomas L. Friedman, "The Messy State," *The Gazette* (Montreal), October 4, 2000: B3.

control measures to buy time and breathing space. In the post–September 2001 era, Russia has made engagement with the West a prominent part of its strategy. Russia's elevated status as a NATO partner, its acquisition of full-fledged membership in the G-8 forum, and its increasing willingness to agree on nuclear arms-control arrangements with the United States, while not challenging the NMD intensely, are noticeable differences in its position. The Russian support for the U.S. war against Al-Qaeda and Taliban terrorists in Afghanistan arises from its desire to have a free hand in crushing the Islamic rebellion in Chechnya. The common enmity with Islamic insurgents has tightened Russia's bond with the West. But beneath this cooperation lies the potential for future conflict, especially if cooperation does not produce substantial dividends over time.

One such area of potential conflict is competition over resources in East and Central Asia.[44] The increasing U.S. military presence in the former Soviet republics and the involvement of U.S. companies in oil exploration in these states generate concerns for Russian planners. Yet Russia's security can no longer be viewed in geopolitical terms alone. Economic and human security issues, migration of people, ethnic conflicts, threats to uninterrupted energy supply, environmental degradation, organized crime, terrorism, and nuclear smuggling are some nontraditional security challenges Russia continues to face.[45] In the near term these challenges will absorb much of Russia's attention, but looming challenges at the systemic level would also remain fundamentally important for this state, although institutionalized engagement with the West could dampen possibilities of conflict. And it is unlikely that it will simply stay in the backwaters of international politics.

The Challenge from Regional Actors

Fundamental challenges to American hegemony are likely to come from a small group of regional states and subnational groups that hold asymmetric capabilities but possess strategies useful to pin down a conventionally dominant power. These strategies include terrorism, guerrilla warfare, and the possession, threat of use, or actual use of weapons of mass destruction. The U.S. effort to stem the spread of nuclear, biological, and chemical weapons has been motivated by these concerns. This assessment is very much evident in the 1993 Bottom-up Review and the 1997 and the 2002 Quadrennial Defense Review by the Clinton and

---

[44] Ian Bremmer, "Russia's Total Security," *World Policy Journal* 16 (Summer 1999): 2.
[45] Ibid., 31–39.

Bush administrations, respectively. These reviews called for the United States to be prepared to fight and win two major regional conflicts simultaneously or in close succession in two distant theaters. The U.S. defense efforts since then have been focused on regional threats more than anything else. This is evident in the 1998 report to the president and Congress by Secretary of Defense William Cohen, which concluded that "the foremost regional danger to the U.S. security is the continuing threat that hostile states with significant military power pose to allies and friends in key regions. Between now and 2015, it is reasonable to assume that more than one such aspiring regional power will have both the motivation and the means to challenge U.S. interests militarily."[46] Terrorist groups that find U.S. policies hostile, especially in the Middle East, are likely to continue their assaults on U.S. targets.

The Asymmetric Challenge of Terrorism

Global networks of terrorist organizations pose major challenges to U.S. security and its international primacy, as evident in the statistics that the United States was the target of over one-third of all international terrorist incidents in the 1980s and 1990s. Terrorists calculate that their strategy could work as an equalizer in the otherwise immensely asymmetric power equation vis-à-vis the United States. The United States is particularly vulnerable to terrorism because of its openness, its active involvement in all conflict-ridden theaters of the world, its support for Israel, and its sometimes unpopular polices in different regions — especially in its sponsorship of regimes that are challenged by ideologically or politically motivated groups.[47] Ideologically motivated opponents want the United States to change its policies or to get out of their regions. In recent years, religious terrorists, as typified in Osama bin-Laden's Al-Qaeda network, have emerged as serious challengers. Part of the problem is that some of these groups originated in the U.S.-led war against the Soviet Union in Afghanistan. After ousting the Soviet Union, the United States left the region in haste, leaving the terrorist groups to multiply in a lawless environment. Allies such as Pakistan offered sanctuaries to these groups, as they found it useful to have terrorism as a weapon in their struggle against stronger regional opponents.

Globalization has in fact helped the growth of transnational terrorism. Technological developments, especially in the information arena,

---

[46] Cited in Daniel Goure and Jeffrey M. Ranney, *Averting the Defense Train Wreck in the New Millennium* (Washington, DC: CSIS Press, 1999), 26–27.

[47] Paul R. Pillar, *Terrorism and U.S. Foreign Policy* (Washington, DC: Brookings Institution Press, 2001), 57, 65–67.

have helped the formation and consolidation of these groups that go unnoticed by state actors. The easy movement of people, money, weapons, and ideas across borders has made it possible for terrorist groups to further their reach globally. The excessive focus of state military and intelligence organizations on threats from other, similar states has diluted their ability to detect terrorist activities early on. The uneven economic development that globalization has brought to different parts of the world has generated millions of unemployed youth in terrorism-breeding societies.

The geographical reach of terrorists has been enhanced by new communication technologies such as the Internet. The United States and other advanced states are vulnerable to terrorism because their vital assets are concentrated in key urban centers. Terrorists realize that surprise strikes or threats of attacks on these targets could affect the national economies.[48] The asymmetric power of terrorism is represented in the successes of Al-Qaeda in penetrating and conducting operations in the United States as well as against U.S. assets abroad. Al-Qaeda has gained strength through stealth, with the ability to carry out attacks and disappear for years to come, while the United States has focused on improving its ability to strike with precision at fixed targets. Military strategies that are relevant in the interstate context, that is, deterrence, offense, compellence, and coercive diplomacy, generally do not work against terrorism. The U.S. reliance on air power and unwillingness to engage in ground operations because of the fear of casualties give terrorist groups such as Al-Qaeda some level of tactical advantage. The presence of a sympathetic population in urban or tribal settings allows terrorist forces to go unnoticed and to conduct their operations secretly. It is likely that, as the years pass, the United States may develop better intelligence and other capabilities to counter terrorism, but terrorism as a scourge is likely to stay. Global social and economic forces, indeed, generate much opportunity for the rise of new groups and causes with asymmetrical strategies to challenge powerful states, especially the United States.

Soft Security Challenges

Although not as significant as hard challenges from other major powers, regional actors, and terrorist groups, soft challenges do matter in the proper management and extension of hegemony. Lesser allies are very much part of the hegemon's strength. When allies loosen their support

---

[48] Thomas Homer-Dixon, "The Rise of Complex Terrorism," *Foreign Policy* 128 (January–February 2002): 52–62.

level or undertake countermeasures, including technological advancements, the hegemonic state's power is challenged in a soft way. The most powerful soft challenges to U.S. hegemony are likely to come from European allies. Having witnessed their ineptitude in Bosnia and Kosovo, the allies have resurrected the European Security and Defense Policy (ESDP), a soft but symbolically powerful challenge to U.S. hegemony, especially because it threatens the very existence of NATO. The United States fears that this initiative may cause the death of NATO altogether as it will have no American representation.[49] The challenge is also driven by the desire of the European states to maintain their technological edge in aerospace and other cutting-edge areas of innovation. The most significant change in this regard has been the increasing integration of European defense industries, unlike during the Cold War period, when "for reasons of promoting intra-NATO rationalization, standardization, interoperability . . . have long pursued an expanded transatlantic partnership when it comes to armaments cooperation. In the past decade, however, intra-European weapons collaboration and defense industry integration have expanded at a rate that far outstrips transatlantic cooperation. . . . Western Europe increasingly views the United States more as a competitor than a prospective partner when it comes to arms production."[50] The U.S. tendency to act unilaterally, while ignoring European preferences for multilateralism, has also caused dissension among the one-time strong allies.

Allies and friends of the United States, such as France, now increasingly speak of a multipolar world. Some French policymakers view America as the "hyper power," or the power above the super power status, which needs to be restrained.[51] The security dimensions of all these are yet to percolate. The United States, if loosened from its hold on NATO and Western Europe, will increasingly focus on technological solutions to solve its security problems. This could generate technological rivalries not just among the United States, Russia, and China, but between the United States and Europe as well.

LOYALTY RARELY WITHERS AWAY!

The view that the state's security function will decline and therefore states will lose the chief rationale for existence is at best premature. As

---

[49] The decoupling of the United States from the European security structure has remained a concern to American decision-makers. See, for example, Madeline Albright, "The Right Balance Will Secure NATO's Future," *Financial Times*, December 7, 1998.

[50] Richard A. Bitzinger, "Globalization in the Post-Cold War Defense Industry: Challenges and Opportunities," in Markusen and Costigan, eds., *Arming the Future*, 321, 325.

[51] Hubert Verdine, *Les Cartes de La France* (Paris: Fayard, 2000), 9.

discussed previously, these arguments are based on several ill-founded assumptions. First, globalization will remove interstate conflicts and intrastate conflicts, thereby dramatically decreasing the role of armed forces. Second, future technology will provide the hegemonic power with overwhelming superiority in offensive, defensive, and deterrent capabilities that will make it irrational on the part of the challenger to take on the hegemonic power. Third, geopolitical conflicts are unlikely to occur in the future because Western (namely, American) military superiority is too high and no new nation is about to catch up with the United States. Fourth, ideology, nationalism, and so forth will increasingly become irrelevant as the benefits of globalization spread throughout the world. Nations and individuals, being rational, will embrace the virtues of globalization, or they will simply be constrained by the mighty forces unleashed by globalization. Finally, state-society tensions will increase in the absence of identifiable external threats as antistatist forces will gain an upper hand.

These assumptions are problematic. First, a challenger can design asymmetric responses to counter the dominant state's power position. These include terrorism, guerrilla warfare, and options such as cyberwar or technological shortcuts. Sustained fear of terrorist attacks can weaken the economic prosperity and domestic tranquility of the wealthy states concerned. Second, technology itself is a cause for conflict because introduction of new technologies can often increase the offensive power of states that gained early access to them. The industrial revolution gave railroads, which enabled key European states to organize mass movements of troops and launch popular mobilization. The rise of the automobile, aircraft, and aircraft carriers improved the offensive capabilities of states that acquired or mastered these technological innovations early on. The nuclear revolution increased the power of the deterrent and, to some extent, defense. We still do not know how the information revolution is going to affect warfare — whether it will result in advantage for the offense, defense, or deterrent. If it helps the offense, conflict behavior of the beneficiaries of the information revolution is prone to increase. Finally, geopolitical conflicts often arise as a result of an unintended consequence of differential growth rates. A state that makes major gains in economic and military capability may attempt to gain a leadership role internationally. As the international system has no nonviolent mechanism to allow peaceful transitions, the likelihood of conflict, even in asymmetric forms, is very much present in the system.

All these elements point to the issue that loyalty is likely to stay with the nation state. Differential growth rates imply that different states provide benefits to the citizens in varying rates. In the example of the

United States, loyalty is a function of the U.S. hegemony, which is largely the reason why Americans enjoy a higher standard of living compared with citizens of other nations. The loyalty to the state is thus very much intertwined with the individual's own interests in seeing this hegemony prolonged as long as possible. Any serious challenge to the American hegemony is likely to spark the individual's sense of nationalism, often claimed to be decreasing at the altar of global forces. In the United States the struggle against terrorism and the plans for homeland security have increased the role of the state. There is no doubt that, as a result of the terrorist challenge, statist forces are on the rise. This trend is likely to continue with no end point in site in the war against terrorism.

With respect to state-society relations, it is often argued that, in the absence of a grave external threat, the cohesiveness of the state will decline, as antistatist forces will emerge powerful. However, this argument assumes that the state elite mismanages foreign policy as it did in the 1960s, that democratic institutions are poorly designed to incorporate change, and that the civil society has weak roots. As Friedberg argues, although the threat of war produced pressures to build a powerful central state in the United States, they were counterbalanced by "strong anti-statist influences that were deeply rooted in the circumstances of the nation's founding." He adds: "The proper balance between statist and anti-statist impulses can sometimes be attained in the American system through convergence and coolly reasoned compromise; more often it will be the product of heated debate and intense, often bitter struggle."[52] My sense is that the end of the Cold War has not yet produced a situation whereby antistatist forces have gained dominance, as the balance in terms of the role of the state is visible in both the Republican and the Democratic parties. The antistatist forces within the Republican Party in fact are stronger proponents of national defense, a contradiction of sorts.

CONCLUSIONS

Several conclusions emerge from this analysis. First, globalization has not ended the core security functions of nation-states, even though some states have scaled back on military spending. Second, globalization is occurring in the backdrop of a near unipolarity in the structure of the international system in which the hegemonic power, the United States, is the leader of the process. This structural condition has been strength-

---

[52] Aaron L. Friedberg, *In the Shadow of the Garrison State* (Princeton: Princeton University Press, 2000), 3–4, 351.

ened by the increased role of U.S. corporations, while these corporations themselves make use of the American power position to reinforce
their economic and political roles across the world. Third, the new security threats have not made states redundant. The major innovation of
states has been the inclusion of the new security threats, such as terrorism, environment, and disease, into national security calculations.

Fourth, state responses in the sphere of security have not been uniform across cases or regions. Global social and economic forces have
affected states in varying degrees. The uneven responses in the security
arena in the face of these new global forces are due largely to the varying contexts of states. Major powers have reduced the level of conflict
vis-à-vis one another since the end of the Cold War, but security competition exists in terms of political influence and weapons innovation. Although several regional conflicts have subsided, traditional security concerns still dominate the behavior of key regional states.

For the United States, the global hegemon, military power bestows
certain key functions. Its role as the extant global protector provides it
with a degree of social-structural power over allies and coercive power
over adversaries. The status a protector gains from anticipated as well
as undefined threats is thus a powerful source of control and collaboration for the United States. In a more negative sense, it does allow it to
control the periphery — those states yet to be co-opted fully in the hegemonic order — that could chip away at the dominant status of the hegemonic power. The United States is likely to remain a national-security
state par excellence, although it may increasingly fashion technological
solutions to gaining dominance over allies and adversaries and avoiding
casualties in active military confrontations. The U.S. hegemony as a systemic condition guarantees adversarial responses from subordinate actors most affected, even when the U.S. elite devises strategies to guarantee that the hegemonic power remains preponderant over all other large
and small challengers.

Revolutionary changes in military technology are a crucial factor that
will determine how states will provide security or respond to security
threats in the future. States tend to worry about technological break-
throughs as the political, military, and economic gains of such changes
may help transform the state or society that acquire the cutting-edge
technology disproportionately. Technology also partially determines
how a state organizes its resources for military security as well as what
strategies and doctrines it will adopt. The type of weapons and technology dictated to a certain extent the adoption of strategies such as the
blitzkrieg and offensive doctrines before World War I and II by European states.[53] Thus, the relationship between technology and military

---

[53] O'Hanlon, *Technological Change and the Future of Warfare.*

strategy is an enduring one, and it will continue into the future inter-state and intrastate relations.

Finally, states tend to adapt to changes in technology and sociopoliti-cal environments in varying degrees. States assume new organizational means to deal with challenges posed by external and internal changes. Some states may innovate rapidly and may succeed in providing security through means other than military/coercive instruments. Military/coer-cive instruments are one of several mechanisms states possess to provide security, and therefore it is incorrect to assert that states have lost their power in the security realm in the era of globalization. Successful adap-tation to new global social forces is a sign of strength of the nation-state, not its weakness.

CHAPTER 6

States and War in Africa

JEFFREY HERBST

SUB-SAHARAN AFRICA is home to most of the armed conflicts today. At the same time, a large percentage of the world's worst performing states are in Africa. The coincidence of conflict and dysfunctional states is hardly surprising. Yet the European experience was that war and state-building were related over the long term. Given the long-term relationship between war and state building in Europe, it is reasonable to ask if the current conflicts will, in the long run, lead to stronger states in Africa. Of course, even if the European experience could be repeated, state building through conflict would not be a complete answer to Africa's problems. While conflict is unusually common in Africa, most states on the continent are not at war. Tanzania, Kenya, Niger, Burkina Faso — among many others — are profoundly troubled states, but they are not experiencing significant conflict. Still, so many countries are currently at war that the state-building ramifications of conflict must be examined.

This chapter concludes that, in fact, most of the conflicts in Africa are within states and therefore do not have the same effects on state building as was the case in Europe. The dynamics of civil war — the type of conflict most prevalent in Africa — differ radically from the interstate war that most contributed to state building in Europe. At the same time, no matter what the realities on the ground, the international community continues to recognize the boundaries of even those states that have lost physical control of their boundaries. As a result, the "filtering" effect that war had in the other periods of history — by eliminating weak or nonviable political arrangements — is not present in Africa.

In the few instances where wars have been between states in Africa, there is some evidence that some of the processes present in Europe are beginning to assert themselves. In particular, those African states that can legitimately claim to be threatened by neighbors have had some notable successes in mobilizing their populations for war. However, this type of violent threat is still rare enough in Africa that it is unlikely that Africa can follow the European path of state development.

WAR AND STATE DEVELOPMENT

Standard narratives of European state development highlight the crucial contribution of war. Thus, Samuel P. Huntington argued that "war was the great stimulus to state building," and Charles Tilly went so far as to claim that "war made the state, and the state made war."[1] Similarly, nomadic states in Inner Asia were forced to acquire a higher level of social organization than would have been required to solve their domestic problems in order to defend themselves from their sedentary neighbors.[2] At the most basic level, war in Europe acted as a filter whereby weak states were eliminated and political arrangements that were not viable either were reformed or disappeared. Weak states do exist in Europe today — Belgium is one example — but the near-constant threat of war prompted most states to become stronger to survive.

More specifically, war in Europe played an important role in the consolidation of many now-developed states in ways that are particularly important to an understanding of how power is broadcast: war caused the state to become more efficient in revenue collection by forcing leaders to dramatically improve administrative capabilities (thereby allowing states to fund nationwide administrative and economic systems), and war created a climate and important symbols around which a disparate population could unify and bond with the state in a manner that legitimized the capital's authority.

Taxes

There is no better measure of a state's reach than its ability to collect taxes. If a state does not effectively control a territory, it certainly will not be able to collect taxes in a sustained and efficient manner. At the same time, a widely distributed tax base helps guarantee consolidation of the state by generating a robust revenue stream. Perhaps the most noticeable effect of war in European history was to cause the state to increase its ability to collect significantly more revenue with greater efficiency and less public resistance. Given the freedom of European states to attack each other, states that could quickly raise money could suc-

---

[1] Samuel P. Huntington, *Political Order in Changing Societies* (New Haven: Yale University Press, 1968), 123; Charles Tilly, "Reflections on the History of European State-Making," in Charles Tilly, ed., *The Formation of National States in Western Europe* (Princeton: Princeton University Press, 1975), 42.

[2] Thomas J. Barfield, *The Perilous Frontier: Nomadic Empires and China* (London: Basil Blackwell, 1989), 7.

cessfully threaten neighbors with a war that might lead to significant damage or even complete destruction. Richard Bean writes, "Once the power to tax had been successfully appropriated by any one sovereign, once he had used that power to bribe or coerce his nobility into acquiescence, that state could face all neighboring states with the choice of being conquered or of centralizing authority and raising taxes."[3] While success in war depends on many factors, including technology, tactics, and morale of the troops, raising sufficient revenue was a necessary condition to prevent defeat. As Michael Mann notes, "A state that wished to survive had to increase its extractive capacity to pay for professional armies and/or navies. Those that did not would be crushed on the battlefield and absorbed into others — the fate of Poland, of Saxony, of Bavaria in [the seventeenth and eighteenth centuries]. No European states were continuously at peace. It is impossible to escape the conclusion that a peaceful state would have ceased to exist even more speedily than the militarily inefficient actually did."[4]

War affected state finances for two reasons. First, it placed tremendous strains on leaders to find new and more regular sources of income. While rulers may have recognized that their tax systems were inadequate, a war may be the only prompt that can force them to expend the necessary political capital and to deploy the coercion required to gain more revenue. For instance, in Mann's study of taxation in England between 1688 and 1815, he finds that there were six major jumps in state revenue and that each corresponds with the beginning of a war.[5] The association between the need to fight and the need to collect revenue is perhaps clearest in Prussia, where the main tax collection agency was called the General War Commissariat.[6]

Second, citizens are much more likely to acquiesce to increased taxation when the nation is at war because a threat to their survival will overwhelm other concerns they might have about increased taxation. In fact, taxation for a war can be thought of as a "lumpy" collective good: not only must the population pay to get the good, but it also must pay a considerable amount more than the current level of taxation, because a small increase in revenue often is not enough to meet the new security

---

[3] Richard Bean, "War and the Birth of the Nation State," *Journal of Economic History* 33 (March 1973): 220.

[4] Michael Mann, *States, War and Capitalism: Studies in Political Sociology* (Oxford: Basil Blackwell, 1988), 109.

[5] Michael Mann, *Sources of Social Power* (Cambridge: Cambridge University Press, 1986), 486.

[6] Michael Duffy, "The Military Revolution and the State, 1500–1800," in Michael Duffy, ed., *The Military Revolution and the State, 1500–1800*, Exeter Studies in History no. 1 (Exeter: University of Exeter, 1980), 5.

threat facing the state.[7] In this way, taxation for a war is like taxation for building a bridge: everyone must pay to build the bridge, and a small increase in revenue will not be enough because half a bridge, like fighting half a war, is useless.

Thus, war often causes a "ratchet effect" whereby revenue increases sharply when a nation is fighting but does not decline to the ante bellum level when hostilities have ceased.[8] Once governments have invested the sunk costs in expanding tax collection systems and routinized the collection of new sources of revenue, the marginal costs of continuing those structures are quite low, and the resources they collect can be used for projects that will enhance the ruling group's support. Ironically, it is under external threat from others that European states were able to consolidate control over their own nations.

War in other societies at other times often played the same kind of role that external conflict did in Europe. For instance, the South Korean and Taiwanese states have been able to extract so many resources from their societies in part because the demands to be constantly vigilant provoked the state into developing efficient mechanisms for collecting resources and controlling dissident groups.[9] A highly extractive state also can cloak demands for greater resources in appeals for national unity in the face of a determined enemy.

It is extraordinarily difficult, outside times of crisis, to reform elemental parts of the governmental system, such as the means of taxation. Since taxes are so consequential to every business decision, over time the tax system reflects a large number of political bargains made by the state with different interest groups. Edward Ames and Richard Rapp's conclusion that tax systems "last until the end of the government that instituted them" and that tax systems in some European countries survived "almost intact" from the thirteenth and fourteenth centuries until the late eighteenth century may be an exaggeration, but it suggests just how much inertia a particular system for collecting government revenue can develop over time.[10] Other than war, no type of crisis demands that the state increase taxes with such forcefulness, and few other situations would impel citizens to accept those demands, or at least not resist them as strongly as they otherwise might have. It is therefore hard to counter Tilly's argument that "the formation of standing armies provided the

[7] "Lumpy" goods are products that are not useful if only part is purchased. Margaret Levi, *Of Rule and Revenue* (Berkeley: University of California Press, 1988), 56–57.

[8] Mann, *Sources of Social Power*, 483–90.

[9] Joel S. Migdal, *Strong Societies and Weak States: State-Society Relations and State Capabilities in the Third World* (Princeton: Princeton University Press, 1988), 274.

[10] Edward Ames and Richard T. Rapp, "The Birth and Death of Taxes: A Hypothesis," *Journal of Economic History* 37 (March 1977): 177.

largest single incentive to extraction and the largest single means of
state coercion over the long run of European state-making."[11]

Nationalism

While critical, taxes are not the only measure of how a state consoli-
dates power. Also important is the far more nebulous idea that the nation and the state are bound together through a series of emotional ties
often expressed in the iconic symbols of nationalism. Nationalism can
be thought of as another way for the state to consolidate its power over
distance, not, as with taxes, through the agencies of coercion but through
the norm of legitimacy.

European nation-states were hardly natural. As the history of France
demonstrates, European states at one time had to deal with, and in
some cases are still coping with, highly diverse populations that did not
have many emotional links with the state. In Europe this problem was
solved in good part by war. Indeed, the presence of a palpable external
threat may be the strongest way to generate a common association between the state and the population. External threats have such a powerful effect on nationalism because people realize in a profound manner
that they are under threat because of who they are as a nation; they are
forced to recognize that it is only as a nation that they can successfully
defeat the threat. Anthony Giddens recounts the effects of World War I:
"The War canalized the development of states' sovereignty, tying this to
citizenship and to nationalism in such a profound way that any other
scenario [of how the international system would be ordered] subsequently came to appear as little more than idle fantasy."[12] Michael
Howard notes the visceral impact of wars on the development of nationalism throughout Europe:

> Self-identification as a Nation implies almost by definition alienation from
> other communities, and the most memorable incidents in the group-mem-
> ory consisted in conflict with and triumph over other communities. France
> *was* Marengo, Austerlitz and Jena: military triumph set the seal on the new-
> found national consciousness. Britain *was* Trafalgar — but it had been a na-
> tion for four hundred years, since those earlier battles Crecy and Agincourt.
> Russia *was* the triumph of 1812. Germany *was* Gravelotte and Sedan.[13]

[11] Tilly, "Reflections on the History," 73.

[12] Anthony Giddens, *A Contemporary Critique of Historical Materialism*, vol. 2 (Berkeley: University of California Press, 1987), 235.

[13] Michael Howard, *War and the Nation State* (Oxford: Clarendon Press, 1978), 9.
Emphasis in the original.

Similarly, in Japan, the Tokugawa Shogunate's armed conquest was "inextricably connected" with the regime's legitimacy.[14] As a result, it is hardly surprising that the critical monuments (e.g., Trafalgar Square, Arc de Triumph, Brandenburg Gates) in so many European capital cities are militaristic. They celebrate the central events that not only preserved the state but also forged its links with the population.

CONFLICT IN AFRICA

Conflict in Africa has a substantially different dynamic from that in Europe during that continent's formative state-building episodes. At the most fundamental level, conflict in Africa does not result in the political destruction of states. The boundary-maintenance regime that African states constructed after independence with the help of the international community has been surprisingly robust. Under this series of formal and informal arrangements, the boundaries inherited from the colonialists are generally assumed to be permanent.[15] Thus, even extremely weak states continue to "exist"; indeed, the only significant boundary change in Africa's independent history has been the creation of Eritrea after a long civil war within Ethiopia. This is a remarkable record in a continent where many countries cannot even physically defend their own boundaries. Conflict has certainly resulted in the physical destruction of many countries in Africa, including Mozambique, Angola, Sudan, Liberia, Democratic Republic of Congo, and Sierra Leone. However, all of these states continue to have a political existence and are still recognized as sovereign states by their neighbors and the international community. For instance, with regard to the conflicts in Democratic Republic of the Congo (DRC), former U.S. Assistant Secretary of State for African Affairs Susan Rice said, "In numerous public statements and through energetic diplomatic action we [the Clinton Administration] have affirmed our strong and unyielding support for the sovereignty and territorial integrity of the Congo."[16] This is despite the fact that it is obvious from the operation of a half dozen foreign armies in the DRC that it has no territorial integrity, has not been an integral unit for many years, and will not be for many more to come. Correspondingly, the

[14] Eiko Ikegami, *The Taming of the Samurai: Honorific Individualism and the Making of Modern Japan* (Cambridge: Harvard University Press, 1995), 152.

[15] See generally Jeffrey Herbst, *States and Power in Africa: Comparative Lessons in Authority and Control* (Princeton: Princeton University Press, 2000), chap. 4.

[16] Susan E. Rice, "The Democratic Republic of the Congo in Crisis," statement before the Subcommittee on Africa, House International Relations Committee, Washington, DC, September 15, 1998. Found at www.state.gov/www/regions/africa/rice—980915.html.

international community has not recognized Somaliland—the break-
away province of Somalia—despite the fact that Hargeisa has physical
control of its territory and there is only the faintest evidence of the state
in Mogadishu.

Indeed, the African reluctance to change boundaries or tolerate the
political elimination of national states stands in sharp contrast to Europe and Eurasia in the 1990s. In Europe since the end of the Cold War,
a relatively large number of states—East Germany, Yugoslavia, Czechoslovakia, and, especially, the Soviet Union—disappeared to be replaced
by presumably more viable arrangements. Europeans also developed new
arrangements that blurred the demarcation and responsibilities associated with sovereignty in Northern Ireland and Kosovo. Finally, the wid-
ening and deepening of the European Union promises to overturn sovereign arrangements across the continent.

If African boundaries do not change to reflect the realities of how
political power is exercised, the continent faces the worst of all possible
worlds. War continues to kill people and level countries, just as they did
in previous times and places. However, since war does not result in the
political destruction of states in modern Africa, the cycle of conflict may
just continue because the institutional arrangement of the state—the
boundaries, location of capital, and territory enclosed by the national
frontiers—cannot change. Thus, even in the Great Lakes region—where
the conflicts in Rwanda, Burundi, and DRC clearly feed off of each
other—there is no movement to address the wars on a regional basis.

Taxes

The evolution of public-sector revenue illustrates just how different
state building has been in Africa compared with Europe, in good part
because African states, while quite weak by world standards, have been
far more secure than many European states during their formative period of development. In the 1960s it was recognized that the structure
of government revenue in Africa was highly problematic. First, the revenue streams produced were clearly inadequate. African states were desperately short of revenue to fund even minimal state services (e.g., pay
nurses' salaries, buy books for schools, supply transport for agricultural
extension services) that their populations had been promised in the
heady days after independence. In addition to these recurrent costs, African countries were in need of more extensive and more efficient tax
systems because the process of development requires large expenditures
on infrastructure (including, of course, roads) to promote economic ac-

tivity throughout the country.[17] W. Arthur Lewis estimated that the public sector in Third World countries should be spending on the order of 20 percent of GDP on services, exclusive of defense and debt repayment.[18] For countries the Economic Commission for Africa (ECA) had data for, government expenditures amounted to only 17 percent of GDP in 1960 and only 22 percent in 1968 before defense (which averaged about 27 percent of government expenditures in both years) and debt payments.[19] While these figures are only rough estimates given the problems associated with African economic statistics in the 1960s, they illustrate the extent of the fiscal problem facing African states at independence.

By 1968 the ECA was already warning that public expenditure in many countries was rising ahead of revenue (despite significant economic growth) and that the share of GDP absorbed by taxes was not related to the growth of the overall economy.[20] The ECA recognized that African countries relied on indirect taxes because they were convenient and relatively inexpensive to collect given the nature of the inherited colonial administrative systems, by then only slightly modified. However, the UN agency noted that income tax still could be applied to some individuals with relatively high salaries and that some people did have substantial savings. It complained with a degree of honesty seldom found in more recent publications that "generally sufficient consideration was not given to the possibilities of developing and strengthening other forms of taxation. The shortage of revenue in most cases was due to the fact that the taxation potential was not fully exploited. In many cases it was not only due to bad tax administration but also the result of resistance from powerful pressure groups who blocked the way to effective tax reform."[21]

In direct contrast to the European experience of states being prompted to collect taxes efficiently due to a threatening external environment, the ECA detected no urgency on the part of African governments to raise money: "the problem of collection lies with the government agency responsible for tax collection. But invariably tax laws are not enforced because of the laxity of government officials." It went on to note that before it was reformed (and undoubtedly since those reforms

[17] W. Arthur Lewis, *The Evolution of the International Economic Order* (Princeton: Princeton University Press, 1978), 39.

[18] W. Arthur Lewis, *Development Planning: The Essentials of Economic Policy* (New York: Harper and Row, 1966), 115.

[19] ECA, *Survey of Economic Conditions in Africa, 1970* (New York: ECA: 1971), 327–28.

[20] ECA, *Survey of Economic Conditions in Africa, 1960–1964* (New York: ECA, 1968), 186–87.

[21] ECA, *Survey of Economic Conditions in Africa, 1970*, 141.

lapsed), the Liberian tax collection agency, like many others across the continent, was "woefully disorganized and painfully demoralized."[22] Similarly, the ECA described the reasons for poor tax collection in the Mid-Western state of Nigeria: "The problem was that a number of leading figures in the society were being allowed to avoid their [tax] obligations. Avoidance has been too easy because big businessmen and self-employed professionals have felt that Government was afraid of them, or that they could 'buy off' tax officials. Sometimes the officials were afraid to take action because they felt that the defaulters might use their social connections to victimize them."[23]

Despite these warnings, African governments did not work energetically to change their revenue structure. Guyer notes, in one of the rare studies of direct taxation, that, in Nigeria, "since independence . . . the taxation systems set up by colonial governments have been all but dismantled, particularly at the local level." She explains that the atrophy of direct tax systems came about because of several different reasons, including populist ideology, civil disorder, and "the increased importance of national wealth coming from large, single sources such as minerals and government loans."[24] Income taxes did increase to 28 percent of government revenue in 1985. However, in the critical period 1985–96, when many African countries were engaged in economic reform, the percentage of government revenue attributable to income taxes actually declined to 25 percent.[25]

Close observers of African public finance today detect the same lack of seriousness with which the ECA was obsessed in the 1960s. For instance, Collier notes the political origins of the public finance problem in Africa:

> [Taxation] is normally constrained by two mechanisms: popular consent and the law. . . . [In independent Africa] the two usual constraint mechanisms failed. . . . In some countries, governments collect taxes in an arbi-

[22] ECA, *Survey of Economic Conditions in Africa, 1972*, part 1 (New York: United Nations, 1973), 232.

[23] Ibid., 233.

[24] Jane I. Guyer, "Representation without Taxation: An Essay on Democracy in Rural Nigeria, 1952–1990," *African Studies Review* 35 (April 1992): 43.

[25] Data are from ECA, "Public Finance in African Countries," *Economic Bulletin for Africa* 1 (June 1961): 16–18, for 1958; World Bank, *African Development Indicators, 1997: Data on Diskette* (Washington, DC: World Bank, 1997). Data for the period 1958 to 1980 on a continental basis are not available, and even the more recent information presented here should be viewed with caution given how poorly many African countries kept their accounts in the 1970s and 1980s. Indeed, one of the manifestations of the reliance on indirect sources of revenues was the retardation of a felt need to make public finance transparent.

trary fashion, because the lack of trustworthy audited accounts has left governments with the choice of failing to collect revenue on profits or collecting it on an arbitrary basis. In many countries, de facto lump-sum assessments are common and so tax rates have little meaning in practice. . . . Thus the fear of high taxation in the private sector goes hand in hand with very low revenues being collected through taxes in many African countries.[26]

The process of tax collection that Collier describes is suggestive, more than anything, of a tribute system where the state has essentially given up on regular tax collection and instead relies on extracting irregular lump sums from corporations and individuals. The political revolution that Africa experienced starting in the early 1960s has yet to lead to a fiscal revolution.

Normally, governments would not have been able to increase spending based almost completely on borrowing. However, donors have been surprisingly generous in the face of African dysfunctionality. While it is often the case, especially in recent years, that external donors have demanded economic reform and prompted greater economic change than would have been generated internally, looking at the current environment in comparative perspective, it is easy to see how much less threatening the world is today for even weak states in Africa compared with Europe during the formative period of many of those countries. Joseph Stiglitz, when he was chief economist of the World Bank, even argued that foreign aid should be treated as a legitimate and predictable source of government revenue.[27] If European states would have had finances as problematic as many African countries, they may not have survived in an era that punished fiscal failure. Instead, in the era of African independence, the international community kept many governments solvent.

The obstacles posed by large peasant populations, significant non-monetarized sectors, and widespread poverty are, of course, important contributors to the revenue crisis of the African state. However, these problems do not fully explain why poor states do not extract greater resources from society in a manner that is less economically harmful. Factors such as political will, administrative ability, and the population's willingness to be taxed—issues that can be affected by the decisions of political leaders—are also crucial in understanding why states are unable to achieve their potential level of taxation in a benign man-

---

[26] Paul Collier, "The Marginalization of Africa," *International Labour Review* 134 (1995): 552.

[27] Joseph Stiglitz, "More Instruments and Broader Goals: Moving towards the Post-Washington Consensus," 1998 WIDER Annual Lecture, Helsinki, Finland, January 7, 1998, found at www.worldbank.org/html/extdr/extme/js-010798/wider.htm, 6.

ner.[28] For instance, Margaret Levi successfully shows that in such diverse cases as republican Rome, France and England in the Middle Ages, eighteenth-century Britain, and twentieth-century Australia, levels of taxation were affected primarily by political constraints faced by rulers, despite the fact that the structure of most of these economies also posed significant barriers to increased tax collections.[29] Anderson estimates that revenue gains in the range of 20–30 percent were possible in Africa in the 1980s if the revenue stream was changed by increasing charges on public services.[30]

What stands out is that Africa did not face the same kind of security threat as Europe, and, therefore, the pressure to mobilize revenue through efficient administration, including efficient nationwide systems to collect revenue, is much lower. It would be foolish to say that significant interstate war would have solved Africa's many fiscal problems. However, it is obvious that African countries have not solved the problem of how to motivate administrative systems to mobilize the maximum amount of revenue efficiently in times of peace. As a result, the spatial structure of revenue, and thus of the state itself, is very much as during the colonial period: concentrated in the capital and the few other areas of the country where it is easy to tax.

Domestic security threats, of the type African countries face so often, may force the state to increase revenue; however, civil conflicts result in fragmentation and considerable hostility among different segments of the population. Public acceptance of tax increases, a crucial factor in allowing European states to extract greater resources in times of war, will be a much more complicated issue in civil disputes. As Mann notes, "the growth of the modern state, as measured by finances, is explained primarily not in domestic terms but in terms of geopolitical relations of violence."[31]

Nationalism

African countries since independence have been unable to rely on the shared experience of war in order to force symbols of national unity

---

[28] Raja J. Chelliah, "Trends in Taxation in Developing Countries," *International Monetary Fund Staff Papers* 18 (July 1971): 312. On the possibility of changing fiscal arrangements in Africa, see Dennis Anderson, *The Public Revenue and Economic Policy in African Countries*, World Bank Discussion Paper no. 19 (Washington, DC: World Bank, 1987), 14–15.

[29] Levi, *Of Rule and Revenue*, 104–5.

[30] Anderson, *The Public Revenue*, 18. See generally Zmarak Shalizi and Lyn Squire, *Tax Policy in Sub-Saharan Africa*, World Bank Policy & Research Series Paper no. 2 (Washington, DC: World Bank, 1988).

[31] Mann, *Sources of Social Power*, 490.

that would bind their disparate populations together. Civil wars generally cannot play this role because the anvil of combat is most directly related to nationalism when the entire population is physically threatened for the same reason. Anthony Smith is absolutely right when he writes, "the central difficulty of 'nation-building' in much of Africa and Asia is the lack of any shared historical mythology and memory on which state elites can set about 'building' the nation."[32] Economic development, which early African leaders identified as the new struggle that Africa would engage in, and presumably the moral equivalent of war in Europe, has largely been a disaster in much of Africa as large parts of the continent are no richer today than they were at independence. As a result, national identity remains highly problematic in many African countries and often has lower salience than membership in other groups. As Ndegwa writes of Kenya, "the socially enacted relationship between ethnic identity, authority, and legitimacy competes with the legally sanctioned membership, authority, and legitimacy of the nation-state."[33]

This is not to argue that nationalism is absent in Africa, or in other parts of the developing world. However, leaders of these states do face a particularly difficult problem in promoting the identification of the nation with the state. Unfortunately, there is no good way to measure nationalistic fervor, much less develop a time series of such sentiments. It is clear that African leaders have yet to systematically develop a strategy of how to build nationalism in times of peace.

The Ability to Mobilize

Both taxes and nationalism are measures of how well the state can mobilize the population. However, they are admittedly measures whose trajectory becomes truly apparent only in the long-term. Tax structures can change only slowly, and the emotional binding of the population to the state is obviously a process that occurs over decades. A more immediate measure of mobilization, and one that may give some hint as to whether there will be the longer-term gains in taxes and nationalism given the type of conflict in Africa, concerns the ability to increase the size of the army in the face of the enemy. Indeed, the ability to mobilize troops is critical to state survival. If it is able to mobilize and deploy the agents of violence, there is some chance that it can crush an insurgency while the rebels are still particularly vulnerable. However, as time goes

[32] Anthony D. Smith, "State-Making and Nation-Building," in John A. Hall, ed., *States in History* (Oxford: Basil Blackwell, 1986), 258.

[33] Stephen N. Nedgwa, "Citizenship and Ethnicity: An Examination of Two Transition Moments in Kenyan Politics," *American Political Science Review* 91 (September 1997): 602.

TABLE 6.1
Unsuccessful Mobilizations during Conflict

| Country | Mobilization during Crisis (soldiers/thousand citizens) | | | | | |
	1	2	3	4	5	6
Congo-Brazzaville	1993	1994	1995	1996	1997	
	4.2	4.1	4	3.9	3.8	
Guinea	1987	1989	1991	1993	1995	1997
	4.5	2.7	2.4	2.2	1.7	1.6
Liberia	1986	1987	1988	1989	1990	1991
	2.6	2.5	2.8	2.7	3.5	2.9
Sierra Leone	1987	1989	1991	1993	1995	1997
	1.5	1	1.1	1.2	1.1	1
Somalia	1982	1984	1986	1988	1990	
	9.2	6.9	7.4	6.7	5.6	
Sudan	1980	1981	1982	1983	1984	1985
	3.4	4.5	4.3	4	2.9	2.8
Uganda	1982	1983	1984	1985	1986	1987
	0.7	0.9	1	1	1	0.9
Zaire	1973	1975	1977	1979	1981	1983
	2.8	2.2	2	0.8	1.5	1.3
Zaire	1993	1994	1995	1996	1997	
	1	.9	.9	1.1		

Source: Calculated from U.S. Arms Control and Disarmament Agency, World Military Expenditures and Arms Transfers, various years.

on, it becomes increasingly difficult to fight an insurgency, and states therefore become vulnerable to outright defeat (especially if they have a relatively small territorial base and face relatively adept rebel fighters) or a prolonged war that neither side can win but will almost surely devastate the country. At the same time, successful mobilization of the citizenry to fight is a clear milestone in the roadmap toward state consolidation. Failure to mobilize in the face of an enemy is a clear indication of state failure.

Table 6.1 presents some instances of unsuccessful mobilization in the face of an enemy while table 6.2 presents instances where African countries were able to mobilize in the face of a growing enemy threat. I have used soldiers per thousand citizens as my major indicator of mobilization because budgetary data on African militaries are completely unreliable and it is at least possible to present a reasonable count of the number of soldiers in an army. As much as possible, I have tried to have column 5 be the year in which the enemy threat became most obvious, although some of the conflicts do not lend themselves to such neat chro-

TABLE 6.2
Successful Mobilizations during Conflict

Country	Mobilization during Crisis					
	1	2	3	4	5	6
Angola	1979	1981	1983	1985	1987	1989
	7.2	7.6	7.4	8.7	9.4	12.9
Ethiopia	1974	1976	1978	1980	1982	1984
	1.3	1.8	6.1	6.5	6	4.5
Mozambique	1979	1981	1983	1985	1987	1989
	2.5	2.4	2.4	2.8	4.6	4.6
Rwanda	1990	1991	1992	1993	1994	1995
	0.8	4.1	4	3.9	6	5.5
Somalia	1973	1975	1977	1979	1981	1983
	8.3	9.4	16.1	15.4	9.2	7.7

Source: Calculated from U.S. Arms Control and Disarmament Agency, *World Military Expenditures and Arms Transfers*, various years.

nologies. For instance, 1990 is the year that Taylor invaded Liberia, 1986 is the year Museveni toppled the government in Kampala, 1997 is the year Angola invaded Congo-Brazzaville, while 1994 is the year that the RFP invaded Rwanda. In other conflicts, it is more difficult to cite a precise time as the conflicts emerged slowly and only gradually built to a crescendo. For instance, the threat to both Sierra Leone and Guinea grew gradually during the 1990s as instability from Liberia spread westward. FRELIMO's war with RENAMO in Mozambique and UNITA's battle with the MPLA government in Angola also gradually became worse throughout the 1980s. Thus, while the ability (or failure) to mobilize is not as clear in countries where the war came gradually, it is still possible to judge if they were able to increase at least the size of their military in the face of a growing enemy threat.

It is notable that of the cases of failed mobilization, most of the wars had a distinctly civil nature, although, as in almost any civil war, there was a significant international element. Thus, when Congo-Brazzaville was invaded by Angola, Luanda was working in support of former President Denis Sassou-Nguesso, who had tried for years to destabilize his successor. Similarly, the wars in Liberia and Sierra Leone are domestic conflicts, albeit fed by outsiders. Somalia in the 1990s, Sudan, and Uganda are civil wars classically understood. The failure to mobilize is quite remarkable. For instance, Siad Barre's army in Somalia actually shrunk significantly as his country slid into civil war, while the authorities in Kampala were unable to increase their army at all in the endgame before Museveni took over. The invasions of Zaire during the Shaba crises of 1977 and 1978 and by Ugandan, Rwandan, and Angolan forces in support of Laurent Kabila in 1996 and 1997 are the clearest examples of a foreign invasion that was not met by significant mobilization.

The cases of successful mobilization are more clearly linked to external invasion, although some of the cases cannot be parsed cleanly. Somalia mobilized to take what it viewed as the Somali portion of Ethiopia in 1977–78, while Ethiopia mobilized slightly later to defend itself. Similarly, the Hutu authorities in Rwanda did mobilize in anticipation of the invasion by the RPF in 1994. Angola and Mozambique are more clearly civil wars, but both Maputo and Luanda had enemies (RENAMO and UNITA) that were directly tied to South Africa. They could thus legitimately claim during at least pleas for mobilization that they were under threat from foreign powers.

There is thus some preliminary evidence to suggest that even relatively short-term mobilization is affected by the type of conflict that Africa experiences. The more common type—civil wars that often result in the physical destruction of much of the country and massive displacement of the population—do not necessarily prompt the state to develop the capacities to expand even the size of the military. The mobilization data, such as they are, suggest that foreign threats do prompt mobilization by the state.

CONCLUSION

African countries face the luxury of escaping the brutal history of continual interstate war that so mars the barbaric European experience. This is a difference with Europe that should be celebrated. However, the problem of state building in times of peace or in the context of civil wars remains largely unexplored. It is not the case that African states cannot grow without the threat of international war. Rather, African states will have to find new ways of mobilizing the population through greater acceptance of taxation, nationalism, and, when facing an enemy, increasing the size of the army. There is no reason to believe that new paths of state consolidation cannot be developed by African leaders. They just need to be absolutely clear that the paradoxical ease of European state development—where the mere effort to insure the physical survival of the state also led to state consolidation—cannot be repeated and that they therefore face a harder task.

Part 3

STATE AUTONOMY

National Legislatures in Common Markets: Autonomy in the European Union and Mercosur

FRANCESCO DUINA

In all cases, whilst the government subsists, the *legislative is the supreme power*: for what can give laws to another, must needs be superior to him.
—John Locke, *Second Treatise of Government*

CLASSICAL AND contemporary scholars have described in great detail the multifaceted and intimate relationship between early capitalist economies and nation-states.[1] Despite their varying views on the nature of that relationship, most scholars have seen the nation-state as a stable and legitimate form of political organization during that period. The arrival of supranational economies, whether on a global or a regional scale, has spurred a heated debate about the continuing stability of nation-states. Numerous scholars have argued for an inevitable decline of the nation-state; others have posited an opposite, strengthening trend. In most cases, the evidence has concerned only some of the key facets of the relationship between supranational economies and nation-states.

This chapter expands our understanding of that relationship by examining the impact of common markets, the European Union (EU) and Mercosur in particular, on the autonomy of national legislatures. In line with the arguments of Rudra Sil and others in this volume, the findings paint a complex picture of change. The legal systems of common markets deprive national legislatures of control over numerous areas related to the trade of goods and, through time, some areas seemingly unrelated

---

[1] John A. Hall and John G. Ikenberry, *The State* (Milton Keynes: Open University Press, 1989); Michael Mann, *States, War, and Capitalism: Studies in Political Sociology* (Oxford: Basil Blackwell, 1988); Karl Marx, *A Contribution to the Critique of Political Economy* (New York: International Publishers, 1970); Charles Tilly, *Coercion, Capital, and European States, AD 990–1990* (Cambridge, MA: Basil Blackwell, 1990); Max Weber, *Economy and Society* (New York: Bedminster Press, 1968).

to the objectives of common markets, such as the environment. But, unpredictably, national legislatures retain significant control over numerous aspects of services, labor, and capital, despite the centrality of those areas to common markets. Moreover, they retain undisputed control over numerous other areas, such as culture and education. We notice, in addition, that the drivers of these observable trends, which include an internal logic of spillover but also the protectionist tendencies of member states in areas such as banking, are complex and often contradictory. Rather than necessitating the decommissioning of national legislatures, then, the arrival of common markets may be giving rise to an enduring division of labor between the supranational and national levels. In the conclusion, we contemplate whether such a change might entail, at the same time, a parallel strengthening of the national executive branch and other national functions.

EXISTING ANALYSES OF STATE AUTONOMY
IN SUPRANATIONAL ECONOMIES

Scholars have generally formulated polarized conclusions about the impact of supranational economies on the autonomy of nation-states. In most cases, as John Campbell notes in his contribution to this volume, only the most obvious facets of that relationship have come under consideration. Typically, attention has turned to the continuing ability of states (more specifically, though often not specified, of the executive and legislative branches) to engage freely in decision making activities (policy making for executives, law making for legislators) in very specific areas of economic life.

When thinking of the *global economy*, scholars have primarily focused on states and decision making with regard to exchange measures, multinational corporations, and macroeconomic problems such as unemployment, inflation, and subsidies. Those proposing the decline of nation-states have accordingly described how states no longer control exchange measures such as tariffs, exchange rates, and protectionist practices.[2] They have described how multinational corporations dictate what initiatives states should pursue.[3] And they have noted how most

---

[2] Gerald Epstein, "International Capital Mobility and the Scope for National Economic Management," in Robert Boyer and Daniel Drache, eds., *States against Markets* (London: Routledge, 1996), 211–24; Kenichi Ohmae, "The Rise of the Region State," *Foreign Affairs* (Spring 1993): 78–87; Vivien Schmidt, "The New World Order, Incorporated," *Daedalus* 124 (1995): 75–106; Jan Aart Scholte, "Global Capitalism and the State," *International Affairs* 73 (1997): 427–52.

[3] Stephen Gill and David Law, *The Global Political Economy: Perspectives, Problems*

states inevitably adopt neoliberal policies[4] when addressing domestic macroeconomic problems.[5]

Defenders of the nation-state have responded in kind. One such group has argued that most exchange measures in fact remain under the control of states.[6] A second group has forcefully argued for the increased role states play in shaping the activities of corporations and international trade organizations.[7] And a third group has argued that states remain free to adopt unique solutions to unemployment, inflation, and other related problems.[8]

Scholars considering the impact of *regional* and especially *common markets* on nation-states have also been polarized in their conclusions and selectively focused in their analyses. In their case, however, atten-

---

and Polices (New York: Harvester/Wheatsheaf, 1988); Matthew Horseman and Andrew Marshall, *After the Nation-State: Citizens, Tribalism and the New World Disorder* (London: HarperCollins, 1994); Susan Strange, "The Defective State," *Daedalus* 124 (1995): 55–74.

[4] John Meyer et al., "World Society and the Nation-State," *American Journal of Sociology* 103 (1997): 144–81; Wolfgang Wessels and Dietrich Rometsch, "German Administrative Interaction and European Union: The Fusion of Public Policies," in Yves Mény, Pierre Muller, and Jean-Louis Quermonne, eds., *Adjusting to Europe: The Impact of the European Union on National Institutions and Policies* (London: Routledge, 1996), 73–109.

[5] Andrea Boltho, "Has France Converged on Germany? Policies and Institutions since 1958," in Suzanne Berger and Ronald Dore, eds., *National Diversity and Global Capitalism* (Ithaca: Cornell University Press, 1996), 89–104; Hervez Dumez and Alain Jeunemaitre, "The Convergence of Competition Policies in Europe: Internal Dynamics and External Imposition," in Berger and Dore, eds., *National Diversity and Global Capitalism*, 216–38.

[6] Eric Helleiner, "Sovereignty, Territoriality, and the Globalization of Finance," in David A. Smith, Dorothy J. Solinger, and Steven C. Topik, eds., *States and Sovereignty in the Global Economy* (London: Routledge, 1999), 138–57; Paul Hirst, "The Global Economy: Myths and Realities," *International Affairs* 73 (1997): 409–25; Robert Wade, "Globalization and Its Limits: Reports of the Death of the National Economy Are Greatly Exaggerated," in Berger and Dore, eds., *National Diversity and Global Capitalism*, 60–88.

[7] Vincent Cable, "The Diminished Nation-State: A Study in the Loss of Economic Power," *Daedalus* 124 (1995): 23–53; Eli Lauterpacht, "Sovereignty: Myth or Reality," *International Affairs* 73 (1997): 137–50; Saskia Sassen, "Embedding the Global in the National: Implications for the Role of the State," in Smith, Solinger, and Topik, eds., *States and Sovereignty in the Global Economy*, 158–71; Linda Weiss, "Globalization and the Myth of the Powerless State," *New Left Review* 24 (1997): 3–27.

[8] Robert Boyer, "State and Market: A New Engagement for the Twenty-first Century," in Boyer and Drache, eds., *States against Markets*, 84–114; Ramesh Mishra, "The Welfare of Nations," in Boyer and Drache, eds., *States against Markets*, 316–33; Vivien Schmidt, "Convergent Pressures, Divergent Responses: France, Great Britain, and Germany between Globalization and Europeanization," in Smith, Solinger, and Topik, eds., *States and Sovereignty in the Global Economy*, 172–92.

tion has turned mostly to the ability of national executives (and not legislators) to engage freely in decision making in international forums devoted almost exclusively to trade. Those espousing a decline in state control have hence argued, from neoinstitutionalist and functionalist perspectives, that the supranational processes, rules, and structures of those forums have pushed states into accepting undesired international agreements.[9] Those arguing otherwise — rational-choice theorists and intergovernmentalists — have instead argued that national preferences are reflected in those agreements.[10]

A smaller set of scholars of regional and common markets has recently turned away from executive and legislative decision making in selected areas and has generated more ambivalent conclusions about the autonomy of nation-states. The works of Burley and Mattli[11] and Guibernau,[12] with their respective focus on judges' autonomy and regional decentralization, are important examples of partial judicial and institutional transformations affecting nation-states. In the same spirit, Mény et al.[13] observe a partial "fusion" of national governmental structures as they cooperate in their effort to implement EU legislation. Mair and Falkner[14] in turn note changes in national party systems, linkages between political representatives and private-sector players, and others spheres of the political system.

These works tend to offer sophisticated assessments of state autonomy. Still, they do not concern themselves with the impact of suprana-

---

[9] Ernst B. Haas, "International Integration: The European and the Universal Process," *International Organization* 15 (1961): 366–92; Paul Pierson and Stephan Leibfried, eds., *European Social Policy: Between Fragmentation and Integration* (Washington, DC: The Brookings Institution, 1995); George Ross, *Jacque Delors and European Integration* (New York: Oxford University Press, 1995); Anne-Marie Slaughter, "The Real New World Order," *Foreign Affairs* 76 (1997): 183–97.

[10] Geoffrey Garrett, "The Politics of Maastricht," *Economics and Politics* 5 (1993): 105–24; Alan Milward, *The European Rescue of the Nation-State* (London: Routledge, 1992); Andrew Moravscik, "Preferences and Power in the European Community: A Liberal Intergovernmentalist Approach," *Journal of Common Market Studies* 31 (1993): 473–524.

[11] Anne-Marie Burley and Walter Mattli, "Europe before the Court: A Political Theory of Legal Integration," *International Organization* 47 (1993): 41–76.

[12] Montserrat Guibernau, *Nations without States: Political Communities in a Global Age* (Cambridge: Polity Press, 1999).

[13] Yves Mény, Pierre Muller, and Jean-Louis Quermonne, eds., *Adjusting to Europe: The Impact of the European Union on National Institutions and Policies* (London: Routledge, 1996).

[14] Peter Mair, "The Limited Impact of Europenon National Party Systems," *West European Politics* 23 (2000): 27–51; Gerda Falkner, "Public-Private Networks in a Multi-Level System: Convergence Towards Moderate Diversity," *West European Politics* 23 (2000): 95–120.

tional economies on the decision making autonomy of national legislators in all areas of social life.[15] Yet such an analysis seems warranted. Legislatures have been at the heart of the nation-state for centuries. As Weber himself argued, legislatures have had the fundamental task of regulating the relationships between civic society and public authority, and between elements of civic society.[16] Locke, in his *Second Treatise of Government*, thought of the legislature as *"the soul that gives form, life, and unity*, to the common-wealth."[17] Generations of writers thereafter echoed his sentiments.[18]

Common to all traditional characterizations of the legislature has been its freedom from both other branches of government, such as the judiciary or executive, and nonstate forces, such as supranational organizations. In the words of Locke, "in all cases, whilst the government subsists, the *legislative is the supreme power*: for what can give laws to another, must needs be superior to him."[19] Such freedom, moreover, has always been interpreted as crucial to modern, democratic states. It has been ensured through two venues. First, as pluralists and liberal theorists have emphasized, elected representatives have owed their positions to the populace (or some of its segments) rather than members of the executive or judiciary.[20] Second, as statists and institutionalists have argued, the domestic legal structures and institutional arrangements that legislators inhabit have themselves been largely insulated from external factors.[21]

Common markets risk, in principle, making the historical autonomy

[15] A few works on the overall autonomy of national legislatures exist. However, they focus exclusively on the EU and tend to assume, rather than analyze, the notion that legislatures have lost much power to supranational decision-making bodies in order to discuss ways to compensate for such a loss. See Tapio Raunio, "Always One Step Behind? National Legislatures and the European Union," *Government and Opposition* 34 (Spring 1999): 180–202; Tapio Raunio and Simon Hix, "Backbenchers Learn to Fight Back: European Integration and Parliamentary Government," *West European Politics* 32 (2000): 142–68; Vivian A. Schmidt, "European 'Federalism' and its Encroachments on National Institutions," *Publius: The Journal of Federalism* 29 (Winter 1999): 19–44.

[16] Weber, *Economy and Society*, vol. 2, chap. 9; vol 3, chaps. 10–13; Theda Skocpol, "Bringing the State Back In: Strategies of Analysis in Current Research," in Peter B. Evans, Dietrich Rueschemeyer, and Theda Skocpol, eds., *Bringing the State Back In* (Cambridge: Cambridge University Press, 1985), 3–37.

[17] John Locke, *Second Treatise of Government* (Indianapolis: Hackett, 1980), 107–8.

[18] Lauterpacht, "Sovereignty: Myth or Reality," 138.

[19] Locke, *Second Treatise of Government*, 78.

[20] Robert A. Dahl, *Dilemmas of Pluralist Democracy: Autonomy versus Control* (New Haven: Yale University Press, 1982); Moravcisk, "Preferences and Power."

[21] Skocpol, "Bringing the State Back In"; Sven Steinmo, *Taxation and Democracy: Swedish, British, and American Approaches to Financing the Modern State* (New Haven: Yale University Press, 1993).

of national legislatures a thing of the past. These markets require that the four basic elements of any economy—goods, labor, services, and capital—circulate free from tariff and nontariff barriers. They also impose a Common External Tariff (CET): a single tariff barrier vis-à-vis the outside world preventing any one participant from having special access to external resources. To realize these objectives, common market officials promulgate obligatory laws intended for faithful adoption into national legal systems. These laws, as Mercosur's constitution and the European Court of Justice have made clear, supercede any competing national law:

> The Common Market Council will promulgate Decisions, whose adoption will be obligatory for the Member States. . . . The Common Market Group will promulgate Resolutions, whose adoption will be obligatory for the Member States. . . . the Member States agree to undertake any measure necessary to ensure, in their respective countries, the realization of Mercosur norms. (Articles 9, 15, and 38 of the Protocol of Ouro Preto of 1995)

> By contrast with ordinary international treaties, the EEC Treaty has created its own legal system which, on the entry into force of the treaty, became an integral part of the legal systems of the member states and which their courts are bound to apply. . . . the executive force of Community law cannot vary from one state to another in deference to subsequent laws. (Case 6/64, *Costa vs. ENEL*, [1964] ECR 1141)[22]

National legislatures do not participate in any of the steps required for the production of these laws. Sets of appointed national representatives belonging to the executive branches of their governments or outright members of supranational bodies, such as the European Commission, control the process instead.[23] Pushed outside of the deliberative space in which common market laws are formulated, domestic legislators have had to accept passively the resulting principles and play an administrative or executive role for transposition and application. That the principles of common market laws may coincide with national interests (and thus strengthen states in certain ways) of course in no way renders the bypassing of the national legislature any less real. The transformation of national legislatures into obsolete or simply executive entities, and their

[22] R. H. Folsom, R. B. Lake, and V. P. Nanda, *European Union Law after Maastricht: A Practical Guide for Lawyers Outside the Common Market* (The Hague: Kluwer Law International, 1996), 23–26.

[23] All EU national legislatures have established European Affairs Committees. In most countries, these only advise national executives on how to vote on EU law. Denmark is the only country where the committee enjoys, and systematically exercises, the right to instruct national executives. Recent changes to the EU treaties have increased information exchanges between national legislatures and EU institutions without, however, granting legislatures more power.

de facto *abdication* of legislative power to representatives of the executive branch working at the supranational level or to outright supranational actors, are bound to happen even when national interests are served.

Yet loss of autonomy by national legislatures has not been pervasive. Such a situation would have occurred only in cases where common markets produced laws so comprehensive and powerful that they would replace national authority in every area. We know, from any cursory review of these laws, that this has not happened. But we know little about the changes that have occurred.

MEASURING THE AUTONOMY OF NATIONAL LEGISLATURES IN COMMON MARKETS

We may state that national legislatures lose most autonomy in those legislative arenas where common market law has intruded the most. In those arenas, the presence of common market law has made national legislative actors and institutions irrelevant, except perhaps for executive purposes. Legislative arenas represent distinct spheres of social actions or the world, such as the environment or industrial production, which are subject to regulation. Arenas can be broken down into legislative "fields" to gain additional specificity.

We can identify approximately 25 major arenas comprising 106 fields representing all areas of traditional national legislative activity.[24] Table 7.1 identifies the arenas and the associated fields. Legislative intrusion refers to the presence of common market law in any one of these fields. Intrusion varies in intensity. It is precisely such variation that we are interested in measuring. Intensity levels may be said to vary across fields as a function of coverage and depth.

Coverage concerns the volume of affected parties, activities, or processes that, out of the total potential volume in a given field, is being targeted by common market laws: Of all parties, activities, or processes belonging to this field, what proportion is being targeted by common market law? To arrive at an understanding of the coverage of a field, each law affecting a given field can be measured in terms of its breadth: specific, broad, or comprehensive. Specific laws target very few of all

---

[24] This is meant to be a comprehensive list of fields and arenas; it is thus based upon, but goes beyond, the list that officials from the EU adopt when classifying existing EU legislation and that scholars rely upon when examining existing common market legislation only; see, for example, Neil Fligstein and Jason McNichol, "The Institutional Terrain of the European Union," in Wayne Sandholtz and Alec Stone Sweet, eds., *European Integration and Supranational Governance* (Oxford: Oxford University Press, 1998), 59–91.

TABLE 7.1

Identification of Legislative Arenas and Fields Historically Controlled by
Nation-States

1. Customs	2. Agriculture	3. Fisheries
A. Classification	A. Definitions	A. Classification
B. Tariffs	B. Production procedures	B. Catching restrictions
C. Nontariffs	C. Subsidies	C. Processing restrictions
D. Border inspection procedures	D. Third-country trade	D. Subsidies
	E. Trade	E. Third-country trade

6. Transportation	7. Competition	8. Taxation
A. Air (infrastructure, safety, procedures)	A. Aid	A. Direct (personal, organizational)
B. Water (ibid.)	B. Private unfair practices (monopolies, dumping, price fixing, etc.)	B. Indirect (personal, organizational)
C. Land (ibid.)	C. Public unfair practices (ibid.)	
D. General	D. Public enterprises	

11. External Relations	12. Energy	13. Industrial Policy
A. International representation	A. Coal (production, aid, prices)	A. Classification
B. Development aid	B. Electricity	B. Manufacturing standards
C. International agreements	C. Nuclear	C. Sectoral intervention
	D. Oil & gas	D. Cooperation
	E. Other sources	

16. Consumers	17. Public Health	18. Science, R&D, Information
A. Health & safety	A. Protective measures	A. Focus
B. Information	B. Intervention measures	B. Funding
C. Economic protection	C. Rights	C. Standards
D. Rights	D. Medical standards	D. Statistics
		E. Registration of products

21. Undertakings	22. Security Policy	23. Justice/Home Affairs
A. Company law	A. Military	A. Civil code
B. Intellectual property	B. Crime & prosecution	B. Penal code
C. Economic & commercial law		C. Court jurisdiction
		D. Legal rights of individuals
		E. Contracts

Note: There are 25 arenas and 106 fields.

4. Labor & Social Policy	5. Services
A. Workers' rights (incl. movement)	A. Classification
B. Pensions	B. Barriers
C. Unemployment	C. Internal & client procedures
D. Migration	D. State guarantees
E. Children & disabled	E. Public contracts
F. Housing	

9. Monetary Policy	10. Capital Movement
A. Freedom of intervention	A. Tariffs
B. Exchange rates	B. Security
C. Accounting methods	C. Stock markets
D. Bank operations	D. International investments
E. Main instruments	E. Other (real estate, assets, start-ups, etc.)

14. Regional Policy	15. Environment
A. Regional rights & responsibilities	A. Air (pollution, protection)
B. Subsidies	B. Water (ibid.)
	C. Land (ibid.)
	D. Animals
	E. Forests
	F. General

19. Education	20. Culture
A. Primary & middle education	A. Funding
B. Minimum age	B. Program content
C. Higher education	C. Museums
D. Special programs	
E. Safety	
F. Professional degrees	

24. Political System	25. Civic Life
A. Constitution	A. Association
B. Party structure	B. Religion
C. Administrative practices & structure	C. Property rights
	D. Citizenship
	E. People movement
	F. Women's rights

the potential targets; broad laws target a sizable amount of potential targets, though they are short of covering the majority; comprehensive laws target the majority of, if not all, targets. Together, the total number of laws targeting a field and the breadth of each law provide us with a good, though surely somewhat imprecise, understanding of the coverage of common market law of any given field. We can then state that overall wide coverage of a field occurs when more than 50 percent of possible targets seem addressed, while overall narrow coverage occurs when less than 50 percent of all targets seem to be addressed by common market law. We then need to turn to depth to understand fully the intensity level with which said laws reach into each field.

Depth refers to the level of control being exerted in a given field over the targeted parties, activities, and processes: Does common market law rely primarily on the principle of mutual recognition (i.e., states must accept each other's regulatory frameworks), or does it assert genuine regulatory requirements of its own? Again, we turn to individual laws and consider three levels of depth, given their target: mostly recognition-related (for example, a law on dark chocolate asking member states to accept each other's definitions of essential ingredients), partly recognition-related and partly regulatory (for example, a law on the training of doctors specifying the content of courses on internal medicine but asking that member states recognize as valid each other's courses on dermatology), and mostly regulatory (for example, a law on corporate taxation defining all different taxation levels). We then consider all laws in a field and state that a field is subject to deep regulation when the majority of affected targets seem subject to regulatory principles. A field is subject to shallow regulation when the majority of affected targets are subject to mutual recognition principles.[25] As with coverage, we recognize the inevitably imprecise nature of the approach.

We will thus notice four types of possible intrusion in any given field (see fig. 7.1). Heaviest intrusion will occur where wide coverage and deep regulation are observable. Selective intrusion occurs as a result of narrow coverage but deep regulation. Nominal intrusion occurs in cases of wide coverage but shallow regulation. No intrusion occurs when coverage is narrow and regulation shallow, and nation-states retain most, if not all, of their legislative autonomy.[26] Secondary works interpreting the legal texts will serve to substantiate the findings of the analysis.

[25] For a potentially alternative method of measuring intensity, see Neil Fligstein and Iona Mara-Drita, "How to Make a Market: Reflections on the Attempt to Create a Single Market in the European Union," *American Journal of Sociology* 102 (July 1996): 1–33.

[26] Throughout, we must of course remember that the absolute size of a field varies. Similarly, we must also recall that the importance of fields for the nation-state varies as well.

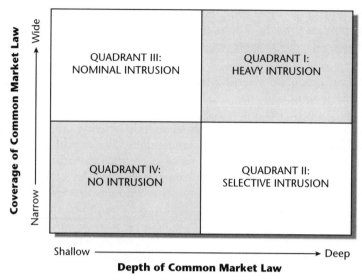

Figure 7.1. Possible intrusion levels in a given legislative field

The resulting analysis can be augmented by a study of the chronological order of intrusion. A sense of the timing of the targeting of different fields may provide us with hints about future trends and, at a more fundamental level, the overall logic driving common market law.

HYPOTHESES ON LEGISLATIVE INTRUSION

With insights from existing works on supranational economies and the nation-state, we can generate initial hypotheses about the nature (intensity and chronological order) of legislative intrusion in common markets. Below are four hypotheses, ranging from full decline of national legislative autonomy to full retention.

According to the first hypothesis, we should witness an irreversible and thorough takeover of the activities of national legislatures on the part of common markets. All fields most intimately related to free trade and a common external tariff are probably targeted first, but heavy intrusion soon expands to all remaining fields as the initial objectives of the project require, for their fulfillment, the realization of other objectives. The hypothesis states:

Hypothesis 1: Common markets begin with wide and deep legislation in strictly economic fields related to the trade of goods, services, labor, and

capital but, after some time, expand their activities into other, apparently unrelated, fields. The national legislature experiences a gradual, continuous decline in most fields.

We can articulate a second, more moderate, hypothesis that begins with the assumption that common markets are by nature economic projects. As such, heavy intrusion may be expected to concern primarily legislative fields directly related to economic activity: trade, industrial production, movement of goods, and others. We should thus witness the heavy targeting of economic fields over time, though this may decrease in intensity as the work nears completion. All other fields are subject to milder forms of intrusion. The hypothesis states:

Hypothesis 2: Common markets begin and essentially end with wide and deep legislative activity strictly in fields concerned with the trade of goods, services, labor, and capital. The national legislature experiences a gradual and continuous decline in those fields only.

The third, also moderate, hypothesis recognizes heavy and even selective intrusion in certain, unpredictable fields. The chronological order of such targeting is unclear. A variety of plausible causes could drive such a pattern, such as nation-states' reactions, spillover, supranational leadership, pressure from interest groups, international events, economic and political crises, poor planning, or misguided beliefs. The hypothesis states:

Hypothesis 3: Common markets produce wide and deep, or narrow and deep, legislation in fields not necessarily related to the trade of goods, capital, labor, and services. The pattern is unpredictable. There seems to be no chronological order to intrusion.

The fourth hypothesis predicts nominal or no legislative intrusion in all fields. There would be, accordingly, little chronological order to notice. The hypothesis states:

Hypothesis 4: Common markets produce little, if any, legislative output that intrudes with national legislatures. Common market law addresses only a very few fields and imposes mutual recognition. The national legislature remains essentially in control. There will be no observable order of legislative intrusion.

The next section turns to the European Union and Mercosur to investigate empirically the nature of common market law and, thus, the continuing relevance of national legislatures.

EMPIRICAL FINDINGS: THE EUROPEAN UNION AND MERCOSUR

The European Union and Mercosur, even despite Argentina's recent crisis, are the two most successful common markets in existence.[27] They are, at the same time, remarkably different in terms of geographic location, length of existence, number of participants, and levels of development. As such, they represent excellent case studies for the unveiling of any general feature of common market law and for generating conclusions about the autonomy of legislatures in common markets.

The European common market began with the formation of the European Coal and Steel Community (ECSC) among France, Germany, Italy, Belgium, Luxembourg, and the Netherlands in 1951. In 1957 the same states signed the two Treaties of Rome establishing the European Economic Community (EEC) (and hence formally asserting the goal of creating a common market) and the European Atomic Energy Community (Euratom). The three treaties together gave birth to the European Community (EC). Denmark, Ireland, and the United Kingdom joined the EC in 1973; Greece, in 1981; Portugal and Spain, in 1986; and Sweden, Austria, and Finland in 1995. Additional treaties have over time expanded the original mandates of the EC. In the most important treaty since inception — the 1992 Treaty on European Union (or Maastricht Treaty) — the European Community renamed itself as the European Union.[28] Today, the EU includes three broad "pillars" or areas of activity: the common market itself, Common Foreign and Security Policy (CFSP), and Cooperation in Justice and Home Affairs (CJHA).

The European Union has depended on *directives* and *regulations* as the main tools for attaining its common market objectives. Directives, generally espousing important and wide-reaching principles, have required transposition and application.[29] Regulations, typically more subject-specific in their scope, have merely required application.[30] The

---

[27] Scholars and journalists alike have for some time admired Mercosur's ability to withstand crisis. For a discussion on Mercosur's survival of Brazil's currency devaluation of 1999, see Nicola Phillips, "Regionalist Governance in the New Political Economy of Development: 'Relaunching' the Mercosur," *Third World Quarterly* 22 (2001): 565–83.

[28] For a history of the EU, see Desmond Dinan, *Ever Closer Union: An Introduction to European Integration* (Boulder: Lynne Rienner Publishers, 1999); John Pinder, *The European Union: A Very Short Introduction* (Oxford: Oxford University Press, 2001).

[29] The CFSP and the CJHA rely on intergovernmental agreements. See article 249 of the Treaty of the European Community.

[30] The EU has also utilized *decisions* to achieve its goals. These, however, are in effect administrative rather than legislative acts (e.g., the decision to initiate a pilot program) and are thus not considered here.

Commission, a supranational institution composed of twenty appointed commissioners, has been the primary formulator and overseer of the implementation of EU directives. The European Court of Justice, also a supranational institution composed of fifteen appointed judges, has been the primary interpreter and enforcer of EU law.[31] The Council of Ministers, an intergovernmental institution composed of national ministers, has had the role of approving legislative proposals. The European Parliament, a supranational institution of directly elected members, has increasingly played a role in the approval process of legislative proposals.

Mercosur resembles the EU in its reliance on foundational treaties and protocols for its design and objectives, and institutions and laws to attain those objectives. The Treaty of Asunción of March 26, 1991, gave birth to Mercosur, with Brazil, Argentina, Uruguay, and Paraguay as its members. It envisioned that by December 31, 1994, a free trade area for labor, services, goods, and capital would be established. After this period, a common external tariff would be specified. The linear and automatic tariff reduction for intra-area trade of goods did occur more or less according to schedule and was partly responsible for an increase in intra-area trade from U.S. $4 billion in 1990 to U.S. $17 billion in 1996. Various political and economic shocks, such as Brazil's currency devaluation in 1999 and Argentina's economic crisis of late 2001 and 2002, have so far challenged, but not undermined, Mercosur's stability. Intra-area trade, which reached a high of 19 percent of all member states' exports in 1994, still accounted for 18 percent of all member states' exports in 2001 (up from 12 percent in 1991).

The protocol of Ouro Preto of January 1, 1995, set out to define Mercosur's institutional structure. The protocol establishes only intergovernmental institutions operating on a consensual basis. The Common Market Council (CMC), composed of the ministers of foreign affairs and finance and the heads of state, is in charge of overall leadership and direction and enacts *decisions*. Like EU directives, these tend to be more abstract and principled than other common market legislation and are to be transposed into national law (article 40, Protocol of Ouro Preto). The Common Market Group (CMG) is composed of four permanent members, the ministries of foreign affairs and the economy, and national central bankers. As the main executive body, its function is

---

[31] Burley and Mattli, "Europe before the Court," 41–76; Rachel A. Cichowski, "Integrating the Environment: The European Court and the Construction of Supranational Policy," *Journal of European Public Policy* 5 (1998): 387–405; Francis Snyder, "The Effectiveness of European Community Law: Institutions, Processes, Tools and Techniques," *The Modern Law Review* 56 (1993): 19–54.

to ensure that the larger principles of the CMC's decisions are practically achieved. To do so, the CMG enacts *resolutions*, intended for incorporation into national law as well.[32] Mercosur's Trade Commission (MTC) aids the CMG in the areas of the trade of goods and customs operations. The Joint Parliamentary Commission is composed of representatives from national legislatures, and its task is to ensure proper acceptance of Mercosur law into national legal systems.

For the purposes of this study, I coded almost two thousand individual laws along the two critical dimensions — breadth and depth — for the period between 1958 and 2000, with Mercosur beginning in 1991. The EU accounts for over thirteen hundred directives and regulations, while Mercosur accounts for over six hundred decisions and resolutions. Laws not coded were repetitions, amendments, and laws in fields already deemed to be under high intrusion.[33] Laws affecting more than one field were coded as such. I relied on the analysis of secondary works on legislation in the EU and Mercosur to corroborate the results of the coding.

The Targets and Intensity of Supranational Intrusion

The following tables report the results from the coding.[34] Let us consider Mercosur first. Table 7.2 identifies the fields that have experienced the most serious intrusion. Heaviest intrusion occurs in fields that we may consider directly related to the trade of goods. Tariffs for goods (1B), agricultural definitions and procedures (2A-B), and industrial classifications and standards (13A-B) have all experienced the production of wide-reaching law rich with regulatory requirements. As Hargain, Duran Martinez, and other legal scholars already noted a few years ago, we can now find definitions in Mercosur for a great number of fruits, vegetables, and industrial products and processes.[35] Resolution 74/93 thus specifies the essential characteristics of onions, resolution 83/93

---

[32] Both decisions and resolutions become effective in Mercosur thirty days after the last member state announces the adoption of the law in question (article 40, Protocol of Ouro Preto).

[33] The number of EU and Mercosur laws coded would otherwise be significantly higher. Note that the data was initially collected for a comparative study of the content of EU and Mercosur law. See Francesco Duina, "Important but Not Pervasive: The Shared Limits of Secondary Law in the Common Markets of Europe and South America," *Current Politics and Economics of Europe* 10 (2001): 351–79.

[34] Coding data are available upon request.

[35] Daniel Hargain, *Circulación de Bienes en el Mercosur* (Buenos Aires: B de F., 1999; Augusto Duran Martinez, *Estudios Juridico a Propósito de Mercosur* (Montevideo: Ingranusi, 1999).

TABLE 7.2
Mercosur — Legislative Fields under Heavy Intrusion

Quadrant I: Wide and Deep Mercosur Legislation

- Customs: tariffs (1B)
- Agriculture: definitions, production procedures (2A-B)
- Industrial Policy: classification, manufacturing standards (13A-B)
- Consumers: health & safety, information (16A-B)

categorizes different types of food additives, resolution 54/92 lays out detailed toy safety requirements, and resolution 18/00 specifies the technical prerequisites of clinical thermometers.

The two remaining fields address consumer rights. These are still related, though perhaps not directly, to the trade of goods. Mercosur has major laws consumer health and safety (16A) and consumer information (16B).[36] Resolutions 123/96, 124/96, 125/96, and 127/96 provide the architecture for a consumer's bill of rights. More specific laws, such as resolution 66/93 on vegetable quarantines, impose modalities and definitions for specific products. Note, therefore, that heavy intrusion does not involve three of the four areas central to common markets: services, capital, and labor.

Essentially all fields in which Mercosur has selectively intervened are related to the trade of goods (see table 7.3). Three fields may be considered directly related: custom classification of goods (1A) and external relations in the form of international representation and agreements for the purposes of trade (11A, 11C). With decision 23/97 and resolution 32/93, for instance, Mercosur begins trade cooperation with the EU. Other laws give Mercosur representation power with Canada, Bolivia, Chile, and other South American countries.

Most of the remaining fields seem indirectly related to the trade of goods. The transportation of goods (6A-C); the environment, specifically with regard to air (15A) and thus the polluting activities of manufacturers; unfair competitive practices (7B, 7C); and science-R&D-information standards, statistics, and product registration (18C, 18D, 18E) are targeted. In the case of pollution, Mercosur has so far concentrated on the automotive and oil and gas industries, asking manufacturers to ensure that products do not pollute beyond certain limits and that combustibles comply with certain chemical properties. Resolution 36/94 specifies, for these purposes, acceptable combustibles. Decision 11/97 in turn regulates the dumping of goods. Again, we notice no serious pres-

[36] Roberto Dromi, *Código del Mercosur* (Buenos Aires: Ediciónes Ciudad Argentina, 1996), 180–81.

TABLE 7.3

Mercosur — Legislative Fields under Selective Intrusion

Quadrant II: Narrow but Deep Mercosur Legislation

- Customs: classification (1A)
- Labor Movement & Social Policy: workers' rights (4A)
- Transportation: air, water, land
  (6A-C)
- Competition: private unfair practices, public unfair practices (7B-C)
- External Relations: international representation, international agreements
  (11A, 11C)
- Environment: air (15A)
- Public Health: protective measures (17A)
- Science, R&D, Information: standards, statistics, registration of products
  (18C-E)
- Undertakings: economic & commercial law (21C)
- Political System: administrative practices and structure (24C)

---

ence in fields related to services, capital, or labor, except for workers' rights (4A), where Mercosur does define some social security rights (health care above all, with decision 19/97) of workers residing outside their home country. Interestingly, though, we note intervention in matters related to public health, an arena removed from commerce, to set protective measures (17A) in airport and at borders in order to prevent the spread of diseases (resolution 27/00).

With table 7.4 we enter the area of nominal intrusion: laws that barely affect national norms by simply accepting the validity of foreign objects, processes, degrees, and so forth. Here capital and labor make an appearance. International investments in fact receive some attention (10D), as do people movement (25E) and higher education degrees (19C). Decisions 7/95 and 8/96, for instance, ask for the recognition, rather than for the harmonization, of numerous types of higher education degrees, making labor movement a little more of a reality. The remaining fields address a mixture of topics: the penal code (23B), public health intervention measures (17B), certain forms of industrial intervention and cooperation (13C, 13D) and consumer protection and rights (16C, 16D).

Table 7.5 includes the majority of fields. All aspects of services (5) remain untouched.[37] Decision 13/97 merely reiterates Mercosur's intention of having a free market for services. Most aspects of capital are

---

[37] The coding thus confirms existing observations by specialists in this area. See Eva Holz, *La Integración de los Sistemas Bancarios* (Montevideo: Fundación de Cultura Universitaria, 1997), 25–26.

TABLE 7.4
Mercosur — Legislative Fields under Nominal Intrusion

Quadrant III: Wide but Shallow Mercosur Legislation

- Customs: border inspection procedures (1D)
- Capital: international investments (10D)
- Industrial Policy: sectoral intervention, cooperation (13C-D)
- Consumer: economic protection, rights (16C-D)
- Public Health: intervention measures (17B)
- Education: higher education (19C)
- Justice, Home Affairs: penal code (23B)
- Civic Life: people movement (25E)

unaffected.[38] Labor, and with it social policy, is unaffected when it comes to most categories (4B-F).[39] The same may be said of fiscal (8), civic (25A-D, F), and political (24A-B) matters.[40]

We may synthesize our findings by stating that Mercosur has heavily or selectively intruded in fields directly related and indirectly related to the trade of goods. Fields related to labor and capital have been mildly targeted or simply ignored. Services and social, cultural, political, and defense matters have been the least targeted.

Let us now turn to the European Union. Tables 7.6–7.9 show the intensity of EU law in different fields. As was the case with Mercosur, many of the fields experiencing heavy legislative intrusion (table 7.6) can be considered directly related to the trade of goods. These include customs (1), product classification and manufacturing standards (13A-B), agriculture (2), production procedures for fisheries (3C), and political representation in the form of international trade agreements (11C). Michael Mann observed this concentration of EU legislation around the trade of goods a few years ago: "The content of European law, especially of the secondary law, overwhelmingly concerns the EEC's two original purposes: trade liberalization and production integration and standardization. It regulates in great detail the *nature* of commodities bought and sold in the Community."[41] A great number of industrial products and procedures, consumer products, agricultural procedures,

[38] One exception could be resolution 53/20 on minimal steps banks must take to prevent money laundering (field 10B).

[39] Maria Carmen Ferreíra and Julio Ramos Olivera, *Las Relaciones Laborales en el Mercosur* (Montevideo: Fundación de Cultura Universitaria, 1997).

[40] The coding confirms Dromi's observations from a few years ago. See Dromi, *Código del Mercosur*, 185.

[41] Michael Mann, "Nation-States in Europe and Other Continents: Diversifying, Developing, Not Dying," *Daedalus* 122 (1993): 115–39.

TABLE 7.5
Mercosur — Legislative Fields under No Intrusion

Quadrant IV: Narrow and Shallow Mercosur Legislation

- Customs: nontariff barriers (1C)
- Agriculture: subsidies, third-country trade, trade (2C-E)
- Fisheries: all (3)
- Labor & Social Policy: pensions, unemployment, migration, children/disabled, housing (4B-F)
- Services: all (5)
- Transportation: general (6D)
- Competition: aid, public enterprises (7A, 7D)
- Taxation: all (8)
- Monetary Policy: all (9)
- Capital Movement: tariffs, security, stock markets, other (10A-C, 10E)
- External Relations: development aid (11B)
- Energy: all (12)
- Regional Policy: all (14)
- Environment: water, land, animals, forests, general (15B-F)
- Public Health: rights, medical standards (17C-D)
- Science, R&D, Information: focus, funding (18A-B)
- Education: primary & middle, minimum age, special programs, safety, professional degrees (19A-B, 19D-F)
- Culture: all (20)
- Undertakings: company law, intellectual property (21A, B)
- Security Policy: all (22)
- Justice, Home Affairs: civil code, legal rights of individuals, court jurisdiction, contracts (23A, 23C-E)
- Political System: constitution, party structure (24A-B)
- Civic Life: association, religion, property rights, citizenship, women's rights (25A-D, 25F)

---

vegetables, and fruits are thoroughly regulated. Thus, directive 2001/110 and regulation 136/66 set stringent labeling and ingredient requirements for honey and olive oil, respectively.

The majority of the remaining fields deal indirectly with the trade of goods. We see legislation on science-R&D-information statistics (18D), land transportation (6C), the environment (15A-B), and consumer health & safety and information (16A-B). Thus, with directive 2000/29, for example, the EU establishes measures to protect plants from harmful organisms in order to increase yields and agricultural productivity, and with directive 70/220 emission requirements for motor vehicles are set.

Differently from Mercosur, however, we also notice heavy legislation

TABLE 7.6
EU — Legislative Fields under Heavy Intrusion

Quadrant I: Wide and Deep EU Legislation

- Customs: all (1)
- Agriculture: all (2)
- Fisheries: processing restrictions (3C)
- Labor & Social Policy: workers' rights, migration (4A,4D)
- Services: barriers (5B)
- Transportation: land (6C)
- Competition: private unfair practices, public unfair practices (7B-C)
- Monetary Policy: intervention, exchange rates, instruments (9A-B, 9E)
- External Relations: international agreements (11C)
- Industrial Policy: classification, manufacturing standards (13A-B)
- Environment: air, water (15A-B)
- Consumers: health & safety, information (16A-B)
- Public Health: protective measures (17A)
- Science & R&D: statistics (18D)
- Undertakings: company law, intellectual property (21A-B)
- Civic Life: people movement (25E)

in the area of labor, especially workers' rights (4A) and migration (4D). Directive 92/85 on the safety and health rights of pregnant workers, and a number of directives and regulations (such as regulation 1408/71) granting migrant workers with jobs the right to enjoy social security benefits, are good examples.[42] Again differently from Mercosur, we note the removal of formal barriers for services (5B) and, related to services, substantial principles around intellectual property (21B). The remaining fields include monetary policy — especially in the areas of intervention (9A), exchange rates (9B), and various instruments such as interest rates (9E). Regulation 1467/97, for example, specifies the meaning and acceptability of excessive budget deficits, while regulation 1466/97 reiterates the convergence criteria for monetary union.[43] Capital is by contrast not heavily regulated at the EU level. We do notice, in the realm of company law (21A), some principles on minimum capital requirements for investment firms (directive 96/3). But such laws are the exception rather than the norm.

[42] See Nicole Busby, "Division of Labour: Maternity Rights Protection in Europe," *Journal of Social Welfare and Family Law* 22 (2000): 277–94.

[43] Principles found in treaties and agreements also specify terms of supranational intrusion in monetary policy. My approach may thus not capture the full degree of lost autonomy by national legislatures.

TABLE 7.7

EU—Legislative Fields under Selective Intrusion

Quadrant II: Narrow but Deep EU Legislation

- Fishing: catching restrictions and subsidies (3B, 3D)
- Services: classification (5A)
- Transportation: air, water, general (6A-B, 6D)
- Competition: aid, public enterprises (7A, 7D)
- Taxation: indirect (8B)
- Monetary: bank operations (9D)
- Capital Movement: tariffs, stock markets (10A, 10C)
- External Relations: international representation (11A)
- Industrial Policy: sectoral intervention, cooperation (13C-D)
- Environment: animals, forests (15D-E)
- Consumers: economic protection, rights (16C-D)
- Public Health: intervention measures (17B)
- Science & R&D: standards, registration of products (18C, 18E)
- Education: higher education, professional degrees (19C, 19F)
- Undertakings: economic and commercial law (21C)
- Justice, Home Affairs: penal code, legal rights of individuals (23B, 23D)
- Civic Life: women's rights (25F)

Table 7.7 includes a large number of fields indirectly related to the trade of goods: air and water transportation (6A-B), consumer protection (16C), certain rights of individuals purchasing consumer products (16D), science and R&D standards (18C), and product registration (18E). Hence, with the important directive 99/44, for example, the EU grants guarantees and warranties to consumers.[44] Again differently from Mercosur, we do observe an effort to classify some services (5A). In the areas of labor, we see a parallel effort at standardizing the preparation of a few higher education and professional degrees (19C, 19F). Directives 84/253 and 80/155, setting standards for certificates for accountants and midwives, respectively, offer good examples. Capital appears here as well: aspects of capital investments related above all to movement are targeted (10A, 10C), making the free circulation of investments more of a reality. Hence, directive 79/279 harmonizes the conditions for admission of securities into stock exchanges. Certain aspects of bank operations (9D) are also affected. Directive 86/635, for example, harmonizes the content and form of consolidated accounts of banks and other financial institutions.

The EU seems careful about targeting fields with mutual-recognition

---

[44] Jennifer Hamilton and Ross D. Petty, "The European Union's Consumer Guarantees Directive," *Journal of Public Policy and Marketing* 20 (2001): 289–96.

TABLE 7.8
EU — Legislative Fields under Nominal Intrusion

Quadrant III: Wide but Shallow EU Legislation

- Monetary Policy: accounting methods (9C)
- Energy: oil & gas (12D)
- Regional Policy: subsidies (14B)

laws (table 7.8), despite common belief that planners have more recently worked towards mutual recognition. Only a few fields appear here. Regional subsidies (14B) are somewhat affected. Accounting methods (9C) are mutually recognized (though this might soon change with monetary union). Energy, especially oil and gas, has been similarly targeted (12D). Hence directive 76/491 merely requests that states make available information on crude oil and other petroleum prices but falls well short of dictating how states should influence those prices.

In the EU, a number of aspects related to capital, services and labor remain under the regulatory domain of nation-states (table 7.9). States control most capital security matters (10B), the treatment of international investments (10D), and capital flows into areas such as real estate and startups (10E). Most aspects related to the regulation of services — client relations and internal procedures, state guarantees to service providers, the assignment of public contracts (5C-E) — are with some exceptions left untouched.[45] As to labor, states continue to control benefits (4B), unemployment compensation (4C), and the protection of children and the disabled (4E). Expectedly, there is also no or only limited legislation on housing (4F), various aspects of civic life (25A–D), culture (20), and numerous other areas related to politics, fiscal policy, and social life. Again, as Mann once noted correctly, "there has been "no attempt at social redistribution" in Europe. The EU also "does not cultivate a real sense of European identity or citizenship. . . . [European] cultural identity exists alongside strong and enduring national loyalties."[46]

Some synthesis about the EU is hence possible. The EU has, like Mercosur, moved with strength in the trade of goods. Fields indirectly related to the trade of goods have also been powerfully targeted: these include transportation, the environment, consumer rights, and many more. The EU has only selectively targeted certain aspects of services,

---

[45] One exception would be the EU's intervention in television broadcasting, where indeed some intervention in client-provider relationships is present (see, for instance, directive 89/552 and its requirements on the broadcasting of advertising and other matters).

[46] Mann, "Nation-States in Europe," 125, 126.

TABLE 7.9
EU — Legislative Fields under No Intrusion

Quadrant IV: Narrow and Shallow EU Legislation

- Agriculture: trade (2E)
- Fisheries: classification, third-country trade (3A, 3E)
- Labor and Social Policy: pensions, unemployment, children/disabled, housing (4B-C, 4E-F)
- Services: all but classification and barriers (5C-E)
- Taxation: direct (8A)
- Capital: security, international investment, other (10B, 10D-E)
- External Relations: development aid (11B)
- Energy: all but oil & gas (12A-C, 12E)
- Regional Policy: rights and responsibilities (14A)
- Environment: land, general (15C, 15F)
- Public Health: rights, medical standards (17C-D)
- Science & R&D: focus, funding (18A-B)
- Education: primary & middle, minimum age, special programs, safety, professional degrees (19A-B, 19D-F)
- Culture: all (20)
- Security Policy: all (22)
- Justice, Home Affairs: civil code, court jurisdiction, contracts (23A, 23C, 23E)
- Political System: constitution, party structure, administrative practices and structure all (24)
- Civic Life: association, religion, property rights, citizenship (25A-D)

labor, and capital. The social, political, moral, defense, and educational spheres of social life are largely left untouched.

The Chronology of Supranational Intrusion

A chronological examination of supranational legislative activity should reveal additional insights into the specific nature of legislative intrusion, especially its logic and possible future direction. Our main findings so far — heavy or selective intrusion in fields related to the trade of goods and of fields indirectly related to such trade in both Mercosur and the EU — leads us to suspect a temporal connection between the two trends: heavy or selective intrusion in the trade of goods leads to later heavy or selected intrusion in indirectly related fields. We can test this supposition by identifying the period or periods in which the bulk of common market law was produced for any field (directly or indirectly related to

TABLE 7.10

Timing of Intrusion in Mercosur

Bulk of Legislation Passed in 1990–1995	Bulk of Legislation Passed in 1996–2000
Customs: classification (1A: 1993–94)	**Competition: private unfair practices (7B: 1996–97)**
Customs: tariffs (1B: 1994)	**Competition: public unfair practices (7C:1996–97)**
Agriculture: definitions (2A: 1994–95)	Environment: air (15A: 1996–97)
Agriculture: production procedures (2B: 1994–95)	Consumers: information (16B: 1996, 1998)
External Relations: international agreements (11C: 1992, 1994)	Science, R&D, Info: standards (18C: 1998–99)
Industrial Policy: classification (13A: 1994–95)	Science, R&D, Info: statistics (18D: 1997–2000)
Industrial Policy: manufacturing standards (13B: 1991–94)	Science, R&D, Info: product registration (18E: 1996)
Consumers: health & safety (16A: 1994)	**Undertakings: economic and commercial law (21C: 1996)**
Transportation: water (6B: 1994–95)	
Transportation: land (6C: 1994–95)	

Note: Fields in bold characters are directly related to the trade of goods; remaining fields are indirectly related.

the trade of goods) deemed to have experienced heavy or selective intrusion.[47]

Table 7.10 shows when individual fields were targeted for Mercosur by considering the periods 1990–95 and 1996–2000. In the early period of 1990–95, Mercosur officials seem to have been predominantly busy targeting areas directly related to the trade of goods (highlighted in bold). Three additional fields indirectly related to such trade were also targeted then: consumer health & safety, water transportation, and land transportation. Attention turned to more of those fields in the period between 1996 and 2000, when the environment and matters related to science, R&D, and information were subject to a number of important laws. Table 7.10 thus suggests that legislative intrusion in Mercosur has indeed followed a progressive expansion of intrusive laws from fields related to the trade of goods to fields related to spillover areas.

[47] Recall that individual laws were coded for coverage in terms of specific, broad, and comprehensive, and for depth in terms of mutual recognition, mutual recognition and regulatory, and regulatory. Thus periods of interest would be those in which, for a given field, (a) several specific/broad and regulatory (rather than mutual recognition) laws were enacted, or (b) a few broad/comprehensive and regulatory laws were enacted. One year and five-year periods are considered for Mercosur and the EU respectively.

We can execute a similar analysis for the EU.[48] In this case, of course, the time span is wider, with the early period stretching from 1960 to 1980, and the later period from 1980 to 2000. Table 7.11 indicates a clear, late expansion of EU legislation into fields indirectly related to the trade of goods. Transportation, the environment, and various aspects of science, R&D, and information were targeted with some intensity only after 1980, probably as Delors pushed for the completion of the common market and the Single European Act of 1986 came into being. The EU certainly continued its legislative activity in fields directly related to the trade of goods during 1980–2000. It is clear, however, that, as with Mercosur, EU law has involved a chronological expansion of intrusive laws from fields related to the trade of goods to fields indirectly related to such trade. We must now synthesize our findings for the EU and Mercosur and articulate, if possible, conclusions about the current autonomy of national legislatures in common markets.

NATIONAL LEGISLATURES IN COMMON MARKETS

The national legislature has been an essential feature of the nation-state for centuries. A review of the impact of common markets on such an institution can help us assess the chances of its continued relevance in the era of supranational economies. Our empirical findings for the EU and Mercosur are similar, despite their differences in age, location, levels of economic development, and size. Let us review these findings and then ponder their implications for other spheres of state power.

Common market law is superior to national law. Its presence decommissions national legislatures. Our findings indicate, however, that common market law concerns primarily legislative arenas and fields directly related (such as industrial production) and indirectly related (such as the environment) to the trade of physical goods. It concerns far less services, capital, and labor, especially in Mercosur. It leaves all other arenas and fields essentially untouched. Common market law, then, causes the displacement of legislative authority in selective and fairly unpredictable areas of social life.[49] On the chronological side, a logic seems apparent, but only as it concerns the trade of goods: once fields directly related to such trade are targeted, other, indirectly related, fields

---

[48] For secondary references on the timing of EU legislation in specific areas, numerous sources abound. See, for example, Richard. L. Leonard, *The Economist Guide to the European Union* (London: Profile Books, 1998); Folsom, Lake, and Nanda, *European Union Law after Maastricht.*

[49] Thus, only with the Treaty of Amsterdam of 1997 did the EU recognize intervention in the environment as an inevitable step toward the creation of a common market.

TABLE 7.11
Timing of Intrusion in the European Union

Bulk of Legislation Passed in 1960–1980	Bulk of Legislation Passed in 1980–2000
Customs: classification (1A: 1965–70)	Customs: classification (1A: 1990–95)
Customs: tariffs (1B: 1965–70)	Customs: tariffs (1B: 1990–95)
Customs: border inspection procedures (1D: 1965–70)	Customs: border inspection procedures (1D: 1985–90)
Agriculture: definitions (2A: 1960–80)	Agriculture: production procedures (2B: 1980–85)
Agriculture: production procedures (2B: 1975–80)	Fisheries: catching restrictions (3B: 1980–85)
Fisheries: catching restrictions (3B: 1975–80)	Fisheries: processing restrictions (3C: 1980–90)
Competition: aid (7A: 1965–70)	Competition: private unfair practices (7B: 1985–95)
Competition: private unfair practices (7B: 1960–70)	Competition: public unfair practices (7C: 1985–90)
Competition: public unfair practices (7C: 1975–80)	Transportation: water (6B: 1980–90)
Taxation: indirect (8B: 1975–80)	Transportation: land (6C: 1990–2000)
External Relations: international agreements ((11C: 1970–80)	Taxation: indirect (8B: 1990–95)
Industrial Policy: classification (13A: 1970–80)	Environment: air (15A: 1980–90)
Industrial Policy: manufacturing standards (13B: 1970–80)	Environment: water (15B: 1980–90)
Environment: animals (15D: 1975–80)	Consumer: health & safety (16A: 1980–90)
Consumer: health & safety (16A: 1975–80)	Consumer: information (16B: 1980–90)
Consumer: information (16B: 1975–80)	Consumers: economic protection (16C: 1980–90)
Science, R&D, and Information: standards (18C: 1965–80)	Science, R&D, and Information: statistics (18D: 1990–2000)
	Science, R&D, and Information: product registration (18E: 1990–2000)

Note: Fields in bold characters are directly related to the trade of goods; remaining fields are indirectly related.

follow. The emerging trend, captured essentially by a combination of hypotheses 1 and 3, is thus as follows: national legislative autonomy is systematically lost in fields related to only one (trade of goods) of the four main official objectives of common markets, and in fields indirectly related to the trade of goods later in time. What does this mean for the autonomy of national legislatures?

First, we can state that national legislatures have been unquestionably transformed. In some areas of law, we may no longer speak of free domestic legislators dedicated, as pluralists and statists once proposed, to the production of an integral legal system. Legislators have instead become the executive arms, along with their national administrations, of supranational bodies to be used for the execution of laws that no longer reflect the resolution to conflicting national preferences pursued democratically through domestic institutions. Our understanding of democracy and representation may thus need revisiting. But this is true for only certain legislative fields—some of which, due to a potentially unforeseen spillover effect, the original planners of common markets did not consider.

Second, we can claim that national legislatures nonetheless retain control of several important legislative arenas. In some instances these are clearly outside the realm of the objectives of a common market, such as culture. But in other cases, as with certain aspects of services or labor, for instance, they are close to the objectives of common markets. This leads one to conclude that national legislatures control more, in a sense, than what one would expect had objectives been pursued with the same zeal throughout. We may even suggest that in fields of least displacement national legislatures enjoy an increased sense of legitimacy, since absence of intrusion may in fact be interpreted as a sanctioning of national authority, in line with the principle of subsidiarity espoused by EU officials. We can thus assert with confidence that the national legislatures retain relevance in the contexts of both the South American and the European markets.

The emerging trend may accordingly be described as a division of labor between supranational and national authorities. Common markets reign supreme in certain areas. In other areas, markets and states share authority. Yet in others, common markets make symbolic claims only. In the remaining areas, national structures continue to have full legislative clout. No sooner is this said than we begin to wonder about the causes of such a pattern: might the observed division of labor one day disappear if markets truly realize their purported end (as free trade areas not only of goods but also of labor, services, and capital) and spillover mechanisms continue their work? What does our analysis reveal about the logic, and thus future, of supranational legal activity?

Our third point concerns the causes and future of common market law. Our findings reveal no evidence that a single logic drives the process of supranational legislative activity. The economic requirements of common markets alone cannot explain why certain economic areas are fully left alone and others mildly targeted, while certain noneconomic areas undergo severe intrusion. Spillover effects as a form of internal market logic hold explanatory power only once common market laws in certain economic areas are introduced. Other factors must therefore be influencing the selection of targets. The commercial interests of certain elements within member states might explain the heavy targeting of goods-related areas.[50] The geopolitical utility of these markets, to prevent wars for instance,[51] might also explain the focus on goods (the EU started, after all, with an agreement on coal and steel). Public ownership of most crucial services, such as banking or energy, in key member states, such as Brazil or France, might explain hesitance in the sphere of services. In addition, other factors may explain, along with spillover, why areas such as education (in the EU especially) and the environment are targeted. One such factor might be the independent desire to create a common citizenry.

No single factor is likely to explain the observed patterns of common market law. Common markets reflect economic, social, and other considerations.[52] There is therefore no reason to believe that observable trends, depicting a mixed and somewhat disorderly division of labor between national and common market structures, are to end in the foreseeable future. Simple claims of either inevitable decline or unperturbed strength in various spheres of the nation-state, so common in the contemporary literature, are inapplicable in the realm of national legislative activity.

New Opportunities for State Power

Given that the continued relevance of the nation-state, in its various functions, is ultimately this volume's topic of interest, we might do well to contemplate whether some decline in the power of traditional national legislative structures does not imply gained strength in other areas. Other contributors to this volume, such as Grzegorz Ekiert, note that loss of state power in some areas may, in some cases, translate into state power in other areas. Can states assert their authority with all the more power in other areas precisely because their national legislative branches are becoming weaker?

---

[50] Andrew Moravcsik, *The Choice for Europe: Social Purpose and State Power from Messina to Maastricht* (Ithaca: Cornell University Press, 1998); Moravcsik, "Preferences and Power."

[51] Milward, *The European Rescue of the Nation-State.*

[52] Just as multiple variables account for the general direction of the European Union and other regional integration efforts. See Neil Fligstein, "Markets as Politics: A Political-Cultural Approach to Market Institutions," *American Sociological Review* 61 (August 1996): 656–73; Fligstein and Mara-Drita, "How to Make a Market," 1–33; Walter Mattli, *The Logic of Regional Integration: Europe and Beyond* (Cambridge: Cambridge University Press, 1999).

States can certainly increase their administrative strength while accepting common market law. The implementation of EU and Mercosur law is left in the hands of nation-states. These must rely on administrative structures strong enough to ensure compliance with the adopted principles. Where administrative units were previously absent, new units emerge. The legitimacy of weaker administrations, such as in Italy or Greece, is also bolstered, as the new mandates legitimize the exercise of authority and the spirit of the law. The executive function of states may thus strengthen as a result of participation in supranational markets.

The executive function may also gain power since members of the executive branches make up the Council of Ministers in the EU and the Common Market Council and Common Market Group in Mercosur.[53] To the extent that these can be said to control the content of common market law, we may state that members of national executives gain strength as the legislative branch loses autonomy. But here we must immediately remind ourselves of the fact that not all ministers of all nations represented in these bodies have their way. German, French, and Brazilian ministers may claim some advantage over national legislatures; the same may not be said as easily of Portuguese, Greek, or Uruguayan ministers. Nation-states may also obtain further power if supranational markets — in part because of their laws — offer them the opportunity to obtain objectives otherwise beyond their reach. As Moravcsik suggests, this may indeed have occurred in the European Union, whose existence has essentially served to promote the commercial power of each member state.[54] More conservative claims could be made about the fact that the European Union and other supranational markets in fact produce outcomes that strengthen some, rather than all, of their member states. Enduring peace, otherwise less secure in a world without the European Union, also allows for the continuation of states as we know them. European states, as Milward reminds us, risked extinction during World War II.[55]

States may even be able to become powerful legislative agents in those areas previously not subject to any type of legislative presence. Supranational law may, in fact, legitimize corollary or tangential national law in spheres hitherto considered beyond the scope of national regulation. Certainly, the limits and scope of such new intervention are set by the

---

[53] In certain countries, such as France, members of the executive can also be members of the legislature. Yet their participation in supranational legislative processes is as members of the executive.

[54] Moravcsik, *The Choice for Europe*.

[55] Milward, *The European Rescue of the Nation-State*. My thanks to John K. Glenn, Executive Director of the Council for European Studies at Columbia University, for insights into this topic.

principles of common market law. This, however, may pose more opportunities than drawbacks from a legislative point of view. An analysis
of national legislative activity following the arrival of supranational law
would be needed to evaluate this thesis.

Finally, we must remember that states can always refuse to implement
common market law, in terms of both transposition into national law
and practical application. In a perverse way, this affords states, and
especially elements within a state, a chance to assert their viewpoints
and independence in the international arena. A look at the EU's implementation record indicates that refusal to implement is certainly pervasive.[56] With the exception of Denmark, no EU member state could
boast, for instance, to have transposed more than 25 percent of the
Single European Act's directives on time.[57]

All of this points to a complex picture of state transformation in the
era of supranational economies. Rather than heralding either the death
of the nation-state or its unperturbed survival, we should examine with
care the intricate changes affecting the nation-state and their multiple,
contradictory implications for the various components of states. We
would also be wise to recall that states have never existed as a fixed
entity in history but have in fact been constantly evolving since their
inception.

[56] Francesco Duina, *Harmonizing Europe: Nation States within the Common Market*
(Albany: State University of New York Press, 1999).

[57] The European Commission has launched more and more noncompliance investigations (1,142 in 1996 alone), and the court has issued more and more judgments. See
Amato Giuliani, "Italy," in Dietrich Rometsch and Wolfgang Wessels, eds., *The European
Union and Member States: Towards Institutional Fusion?* (Manchester: Manchester University Press, 1996), 157–74.

CHAPTER 8

The Tax State in the Information Age

CHRISTOPHER HOOD

THE TAX STATE'S "GOOD TWENTIETH CENTURY"?

Ability to tax is central to state capacity as ordinarily conceived, since states that cannot levy effective taxes will have only limited capacity to do anything else (unless they can find workable substitutes for taxation, such as military conscription).[1] Hence tax capacity provides a — perhaps the — key test of state capacity.[2] And at first sight, the twentieth century seems to have been a notably "good century"[3] for the tax state.[4] In most of the major developed countries the tax take as a proportion of GDP rose dramatically, from around 10 percent or less before World War I to between 25 and 50 percent at the end of the century. Even in the United States, a state born through a colonial tax revolt and often seen as containing particularly strong political resistance to high taxation, taxes as a proportion of recorded national income rose from under 5 percent before the Civil War to nearly 25 percent a century later. They never fell below that point even at the height of the "Reaganomic" era of the 1980s, in spite of the tax-cutting small-government ambitions of that era.[5] Indeed, OECD notes: "Over the past three decades in the OECD area as a whole, the tax level — including social security contributions — has risen almost continuously, up from 25.8 percent of GDP in 1965 to

---

[1] Margaret Levi, *Of Rule and Revenue* (Berkeley: University of California Press, 1988), 2.

[2] See Christine Fauvelle-Aymar, "The Political and Tax Capacity of Government in Developing Countries," *Kyklos* 52 (1999): 391.

[3] If "a good century" for taxes is taken (tendentiously) to mean a century in which the fiscal tightened its grip on the economy.

[4] "Tax state" is the term used by the Vienna school and particularly Rudolf Goldscheid to denote states dependent on taxation rather than on the exploitation of their own property. See Rudolf Goldscheid, "A Sociological Approach to Problems of Public Finance," in Richard A. Musgrave and Alan T. Peacock, eds., *Classics in the Theory of Public Finance* (New York: Macmillan, 1967), 205. The term is used without attribution by other writers such as B. Guy Peters, "The Development of the Tax State," *Studies in Public Policy* 146 (Glasgow: Centre for the Study of Public Policy, University of Strathclyde, 1985).

[5] See OECD, *Revenue Statistics 1965/1998* (Paris: OECD, 1999), table 3, 65–66.

37.2 percent of GDP in 1997 (unweighted averages), or by 11.4 percentage points."[6]

This picture needs to be qualified in several ways. By no means all states saw the dramatic rise in GDP claimed by taxation in much of Western Europe over the century. As Minxin Pei shows in this volume, tax revenue in China fell sharply in recent decades, and even in the OECD states, major differences remained in their tax profiles, notably in the relative shares of direct and indirect taxes in the tax structure[7] and in the relative size of their "shadow economies," as far as that can be gauged.[8] Among the older affluent democracies, tax-to-GDP levels varied widely, from around 50 percent in Sweden to 30 percent or less in countries like the United States, Japan, Australia, and Switzerland.[9] The tax take as a proportion of GDP tended to be substantially lower (but also with large variations) in the less developed states. And the Asian "little tiger" newly industrialized countries (NICs) remained fairly low-tax economies, with total tax revenue below 15 percent of GDP in the 1980s.[10] The era of communist rule in Russia and Eastern Europe is hard to interpret from a tax capacity perspective, though communist states are not "tax states" in the normal Vienna-school sense.[11]

However, no major state seems to have entered the twenty-first century with a proportionate tax take much lower than a century earlier, even though some states' overall tax-to-GDP ratios fell back at the end of the twentieth century, as in the Chinese case (or less dramatically in cases such as Sweden, the Netherlands, Japan, and Ireland). Even Hong Kong, often considered "the classic example of a Reagan-type supply-side economy"[12] and indeed scarcely a "tax state" at all in the twentieth

---

[6] Ibid., 17.

[7] See Richard Rose, "Maximizing Revenue and Minimizing Political Costs," *Studies in Public Policy* 142 (Glasgow: Centre for the Study of Public Policy, University of Strathclyde, 1985); Sven Steinmo, "Political Institutions and Tax Policy in the United States, Sweden and Britain," *World Politics* 41 (1989): 502; Steinmo, *Taxation and Democracy* (New Haven: Yale University Press, 1993); OECD, *Revenue Statistics*: 17ff.

[8] See Friedrich Schneider and Dominik Enste, "Shadow Economies: Size, Causes and Consequences," *Journal of Economic Literature* 38 (2000): 77–114.

[9] For explanations of those variations, see Sven Steinmo and Caroline Tolbert, "Do Institutions Really Matter? Taxation in Industrialized Democracies," *Comparative Political Studies* 31 (1998): 165–87.

[10] See Vito Tanzi and Parthasarathi Shome, "The Role of Taxation in the Development of East Asian Economies," in Takatoshi Ito and Anne O. Krueger, eds., *The Political Economy of Tax Reform* (Chicago: University of Chicago Press, 1992), 45.

[11] Such states become "tax states" in the Vienna-school sense when privatization of their assets makes them dependent on taxation. For discussion of taxation in postsocialist Russia, see Federico Varese, "The Transition to the Market and Corruption in Post-Socialist Russia," *Political Studies* 45 (1997): 579–96.

[12] See Tanzi and Shome "The Role of Taxation," 57.

century,[13] seemed to be heading inexorably VAT-ward by the end of the century. That experience contrasts with that of earlier historical eras, such as the way Roman Empire's tax system eventually self-destructed by encouraging the development of a subsistence economy, as noted by Max Weber.[14]

Inflation, economic development and population growth, changing technology and lifestyles all seem to have contributed to the tax state's "good twentieth century."[15] Such changes combined to broaden the base of the four major taxes (income tax, social security tax, VAT and sales taxes, and other specific taxes on consumption) that together accounted for most tax revenue in OECD states by the 1980s.[16] At the start of the century, income taxes were paid, if at all, by a small, wealthy minority in most developed countries, and effective, broad-based sales taxes were rare.[17] Taxes on oil and vehicles were likewise in their infancy but became a mainstay of almost every fiscal system by the end of the century.

Of course, it was also a good century for tax havens, and even among the developed high-tax countries spending commitments in many cases matched or outran revenue increases, producing fiscal squeezes, especially in the 1920s, 1930s, and 1970s. Nevertheless, the long-term increase in the relative tax take in the developed countries merits some attention, to provide a basis for assessing the prospects for the tax state in the information age. Is the twentieth-century advance of the tax state in the developed countries best seen as a historical aberration, from which we might expect a reversion to more historically normal levels? How should we interpret and explain the tax state's "good twentieth century"?

INTERPRETING THE TWENTIETH-CENTURY GROWTH OF THE TAX STATE: A RISE IN STATES' EXTRACTIVE CAPABILITY?

The obvious interpretation of the proportionate long-term growth in tax revenue is that states' "extractive capability" at least in developed countries increased dramatically in the twentieth century, far exceeding

[13] With a tax/GDP ratio of under 12 percent in the 1980s (ibid., 38), no general sales tax or VAT, an income tax paid only by a small minority of employees, and a general dependence on sales of state-owned land.

[14] See Hans Gerth and C. Wright Mills, *From Max Weber* (London: Routledge, 1948), 210. Indeed, the tax take in the Britain at the start of the twentieth century as a proportion of national income was only half what it had been at the start of the nineteenth.

[15] For a predictive model of revenue yield, see Terence Karran, "The Determinants of Taxation in Britain: An Empirical Test," *Journal of Public Policy* 5 (1986): 365–86.

[16] See Rose, "Maximizing Revenue," 21.

[17] For an analysis of tax structure changes in six developed states between 1900 and 1978, see Peters, "The Development of the Tax State," 22–23.

what was achieved by many earlier despotic or absolutist states and empires.[18] However, such a conclusion depends on what counts as the key test of states' extractive capability. The tax share of GDP is only one possible indicator of such capability, and arguably a limited one, for at least three reasons.

First, extractive capability is not necessarily indicated by the taxes that states choose to impose at any given time but crucially concerns the taxes they could impose in defined conditions (such as war or social crisis). Unless it is assumed that states always tax up to their full capacity, as in variants of the "predatory state" thesis, thus eliminating the problem by definition, current tax take cannot be automatically equated with tax capability. Some political scientists have therefore used "tax effort" indices that measure the ratio of actual tax share to the tax share that would be predicted on the basis of economic data, but those indices are still in their infancy as tools of comparative political analysis.[19]

Second, if extractive capability is taken to mean the proportion of a society's income above basic subsistence level that the state is able to draw from its citizens or subjects, the conclusion that extractive capability rose over the twentieth century becomes more questionable. (As would be the conclusion that such capability tends to be higher in developed democracies than in less developed countries.) As real incomes rise with economic development, the proportion of GDP that represents the above-subsistence level increases by definition, so the tax-to-GDP ratio would need to rise substantially simply to stand still relative to above-subsistence income. Such a sum cannot be calculated precisely, because what counts as a pure subsistence level of income is not necessarily a constant.[20] But to take an illustrative and anything but far-fetched example, imagine that aggregate real income quadruples over a long period of economic growth[21] and that the proportion of that income needed to maintain bare subsistence falls from four-fifths to a quarter. In those conditions, the state's tax take of overall income would need to rise nearly fourfold just to

[18] Almond and Powell define "extractive capability" as the performance of political systems in "drawing material and human resources from the domestic and international environments," declaring, "The capacity to obtain such resources underlies the other capabilities." See Gabriel Almond and G. Bingham Powell, *Comparative Politics* (Boston: Little, Brown, 1966), 195. See also Joel Migdal, *Strong Societies and Weak States* (Princeton: Princeton University Press, 1988); Bertrand de Jouvenel, *Power*, tr. J. F. Huntingdon (Indianapolis: Liberty Fund, 1993), 8–12.

[19] See Fauvelle-Aymar, "Political and Tax Capacity," 393.

[20] Not just because the definition of basic subsistence is debatable, but also because development alters the conditions in which subsistence-level existence is possible.

[21] Even in Britain, an economic tortoise compared to the Asian "little tigers" in the late twentieth century, real GDP per head rose by nearly 150 percent between 1948 and 1981. See Karran, "The Determinants of Taxation in Britain," 369.

maintain the same level of extractive capability over above-subsistence income. So if extractive capability is defined in that proportionate way, we might conclude that such capability did not rise and in fact fell back sharply in the developed countries, particularly in the affluent decades of the late twentieth century. And the idea of a rise in extractive capability may need to be further qualified if we accept the claim made by several scholars that the official GDP against which the size of the tax state is conventionally measured was a declining proportion of total economic activity, with a growth in shadow economies in some of the developed countries in the late twentieth century.[22]

Third, state extractive capability might reasonably be taken to include the shape or structure, as well as the overall size and scope, of taxation. A banana republic that can only tax bananas might be judged to have an extractive capability different from a state with a more varied or compound tax structure, even if the two states' overall tax take is the same, since the former's extractive capability is wholly tied to the banana crop or the willingness of banana farmers to stay and pay. More generally, if the variety of the tax base narrows, or circumstances limit the range of taxes that can be levied by the state or restrict its capability to act unilaterally in setting taxes, the "shaping" aspect of tax capacity can be weakened even if overall tax take is maintained or increased.[23] And indeed the twentieth century saw numerous developments limiting that aspect of tax capacity for the capitalist democracies — notably the extension of global free trade regimes restricting the scope of customs taxes and pressures to limit taxes on business profits or to use state-owned enterprises as fiscal or economic policy instruments. And just as the development of earlier federations and customs unions (such as the United States and the German *Zollverein* and empire) restricted important aspects of the extractive capacity of the individual states, so did the European Union and other regional trade blocs such as Mercosur over indirect taxation and tariffs, as shown by Francesco Duina in this volume.

Indeed, for egalitarians the failure of the twentieth-century tax state was its limited impact on income distribution in most countries, in spite of occasional attempts or claims to use taxes for that purpose. (Cases in point include land taxes in pre–World War I Britain, the progressive tax ambitions of postcolonial India,[24] and inheritance taxes imposed under the U.S. occupation regime in post–World War II Japan.) Sven Steinmo and other scholars argue that the 1980s' tax reforms enacted by many

[22] Particularly using the "currency demand" method of estimating the size of shadow economies. See Schneider and Enste, "Shadow Economies."

[23] Almond and Powell note that extractive capability is characterized by the breadth of the revenue base and not just by the size of the tax take. See Almond and Powell, *Comparative Politics*, 196.

[24] Nani Palkhivala, *The Highest Taxed Nation* (Bombay: Manaktalas, 1965).

developed countries, incorporating declining taxation of capital and reductions in marginal income and corporate tax rates, were heavily conditioned by increased mobility of international capital.[25] Steinmo claims that opinion poll evidence from the three countries in his study (United States, Sweden, and Britain) suggests "most people felt that what was wrong with their [tax] systems was that the wealthy and the corporations paid too little in taxes."[26] But in all cases governments took tax policy in the opposite direction, cutting rather than raising taxes on corporations and higher income brackets. Such observations suggest that the extractive capability of capitalist democracy in this era was limited in important qualitative ways by international competition for investment and jobs.

For these and other reasons,[27] the conclusion that the twentieth century saw a general growth in the extractive capability of the wealthy democracies depends heavily on what the key measure of extractive capability is taken to be and what weight is to be given to overall size as against shape and structure. Nevertheless, overall taxation did grow over the century as a proportion of official GDP in the developed countries, and that growth can be explained in several possible ways, rounding up some familiar suspects in political science.[28] Three of those suspects include accounting for policy change in terms of state responses to changing public attitudes, explaining policy change by transformations in policy habitat affecting enforceability and ease of collection, and hybrid approaches that stress inertia or *mortmain* effects.

EXPLAINING THE DEVELOPMENT OF THE TWENTIETH-CENTURY TAX STATE: THREE APPROACHES

Attitudinal Change and Democratization

The first of those "usual suspect" explanations would associate increased taxation with attitudinal changes, perhaps linked with constitutional changes. Candidates for attitudinal shift include an extension of "egalitarian" attitudes, as claimed by the late Aaron Wildavsky to char-

---

[25] See Steinmo, *Taxation and Democracy*, 158.

[26] Ibid.

[27] For instance, there are differences in the extent to which states use "tax expenditures" as a policy instrument, the relative sizes of the shadow economy, and the way GDP is counted. Such differences can affect the numerator or denominator (or both) of the tax/GDP ratio. See OECD, *Revenue Statistics*, 27–28.

[28] See B. Guy Peters, *The Politics of Taxation* (Oxford: Blackwell, 1991); Christopher Hood, *Explaining Economic Policy Reversals* (Buckingham: Open University Press, 1994), chap. 6.

acterize much of twentieth-century fiscal history in Western Europe and North America.[29] A related idea is that the size and shape of taxation reflects the degree of legitimacy and popular support of political regimes, and hence that democratization shapes tax capacity (a classical theme in political thought, going back at least to Jean Bodin).[30] It is epitomized in Sidney Ratner's heroic interpretation, originally put forward in 1942, of the introduction of the graduated income tax in the United States in 1913 after the passing of the sixteenth amendment to the U.S. constitution, as a product of democratization.[31] If such interpretations are accepted, the twentieth-century advance of the tax state might be seen as a reflection of increased state legitimacy produced by the development of mass-franchise democracy and the associated advance of welfare-state policies in the wealthy countries.[32] On this hypothesis, increased tax capacity might reflect democratization in several possible ways, including increased state legitimacy producing greater willingness to pay, a dominant electoral coalition supporting tax-financed state expenditure, and a growth of egalitarian attitudes that may accompany or cause pressures for democratization.[33]

The Development of New Tax Handles
in a Changing Fiscal Environment

However, those who are schooled in rational-choice analysis of political action[34] will be skeptical of the idea that extension of the franchise and

[29] See Carolyn Webber and Aaron Wildavsky, *A History of Taxation and Expenditure in the Western World* (New York: Simon and Schuster, 1986); Aaron Wildavsky and Brendan Swedlow, "Is Egalitarianism Really on the Rise?" in Aaron Wildavsky, ed., *The Rise of Radical Egalitarianism* (Washington, DC: American University Press, 1991), 63–98.

[30] See Martin Wolfe, "Jean Bodin on Taxes: The Sovereignty-Taxes Paradox," *Political Science Quarterly* 83 (1968): 279.

[31] See Sidney Ratner, *Taxation and Democracy in America* (New York: Wiley, 1967).

[32] States where fiscal burdens and benefits are more equally shared might be expected to encounter less popular opposition to tax increases than states like prerevolutionary France (where the nobility and clergy were exempt from tax) or the Ottoman Empire in 1900, when almost the entire tax revenue went to pay foreign creditors and support the imperial court. See Paul Leroy-Beaulieu, "On Taxation in General," in Richard A. Musgrave and Alan T. Peacock, eds., *Classics in the Theory of Public Finance* (New York: Macmillan 1967), 152.

[33] That hypothesis would fit with observations of tax-to-GDP ratios in cases like Greece before and after 1974 and South Korea before and after 1987 (where tax-to-GDP ratios rose faster in the years after the end of authoritarian regimes than in the preceding years) but remains to be systematically tested.

[34] See Mancur Olson, *The Logic of Collective Action* (Cambridge: Harvard University Press, 1965).

competitive party systems will necessarily produce increased individual willingness to pay taxes, instead of "free riding" behavior.[35] They will note that tax increases relying on feelings of patriotism or solidarity[36] tend to be much less successful than tax increases underpinned by coercive administration, and they may conclude that the effect of democratization on taxable capacity in "soft states" — those with limited autonomy and administrative power — may be limited.[37] A "soft public choice" account of state tax capacity has been offered by Margaret Levi,[38] who assumes rulers — those in the topmost positions of the state — normally tend to be "predatory" revenue-maximizers but face varying environmental constraints in realizing those predatory ambitions.[39] In this vein, a second broad way of explaining the proportionate increase in taxability in the wealthy democracies in the twentieth century focuses on tax handles. It looks for changes in tax "habitat" (not just the general climate of opinion) that made it easier for governments to levy broad-based taxes and harder for those they rule to evade such impositions.

A habitat-change interpretation suggests that economies developed in ways that increased the number of extractive "niches" available to the tax state.[40] In traditional societies largely based on agriculture, above-subsistence income is readily held in kind, and particularly in the form of livestock, whose numbers and increase are notoriously hard for the state's bureaucrats to keep track of (as even Stalin discovered). The technological changes, rising scale of employment and production, and increased monetization of income that tended to go along with indus-

[35] However, neither the public-choice literature nor the voluminous literature that has recently emerged on democratization in political science contains much discussion of the link between democratization and tax capacity.

[36] As with attempts to raise income taxes in Britain in the early years of World War II, before the introduction of the PAYE scheme for income taxation at source in 1944.

[37] The idea of "soft states" has a history in political science but has been used most recently by John Eatwell and his colleagues to characterize postcommunist central and Eastern European states. See John Eatwell et al., *Hard Budgets in Soft States* (London: Institute of Public Policy Research, 2000), 3. The size of the shadow economy in such states rose rather than fell after democratization, according to Schneider and Enste, "Shadow Economies."

[38] See Levi, *Of Rule and Revenue.*

[39] For all its public-choice trappings, Levi's approach is relatively indeterminate and overlaps with a responsive-government account of tax change, since it places heavy emphasis on what she calls "quasi-voluntary compliance" with the predatory rulers' tax demands. It also overlaps with themes advanced by historical institutionalists. See, for example, Steinmo and Tolbert, "Do Institutions Really Matter?" 168–71.

[40] For "niche theory," see Glendon Schubert, "Politics as a Life Science: How and Why the Impact of Modern Biology Will Revolutionize the Study of Political Behavior," in Albert Somit, ed., *Biology and Politics* (Paris/the Hague: Mouton and Maison des Sciences de l'Homme, 1976), 185.

trialization open up new sources of taxation. For instance, the replacement of horses and other draught animals by motor vehicles sets the stage for the development of fuel taxes as a major source of state revenue, since oil is easier to tax at bottlenecks in the production and distribution chain than hay and oats. The growth of "Fordist" factory production systems from the early part of the century produces standardized mass employment for money wages by enterprises above the family firm (or farm) level, employing standardized accounting systems that the state can draw on to levy income taxes. The development of large-scale retail and distribution structures with similar properties (such as supermarkets replacing family-run stores, or large-scale gambling structures replacing more localized gambling outlets) also had tax-handle implications later in the century. It set the scene for the development of VAT and sales taxes — another of the "success stories" for the tax state in the twentieth century.[41]

Historical Institutionalist Accounts: Inertia Politics and Keeping the Saddle on the Horse

In what would now be termed a "historical institutionalist" analysis, Alan Peacock and Jack Wiseman offered an account of the development of the twentieth-century tax state that combines "legitimacy" and "tax niche" explanations.[42] As they put it, "It is harder to get the saddle on the horse than to keep it there." While Adam Smith and other classical economists expected states to raise tax burdens during wars or other crises, they thought those burdens would subsequently return to approximately the previous level. But Peacock and Wiseman noted that twentieth-century experience did not fit that expected pattern. Rather, tax levels associated with the world wars of the first half of the twentieth century in the developed countries declined only slightly (in aggregate terms) over a subsequent half-century of economic development uninterrupted by major wars. Peacock and Wiseman put this pattern down to inertia: public opinion sanctions tax increases in a crisis, but tax levels tend to stay at the new plateau until the next crisis rather than reverting to precrisis level, as Adam Smith expected. Richard Rose also places heavy emphasis on inertia as a key theme in tax policy development, offering a variant of 'punctuated equilibrium' theory to account for long-term processes of tax change.[43]

[41] Particularly over recent decades. See OECD, *Revenue Statistics*, 20.

[42] Alan Peacock and Jack Wiseman, *The Growth of Public Expenditure in the UK* (Oxford: Oxford University Press, 1961).

[43] Richard Rose, "Inheritance before Choice in Public Policy," *Journal of Theoretical*

For the purpose of this analysis, we can adopt the eclectic position of regarding each of these approaches as having something to contribute to an account of the tax state's good twentieth century, without needing to choose sharply among them.[44] Accordingly, the next section considers the implications of each of those accounts for critical success factors affecting the capacity of the tax state in the information age. The subsequent section considers possible strategies that might be available to the tax state to counteract threats to its position in the information age.

IDENTIFYING CRITICAL SUCCESS FACTORS

The accounts discussed in the last section at least provide pointers to some of the critical success factors that would need to be satisfied for the tax state to repeat, sustain, or exceed its good twentieth century performance in the information age. At least three such factors can be identified. One, recalling both Ratner's "taxation and democracy" thesis and Levi's idea of "quasi-voluntary compliance," is the capacity of the affluent democracies to produce ruling electoral coalitions sustaining a continuation or increase of twentieth-century tax ratios. That means structures in which tax losers are capable of being politically dominated by winners and more general climates of public opinion producing a "tax culture." A second, also relating to what underpins quasi-voluntary compliance and to analyses of the administrative ecology of feasible taxation, is that technological-economic development continues to produce readily graspable tax "handles" in the information age. A third, recalling Steinmo's discussion of what shaped 1980s tax reform, is the existence of broader international conditions capable of sustaining or augmenting the tax state. How far can we expect those success factors to continue to sustain a long-term trend[45] to increased scale of taxation and taxation becoming steadily more sophisticated, broader in scope, and more bureaucratic in form?

Sustaining a Tax Culture

First, for the tax state to repeat or exceed its twentieth-century performance in the information age, domestic political conditions must pro-

---

Politics 2 (1990): 263–91; Richard Rose and Terence Karran, *Taxation by Political Inertia* (London: Allen and Unwin, 1987).

[44] Though my own work stresses the second interpretation. See Hood, *Explaining Economic Policy Reversals.*

[45] Identified by Levi, *Of Rule and Revenue,* and de Jouvenel, *Power.*

duce a tax culture or coalition that sustains it. It is often claimed that tax growth in the mid-twentieth century in the industrialized democracies reflected broader popular support for more interventionist government, against the experience of the 1930s' Depression and two world wars.[46] The voter resistance to extra taxation that appeared in the United States and some other wealthy democracies from the 1970s (when real income growth slowed and inflation formed a larger part of fiscal drag) was not strong enough to reduce overall tax-to-GDP ratios, though it shook or unseated several governments and political leaders.[47] As already noted, several studies have suggested that shadow economies slightly increased in many of the OECD countries in the late twentieth century, and large-scale tax evasion was not unknown (for instance, one in five adults in England and Wales had to be issued a court summons to pay the ill-fated poll tax during its brief existence from 1988 to 1992). But it is not clear whether such activity matched the scale and incidence of tax riots and revolutions in earlier eras.[48]

We do not know whether the information age will produce equivalents to the Great Depression and world wars of the twentieth century in stimulating or reviving a tax culture or statist egalitarianism. But we do know that the demography of many of the wealthy democracies, with long-term increases in longevity and falls in fertility rates, brings the prospect of ageing and later falling populations across many of those countries in this century if immigration or fertility does not increase. Orthodox projections show substantial increases in the proportion of the population over sixty in many of the developed democracies in the early 2000s, going from around 20 percent in 1990 to 30 percent or so in 2025 in Germany and Japan.[49] The effect of this change on state tax capacity is hard to assess and is unlikely to be uniform, since there are considerable differences in the projected speed of ageing across different states and also in the way health care and retirement pensions are funded. The effect is likely to be greatest in countries like Germany, which combine high expected "age bomb" effects with a tradition of funding state-sector retirement pensions from general taxes rather than contributory pension funds.

The point is that as the numbers of retirees relative to those of work-

---

[46] See Webber and Wildavsky, *A History of Taxation*, 562–63.

[47] They include "read my lips: no new taxes" U.S. President George Bush, who failed to secure reelection in 1992; "poll tax" U.K. Prime Minister Margaret Thatcher, who was removed in 1990; and the Japanese Liberal Democratic Party, defeated for the first time in nearly fifty years after its introduction of an unpopular general sales tax in 1986.

[48] See Peters, *The Politics of Taxation*, 286.

[49] See Yukio Noguchi, "Aging of Population, Social Security and Tax Reform," in Ito and Krueger, eds., *The Political Economy of Tax Reform*, 31–61.

ing age change, the attitudes of each group toward paying a bigger share of the state's total tax revenue to limit the burden on the other group are likely to be tested. That test would be severe if (as many have suggested) those of working age were obliged to save more to finance their own retirement pensions and old-age care and/or pay more tax to support current retirees. Covering the gap by inflation (a traditional "stealth tax"[50]) would be politically difficult if a larger proportion of voters was made up of retirees who made their financial plans on the basis of past levels of taxation and inflation. Unless the economies, stock and real estate markets of the wealthy democracies turn out to boom for decades, defying all historical patterns, one or both of these age groups would need to be more collectivist than they were in the past if the tax state was to escape major political stresses in those countries combining the greatest age bomb effects with the least contributory approaches to pensions and health care. If neither age group exhibits more collectivist, willingness to pay tax, tendencies in such circumstances, and state managers cannot cover the gap by stealth taxes, the early-to-middle decades of this century may prove more of a challenge for at least some tax states than was the industrial age.

A Supply of Graspable Tax Handles

Second, for the tax state to be maintained or expanded in the information age, economic and technological development must produce suitable tax handles — forms of production, distribution, or employment that can be readily identified, valued, and controlled through intermediary organizations that can be economically overseen by state bureaucracy and thus enable taxes to be collected at relatively low cost. Drawing on earlier authors such as Jeremy Bentham, I have argued that the features of low-cost and effective tax collection can be broken down into five properties of administrative feasibility.[51] Those properties are listability, conduitability, standard clarity, cross-sanctions, and reinforceability. *Listability* means easy identifiability of the population to

[50] Currently, a term of abuse used by the British Conservative Party to highlight hidden tax rises (that is, taxes other than income tax and VAT) under the New Labour government. But many classical writers on taxation saw taxation by stealth as the key to fiscal success. Indeed, a medieval English feudal lord saw the ideal tax as one "providyng as it weare of some sewers or channelles to drawe and sucke from them theyr money by subtyle and indirect means to be handled insensiblye." See Edward E. Hughes *Studies in Administration and Finance 1558–1825* (Manchester: Manchester University Press, 1934), 303.

[51] See Christopher Hood, "British Tax Policy Change as Administrative Adaptation," *Policy Sciences* 18 (1988): 3–31; Hood, *Explaining Economic Policy Reversals*.

which taxes apply. *Conduitability* means the ability to channel taxes through a manageable number of stable intermediaries. *Standard clarity* means capacity to specify and assess tax bases with limited effort and ambiguity. *Reinforceability* means taxes can be cross-checked from different administrative vantage points, and *cross-sanctions* means that evasion of one tax brings extra liability to another (or other corresponding disadvantages, such as no legal validity of titles to property without payment of stamp taxes). The administratively "perfect" tax base (combining high effectiveness and low collection cost) would possess all of these properties, and a tax with none of them can be expected to fail, on some approximation of a niche theory explanation of tax survival.[52]

Nevertheless, a tax handle can still be satisfactory with only a few of them, and, as noted earlier, a number of tax handles with two or more of these properties were available to the twentieth-century tax state, especially for the first two Kondratieff cycles of the century. In particular, those two cycles produced technological-economic conditions favorable for the development of mass income taxation, oil taxes, and mass VAT or sales taxation. Those conditions include the development of middle- and large-scale public and private employers (satisfying the listability and conduitability conditions for mass income taxation) and the later rise of large-scale retailers (satisfying the same conditions for sales taxation). Other developments, like mass motoring and mass tourism, also provided low-cost, high-effectiveness tax handles.

If the information age lived up to its name, we might expect state authorities to know more about the economic circumstances and transactions of their citizens, in ever more sophisticated ways, and thus to have more low-cost capacity for reinforceability and cross-sanctions. But it seems far from certain that such an outcome can be expected, since, as Margaret Levi has observed, technological change is apt to be double-edged for tax capability.[53] Indeed, there are several potential challenges to the administrative feasibility and collection cost of established taxes in the information age. For instance, a declining "Fordist" mass-employment base may raise the cost of collecting income taxes. A society in which most employees work exclusively for a single medium or large-sized organization makes an income tax handle with greater listability and conduitability than an employment structure with a substantial proportion of self-employment, part-time employment, subcontracting, "portfolio workers," and small-scale boutique operations. More enterprises operating across frontiers (as in e-commerce) also

---

[52] See Schubert, "Politics as a Life Science."
[53] See Levi, *Of Rule and Revenue*, 28–29.

means rising collection costs due to decreasing listability and standard clarity.[54]

Moreover, an increase in the ratio of retired older people coupled with a general increase in affluence in the wealthy democracies may mean a rising proportion of total income derived from mobile capital. And such income is potentially more capable (thanks to the information age) of being switched away from readily taxable channels.[55] To that may be added the increasing scope for trade and investment across borders that so many observers have commented on, and a squeeze on traditional middle-sized firms least able to follow a "capital exit" strategy in response to tax pressure. Even though direct taxation of corporate earnings was not one of the four main twentieth-century props of the tax state in many countries, corporations were major tax intermediaries, and the maintenance of that role seems important. Further, if e-commerce develops in the coming decades on the scale predicted by some of the information-age prophets, it could potentially weaken the rich VAT or sales tax base that was so marked a feature of the tax state's late-twentieth-century development.[56] That base could be squeezed between hard-to-tax e-selling and informal selling below VAT thresholds. The recent demise of the betting tax in Britain as a result of gambling on the Internet is an example of this kind of vulnerability. The idea of individual states as "fiscal concentration camps"[57] could never be fully realized even at the height of the Fordist or Keynesian-state era; but the information age seems as likely to open up new exits out of the established tax bases as to close them off.

International Regimes That Support the Tax State

A third condition for survival and development of the tax state is an international regime that is benign for that type of state. The earlier discussion suggested that the twentieth-century tax state in the wealthy democracies developed within an international regime that permitted increasing income and sales taxation. Such regimes may well have constrained the shape of the tax structure, particularly in the 1980s, as

[54] See Peter N. Grabosky and Russell G. Smith, *Crime in the Digital Age* (New Brunswick: Transaction Publishers, 2000), on what the authors claim to be increasing criminal opportunities offered by digitization and telecommunications changes, some of which directly affect tax capacity.

[55] See Henry J. Aaron, "Richer Means Harder to Tax," in Herbert Stein, ed., *Tax Policy in the Twenty-First Century* (New York: Wiley, 1988), 232–48.

[56] See Gary Richards, "E-commerce — a Snapshot," *British Tax Review* 2000, no. 3 (2000): 137–43.

[57] See *Financial Times*, January 16, 1969, letter by A. W. Nelson.

Steinmo, Peters, and others argue,[58] but as noted earlier they did not restrict the aggregate growth of the mainstays of the tax state. Again, there is no obvious reason why such conditions might be expected to alter in the information age. After all, the ideas of world government that were advanced after World War II have long receded, and even in the EU the road to direct tax harmonization has been slow and rocky since the 1960s.[59]

In what sense or in what ways might the much-debated phenomenon of globalization — whose relation to state capacity is discussed in many other chapters in this book — work to shape tax capacity in ways different from the past? Those "soft" versions of globalization that stress convergence through policy diffusion and mutual learning among states do not necessarily imply weakening of tax capacity, though in fact there is nothing new about international borrowing in tax policy (for instance, over stamp taxes, sales taxes, income taxes, or state lotteries). However, the harder "capital exit threat" version of globalization, as expounded by John Ikenberry, in which mobile capital forces convergence of state policies, poses a sharper potential challenge to state tax capacity. And if globalization puts a rising share of economic activity into the hands of multinational corporations, the ability of those corporations to escape tax on their earnings could further limit the tax capacity of developed states, as it has done for the less developed ones.

Up to now any such change seems to have had limited impact on aggregate tax capacity, because taxes on business income and profits were not major sources of tax revenue in the developed countries in the twentieth century. To hit the tax state where it hurts most — in overall revenue yield — increasing corporate size and capital mobility would need to threaten one or more of the tax state's main sources of tax revenue, or prevent the development of equally productive successor taxes.

There are at least two possibilities of that type. One could be the intensification of international competitive challenge to the wealthy democracies from NICs, penetrating the regional trade blocs through more liberal international-trade regimes. Were it to eventuate, such a development could put more pressure on the reduction of business overheads in general and the tax component of those overheads (such as fuel and energy taxes) in particular.

Another possibility consists of a threat to sales tax regimes through the growth of international e-commerce (and indeed business-to-business transactions), if, as many claim, e-commerce comes to be a major trading (and criminal) medium in the information age, with more dig-

---

[58] See Steinmo, *Taxation and Democracy*; Peters, *The Politics of Taxation*.
[59] See Kenneth Dyson, *Elusive Union* (London: Longman, 1994).

itized crime and more information products delivered on a virtual basis.[60] Such taxation cannot be expected to operate smoothly unless all states (or at least a sufficient number of states) can agree on a regime or act simultaneously on the same lines, given the possibilities for migration of transactions across frontiers that virtual transactions offer. Commentators such as Gary Richards expect the result to be pressures for international (and certainly EU) convergence over VAT or sales taxes.[61] The OECD has worked on such issues for some years, but OECD countries differ in their approach, and developing countries outside the OECD may well adopt different rules over issues such as "permanent establishment."[62] Certainly, political resistance to taxation of Internet transactions in a single powerful state (notably through the power of the e-commerce and technology lobby in the U.S. Congress) could have major consequences for the tax state generally in the information age over e-commerce in virtual products.

COUNTERACTIVE STRATEGIES TO SQUEEZES ON THE TAX STATE

If the information age poses possible threats to the tax state, it can also be expected to offer opportunities. If a new age of economic growth and development occurs, it might well produce absolute increases in tax revenue, and some soft targets for revenue are likely to remain from the earlier era even if tax collection costs rise in some fiscal areas. Moreover, as suggested earlier, the new age offers a range of potential new revenue niches for the tax state to occupy. Indeed, at least three general strategies could be identified for the tax state to deploy against possible squeezes on one or more of its four main twentieth-century sources of income. Those possible strategies include going outside the "big four" major sources of tax revenue, developing a "two-tier" political economy, and going outside the traditional boundaries of the tax state in other ways.

Look Outside the "Big Four" for New Major Tax Sources

If governments in the wealthy democracies wished to increase the load carried by taxes outside the "big four" that underpinned the twentieth-

---

[60] As with U.S. attempts to levy "use taxes" to supplement sales taxes where providers can supply goods out-of-state.

[61] See Richards, "E-commerce—a Snapshot."

[62] For instance, the issue of whether and when a website counts as a permanent establishment for tax purposes (ibid., 139).

century tax state, those governments would need to find either new fiscal niches or a way of stepping up existing minor taxes. That would mean departing from what Richard Rose claims to be a normal pattern of "taxation by inertia" (meaning little change in tax structures over long intervals, with reliance on tax buoyancy to lift or maintain overall revenue).[63] Potential new niches for the tax state offered by the information-age economy include placing tollgates on the information super-highways, taxes on websites, virtual stamps on e-mail, or (more likely) increasing use of telecom companies and Internet service provider (ISP) companies as the key tax collectors of the information age. Moreover, one of the state's central and traditional functions — the capacity to identify its citizens — could be of even greater economic value for commercial transactions precisely because of the potential for increased anonymity in the Internet age.

There are certainly major technical and legal challenges that would need to be overcome before the tax state could successfully occupy such niches. As noted earlier, it is easy to see how tax havens could frustrate attempts to tax websites (although a cross-sanctions facility could be provided by denial of legal rights to transactions conducted through tax haven websites). Some such taxes might prove unpopular with voters, particularly where alternatives to the web dry up for some types of transactions, for instance in banking. But the main limit to the pursuit of a strategy of developing Internet-specific taxes seems likely to come at the international-regime level from a mixture of divergent state strategies and organized business pressure, given the power of telecom multinationals and ISPs.

Develop a Two-Tier Tax Strategy

Such political limits to attempts to break out of the tax state's four main twentieth-century boxes may be substantial. If so, another strategy might be to accept in effect a two-tier political economy. What that means is a lightly taxed or untaxed "virtual economy," but heavier taxes levied on physical routes in and out of that economy. After all, even, and perhaps especially, in the information age, virtuality has its limits. While the frontier shifts between products and services that are distributable virtually and those that are not (with more entertainment, publications, banking, advice, training, and counseling services migrating into the former category), energy, food, clothes, hardware, and many other products and services must inescapably be physically consumed, transported,

---

[63] See Rose, "Maximizing Revenue."

and distributed. A tax state that concentrates on the physical margins of the virtual economy would merely be following an information-age parallel to the strategy pursued by many early modern states and their developing-country counterparts today — that is, placing more reliance on taxing the export or import of primary products (or taxing markets by franchising or levying tolls on their entry points) than on trying to tax all transactions and earnings within domestic markets.[64] If the tax state finds it harder to keep track of what we buy and sell through our screens and WAP phones, it can still tax the electricity that powers them, the radio masts or Integrated Services Digital Network (ISDN) lines that relay the signals, and the physical delivery process.

That two-tier approach to fiscal extraction by the tax state in the information age is likely to encounter limits, too. Higher energy taxation can encounter political resistance,[65] and such taxes tend to be regressive in the absence of counteracting subsidies to the least well-off individuals or regions. It would take major growth in green values in the wealthy democracies to overcome such resistance. Attempts to put additional taxes on distribution would be both vulnerable to political resistance orchestrated by national and international courier companies and possibly difficult administrative logistics in a world where multiple private courier and distribution services have replaced old-style post office delivery monopolies.

Go Outside the Traditional Boundaries of the Tax State

A third option is for governments to pursue strategies that go outside the traditional boundaries of the tax state altogether, for instance, by using inflation to fill revenue gaps. Printing money, after all, is a traditional standby of governments facing tax constraints and historically has often been adopted during wars and other periods of fiscal squeeze. In effect, such a strategy would be a backdoor way of raising taxes on the rising proportion of retired elderly the wealthy democracies are likely to contain in the coming decades — but the rising share of the electorate comprising the "grey vote" might make such a strategy less politically infeasible. Moreover, the "capital exit threat" version of globalization could limit such a strategy, to the extent that the informa-

---

[64] See Harvey Hinrichs, *A General Theory of Tax Structure Change during Economic Development* (Cambridge: Harvard University Law School, 1966); Fauvelle-Aymar, "Political and Tax Capacity," 392ff.

[65] As shown by anti–fuel tax campaigns in parts of Europe and Asia against a backdrop of a doubling of oil prices in 2000.

tion age makes it easier for individuals and companies to use arbitrage formulas to shift their liquid wealth among currencies, meaning that governments or currency unions seeking to tax by inflation could face even greater currency outflow than in the 1970s. If so, there would be a greater risk of nominal currencies being shouldered aside by others as the preferred units for transactions or saving, and the inflation "tax" falling hardest on public servants and those dependent on state pensions or welfare payments (a situation that is all too familiar in less developed countries).

Another strategy at or beyond the traditional borderlines of the tax state is to place more emphasis on the revenue government can obtain from its assets. This strategy might also be limited: as the recurring privatization-age metaphor of "selling the family silver" suggests, state assets once sold in a conventional way cannot be readily recovered, and rent-seeking processes often mean public assets are sold permanently and at "fire sale" prices. But as auctions of new-generation mobile phone licenses in Britain and Germany in 1999 and 2000 showed, some of the resources commanded by the state can be franchised or sold on a recurrent basis (albeit in both cases at ruinous cost to the successful bidders), and some of those resources may assume particular importance in the information age.

A further possible way of breaking out of the traditional tax state framework is to alter the boundaries or structure of the tax state itself, either by passing more tax powers down to lower levels of government or by a shift toward more international tax structures and agencies, or both. Greens have long argued that small, self-governing communities have greater capacity to detect tax evasion than conventional, central state organizations (implying a return to the origins of modern tax collection in parish units in many states).[66] Twentieth-century developments in many states went in the opposite direction, with the more buoyant taxes collected by central or federal governments, but the information-age challenges to the tax state sketched out earlier could erode the informational advantages possessed by central or federal governments in collecting income or sales taxes. Indeed, some argue that the only way to take a decisive step toward more redistributive taxation and/or to extend state capacity over tax structure is to change the boundaries of the "tax state" in the direction of a more international approach to tax collection. Such ideas include the "Tobin tax" proposal, the argument by Ronald Dore and others for a global tax author-

[66] See Robert Goodin, *Green Political Theory* (Cambridge: Polity, 1992).

ity to tax major multinational corporations on their global earnings,[67] and the argument of EU "federalists" for a move toward substantive harmonization of direct taxes in the EU (a cause that has made relatively little progress over the past thirty years, as Francesco Duina's analysis in this volume shows). Such proposals remain on the drawing board, and the political constraints to their realization are substantial.

CONCLUSION

If the tax state had a good twentieth century, it is less clear that the information age presents such a benign environment for continuing advance of tax-to-GDP ratios or even their maintenance. Although social science is better at retrodicting the past than predicting the future, we may still be able to identify some conditions on which the future of the tax state in the information age will depend. There are no strong reasons for expecting the tax state to face a sudden major loss of overall taxable capacity, unless the threats to the three critical success factors identified earlier were to materialize simultaneously.

Over time several factors could combine to erode the pillars on which the twentieth-century tax state was built, as has been suggested above. Indeed, if tax capacity is taken to include the state's power over the shape as well as the size of taxation, that capacity — far from complete even in the past — may well be further attenuated. The dilemma of choosing between taxes that are fiscally productive and easy to levy and taxes that are redistributive or serve broader political aims is not new but seems unlikely to go away in the information age, and indeed may sharpen rather than diminish.

Possible counterstrategies to erosion can be identified, though those discussed earlier all appear limited, most are likely to be regressive in their effects even if they could help to plug revenue gaps, and several involve legal and administrative difficulties. But the key constraints seem likely to lie more in domestic politics and international regimes rather than in an absence of administratively feasible tax handles.

Moreover, it was noted earlier that the significance of tax capacity depends on expenditure demands, and this chapter has focused on revenue rather than spending. If the possible threats to the tax state sketched out earlier were real, and expenditure demands on state capacity were maintained or increased, tax capacity would fall and the tax state would need "to accommodate her future views and designs to the real mediocrity of her circumstances" (to borrow and adapt the final words

[67] See *The Independent*, October 26, 1995.

of *The Wealth of Nations*).[68] However, if expenditure demands on state capacity were to fall in the information age — for instance with an absence of world wars of the twentieth-century type — there could be a nineteenth-century pattern of taxation falling as a proportion of GDP but state capacity being maintained or even increased.

[68] Adam Smith, *The Wealth of Nations*, vol. 2, ed. Edwin Cannan (London: Methuen, 1961), 486.

CHAPTER 9

States, Politics, and Globalization:
Why Institutions Still Matter

JOHN L. CAMPBELL

IT IS ALMOST impossible to open a newspaper today and not see a story about "globalization." Although the term means many things, scholars often use it to refer to sharp increases since the mid-1970s in trade, production, and capital flows across national borders due to tariff liberalization, reductions in capital controls, and dramatic improvements in telecommunications and transportation. Many of them argue that the pressures of globalization are forcing nation-states either to reduce taxes, spending, budget deficits, and regulatory control of their economies, or to pay the consequences in terms of higher unemployment, rising interest rates, lower rates of economic growth, and the like. Politicians often invoke this argument to justify such policies, claiming that their hands are tied to do otherwise by the overwhelming pressures of globalization. States, it would seem, have become weakened significantly by globalization. In the vernacular of state theory,[1] they have lost a good deal of their autonomy from the influences of capital and have experienced a decline in their capacities to manage their economies.[2]

These arguments also suggest that economic globalization is leading to a neoliberal convergence not only in policy, but also in the political and economic institutions of advanced capitalist countries.[3] That is,

[1] John A. Hall and G. John Ikenberry, eds., *The State* (Minneapolis: University of Minnesota Press, 1987); Theda Skocpol, "Bringing the State Back In: Strategies of Analysis in Current Research," in Peter Evans, Dietrich Rueschemeyer, and Theda Skocpol, eds., *Bringing the State Back In* (New York: Cambridge University Press, 1985), 3–44.

[2] Throughout this chapter by state capacities I refer to *infrastructural* capacities, that is, the ability of states to penetrate society and organize social relations, such as by taxing, spending, and regulating economic activity. These capacities are conceptually distinct from *despotic* capacities, those that afford states the ability to act with impunity from society. See Michael Mann, "The Autonomous Power of the State: Its Origins, Mechanisms and Results," *Archives Europeennes de Sociologie* 25 (1984): 185–213.

[3] Philip G. Cerny, "International Finance and the Erosion of Capitalist Diversity," in Colin Crouch and Wolfgang Streeck, eds., *Political Economy of Modern Capitalism:*

there is a shift underway, first, in cognitive and normative orientation in favor of politically unfettered markets where states are simply referees enforcing the rules of fair competition and, second, in formal governance arrangements toward privatization, the dismantling of welfare states, and the demise of neocorporatism and other forms of social partnership.[4] By extension, institutions matter less and less as important determinants of political economic performance.[5]

How much truth is there to this economic globalization thesis? Critics claim that divergence remains the rule rather than the exception because nationally specific institutions mediate the degree to which global pressures affect policy making by states as well as private actors in ways that militate against convergence.[6] By mediation I mean that political

---

Mapping Convergence and Diversity (Thousand Oaks, CA: Sage, 1997), 173–81; William Greider, *One World Ready or Not: The Manic Logic of Global Capitalism* (New York: Simon and Schuster, 1997); Bob Jessop, "The Future of the National State: Erosion or Reorganization? General Reflections on the West European Case," paper presented at the Conference on Globalization: Critical Perspectives, University of Birmingham, 1997; Kenichi Ohmae, *The Borderless World: Power and Strategy in the Interlinked Economy* (New York: Harper Collins, 1990); Robert Reich, *The Work of Nations* (New York: Vintage, 1991); Susan Strange, "The Future of Global Capitalism; Or, Will Divergence Persist Forever?" in Crouch and Streeck, eds., *Political Economy of Modern Capitalism*, 182–91; Malcolm Waters, *Globalization* (London: Routledge, 1995). For a review, see Geoffrey Garrett, "Global Markets and National Politics: Collision Course or Virtuous Circle?" *International Organization* 52 (1998): 787–824.

[4] Scott Lash and John Urry, *The End of Organized Capitalism* (Madison: University of Wisconsin Press, 1987).

[5] Others maintain that the rise of international political organizations, such as the United Nations and other nongovernmental organizations, is leading to the diffusion of common political culture and practices among nation-states—another argument about global convergence but one that stresses political rather than economic causes and does not suggest that convergence is necessarily neoliberal in outcome. See John Boli and George M. Thomas, *Constructing World Culture* (Stanford: Stanford University Press, 1999); Margaret Keck and Kathryn Sikkink, *Activists Beyond Borders: Advocacy Networks in International Politics* (Ithaca: Cornell University Press, 1998); John Meyer et al., "World Society and the Nation State," *American Journal of Sociology* 103 (1997): 144–81; Meyer et al., "The Structuring of a World Environmental Regime, 1870–1990," *International Organization* 51 (1997): 623–51.

[6] Suzanne Berger, "Introduction," in Suzanne Berger and Ronald Dore, eds., *National Diversity and Global Capital* (Ithaca: Cornell University Press, 1996); Paul Hirst and Grahame Thompson, *Globalization in Question* (Cambridge: Polity Press, 1996); Geoffrey Garrett, *Partisan Politics in the Global Economy* (New York: Cambridge University Press, 1998); Garrett, "Global Markets"; Geoffrey Garrett and Peter Lange, "Internationalization, Institutions and Political Change," in Robert O. Keohane and Helen V. Milner, eds., *Internationalization and Domestic Politics* (New York: Cambridge University Press, 1996), 48–75; Herbert Kitschelt et al., "Convergence and Divergence in Advanced Capitalist Economies," in Herbert Kitschelt et al., eds., *Continuity and Change in Contemporary Capitalism* (New York: Cambridge University Press, 1999), 427–60; Helen

institutions create incentives for policymakers to maintain the status quo with regard to tax, welfare, regulatory, and other policies rather than succumb to the incentives for neoliberal reform that stem from globalization pressures. These criticisms constitute an institutional thesis with which I am largely sympathetic. However, I argue in this chapter that there is still some truth to the globalization thesis and that the truth needs to be more carefully distinguished from the fiction. Furthermore, although politics and political institutions do mediate how states and economic actors respond to global pressures when they occur, critics of the globalization thesis have not systematically specified the full range of mechanisms or processes by which this mediation occurs. This chapter does that and, as a result, fills an important gap in the literature.

The argument proceeds as follows. First, I review evidence that indicates that the extent of economic globalization has been exaggerated as have its effects, particularly the rise of neoliberal state policies. In other words, neither state autonomy nor state capacities, respectively, have been eroded nearly as much as the globalization thesis suggests. Second, I suggest briefly why the economic globalization thesis has been overstated and argue that some of the problem lies in the fact that its proponents neglect the importance of national political and institutional differences among countries. Third, I identify seven important mechanisms whereby states respond to globalization in important ways — all of which suggest that states are far from being incapacitated in the face of global economic pressure. Finally, I conclude with some reflections on whether the globalization thesis might eventually be vindicated and why it has remained such an accepted part of our political discourse despite its shortcomings.

HOW EXTENSIVE IS ECONOMIC GLOBALIZATION?

Central to the globalization thesis is the claim that international trade has expanded dramatically among the advanced capitalist countries during the last few decades. Indeed, figure 9.1 shows that since 1960 in the seventeen richest OECD countries, average exports and imports as a percentage of GDP, a standard measure of a national economy's openness to international trade, increased from 24 percent to 30 percent.[7] Yet it is difficult to see this as an overwhelming force, particularly given

---

V. Milner and Robert O. Keohane, "Internationalization and Domestic Politics: An Introduction," in Keohane and Milner, eds., *Internationalization and Domestic Politics*, 3–24.

[7] The time periods represented in figure 9.1 correspond with business cycles in the OECD. The same is true for figures 9.4 and 9.5 below. See Lane Kenworthy, "Globalization and Economic Convergence," *Competition and Change* 2 (1997): 1–64, for details.

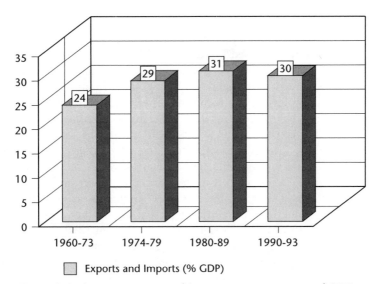

Figure 9.1. Average exports and imports as a percentage of GDP
for the 17 richest OECD countries. *Source:* OECD, reported in
Kenworthy, "Globalization."

the fact that between 1974 and 1993 these figures remained virtually
constant. Instead, it appears that the increase in international trade occurred prior to 1973, at least insofar as the OECD is concerned. If we
take a longer and more encompassing view, we find that although international trade increased substantially in absolute terms during the twentieth century, in relative terms it rose only slightly. In 1913, 15 percent
of all world economic activity involved international trade — a figure
that remained the century's high water mark until it was surpassed in
the mid-1990s, reaching 17 percent in 1996.[8] In other words, by the
mid-1990s about 83 percent of the world's economic activity was still
domestically based.

Two additional points about trade require brief mention. First, by 1995
roughly 67 percent of world trade was among the developed countries —
the so-called triad region of North America, Western Europe, and Japan — and represented only a very slight increase since 1980. This may
seem remarkable insofar as the emerging Asian economies contributed
increasingly to international trade during this period, but this effect was
offset by declines in trade from the Middle East, Africa, Eastern Europe,
and the former Soviet Union.[9] Second, there is significant variation
across advanced countries in how open their economies are and, thus,

[8] Neil Fligstein, *The Architecture of Markets* (Princeton: Princeton University Press,
2001), chap. 9.
[9] Ibid.

how vulnerable they might be to the pressures stemming from global trade. For example, between 1960 and 1994, exports and imports as a percentage of GDP increased in the Netherlands from 42 percent to 50 percent, in France from 14 percent to 22 percent, and in the United States from 5 percent to 11 percent.[10] Of course, many of the smaller OECD economies have been much more open than the larger ones for a long time.[11] This makes sense insofar as the larger economies have much larger domestic markets within which their companies can operate, so there may be less incentive to tap international markets. The point is that these differences show little sign of change.

Another global factor alleged to be weakening states and precipitating policy convergence is the tendency for companies to shift their investments in production and marketing capacity to other countries. Indeed, figure 9.2 shows that foreign direct investment (FDI), that is, the money firms spend buying shares in foreign companies, building plants abroad, and merging with foreign firms, has increased sharply since 1985 and certainly much faster than trade. Of this, 75 percent of the total accumulated stock and 60 percent of the flow of FDI were concentrated in the triad region.[12] In other words, the vast bulk of FDI remained within the advanced capitalist countries. Despite the increase, however, FDI remained only a small fraction of total firm investment during this period. Even for firms in smaller, more open economies, which typically have the highest rates of FDI, this amounted to only about 20 percent of total firm investment.[13] Given the fact that most investment remained in firms' home countries, one must wonder how much of an effect rising FDI really had on states. Furthermore, while it is true that companies can exert power over states to grant favorable tax treatment, trade protection, and the like when they are deciding where to invest internationally, once the decision is made the host country gains considerable power in future bargaining because it is often hard for firms to pull out once they have made their investments, so the threat of capital flight diminishes.[14]

Perhaps the clearest indicator of increasing global economic activity is international portfolio investment, that is, foreign investment in equities, bonds, currencies, and the like, especially insofar as these invest-

[10] Kenworthy, "Globalization," 9.

[11] Peter J. Katzenstein, *Small States in World Markets* (Ithaca: Cornell University Press, 1985).

[12] Hirst and Thompson, *Globalization*, 63.

[13] John A. Hall, "Globalization and Nationalism," ms., Department of Sociology, McGill University, 2000.

[14] Robert Gilpin, *The Challenge of Global Capitalism* (Princeton: Princeton University Press, 2000), 173–74.

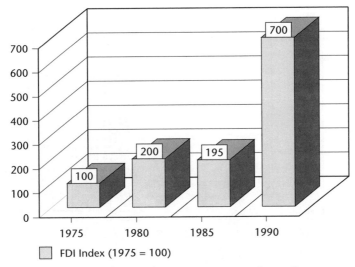

FDI Index (1975 = 100)

Figure 9.2. World foreign direct investment outflows. *Source:* Adapted from Hirst and Thompson, *Globalization*, 55.

ments are more liquid and potentially volatile than FDI. In fact, figure 9.3 shows that international portfolio investment grew much faster than FDI during the 1980s and early 1990s. In 1993, these investments were three times larger than FDI. Nevertheless, domestic investment remained the norm, at least insofar as stocks and bonds were concerned. Investors still preferred to keep almost all of their investments at home, even though the possibility for international investing increased as barriers to overseas participation were lifted. For example, foreign participation in stock markets increased during the 1980s but remained quite small. Foreign listings on the New York Stock Exchange increased from 2.5 percent to 5.4 percent of total listings; on the London Stock Exchange, from 13 percent to 22 percent; and on the Tokyo Stock Exchange, from 1 percent to 7 percent. Notably, even though the most dramatic increase in international listings occurred on the Tokyo exchange, the volume of trade in foreign securities there remained quite modest.[15]

In sum, although the world economy has become more open, at least since World War II, it is less internationally integrated than often suggested by the globalization thesis. Domestic markets remain the location for most firms' production and capital investments as well as for general portfolio investment. Most international economic activity, notably

[15] Beth Simmons, "The Internationalization of Capital," in Kitschelt et al., eds., *Continuity and Change*, 51–56.

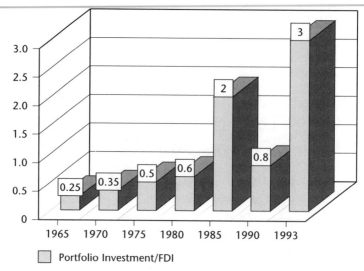

Figure 9.3. Ratio of OECD long-term portfolio investment to FDI.
Source: Adapted from Hirst and Thompson, *Globalization,* 55.

trade and FDI, is located among the advanced capitalist countries, but even here there is considerable cross-national variation. Some aspects of economic activity have become more globally oriented than others. The point of all this is rather simple. Economic globalization has not been so extensive as to obliterate the autonomy of states from international economic forces. Because globalization is not as pervasive and ubiquitous as often assumed, it should not be surprising if its effects on state capacities are also less pronounced than often claimed.

WHAT EFFECTS HAS GLOBALIZATION HAD ON STATE POLICIES?

Many observers have bemoaned the fact that globalization has increased the possibility for capital to flee to countries where it can enjoy the most favorable investment conditions, notably low tax rates. In turn, they have claimed that this would cause states to compete in order to attract capital by lowering tax rates, thus precipitating a "race to the bottom," the result of which would be an international convergence on relatively low tax rates.[16] Generally speaking, this has not happened. Figure 9.4

[16] For reviews, see Garrett, "Global Markets"; Edgar Kiser and Aaron Laing, "Have We Overestimated the Effects of Neoliberalism and Globalization? Some Speculations on the Anomalous Stability of Taxes on Business," in John L. Campbell and Ove K. Pedersen,

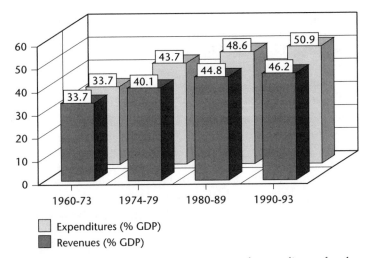

Figure 9.4. Average government revenues and expenditures for the 17 richest OECD countries. *Source:* Adapted from Hirst and Thompson, *Globalization,* 55.

reveals that taxes as a percentage of GDP increased steadily between 1960 and 1993 among OECD countries. The same is true specifically for taxes on business, where most of the increase stemmed from higher employers' social security taxes although corporate income taxes increased slightly as well. There is also little evidence for a convergence in business taxes. For example, business taxes in the Scandinavian social democracies rose most dramatically, from about 4 percent to 10 percent of GDP between 1965 and 1995, while taxes in more neoliberal countries, such as the United States and Britain, increased from about 5 percent to 6 percent. If anything, movement has been away from convergence.[17] Why? Some have argued that a tradeoff occurred where in exchange for higher business taxes social democratic governments were also more likely to increase spending on education, research and development, and the like. Because business benefited from this spending, it was willing to help pay for it through higher taxes.[18] Others have noted that higher rates of taxation fund spending for programs that contribute to political stability — another collective good that business values and is

eds., *The Rise of Neoliberalism and Institutional Analysis* (Princeton: Princeton University Press, 2001); John L. Campbell, "Fiscal Sociology in an Age of Globalization: Comparing Tax Regimes in Advanced Capitalist Countries," paper presented at the Conference on Economic Sociology in the 21st Century, Cornell University, 2001.

[17] Kiser and Laing, "Overestimated"; Kenworthy, "Globalization."
[18] Kiser and Laing, "Overestimated."

willing to help support, especially during a time when greater international market integration may threaten the economic security among broader segments of society.[19] In sum, business may be willing to support policies whereby states socialize some of the risks that would otherwise prevent them from investing.[20]

Globalization is also said to trigger a convergent race to the bottom in government spending. Lower taxes mean that governments will eventually have to reduce expenditures in order to maintain some semblance of fiscal responsibility, or pay the price through higher interest rates and inflation. But OECD social expenditures increased between 1960 and the early 1990s, although the rate of increase declined since 1980 (see fig. 9.4). The globalization thesis also suggests that capital is supposed to move in search of not only cheap labor but also a lower social wage, including social security, unemployment benefits, and various transfer payments, the costs of which business helps cover through taxes. Thus, even if overall government expenditures remain steady or even rise, we should at least see states cutting these social programs in order to attract investment and mitigate capital flight. Instead, Figure 9.5 shows that OECD social welfare transfers increased from 1960 to 1993, and figure 9.6 indicates that, although countries that often had social democratic governments spent more than their Christian democratic or liberal counterparts, this trend held for all three types of governments at least through 1986, the most recent year for which I have data.[21]

But were these countries punished for their fiscal behavior? First, budget deficits in most OECD countries increased during the early 1990s, and where they did, countries tended to incur slightly higher real long-

[19] Garrett, *Partisan Politics*; Garrett, "Global Markets."

[20] See Linda Weiss, *The Myth of the Powerless State* (Ithaca: Cornell University Press, 1998). This is not to say that Scandinavian firms were completely enthralled with all forms of state spending. Indeed, in Sweden there was a strong backlash against many welfare state policies that business believed had sparked inflation. See Mark M. Blyth, "The Transformation of the Swedish Model: Economic Ideas, Distributional Conflict and Institutional Change," ms., Department of Political Science, Johns Hopkins University, 1999. However, these were likely to be transfer programs rather than those that benefited business directly, such as business subsidies that increased during the 1980s and early 1990s. See Kenworthy, "Globalization," 33. However, in some countries, such as Denmark, business has actually been quite supportive of social programs. See Duane Swank and Cathie Jo Martin, "Employers and the Welfare State: The Political Economic Organization of Firms and Social Policy in Contemporary Capitalist Democracies," *Comparative Political Studies* 34, 8(2001): 889–923.

[21] It is worth noting that within the OECD the country that has undertaken the most dramatic reduction in social spending has been the United States, the most closed economy (except for Japan) in terms of trade and, thus, the country for which globalization theorists might have been *least* likely to expect such cuts. See Fligstein, *The Architecture of Markets*, chap. 9.

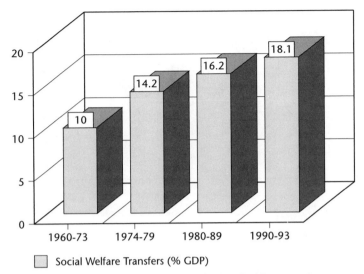

Figure 9.5. Average social welfare transfers for the 17 richest
OECD countries. "Social welfare transfers" include social security
and social assistance programs. *Source:* OECD, reported in
Kenworthy, "Globalization."

term interest rates, as globalization theorists predict. Still, it is important to note that governments with higher levels of spending were no
more likely to experience increased deficits than countries with lower
levels of spending.[22] Second, the OECD also tended toward lower, not
higher, rates of inflation.[23] Third, there is little evidence that higher
levels of spending, taxation, or budget deficits caused capital to flee to
other countries.[24] Fourth, nor is there much evidence that higher taxing
or spending, typical for social democratic and Christian democratic
governments, undermined economic growth.[25] Fifth, the literature is unclear regarding whether social democratic and Christian democratic
governments are any more prone to unemployment than neoliberal ones,
although it does appear that disinvestment causes unemployment to increase.[26] In sum, the evidence is again far from overwhelming in its sup-

[22] Garrett, *Partisan Politics*, chap. 6.

[23] Kenworthy, "Globalization," 17, 24, 48.

[24] Garrett, "Global Markets."

[25] Alexander Hicks and Lane Kenworthy, "Cooperation and Political Economic Performance in Affluent Democratic Capitalism," *American Journal of Sociology* 103 (1998):
1631–72.

[26] Ibid.; Bruce Western and Katherine Beckett, "How Unregulated Is the U.S. Labor
Market? The Penal System as a Labor Market Institution," *American Journal of Sociology*

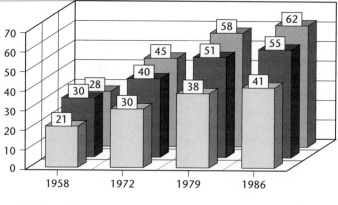

Social Democratic
Christian Democratic
Liberal

Figure 9.6. Average OECD social welfare payments. "Social welfare payments" include social security, consumption payments (in-kind benefits such as health and education), and transfer payments (cash benefits such as income support and unemployment benefits). *Source:* Adapted from John Stephens, Evelyn Huber, and Leonard Ray, "The Welfare State in Hard Times," in Kitschelt et al., eds., *Continuity and Change.*

port for the globalization thesis. Governments were punished by the financial markets (through higher interest rates), but then only for larger budget deficits, not for increased spending or taxation per se; higher levels of taxation, spending, or deficits did not generally bring serious retribution from capital engaged in multinational trade or production. But even higher interest rates did not seem to deter governments from running deficits. Indeed, governments seemed to be quite willing to incur slightly higher interest rates if the deficits that caused them helped these governments to remain in power and maintain political stability.

Finally, does globalization cause states to engage in economic deregulation and a more free-market model as capital becomes more footloose? The evidence here is a bit more sketchy, but some have suggested that if there is a trend, it is toward a reorganization — not a reduction — in regulatory capacities. First, in the important area of monetary control there has been since the breakdown of the Bretton Woods accord in

104 (1999): 1030–60; Bruce Western, "Institutions, Investment and the Rise in Unemployment," in Campbell and Pedersen, eds., *The Rise of Neoliberalism.*

1971 a tendency for governments to grant their central banks more autonomy to set interest rates and regulate the money supply in order to better control inflation and defend currencies in the face of increasingly mobile international capital and currency speculation—a trend that has removed monetary policy from national politics and led to generally more austere monetary policy.[27] However, this appears to have been matched with important changes in bankruptcy law whereby governments eventually recognized that stringent monetary policy increased the possibilities of recession, business failure, and unemployment, so, out of concern for the political ramifications, many governments revised their bankruptcy laws to facilitate corporate reorganization rather than liquidation. In other words, neoliberal deregulation in monetary policy was counterbalanced with non-neoliberal reregulation in bankruptcy policy.[28]

Moreover, initial efforts to deregulate many economies turned out quite differently in the end. Often reforms were implemented by policymakers and bureaucrats who struggled over the specifics of reform and managed to shape them according to their institutionally and organizationally defined interests. The Japanese telecommunications industry is a good example. According to Steven Vogel, the Japanese had long believed in a strong managerial role for government in the economy, and, as a result, the state had developed institutional capacities to restructure markets and guide industrial development. But in 1980, motivated in part by the example of U.S. deregulation a decade earlier, the legislature started to talk about liberalizing the use of telephone lines, and in 1984 it privatized the national telecommunications carrier, Nippon Telegraph and Telephone Public Corporation (NTT). Neoliberal deregulation appeared to have arrived. However, the Ministry of Posts and Telecommunications used this as an opportunity to enhance its role as protector and promoter of the industry and thus reassert the state's control over the industry albeit in a new form. Previously, the ministry enjoyed only limited supervisory control over NTT, but as privatization proceeded it played a key role helping to craft legislation that left it with extensive capacities to regulate prices and the introduction of new services—a maneuver that elevated it to a position of power and prominence among Japan's elite ministries, including the mighty Ministry of International Trade and Industry. Reform ended up conforming less to some neoliberal ideal and more to the institutional traditions (cognitive, norma-

---

[27] Kathleen R. McNamara, *The Currency of Ideas* (Ithaca: Cornell University Press, 1998); Simmons, "Internationalization."

[28] Bruce G. Carruthers, Sarah L. Babb, and Terence C. Halliday, "Institutionalizing Markets, or the Market for Institutions? Central Banks, Bankruptcy Law and the Globalization of Financial Markets," in Campbell and Pedersen, eds., *The Rise of Neoliberalism.*

tive, and organizational) of strong, centralized, state bureaucracies holding sway over industrial development and operation. Because regulatory reform in other countries in telecommunications, finance, and other industries also matched long-standing national institutional traditions, Vogel shows that there has not been a convergence toward neoliberal deregulation but rather the development of new styles of regulation and new regulatory capacities that vary across countries.[29]

I am not arguing that the evidence here is conclusive, only that it raises questions about the adequacy of the globalization thesis. Definitive tests require far more data and sophisticated analytic techniques. Nevertheless, the argument is that states may not have rushed to cut taxes and spending and deregulate their economies as much as the economic globalization thesis would have us believe. Nor has there been as much of a convergence on the neoliberal ideal — a race to the bottom — as we might expect.[30] Certainly, some states have pursued neoliberal policies more than others, but some states have done so for a long time anyway. That is, the capacity of states to extract revenue, provide welfare and other benefits, and regulate economic activity has always varied considerably and continues to do so. Why has the globalization thesis apparently missed the mark?

WHY HAVEN'T GLOBALIZATION PRESSURES
HAD GREATER EFFECT ON STATES?

In addition to having exaggerated the extent of global pressure and the decline of state autonomy, as noted above, there are several reasons why globalization has not had as great an impact on state capacities as the globalization thesis predicts. First, the trends in question are not irreversible. For instance, the period from 1920 to 1945 witnessed declines in international trade and investment for reasons having much to do with states and politics, particularly war but also the creation of tariffs and other trade barriers. International political agreements continue to have such effects. While the development of the European Union, the North American Free Trade Agreement (NAFTA), Mercosur, and similar agreements increase international trade and capital flows within regions, they may also create barriers and incentives that inhibit trade between regions. For instance, since NAFTA, U.S. foreign direct investment has shifted away from the East Asian economies to Mexico.[31]

[29] Steven K. Vogel, *Freer Markets, More Rules* (Ithaca: Cornell University Press, 1996).
[30] See especially Kitschelt et al., "Convergence."
[31] Gilpin, *Challenge*, 181.

There is also always the possibility that national governments will invoke trade sanctions when they perceive that other countries are engaged in "unfair" economic practices. For years the United States refused to extend most-favored nation status to China in order to force
the Chinese to change their labor and human rights policies, and the
United States is now considering trade sanctions against the Japanese
for hunting whales. As these examples illustrate, one very important
reason why the forces of globalization ebb and flow is that states actually have some control over them. Rather than just suffering the consequences of globalization, states may actively contribute to globalization
itself.[32] Indeed, T. V. Paul argues in chapter 5 in this volume that the
advanced capitalist states in general and the United States in particular
have contributed to the rise of globalization in many ways.

Second, the globalization thesis neglects the importance of institutional legacies and how they mediate international pressures with important effects. Vogel has shown that differences in normative and cognitive understandings among policymakers and state bureaucrats led to
important variations in the manner in which regulatory reforms were
implemented in Britain, Japan, and several other advanced capitalist
countries.[33] More formal institutional arrangements also mediated how
these reforms proceeded. He explains that because Britain's constitution
tends to concentrate policy control in the executive branch, Margaret
Thatcher had an easier time pursuing a more draconian deregulatory
program than Ronald Reagan did in the United States, where constitutional provisions fragmented control between Congress and the executive branch, thus muting reform. For similar reasons, neoliberal tax cuts
were more sustained in Britain during the 1980s than in the United
States, where the deep cuts advocated by the president and passed by
Congress in 1981 were partially restored a year later after various interest groups, including some members of the business community, who
enjoyed relatively easy institutional access to policymakers, convinced
them that the cuts had triggered budget deficit problems.[34] Indeed, political-institutional factors continued to reinforce differences in national

[32] Weiss, *Myth*, 11.

[33] Vogel, *Freer Markets*. See Gosta Esping-Anderson, *Social Foundations of Postindus-
trial Economies* (New York: Oxford University Press, 1999), for discussion about how
normative institutions limit neoliberal reform in welfare policy.

[34] John L. Campbell and Michael Allen, "Indentifying Shifts in Policy Regimes: Cluster
and Interrupted Time-Series Analyses of U.S. Income Taxes," *Social Science History* 25
(2001): 37–65; Cathie J. Martin, *Shifting the Burden: The Struggle over Growth and
Corporate Taxation* (Chicago: University of Chicago Press, 1991), chap. 6; Sven Steinmo,
Taxation and Democracy (New Haven: Yale University Press, 1993).

tax policies and the amount of revenues states collected throughout the OECD.[35]

Finally, national politics exert similar effects. For example, once established, social programs tend to develop constituencies over time who will defend them if they come under siege. In the United States, when social security became a budget-cutting target during the 1980s, the American Association of Retired Persons, one of the most powerful lobbying organizations in Washington, successfully repelled the attack.[36] The effort to cut old-age pensions was more successful in Britain because the pension system was more fragmented institutionally, consisting of both universal flat-rate and means-tested components, so opposition to retrenchment was divided.[37]

Similarly, labor unions, which have been organized differently throughout Europe and developed different collective identities, reacted in unique ways to the efforts of employers and governments to shift labor-management relations in a neoliberal direction due to globalization pressures. Swedish unions, for instance, focused their attention, albeit unsuccessfully, on defending the central wage bargain; German unions sought to protect wages and the length of the work week; Italian unions struggled to preserve cost-of-living increases; and U.S. unions wanted to defend control over shop-floor relations.[38] The degree to which unions were successful varied in each case, but labor politics played a key role in mediating whether globalization resulted in neoliberalism or not. Of course, as Rudra Sil notes in chapter 10 in this volume, states were also culpable in all of this insofar as they helped shape and sustain various industrial relations systems.

Lastly, even though some members of the business community sought neoliberal responses to the pressures of globalization, others did not. German employers associations were deeply divided about dismantling co-determination practices. In particular, large firms wanted to preserve neocorporatist wage bargaining in order to keep wage conflicts out of the cooperative shop-floor relations they had historically kept with workers and that they believed were crucial for maintaining the kind of flexibility in production that was still required to compete interna-

[35] Sven Steinmo and Caroline J. Tolbert, "Do Institutions Really Matter? Taxation in Industrialized Democracies," *Comparative Political Studies* 31 (1998): 165–87.

[36] Theda Skocpol, *The Missing Middle: Working Families and the Future of American Social Policy* (New York: Norton, 2000).

[37] Paul Pierson, *Dismantling the Welfare State? Reagan, Thatcher and the Politics of Retrenchment* (New York: Cambridge University Press, 1994).

[38] Richard M. Locke and Kathleen Thelen, "Apples and Oranges Revisited: Contextualized Comparisons and the Study of Comparative Labor Politics," *Politics and Society* 23 (1995): 337–67.

tionally. So far they have managed to defend against the neoliberal alternatives that small and medium-sized firms have advocated[39] On the same note, during the last thirty years when employers were organized collectively, such as through national employers associations, they tended to support, not attack, social spending programs in the OECD countries. This was probably because they saw these policies as contributing to human capital development, helping to cultivate trust with workers and the general public, and facilitating a well-functioning economy in other ways.[40]

To digress briefly, not only can domestic interests help preserve corporatist and other institutionalized forms of bargaining, they may sometimes create pressure to expand or build these institutions anew. For instance, Brendan O'Leary in chapter 2 in this volume suggests that domestic conflicts over nationalism may lead to the development of consociational bargaining. The implication is that this and other sorts of domestic pressure may act as a counterweight to whatever global pressures there may be to move away from such institutions.

Certainly the relationship between institutional legacies and politics is an important one insofar as national-level institutions help organize politics and thus the degree to which political opposition emerges and prevents neoliberal reforms from proceeding when proponents of the globalization thesis advocate them. As a result, neglecting these political-institutional effects obscures the mechanisms that determine how national actors respond to the pressures of globalization when they arise or are otherwise invoked. But can we be more specific about what these mechanisms are?

SEVEN MECHANISMS THAT MEDIATE
THE EFFECTS OF GLOBALIZATION

Several scholars on both the left and right have argued that nation-states are increasingly incapacitated or hollowed out as a result of their inability to cope with the globalization of economic activity and, thus, are forced to pursue neoliberal policies.[41] Others have disagreed.[42] How-

---

[39] Kathleen Thelen, "Why German Employers Cannot Bring Themselves to Dismantle the German Model," in Torben Iversen, Jonas Pontousson, and David Soskice, eds., *Unions, Employers and Central Banks* (New York: Cambridge University Press, 2000), 138–69.

[40] Swank and Martin, "Employers."

[41] Crouch and Streeck, eds., *Political Economy of Modern Capitalism*; Jessop, "Future"; Ohmae, *Borderless*; Reich, *Work of Nations*.

[42] Peter A. Hall, "Organized Market Economies and Unemployment in Europe: Is It

ever, the evidence suggests that states respond to shifting international
economic pressures in various ways that often prevent them from being
incapacitated by neoliberal currents.

To begin with, states can block pressures for neoliberalism for long
periods of time.[43] Scandinavia is a case in point where states have persis-
tently maintained high levels of business taxation and government spending. Others have shown that countries with strong unions and social
democratic governments have held out against the neoliberal juggernaut, sometimes even managing to strengthen traditional social democratic policies insofar as they provide the security and stability businesses seek in the face of rising international economic competition and
risk.[44] Of course, the ability of states to block pressures for neoliberalism is not restricted to the OECD. A cogent argument can be made that
the institutions of the Soviet command economy buffered the Soviet
Union from the vicissitudes of the international economy for decades.[45]
Notably, the state monopoly on foreign trade and the administrative
command system of central planning long protected key industries, such
as energy, from fluctuations in international prices. Even after several of
the largest energy companies were privatized after the fall of the communist regime, high-ranking state officials retained firm control over the
post-Soviet energy sector, continued to block neoliberal reform and the
development of efficient energy markets, and perpetuated much of the
centralized, bureaucratic management of the Soviet era, including its
institutional legacy of inefficiency and corruption.[46] Indeed, political and
institutional legacies die hard and, as a result, may block neoliberal
reform even when it may be desirable.

States can also translate neoliberalism into their own long-standing
institutions without abandoning them entirely. In Denmark, pressures of
international competition led policymakers to search for ways to incorporate neoliberal principles into traditional Danish institutions where
economic policy was the product of elaborate negotiations between the
state and private actors. Rather than abandoning industrial policy and

---

Finally Time to Accept Liberal Orthodoxy?" paper presented at the 11th International
Conference of Europeanists, Baltimore, 1998; Garret, *Partisan Politics*; David Soskice,
"Divergent Production Regimes: Coordinated and Uncoordinated Market Economies in
the 1980s and 1990s," in Kitschelt et al., ed., *Continuity and Change*, 101–34; Weiss,
Myth.

    [43] Garrett and Lange, "Internationalization."

    [44] Garrett, *Partisan Politics*.

    [45] See also Susan Shirk, "Internationalization and China's Economic Reforms," in Keo-
hane and Milner, eds., *Internationalisation and Domestic Politics*, 186–208, for China.

    [46] Matthew Evangelista, "Stalin's Revenge: Institutional Barriers to Internationalization
in the Soviet Union," in Keohane and Milner, eds., *Internationalisation and Domestic
Politics*, 159–87.

absolving the state of its responsibilities for industrial development, Danish leaders reorganized both by establishing a more decentralized set of institutional links among the national government, local authorities, business, labor, and other private organizations. The result was a new, but still negotiated, form of policies that encouraged firms to adopt new technologies and production practices.[47] Neoliberalism was translated into traditional Danish practices rather than replacing them. Similarly, the Danish state reformed nationally coordinated labor market policy but decentralized it rather than abandoning it entirely so that labor market policy is now coordinated through negotiations between employers and state authorities at the regional level.[48] In this regard, recall that Vogel also identified translation processes in other countries when neoliberal pressures for deregulation emerged and policymakers tailored them to fit the political interests as well as institutional and normative configurations of prevailing regulatory bureaucracies.[49] Finally, and perhaps most revealing, Francesco Duina notes in this volume and elsewhere that even when organizations like the European Union and Mercosur issue directives that are intended specifically to harmonize the regulation of trade among states, national governments often translate them into their own law in unique ways—and in some cases refuse to translate them at all—thereby leaving more heterogeneity than might otherwise be expected.[50]

It is worth mentioning that translation also occurs in the private sector. Even when capital moves across borders in search of mergers and acquisitions, it tends to operate in ways that are similar to how it did at home.[51] When Daimler-Benz merged with Chrysler in 1998, it kept its legal status as a German firm and continued to use German institutions of social partnership in the United States by including a representative of the United Auto Workers on the supervisory board of the new entity. And although Deutsche Bank now advocates more openness and transparency in the banking community in order to compete effectively in an

---

[47] Peter Kjaer and Ove K. Pedersen, "Translating Liberalization: Neoliberalism in the Danish Negotiated Economy," in Campbell and Pedersen, eds., *The Rise of Neoliberalism.*

[48] Swank and Martin, "Employers."

[49] Vogel, *Freer Markets.*

[50] See Francesco Duina, *Harmonizing Europe: Nation States within the Common Market* (Albany: State University of New York Press, 1999). Scholars have noted that the same sort of institutionally mediated translation process occurs for the global diffusion of new models and ideas for policy areas less directly linked to economics, such as citizenship and human rights. See Yasemin Soysal, *Limits of Citizenship* (Chicago: University of Chicago Press, 1994); and Keck and Sikkink, *Activists.*

[51] Paul Doremus et al., *The Myth of the Global Corporation* (Princeton: Princeton University Press, 1998).

environment of increasingly international capital markets, it still tries to retain its privileged ties with the largest German firms. Finally, when firms in the steel industry were pressed by German banks to cut costs and raise productivity through mergers in order to compete better internationally, they did so in ways consistent with German tradition. Notably, large firms, such as Krupp and Hoesch, continued to negotiate with works councils and the union over organizational structures and practices for the new firm — negotiations that both labor and management advocated. All of this contradicts the argument that Germany's economic institutions are inexorably converging on the neoliberal model. Despite the fact that German firms espouse economic liberalism, they continue to invest in the social partnerships and long-term relationships that have characterized their behavior for decades.[52]

Of course, just as globalization pressures are reversible, even when states experiment with neoliberal programs it is entirely possible that they may reverse course to correct for the political fallout that results. For example, in some East European countries, such as Poland, political elites adopted neoliberal reforms, such as lower levels of government spending and balanced budgets, during the early 1990s under pressure from the international financial community. However, these were later eased when unions protested that the effects of these policies in terms of lower wages and benefits were unacceptable. Neoliberal reform was also quickly moved to the back burner in Hungary after local elections indicated that the first postcommunist ruling coalition would likely be punished politically for the sacrifices neoliberal reform would require of the general population. Even after the country's budget deficit and international debt situation deteriorated, thus forcing the government to push hard for neoliberal reform, the courts rescinded several of these measures, including important welfare benefit reductions. In the Czech case, for institutional reasons unions were weaker and electoral competition was relatively subdued, so there was less opposition to fiscal reform during the first half of the decade. Eventually, of course, reforms did proceed, but often only after bargaining between state and private actors helped to accommodate these concerns.[53] Similar stories have been told about the reversal of neoliberal reform in some Latin American countries during the 1980s.[54] The point is that even in the face of

---

[52] J. Nicholas Ziegler, "Corporate Governance and the Politics of Property Rights in Germany," *Politics and Society* 28 (2000): 195–221.

[53] John L. Campbell, "Convergence or Divergence? Globalization, Neoliberalism and Fiscal Policy in Postcommunist Europe," in Steven Weber, ed., *Globalization and European Political Economy* (New York: Columbia University Press, 2001).

[54] Jack Knight, "Explaining the Rise of Neoliberalism: The Mechanisms of Institutional Change," in Campbell and Pedersen, eds., *The Rise of Neoliberalism.*

international pressure, political elites do not automatically respond with neoliberalism; political and institutional arrangements help determine whether neoliberalism proceeds or retreats.

Sometimes even if states choose not to reverse neoliberal reform, they may compensate for it in other ways. This is essentially what occurred when states eased bankruptcy law and made corporate reorganization a more likely option than liquidation when it became clear that relinquishing control over monetary policy to central banks increased business failures. Compensation may be at work elsewhere as well. Scholars often point to the comparatively low rate of unemployment in the United States during the 1990s as evidence of how successful a country can be if it adopts neoliberal reforms. Indeed, the United States did initiate several such reforms during the 1980s, notably tight monetary policy, but they led to two recessions before unemployment dropped to historic lows in the mid-1990s. Meanwhile, however, rates of incarceration skyrocketed, increasing 300 percent since 1980, reaching rates five to ten times greater than in Western Europe and, as a result, lowering unemployment statistics significantly by reducing the pool of available labor in the first place. This should not be surprising because those most likely to be jailed in the United States were also those most likely to be unemployed during economic downturns, that is, poor, uneducated, men of color. In effect, incarceration served as an insidious form of labor market policy and was, therefore, a major deviation from neoliberalism that compensated albeit unintentionally for the otherwise deleterious effects of neoliberalism.[55]

Similarly, even when states lose some capacities they may be able to build new ones. For instance, Christopher Hood argues in chapter 8 in this volume that although increased international capital mobility may pose problems for the capacity of states to extract revenue by traditional means, states may develop new capacities, such as leasing state assets, shifting tax burdens to domestic industries, and imposing new taxes on the Internet economy. Furthermore, Grzegorz Ekiert shows in chapter 11 that an important way the postcommunist Polish state coped with pressures for neoliberalism was to build new state capacities by shifting power to the prime minister, creating a professional civil service, increasing the number of public sector employees, and raising— not lowering—the level of revenue extraction and social expenditures.

Much of the preceding discussion draws attention to the important ways in which institutions affect how states deal with the pressures of globalization. Indeed, warnings about the neoliberal juggernaut are exaggerated in part because they neglect the stickiness or path-dependence

[55] Western and Beckett, "Unregulated."

of institutional legacies. However, states can also utilize quite self-consciously existing institutional arrangements to cope with these pressures. In this sense institutions "enable" political elites by affording them unique opportunities for action. Peter Hall has argued that advanced capitalist political economies assume a variety of institutional forms, each with its own "comparative institutional advantages" when it comes to dealing with increased international economic competition.[56] For instance, so-called liberal market economies (LME), such as the United States, are adept institutionally at rapidly moving capital, labor, and other resources among firms and across sectors, thus facilitating radical and successful product innovation, as has been the case in biotechnology, computers, and software. Among other things, this is because labor unions are weak, corporate managers enjoy unilateral decision-making power, and capital markets favor shareholder interests and short-term profitability.[57] On the other hand, organized market economies (OME), including Germany and some of the smaller West European countries, are better suited institutionally for maintaining high product quality, flexible production, and more incremental kinds of innovation in industries like machine tools. This is because unions are strong and under law workers are guaranteed a role in cooperative decision making with managers and finance capital takes a more long-term view of profitability because stakeholder rather than shareholder interests receive top priority.[58]

Hall's point is that in addition to cutting costs to cope with globalization, countries can compete effectively by utilizing their comparative institutional advantages. Indeed, this is precisely why some German industrialists have fought to preserve rather than scrap co-determination and corporatist wage bargaining, and why Scandinavian capital may have been willing to continue paying high taxes for substantial govern-

[56] Hall, "Organized Market Economies." See also Hicks and Kenworthy, "Cooperation"; J. Rogers Hollingsworth and Streeck, "Concluding Remarks on Performance, Convergence and Competetiveness," in J. Rogers Hollingsworth, Philippe Schmitter, and Wolfgang Streeck, eds., *Governing Capitalist Economies* (New York: Oxford University Press, 1994); Soskice, "Divergent Production Regimes"; Weiss, *Myth*.

[57] See Mark J. Roe, *Strong Managers, Weak Owners: The Political Roots of American Corporate Finance* (Princeton: Princeton University Press, 1994); Bruce Western, *Between Class and Market: Postwar Unionization in the Capitalist Democracies* (Princeton: Princeton University Press, 1997); John Zysman, *Governments, Markets and Growth: Financial Systems and the Politics of Industrial Change* (Ithaca: Cornell University Press, 1983).

[58] See Joel Rogers and Wolfgang Streeck, "Workplace Representation Overseas: The Works Councils Story," in Richard Freeman ed., *Working under Different Rules* (New York: Russell Sage Foundation, 1994), 97–156; Western, *Class and Market*; Zysman, *Governments*.

ment spending. Certainly in the area of technology development, perhaps one of the most important insofar as global competition is concerned, differences in institutional arrangements offer policymakers both advantages and disadvantages upon which they can capitalize, if they recognize them.[59] Whether they recognize them and react effectively is another question, particularly insofar as the ideology of globalization and neoliberalism is so pervasive. In any case, these sorts of institutional differences are another important reason why there has not been more convergence toward the neoliberal norm.[60]

This discussion underscores one final, but very important institutional mechanism: institutions play a key role in actors' preference formation[61] and may do so in ways that do not support neoliberalism. Two examples will suffice. First, as noted above, one reason why German firms persist in defending the institutions of social partnership is that they perceive that it is in their interests to do so. However, this was not always the case. Indeed, it was only after the government enacted codetermination legislation over the objections of business and firms were forced to live with it for awhile that they began to appreciate the benefits such institutions might afford them — the sort of x-efficiencies often neglected in neoliberal rhetoric.[62] Second, one reason why centralized employer associations tend to support social spending is that associations see the potential benefits and try to educate their members about them, thereby transforming members' perceptions of their interests.[63] Of course, sometimes institutions affect preferences in surprising ways. Minxin Pei argues in chapter 12 in this volume that decentralizing state capacities may create incentives that undermine political and economic efficiency — an outcome quite the opposite from that predicted by neoliberalism. He shows that in China the decentralization of revenue ex-

---

[59] J. Nicholas Ziegler, *Governing Ideas: Strategies for Innovation in France and Germany* (Ithaca: Cornell University Press, 1997); John L. Campbell, *Collapse of an Industry: Nuclear Power and the Contradictions of U.S. Policy* (Ithaca: Cornell University Press, 1988), chaps. 8–9.

[60] Soskice, "Divergent Production Regimes."

[61] For example, see Kathleen Thelen and Sven Steinmo, "Historical Institutionalism in Comparative Politics," in Sven Steinmo, Kathleen Thelen, and Frank Longstreth, eds., *Structuring Politics* (New York: Cambridge University Press, 1992).

[62] Wolfgang Streeck, "Beneficial Constraints: On the Economic Limits of Rational Voluntarism," in J. Rogers Hollingsworth and Robert Boyer, eds., *Contemporary Capitalism: The Embeddedness of Institutions* (New York: Cambridge University Press, 1997), 197–219. See also Michael Best, *The New Competition: Institutions of Industrial Restructuring* (Cambridge: Harvard University Press, 1990); William Lazonick, *Business Organization and the Myth of the Market Economy* (New York: Cambridge University Press, 1991).

[63] Swank and Martin, "Employers."

traction created principle-agent problems that precipitated tax evasion, corruption, and thus revenue loss for the state.

CONCLUSION

I have argued that nationally specific institutions mediate the degree to which the pressures of globalization result in an erosion of state capacities within the advanced capitalist world and that there are seven mechanisms that are responsible for this mediation. Some of these mechanisms are well known in the literature, but some are not. In particular, relatively little attention has been paid to how bits and pieces of the neoliberal model are translated into local contexts or how states compensate for neoliberal reform in one policy area with non-neoliberal reform in another. We would do well to specify more clearly the processes involved. For instance, it would be useful to know why some parts of the neoliberal model are selected for translation while others are not, and how these decisions are made. Similarly, one wonders how decisions are made whereby policy adjustments are made in one area to compensate for those made in others, or whether compensatory actions are more unintentional than deliberate.

Much of the literature advocating an institutional critique of the globalization thesis focuses on how the formal aspects of institutions, such as the arrangement of bureaucratic and regulatory agencies, are important in all of this. Much less attention has been devoted to how the normative and cognitive aspects of political institutions come into play. This is surprising because there is a substantial literature arguing that a common set of normative prescriptions and cognitive assumptions have diffused among nation-states and are exerting pressure for convergence in political practices (see note 5 above). I support the idea that nationally specific normative and cognitive factors are important but suggest, following others in this volume who recognize how persistent and powerful national identities can be, that normative and cognitive factors also operate in ways that contribute to the resilience of national policy differences despite globalization pressures. In this regard, I see less convergence in norms and cognition across countries than those who adopt the strict diffusion perspective. Indeed, I have provided examples above, such as the adoption of neoliberal reforms in Japan, which indicate how important these factors may be. Certainly one reason why the Danes decentralized, rather than jettisoned, their corporatist policy-making institutions was that these institutions have become so much a part of Danish political culture and so taken-for-granted as the

appropriate way of conducting policy making that it was virtually un-
thinkable for Danish policymakers to fully dismantle them.[64]

Let me raise three last issues by way of conclusion. First, the identification of these mechanisms is important because it helps explain why
state capacities have not been corroded as much as the globalization
thesis predicts. Many states remain quite capable of taxing, spending,
and regulating economic activity within their borders. Indeed, when the
circumstances that states face change, they are often flexible enough to
transform their instruments and activities in ways that preserve their
strength.[65] Of course, this is not to say that states will necessarily act in
ways that benefit their economies. Institutional legacies and politics are
a double-edged sword. Thanks to them, political elites may misread situations, make mistakes, or simply respond too slowly (or too rapidly)
to situations in ways that cause more harm than good.[66] In the long run,
this may even contribute to their own incapacitation and hollowing out
if their tax base crumbles, inflation rises, productivity lags, unemployment grows, and political turmoil and electoral backlash ensues. However, my point is that none of this is as inevitable as the globalization
thesis suggests, precisely because institutions and politics matter in the
ways suggested earlier.[67]

Second, despite the arguments I have offered, proponents of the globalization thesis might still insist that their view will be born out if we
wait a little longer. They might suggest that for political and institutional reasons, states may refuse to cut taxes, spending, and regulations,
but they will be punished eventually by global forces beyond their control. In particular, corporations will eventually flee to more favorable
environments; jobs will eventually be lost; and unemployment will eventually rise. In other words, the autonomy of states really has deteriorated, but the full effects have yet to appear. I doubt that this is so
because this view rests on several shaky assumptions. (1) It assumes that
all firms are alike insofar as they are driven primarily by the quest to
reduce the costs of labor, raw materials, taxes, and the like. In fact,
some firms are more interested in skilled labor, just-in-time delivery,
quality control, flexible specialization, government investment pro-

[64] See Klaus Nielsen and Ove K. Pedersen, "From the Mixed Economy to the Negotiated Economy: The Scandinavian Countries," in Richard M. Coughlin, ed., *Morality, Ra-
tionality, and Efficiency: New Perspectives on Socio-Economics* (New York: M. E. Sharpe,
1991).

[65] Hall and Ikenberry, *The State*, 96.

[66] Michael R. Smith, *Power, Norms and Inflation: A Skeptical Treatment* (New York:
Aldine de Gruyter, 1992), chap. 9.

[67] For further discussion of why neoliberal convergence is unlikely, but for reasons other
than institutional ones, see Hollingsworth and Streeck, "Concluding Remarks."

grams, and other far more institutionally specific factors because they see them as being more important for their competitive success than cheap factor inputs.[68] The computer and software industries are especially pertinent examples.[69] (2) It assumes that the financial markets and multinational firms care about the same thing when deciding where to invest when, in fact, the former are concerned principally with government budget deficits rather than levels of spending, taxing, and regulation per se, and the latter do not appear especially obsessed with any of this.[70] (3) It assumes that states are passive recipients of globalization pressures when, in reality, they are often able to wield significant power over them. (4) It assumes that states are unwilling to suffer the costs of whatever punishments the financial markets and firms dispense when, as it turns out, they may be willing to tolerate some castigation, at least insofar as interest rates are concerned, if it enables them to ensure the economic security of the citizenry. To the extent that these assumptions remain flawed, there is good reason to suspect that neoliberal convergence is not likely and that states will retain considerable capacities for managing their economies no matter how long we wait.

Finally, if the evidence favoring the globalization thesis is so specious, why does it continue to attract so much attention and be taken for granted as the truth? This is a complicated question, well beyond the scope of this chapter, but a few thoughts are in order. The idea of globalization has been used by conservatives to create an ideological climate that suggests that government intervention is futile and could even hurt national economic competitiveness.[71] Some leftists have also accepted the globalization thesis and used it as justification for various socialist projects.[72] Furthermore, arguments about globalization are simple so they afford policymakers as well as business leaders some justification for making decisions that are unpopular with the general public. Indeed, in 1993 the Clinton administration invoked the pressures of globalization to legitimize painful spending cuts that it claimed were necessary to reduce federal budget deficits.[73] Of course, the globalization

[68] Best, *New Competition*; Lazonick, *Business Organization*; Hall, "Organized Market Economies."

[69] Annalee Saxenian, *Regional Advantage: Culture and Competition in Silicon Valley and Route 128* (Cambridge: Harvard University Press, 1994).

[70] Garrett, "Global Markets."

[71] Gilpin, *Challenge*, 313; Frances Fox Piven, "Is It Global Economics or Neo-Laissez-Faire?" *New Left Review* 123 (1995): 107–14.

[72] David M. Gordon, "The Global Economy: New Edifice or Crumbling Foundations?" *New Left Review* 168 (1988): 24–65.

[73] Paul Krugman, "Competitiveness: A Dangerous Obsession," *Foreign Affairs* 74 (1994): 28–44.

thesis also provides scholars with exciting subject matter that sells books! The point is that the globalization thesis is politically and perhaps intellectually expedient; not only does it constitute a cognitive paradigm that constrains how people view the world, but it can be used as a frame for legitimizing a variety of activities and interests. Until we think more carefully about the relationships between international economic activity and national-level institutions and politics, its power will remain unchecked.

Globalization, the State, and Industrial Relations: Common Challenges, Divergent Transitions

RUDRA SIL

THE EMPIRICAL processes frequently associated with "globalization"—notably, the sharply increased levels of transnational capital mobility, technology flows, communications, and migration—are frequently linked to hypotheses about the dramatic consequences of these processes for existing institutions and analytic concepts. In particular, public discourse is replete with references to the obsolescence or relative insignificance of the nation-state, regarded by many as a key source of variation in development processes,[1] in the face of worldwide pressures to adopt standard practices, institutions, and technologies appropriate for a supposedly unprecedented "global" era. To some extent, this is because such discourse implicitly proceeds from universalist presumptions not fundamentally different from those undergirding past theories of convergence insofar as epistemological and causal primacy is a priori accorded to sources of *uniformity across space and change over time* (as opposed to sources of variation across space and continuity over time). The tendency to regard globalization as inevitably leading to the homogenization of institutions and the obsolescence of the nation-state is but one consequence of such an epistemology.

As an increasing number of scholarly studies have begun to emphasize, however, the pressures created by globalization on existing institu-

This chapter has benefited from helpful comments and suggestions from John Bendix, Calvin Chen, Atul Kohli, and Axel Van den Berg, as well as from this volume's editors and reviewers. Portions of the chapter build upon Rudra Sil and Christopher Candland, "Institutional Legacies and the Transformation of Labor: Late-Industrializing and Post-Socialist Economies in Comparative-Historical Perspective," in Candland and Sil, eds., *The Politics of Labor in a Global Age* (New York: Oxford University Press, 2001).

[1] On the causal significance of varying state structures and national political dynamics, see, e.g., Peter Evans, Theda Skocpol, and Dietrich Rueschemeyer, eds., *Bringing the State Back In* (Cambridge University Press, 1985); Peter Evans, *Embedded Autonomy: States and Industrial Transformation* (Princeton: Princeton University Press, 1995); Meredith Woo Cummings, ed., *The Developmental State* (Ithaca: Cornell University Press, 1999); and David Waldner, *State Building and Late Development* (Ithaca: Cornell University Press, 1999).

tional arrangements and social relations may not be so sweeping as to justify the dismissal of existing concepts and units of comparison.[2] Drawing upon patterns of electoral politics and social and macroeconomic policy among advanced industrial economies, these studies recognize that new patterns have emerged everywhere while emphasizing the continuing significance of national politics and cross-national diversity. The distinctive contribution of this chapter lies in the effort to build on these analyses along three lines. First, given that genuinely comparative studies of political economy have been conducted largely across advanced industrial economies (or within specific regions),[3] the chapter shifts the attention to the wide-ranging experiences of what I refer to here as "transitional late industrializers" (TLIs)[4] to capture the more varied landscape upon which the vast majority of the global labor force happens to live and work. A balanced appraisal of the significance of globalization requires greater attention to the experiences of TLIs especially since strong arguments about globalization implicitly suggest that the more dramatic exposure to global economic forces in a transitional setting will likely produce a more dramatic narrowing of policy options and, subsequently, a more rapid erosion of the authority of the nation-state.[5] Second, the

[2] For example, Suzanne Berger and Ronald Dore, eds., *National Diversity and Global Capitalism* (Ithaca: Cornell University Press, 1996); Robert Boyer and Daniel Drache, *States against Markets: The Limits of Globalization* (New York: Routledge, 1996); H. Kitschelt et al., eds., *Continuity and Change in Contemporary Capitalism* (Cambridge: Cambridge University Press, 1999); Geoffrey Garrett, *Partisan Politics in the Global Economy* (New York: Cambridge University Press, 2000); Paul Pierson, ed., *The New Politics of the Welfare State* (New York: Oxford University Press, 2001).

[3] This is true of the studies cited in note 2 above, but on industrial relations specifically, see, e.g., Sanford Jacoby, ed., *The Workers of Nations: Industrial Relations in a Global Economy* (New York: Oxford University Press, 1995). One recent exception is the volume by Candland and Sil, which includes similarly structured essays covering Latin America, South Asia, East Asia, and postcommunist Europe.

[4] While the category of "late-industrializer" is general enough to encompass West European or East Asian economies at an earlier period of history, the category of TLI here is reserved for countries, including postsocialist ones, where state elites still consider themselves to be in the process of "catching up" but believe that further progress is at present dependent on some form of economic liberalization and increased participation in the international economy.

[5] This is what Thomas Friedman, in his popular but simplistic paean to globalization, has referred to as the "golden straitjacket" (acceptance of a fully marketized economy along with the institutions to guarantee transparency and predictability) that developing countries must don in order to survive in the post–Cold War "global system"; see his *The Lexus and the Olive Tree* (New York: Anchor, 1999). More scholarly treatments that also tend to presume that globalization will have a more powerful impact in transitional settings include Gerald Helliener, *The New Global Economy and the Developing Countries* (Brookfield, VT: Edward Elgar, 1990); Shigeru Otsubo, *Globalization: A New Role for Developing Countries in an Integrating World* (Washington, DC: World Bank, 1996);

chapter focuses squarely on industrial relations, a field that, in spite of major contributions to general theories of political economy and social change,[6] has tended to be relegated to the margins in recent studies of political and economic transition. This is unfortunate as no other field focuses as comprehensively or directly on the range of institutions and social relations that mediate the way in which transnational processes and national policies might affect millions of working individuals in every state; and, it is, after all, the behaviors of, and relations among, these actors that ultimately determine both what globalization *is* and what it *does*. Third, and most generally, there is an explicit attempt at contextualizing the epistemological assumptions undergirding strong claims about globalization vis-à-vis social theory writ large, with an eye to generating further insights into the prospects of the nation-state as an institution, a unit of comparison, and a theoretical construct.

While the survey of industrial relations across TLIs is neither comprehensive nor systematic, it does reveal sufficient diversity in worldwide trends to support the three related theoretical arguments advanced in this chapter. First, globalization is best understood not as a qualitatively different homogenizing force but as a new, particularly pervasive, manifestation of a *recurrent* dynamic whereby external pressures periodically prompt states and nonstate actors to revise previous institutional arrangements, but along trajectories that reflect the resilience of diverse social understandings and institutional legacies. Second, the recent spike in transnational flows of capital, technology, people, and practices over the past decade, while perhaps unprecedented in absolute terms, reveals the pivotal significance of the interests, capacity, and autonomy of states in determining the extent to which, and manner in which, external pressures and influences are affecting different segments of the citizenry of

---

Ralph Bryant, "Global Change: Increasing Economic Integration and Eroding Political Sovereignty," *Brookings Review* 12 (Fall 1994); Jeffrey Sachs and Andrew Warner, "Economic Reform and the Process of Global Integration," *Brookings Paper on Economic Activitiy*, no. 1 (1995); Sachs and Warner, "Achieving Rapid Growth in the Transition Economies of Central Europe," discussion paper 544, Harvard Institute for International Development (July 1996).

[6] One recent study that views labor as central to the story of democratization is Ruth Berins Collier, *Paths Toward Democracy: The Working Class and Elites in Western Europe and South America* (New York: Cambridge University Press, 1999). Past examples of studies in industrial relations that I view as major contributions to different strands of social theory include Reinhard Bendix, *Work and Authority in Industry* (New York: John Wiley, 1956); Clark Kerr et al., *Industrialism and Industrial Man* (Cambridge: Harvard University Press, 1960); Ronald Dore, *British Factory, Japanese Factory: The Origins of National Diversity in Industrial Relations* (Berkeley: University of California Press, 1973); Charles Sabel, *Work and Politics* (New York: Cambridge University Press, 1982); Michael Burawoy, *The Politics of Production* (London: Verso, 1985). More recently, see Rudra Sil, *Managing "Modernity": Work, Community, and Authority in Late-Industrializing Japan and Russia* (Ann Arbor: University of Michigan Press, 2002).

different states. And third, while weaker states may be less capable of enforcing laws and contracts in the face of globalization, differences in the ability of states in managing external pressures are nothing new; what is more significant here is that there has yet to emerge an alternative *form* of organization that cares to assume the nation-state's claimed right to invoke the threat of coercion in guaranteeing public agreements, particularly employment contracts — which may explain why both business and labor continue to focus on national laws and institutions in their attempts to expand their relative influence in TLIs.

Below, the first section outlines what is meant by "universalist" social theory, identifying the kinds of arguments about globalization and industrial relations that might be considered such. The second section considers the extensive role of the state in managing industrial relations among late industrializers prior to economic liberalization, noting both the common effects of pressures to "catch up" as well as the dimensions along which variations emerged across national industrial relations systems. The third section argues that, despite the common pressures stemming from global economic forces for "flexibilization" of contracts, labor markets, and production processes, states remain the focal point of industrial relations in TLIs in at least three capacities: as the most relevant actor in engineering whatever shifts are taking place in national industrial relations, as the ultimate guarantor of whatever social pacts are negotiated at whatever level, and as the chief mediator in the rationalization of relations between transnational firms and local subsidiaries enmeshed in informal labor markets. The fourth section notes the substantial variation across TLIs in the extent and trajectories of change in industrial relations systems and suggests that differences in inherited institutional arrangements and variable state capacities and interests have contributed to this variation. The conclusion draws upon these observations to emphasize the need for a more comprehensive theoretical framework in which attention to the common pressures associated with a more densely integrated global economy are accompanied by due consideration to the state's continuing role as the enforcer of laws and contracts; the capacity, autonomy, and interests of state elites; and the influence of institutional and normative legacies embedded in national and subnational social relations.

"UNIVERSALIST" PERSPECTIVES ON GLOBALIZATION AND INDUSTRIAL RELATIONS

What I refer to as "universalist" research programs, whatever substantive claims they may yield, are distinguished by two underlying assumptions: first, that indicators of *change* over time are more indicative of the invariable laws of history than indicators of continuity over time; and second, that the forces propelling this change are *ubiquitous*, producing convergent trajectories in the defining elements of social life in spite of long-standing local particularities. In effect, adapting Lakatos, we might identify a universalist research program as one in which the "hard core" contains the unquestioned assumption that observations indicating changes over time and similarities across space have greater epistemological significance in the interpretation of history vis-à-vis factors thought to account for local particularities or variations across space.[7] Such assumptions are evident in theoretical projects as diverse as Marx's historical materialism, Spencer's social evolution, and Parsonian theories of modernization.[8] In all these theoretical enterprises, change across time and space could not but be interpreted as a progression toward a uniform pattern of social order. Features of the most "developed" social systems were expected to be inherently and functionally linked to progressively higher levels of technology and organizational complexity, whatever the historical inheritance or cultural orientation of a particular collectivity. And, in all these projects, the state was little more than a manifestation or facilitator of larger social forces, playing out standard, predetermined roles in the unfolding of history—for example, by aiding in the social mobilization of previously parochial communities or facilitating the rationalization of economic production.

Although the 1970s and 1980s witnessed a significant retreat from universalism in that greater attention was paid to political institutions as indicators or sources of diverse historical trajectories,[9] the end of the Cold War and concurrent trends toward economic and political liberalization appear to have provided fertile ground for a return to universalist theorizing. This time, however, the operative assumption is not about the inevitability and uniformity of "modernization" worldwide but the inescapable consequences of "globalization"—a term that has become ubiquitous as scholars, policymakers, corporations, and individuals worldwide try to interpret the significance of the increasingly rapid movement of capital, technology, institutions, and people across national bor-

---

[7] Imre Lakatos, "Falsification and the Methodology of Scientific Research Programmes," in Lakatos and Alan Musgrave, eds. *Criticism and the Growth of Knowledge* (New York: Cambridge University Press, 1970), 91–196.

[8] For an extensive discussion of the universalist assumptions underpinning much of nineteenth-century European social theory, early-twentieth-century organization theory, and postwar modernization theory, see Sil, *Managing "Modernity,"* 56–68.

[9] See James March and Johan Olsen, *Rediscovering Institutions: The Organizational Basis of Politics* (New York: Free Press, 1989); Sven Steinmo, Kathleen Thelen, and Frank Longstreth, eds., *Structuring Politics: Historical Institutionalism in Comparative Analysis* (New York: Cambridge University Press, 1992).

ders. While some treat these indicators of globalization as an extension or intensification of the same processes once labeled "complex interdependence," more explicitly universalist are those perspectives that view globalization as an unprecedented, qualitative transformation of the international economy and, in more holistic treatments, of the very structure of collective consciousness and social relations worldwide.[10]

Variations in the precise definition of globalization notwithstanding, the term inherently draws attention to aspects of social reality that are experienced, in principle, by the entire social world. This is not, in itself, a problem: the very search for theory in the social sciences is predicated on some intersubjective understanding of commonly experienced aspects of social reality, and it is not hard to imagine one of these aspects being exposure to peoples, ideas, practices, and technologies beyond one's usual social horizon. Contemporary universalist theories are distinguished by assumptions about the epistemological and causal significance of the trends associated with globalization, not the fact that these trends represent a part of whatever social reality is commonly experienced by individuals and communities worldwide. In effect, as we move from common-sense statements about what globalization *is* to claims about what globalization *does*, both to the social world and to our attempts to understand it, we run across a tendency to assume that the empirical observations matched with the concept cannot be meaningfully understood in terms of previously constructed categories, and that these observations encompass novel phenomena that are causally more significant than sources of diversity across space, particularly state structures and national policy.

To be sure, such universalism has been subject to much scholarly criticism by those proceeding from other epistemological perspectives — for example, realists emphasizing the primacy of state sovereignty and security, and historical institutionalists emphasizing diverse trajectories of path dependent change. But public and academic discourse on globaliz-

---

[10] On "complex interdependence," see Robert Keohane and Joseph Nye, *Power and Interdependence* (Boston: Little, Brown, 1977). On economic globalization, see, e.g., Richard McKenzie and David Lee, *Quicksilver Capital: How the Rapid Movement of Wealth Has Changed the World* (New York: Free Press, 1991); Kenichi Ohmae, *The Borderless World: Power and Strategy in the Interlinked Economy* (New York: Harper Perennial, 1993); Saskia Sassen, *Losing Control: Sovereignty in the Age of Globalization* (New York: Columbia University Press, 1996); Vivien Schmidt, "The New World Order, Incorporated: The Rise of Business and the Decline of the Nation-State," *Daedalus* 124 (1995): 75–106; "The World Economy: Who's in the Driving Seat?" *The Economist* (October 7, 1995). More holistic perspectives on globalization include Martin Albrow, *The Global Age* (Stanford: Stanford University Press, 1996); Anthony Giddens, *Runaway World: How Globalization is Reshaping Our Lives* (2000); Ronald Robertson, *Globalization: Social Theory and Global Culture* (London: Sage, 1992).

ation continues to evince the same kind of triumphalism that once per-
meated modernization theories predicated on a single "end of history."[11]
In typical articulations of this thesis in the field of political economy,
"the structural characteristics of a much larger-scale, global economy"
are thought to have progressively undermined the capacity of states to
provide the public goods they alone could once provide, with the result
that "today's 'residual state' faces crises of both organizational efficiency and institutional legitimacy."[12] In more pessimistic treatments,
states are characterized as playing a "courtesan role," serving the dominant interests of global market forces while neglecting to attend to the
material welfare or cultural life of many of its citizens.[13] Despite the
shift in attention from developmental processes to transnational ones,
such understandings of globalization automatically assign causal and
epistemological priority to ubiquitous processes and their likely sources
while discounting any evidence of historical variation and local distinctiveness.

In the study of comparative industrial relations, these universalist
treatments of globalization have provided the bases for arguments linking the distinguishing features of the contemporary international economy to seemingly convergent shifts in patterns of industrial relations
worldwide. Although inspired originally by trends in advanced industrial economies, the logic of the argument is more general. Intensifying
global competition and technological innovation are thought to produce
a shift from traditional mass production toward more "lean" forms of
production, characterized by less rigidly demarcated individual tasks,
shifting work organization and skill requirements, and just-in-time schedules and supply networks that enable production to keep up with more
rapidly changing markets and technologies. With the transnational diffusion of lean production, preexisting national industrial relations systems everywhere are thought to be under pressure to restructure preexisting social pacts and institutions so as to accommodate greater
"flexibility" in labor markets and production practices. In practice, this

---

[11] The term "end of history," borrowed from Hegel via Fukuyama, aptly captures this
universalist treatment of diverse histories; see Francis Fukuyama, *The End of History and
the Last Man* (New York: Free Press, 1992).

[12] Philip Cerny, "Globalization and the Changing Logic of Collective Action," *Interna-
tional Organization* 49 (Autumn 1995): 598. For a critique of this type of argument, see
Robert Boyer, "The Convergence Hypothesis Revisited: Globalization but Still the Cen-
tury of Nations?" in Berger and Dore, eds., *National Diversity*, 29–59; and Robert Wade,
"Globalization and Its Limits: Reports of the Death of the National Economy Are Greatly
Exaggerated," in Berger and Dore, eds., *National Diversity*, 60–88.

[13] James Mittelman, *The Globalization Syndrome: Transformation and Resistance*
(Princeton: Princeton University Press, 2000), 25.

is thought to require more decentralized forms of collective bargaining—with global corporations and their workers becoming more directly responsible for renegotiating wages and social pacts as national employers' associations, trade union federations, and labor ministries become correspondingly less active—as well as a general decline in union density and influence, intensifying pressures for wage restraint, a sharp reduction in employment guarantees and benefits even in the public sector, and the elmination of laws that restrict the mobility of workers or limit the rights of employers in relation to the hiring and firing of workers.[14] Even the International Labor Organization—the only specialized body of the United Nations in which national governments, business associations, and trade unions are all represented—now takes for granted that national borders and institutions cannot protect workers or enterprises from the "harsh competitive pressures" associated with globalization."[15] Under these conditions, those who sympathize with the plight of workers call not for the strengthening of state action or national welfare provisions but for greater international standardization of social and economic policy, along with transnational coordination among organized labor.[16]

These projections of an eventual convergence in industrial relations all take for granted the irreversibility and uniformity of the effects of

[14] On the supposed erosion of centralized collective bargaining and of the influence of organized labor, see Cerny, "Globalization," esp. 612; Ethan B. Kapstein, "Workers and the World Economy," *Foreign Affairs* 75 (May/June 1996): 16–37; Scott Lash, "The End of Neo-Corporatism? The Breakdown of Centralised Bargaining in Sweden," *British Journal of Industrial Relations* 23 (1985): 215–39; Peter Swenson, *Fair Shares: Unions, Pay and Politics in Sweden and Germany* (Ithaca: Cornell University Press, 1989). On new forms of lean production and workplace participation, see Charles Heckscher, *The New Unionism: Employee Involvement in the Changing Corporation* (New York: Basic Books, 1988); Harry Katz and Owen Darbishire, *Converging Divergences: Worldwide Changes in Employment Systems* (Ithaca: Cornell University Press, 1999); John Paul MacDuffie, "International Trends in Work Organization in the Auto Industry: National-Level vs. Company-Level Perspectives," in Kirsten Wever and Lowell Turner, eds., *The Comparative Political Economy of Industrial Relations* (Madison: Industrial Relations Research Association, 1995); J. Womack, D. Jones, and D. Roos, *The Machine That Changed the World* (New York: Rawson Macmillan, 1990).

[15] International Labor Organization (Muneto Ozaki, general editor), *Negotiating Flexibility: The Role of the Social Partners and the State* (Geneva: International Labor Office, 1999), henceforth cited as ILO, *Negotiating Flexibility*.

[16] See Kapstein, "Workers"; Terry Collingsworth, J. William Goold, and Pharis J. Harvey, "Time for a Global New Deal," *Foreign Affairs* (January/February 1994): 8–13; Ellen Meiksins Wood, Peter Meiksins, and Michael Yates, eds. *Rising from the Ashes? Labor in the Age of "Global" Capitalism*, special issue of *Monthly Review* 49 (July–August 1997); Terry Boswell and Dimitris Stevis, "Globalization and International Labor Organizing: A World-System Perspective," Special Issue on Labor in the Americas, *Work and Occupations* 24 (August 1997): 288–307.

the global economy, ignoring the role of the nation-state in engineering economic transition and discounting the significance of variations in national social policy and institutional legacies relative to the pressures for homogenization. A critical exploration of the assumptions undergirding such conclusions, however, suggests the need for a more nuanced perspective, especially in the case of TLIs. Following a brief review of the past role of late-industrializing states in managing industrial relations, the remainder of this chapter turns to the question of whether and how this role has been transformed, and what this suggests for the extent of variation across TLIs.

LATE INDUSTRIALIZATION, THE STATE, AND NATIONAL INDUSTRIAL RELATIONS

Historically, the process of industrialization—from England and Germany to India and Brazil—has witnessed a significant role for the state in managing the emergence of a new class of industrial workers coping with new kinds of tasks in new kinds of production systems. National elites eager to preserve social peace and facilitate industrialization have everywhere relied on state intervention of one form or another for such purposes as the creation and regulation of labor markets, the mediation and suppression of labor disputes, and the establishment of standard rules governing rights and obligations of workers and managers. For their part, businesses and managers everywhere have relied on states to provide an orderly and predictable environment in which to pursue their production activities while the political mobilization of workers has focused on rights and protections only the state can guarantee. The emergence of national systems for managing industrial relations is thus an integral element of the process of industrialization.

The point of departure for the argument to follow is that significant differences eventually appeared in the extent and character of state involvement, some of which were tied to the dynamics and pressures of late industrialization in the non-Western world.[17] Among the earlier industrializers of the West, while the state was crucial to the formation of key aspects of industrial relations, by the middle of the twentieth century, it came to assume a relatively less conspicuous posture. This is most obvious in the case of the minimal involvement of governments in the decentralized industry-wide bargaining in the United States or in the

---

[17] The implications of late industrialization for industrial management have been captured by Dore's *British Factory, Japanese Factory*. While Dore downplayed the potential diversity of industrial relations among late industrializers, his analysis does draw attention to how the imperatives of belated industrialization affect national industrial relations.

bipartite consultations in Britain and Canada; but it is also true of the corporatist institutions that emerged across continental Europe, where organized welfare states, while important actors, have generally refrained from imposing social pacts, acting instead as facilitators of social dialogue between peak organizations of business and labor.[18] By comparison, late-industrializing states, particularly those embracing socialism or emerging from decolonization, have consistently played a more conspicuous role in the coordination and management of industrial relations as part of their broader mission of building coherent nations, maintaining social peace, and acting as a "historical substitute" for a well-established entrepreneurial class in spearheading economic development.[19]

As part of this process, state elites typically relied heavily on large public-sector firms to spur industrialization and paid close attention to the activities of the increasingly concentrated workforce in key sectors. To discourage excessive turnover and meet the collective needs of industry, states introduced legal and institutional mechanisms to regulate labor markets, for example, by linking employment status to access to key resources and welfare provisions. Given the urgency with which state elites sought to boost industrial production, states also stepped in to facilitate the training and placement of managerial personnel and employees whose skills were in short supply, with an eye to borrowing applying technologies and management techniques from more "advanced" economies. Moreover, eager to bypass the more conflictual pattern of labor relations they associated with earlier industrialization in the West,[20] state elites also took the lead in defining the scope and character of labor incorporation, either by establishing national trade union centers to co-opt the labor movement or by preemptively delimiting the scope of organized labor's activities by introducing paternalistic management practices. The small size and relative weakness of the business classes and organized labor at the early stages of industrialization gener-

[18] Borrowing Schmitter's distinction, what we see in much of Western Europe is "societal corporatism," whereby employers' associations and trade union federations are well-organized, relatively autonomous, and voluntarily interested in the services of the state to facilitate collective bargaining. This may be distinguished from "state corporatism" where tripartitism is essentially organized and managed by the state. See Philippe Schmitter, "Still the Century of Corporatism?" in Schmitter and Gerhard Lehmbruch, eds., *Trends Towards Corporatist Intermediation* (Beverly Hills: Sage, 1979), 13, 22–23.

[19] The concept of "historical substitute" is from Alexander Gerschenkron, *Economic Backwardness in Historical Perspective* (Cambridge: Harvard University Press, 1962).

[20] Elites in nineteenth-century Japan and Russia, for example, engaged in remarkably similar debates over whether labor relations in their respective countries were destined to be more harmonious than had been the case among earlier industrializers in Europe; see Sil, *Managing "Modernity,"* chaps. 3–4.

ally left states in a central position to shape the terms of collective bargaining, either through the establishment of some variant of state-cor-
poratism (as in much of Latin America in the 1970s and 1980s) or
through less formal mechanisms of "guidance" in the case of decentralized firm-level or sectoral wage bargaining (as in Korea and Singapore).

The common imperatives related to belated industrialization do not,
however, suggest any uniform pattern of state intervention in late industrialization. In fact, differences in historical inheritances, ideological
commitments, resource bases, and levels of state autonomy and capacity
led to a great deal of variation across national industrial relations.[21] One
broad distinction in industrial relations emerges from the contrast between socialist regimes and other late industrializers with a more mar-
ket-oriented or "mixed" economy. In the case of socialism, direct state
ownership of the means of production meant that jobs, wages, and welfare were determined by central planners, while official ideology denied
the very idea of industrial conflict or independent workers' interests in a
"workers' state." Thus, while union density may have been high (often
as high as 90 percent) in the industrial sector, the only legal trade
unions were those incorporated into the party-state apparatus. At the
factory level, the trade union committees occasionally acted upon workers' grievances, but more often than not they operated as "transmission
belts," responsible for implementing the directives of central planners
and party functionaries, assisting in the implementation of production
schedules, and managing the distribution of an extensive set of welfare
provisions, such as housing, education, healthcare, subsidized food-
stuffs, and recreational facilities. Also, an internal passport system,
which restricted access to key resources and employment opportunities
to residents of particular locales, served as a means to discourage turnover and channel labor mobility. While some have invoked the language
of "corporatism" to characterize socialist regimes' commitment to full
employment, rising wages, and access to necessities (in exchange for
passivity and cooperation at the workplace),[22] the absence of an independent labor movement and an independent set of business interests
meant that any real bargaining between workers and managers had to
be hidden and informal.

In late-industrializing economies where a private sector accounted for
a substantial portion of the GDP, states remained central actors, but in

[21] For an extensive discussion of the sources of national diversity in industrial relations,
see ibid., chap. 2.

[22] For example, Valerie Bunce, "The Political Economy of the Brezhnev Era: The Rise
and Fall of Corporatism," *British Journal of Political Science* 13 (April 1983): 129–58;
Anita Chan, "Revolution or Corporatism? Workers and Trade Unions in Post-Mao
China," *The Australian Journal of Chinese Affairs* 19 (1993): 31–61.

the absence of a unified party-state apparatus and a command economy, they pursued less direct and more heterogeneous forms of intervention in labor relations. Even where organized labor was effectively co-opted by the state, unions were theoretically presumed to represent the separate interests of workers; this meant that unions could not be treated as merely facilitators of production conferences or the distributors of welfare provisions as in socialist economies, and that the state had to rely more on labor legislation, political maneuvering, and even overt coercion to defuse industrial disputes. Moreover, the existence of a private sector, however small, also meant that the state had to rely on indirect means to create standardized employment practices — for example, by positing public-sector contracts as models for contracts in firms in the private sector. Also, the presence of alternative employment opportunities, along with the limited effectiveness of organized labor outside of large firms in key sectors, meant that labor mobility was higher and union density was substantially lower (often as low as 10 percent of the workforce) than in socialist economies, with organized labor mainly acting on behalf of a relatively less mobile and more privileged stratum of workers in economically or strategically important sectors. Thus, the state remained the central actor in organizing industrial relations, but the more diverse experiences, conditions, and interests of different categories of workers and firms in different sectors meant that states had to adopt more complicated strategies for preserving industrial order.

Finally, it is necessary to bear in mind the substantial variation in patterns of national industrial relations systems related to the particular inheritances, resources, and objectives of individual states. Among socialist countries, there was considerable variation in the extent of hierarchical control imposed by the communist party-apparatus over local workers' bodies. For example, in contrast to Russia and China, where communist parties took power in the course of indigenous proletarian revolutions and proceeded to completely subsume trade unions and other workers' bodies, in Eastern Europe and southern Vietnam, newly formed communist governments had to find different ways to secure the submission of preexisting workers' organizations to party-state control, sometimes allowing a greater degree of autonomy to unions.[23] Among other late industrializers, substantial variation is evident in such factors as the content and enforcement of national labor legislation, the extent

---

[23] For example, the Vietnamese Communist Party, coping with the legacy of independent labor militancy in southern Vietnam, decided to allow unions to participate in management functions, independently represent workers' interests, and join international federations without official approval. See Anita Chan and Irene Norlund, "Vietnamese and Chinese Labour Regimes: On the Road to Divergence," *The China Journal* 40 (July 1998): 173–98.

to which states intervened in collective bargaining, and the autonomy and influence of organized labor. Most Latin American states, for example, typically eschewed both formal and informal coordination of wage bargaining, relying frequently on national legislation to cover minimum labor standards across individual firms. Japanese industrial relations, following a crackdown on militant leftist unions in the late 1940s, came to be characterized by enterprise-level bargaining with both white- and blue-collar workers joining company unions; the state's intervention was important but largely informal, achieved through the participation of relevant government ministries in annual industry-wide consultations over appropriate rates of wage increases. In Southeast Asia, whereas the state aimed to divide and marginalize organized labor in Thailand and Malaysia, in Singapore it co-opted labor through the ruling party's control over a single peak trade union association. Industrial relations in India could be distinguished by the fact that unions across sectors, while formed independently, joined federations that were affiliated with one of the national political parties; while this gave trade unions some clout on less divisive issues, it also meant that rivalries between parties limited what organized labor could collectively achieve.

Thus, the late-industrializing state generally played a pivotal role in establishing national systems of industrial relations, influencing the character of labor markets, the structure of organized labor, and systems of collective bargaining relations; at the same time, significant variations in development strategies and ideologies, the mechanisms of governance, and particular historical circumstances combined to produce considerable diversity in national patterns of industrial relations. The question to be asked now is how the role of the state and extent of cross-national diversity in industrial relations have been affected by economic liberalization and the resulting increase in exposure to global market forces.

STATES AND THE TRANSFORMATION OF INDUSTRIAL RELATIONS: ENGINEERING "FLEXIBILIZATION"

With the dismantling of command economies in postsocialist settings and economic liberalization in other TLIs, the heightened exposure to global economic forces have forced state elites to confront tradeoffs between the imperatives of creating the conditions conducive to economic competitiveness and preserving the degree of social protection accorded by previously negotiated social pacts. To varying degrees, most TLIs have thus far responded to this tradeoff in favor of competitiveness, scaling back the production activities of the state, engineering cuts in social spending, promoting a more dynamic business environment, and reconsidering crucial features of existing systems of industrial relations. The shift is most dramatic in the case of postsocialist transitions where official party-controlled trade union bodies of the communist era have given way to independent unions, each claiming to represent workers' interests in an environment where private exchange relations and contracts have only recently been legalized. But economic liberalization in other TLIs has also led to proposals for a fundamental restructuring of industrial relations in response to the expansion of the private sector and heightened competitive pressures. In more concrete terms, TLIs have faced common pressures to embrace "flexibility" in various dimensions of industrial relations: flexibility in labor markets so as to reduce redundancy and permit the redeployment of labor into more competitive sectors; flexibility in the negotiation of contracts, permitting more part-time and temporary work while allowing firms to devise their own pacts with workers depending on changing needs and competitive pressures; and, flexibility in work organization in order to be more responsive to rapidly changing technologies and demands.

That the present international economic environment is spurring TLIs to respond to these common pressures for "flexibilization" is neither surprising nor controversial. And it certainly would not be the first time that late industrializers seeking to "catch up" and improve their international position are constrained by the pressures to adopt methods and practices that appear to have contributed to the success of more "advanced" powers.[24] What is less clear, however, is whether or not the particular transformations evident in national industrial relations systems across TLIs at present constitute evidence in support of "strong" versions of the globalization thesis that suggest that the present international order is *qualitatively* different from any other in history, contributing to the steady erosion of state capacities and cross-national variations. In fact, there are good reasons to be cautious about translating universalistic assumptions about the consequences of globalization into specific hypotheses about trajectories of change in national systems of industrial relations and in the role of states therein.

Especially significant in this regard is the fact that the transnational mobility of labor, although higher than at any other point in history, is lower by a different order of magnitude in comparison to the rate at which the transnational mobility of capital has increased. While "capi-

---

[24] The emulation of industrial relations practices elsewhere was quite prevalent, for example, in the 1920s and 1930s when Taylorism and "scientific management" were widely promoted, even by socialist late industrializers; on how this process evolved in Japan and the Soviet Union, see Sil, *Managing "Modernity,"* esp. 138–60, 215–41

tal . . . is becoming more international, . . . labor remains rooted in particular places called nations."[25] This means that whatever else economic globalization might entail, workers are likely to look to the state to mitigate the effects of global competition on wages and benefits, employers are likely to rely on the state to create conditions that will make labor cooperative and productive, and, as a consequence, national regulatory frameworks are likely to remain relevant even where collective bargaining is being decentralized. This also means that one can reasonably expect continuing variations across national industrial relations systems since external pressures may not be equally pervasive or intense for all countries, since existing bargaining arrangements and different starting points will engender different expectations and dynamics in the renegotiation of social pacts, and since the meaning or salience of particular pressures or practices will vary across industrial cultures.[26] In fact, even among the advanced industrial economies of Western Europe, where economic globalization, privatization, and supranational regulatory frameworks have had the greatest impact on preexisting national institutions, a growing body of evidence now documents the resilience and continuing diversity of welfare states, national labor legislation, political unionism, worker participation schemes, and collective bargaining practices involving a role for the state.[27] In the case of TLIs, a preliminary survey of recent trends suggests that states continue to be the dominant actors in engineering shifts in the laws and institutions that comprise national labor relations; that states continue to be the only authoritative guarantor of formal contracts between employers and

[25] Sanford Jacoby, "Preface" to Jacoby, *The Workers of Nations*, ix.

[26] See Richard Locke and Kathleen Thelen, "Apples and Oranges Revisited: Contextualized Comparisons and the Study of Comparative Labor Politics," *Politics & Society* 23 (September 1995): 337–67.

[27] See, e.g., Garrett, *Partisan Politics*; Anke Hassel and Thorsten Schulten, "Globalization and the Future of Central Collective Bargaining: The Example of the German Metal Industry," *Economy and Society* 27 (1998); Peter Lange, Michael Wallerstein, and Miriam Golden, "The End of Corporatism? Wage Setting in Nordic and Germanic Countries," in Jacoby, *The Workers of Nations*, 76–100; Richard Locke, Thomas Kochan, and Michael Piore, "Reconceptualizing Comparative Industrial Relations: Lessons from International Research," *International Labour Review* 134 (1995); Fritz Scharpf, "The Viability of Advanced Welfare States in the International Economy: Vulnerabilities and Options," *Journal of European Public Policy* 7 (2000): 190–228; Wolfgang Streeck, "The Internationalization of Industrial Relations in Europe: Prospects and Problems," *Politics & Society* 26 (December 1998): 429–59; David Swank, "Social Democratic Welfare States in a Global Economy: Scandinavia in Comparative Perspective," in J. Moses, R. Geyer, and C. Ingebritsen, eds., *Globalization, Europeanization and the End of the Scandinavian Social Democracy?* (New York, St. Martins Press, 2000), 85–138; Kathleen Thelen and Ikuo Kume, "The Effects of Globalization on Labor Revisited: Lessons from Germany and Japan," *Politics & Society* 27 (December 1999): 477–505.

workers; that states alone can serve to mediate the relations between transnational corporations and local labor markets; and that, in all of these roles, differences in state capacities and institutional legacies have contributed to substantial variation in the extent and direction of restructuring in industrial relations.

Just as states had previously played a conspicuous role in organizing labor relations under conditions of belated industrialization, under the more complex pressures associated with globalization, states continue to be the pivotal actor in the restructuring of industrial relations in TLIs—even where collective bargaining appears to be becoming decentralized or labor market regulations are being lifted. This is true of Latin America, where postauthoritarian governments have been the main agents in efforts to change national laws and remove obstacles to labor market flexibility; it is true of the newly industrializing economies of Southeast Asia where states have continued either to co-opt (e.g., Singapore) or to divide (e.g., Malaysia) organized labor in the interest of spurring more rapid economic growth; it is also true of developing countries like India and the Philippines, where competing coalitions of national political and economic actors have been engaged in struggles over legislative reform, but where states have sought to reduce labor market rigidities through lax enforcement of laws; and it is true of postsocialist economies where efforts to negotiate new social pacts (as in Poland, Hungary, and the Czech Republic) or establish new labor codes to regulate the activities of organized labor (as in China and Russia) are being spearheaded by state elites.[28] This does not suggest that the state is everywhere an autonomous actor able to identify and implement optimal solutions to problems created by the encroachment of global economic forces. It does, however, suggest that the increased exposure to global forces cannot be automatically presumed to have eroded the significance of the state vis-à-vis other industrial relations actors. Even if states are generally behaving as if they are favoring business at the expense of organized labor, it must be remembered that states have never

[28] On Latin America, India, and the Philippines, see ILO, *Negotiating Flexibility*, 82–83, 87. On Southeast Asian NICs, see Stephen Frenkel, "Variations in Patterns of Trade Unionism," in Frenkel, ed., *Organized Labor in the Asia-Pacific Region: A Comparative Study of Trade Unionism in Nine Countries* (Ithaca: Cornell/ILR Press, 1993). On post-communist East-Central Europe, see Mitchell Orenstein and Lisa Hale, "Corporatist Renaissance in Post-Communist Europe?" in Candland and Sil, eds., *The Politics of Labor*; David Ost, "Illusory Corporatism in Eastern Europe: Neoliberal Tripartism and Postcommunist Class Identities," *Politics & Society* 28 (December 2000): 503–30. On China and Russia, see Calvin Chen and Rudra Sil, "Post-Communist Transitions and the Fate of Labor in China and Russia," presented at the Annual Meeting of the International Studies Association, Chicago, February 20–24, 2001.

been completely autonomous from social classes, and it is not clear that they are now becoming *more* beholden to business interests than they were previously in their dealings with particular firms in the private sector. And even if some states may be less able to intervene in the activities of firms, their *relative* influence cannot be said to be irreversibly declining given the tensions *within* both business and labor related to sectoral effects of increased capital mobility.[29]

In the case of business, the deregulation of labor markets and the accommodation of more flexible contracts will be welcomed in high-tech sectors or in sectors where firms enjoy a competitive advantage (the software industry in India, for example), but large enterprises in traditional heavy industrial sectors — such as mining, chemicals, and steel — may have an interest in resisting changes in labor laws that will be detrimental to their ability to maintain a surplus workforce and preserve labor-intensive production practices. In postsocialist economies, some members of the new business elite have been aggressive in supporting new employment practices labor codes, while others have sought to preserve informal pacts with workers and municipal administrators, or with existing production and distribution networks developed by former state enterprise directors.[30] Moreover, those small- or medium-sized enterprises that are more enmeshed in regional production and distribution networks will typically have more to lose from the arrival of new corporate competitors; for such enterprises, the deregulation of labor markets or the absence of state intervention in enforcing social pacts would have the impact of enhancing the competitiveness and relative strength of those corporations that are part of national or global production and distribution networks. Thus, while all business actors have a common interest in political stability and greater control over production, there is considerable variation in terms of the effects of economic liberalization on the interests and influence of firms of different sizes or in different sectors. This, in turn, represents another potential source of variation across TLIs as industrial relations systems are restructured.

Organized labor, for its part, has also been struggling of late to maintain a unified position and pursue a coherent agenda in TLIs. In many countries with a tradition of independent unionism, union membership rates have either dropped or national-level unions are finding them-

[29] This presumption follows a logic akin to that in the Stolper-Samuelson theorem as articulated in Ronald Rogowski, *Commerce and Coalitions: How Trade Affects Domestic Political Alignments* (Princeton: Princeton University Press, 1989).

[30] This dynamic is most obvious in Russia; see Rudra Sil, "Privatization, Labor Politics, and the Firm in Post-Soviet Russia: Non-Market Norms, Market Institutions, and the Soviet Legacy," in Candland and Sil, eds., *The Politics of Labor.*

selves having to compete with local, firm-level or sector-level workers' organizations in order to remain relevant. In the case of India, although unions were able to effectively slow down legislative reform that would threaten employment security, membership rates among the different trade union federations, each linked to a national political party, have dropped because the political cleavages within organized labor have rendered unions less able to develop a coherent strategy to address the concerns of more recently hired workers outside of the traditionally powerful heavy industry sectors.[31] In Malaysia and Thailand, union density in 1990 had already declined to the point that less than 5 percent of employees were covered by collective bargaining agreements, with most workers relying more on spontaneous local-level forms of industrial action than on union-led organized strikes or protests.[32] Similarly, in Mexico, while the relationship of the leading union federation (Mexican Workers' Confederation or CTM) to the former ruling party (Institutional Revolutionary Party or PRI) made it generally supportive of economic liberalization policies initiated by Salinas, some of the CTM's sectoral affiliates (electricity, for example) have opposed economic reform for fear of losing the benefits guaranteed by the existing terms of employment.[33] In postsocialist settings where the party-state apparatus collapsed, new battle lines have formed between unions descended from the old state-controlled union apparatus and the new alternative unions. This dynamic is most pronounced in Russia where the Federation of Independent Trade Unions (FNPR), the descendant of the official Soviet trade union apparatus, has attempted to protect its initial advantages by supporting a new labor code that, ironically, was opposed vigorously by new alternative unions who dismiss the FNPR as a remnant of the Soviet state and embrace the employment guarantees and labor standards written into the old Soviet-era labor code.[34] In all of these diverse contexts, workers in internationally competitive sectors, whether unionized or not, have succeeded in obtaining superior packages of wages, benefits, and working conditions largely because state elites have identified these sectors as economically or strategically important. Thus, with business associations and organized labor across TLIs more fragmented as a result of the differential impact of economic

[31] For a more detailed examination of this problem, see Christopher Candland, "South Asian Trade Unionism and the Cost of Incorporation: Labor Institutions, Industrial Restructuring, and New Trade Union Strategies in India and Pakistan," in Candland and Sil, eds., *The Politics of Labor*.

[32] Frenkel, "Variations in Patterns of Trade Unionism," 315.

[33] See M. Victoria Murillo, "Macroeconomic Adjustment, Industrial Restructuring and Union Response in Mexico," in Candland and Sil, eds., *The Politics of Labor*.

[34] Chen and Sil, "Post-Communist Transitions."

liberalization on different sectors and locales, even a "downsized" state effectively remains the pivotal actor in the process of engineering and managing shifts in national patterns of industrial relations.

Beyond being the most influential actor in restructuring industrial relations, states remain the most authoritative mediator and guarantor for contracts and social pacts in TLIs. Even where it is no longer directly coordinating the negotiation of national or industry-wide pacts, the state continues to serve as the most significant arena within which various business and labor actors are attempting to compete for influence or settle their differences. To the extent that private sectors throughout TLIs are larger and more active, they remain constrained in their ability to conclude formal pacts with organized labor without the state's services as guarantors of firm-level or industry-wide contracts. Even where workers may be increasingly looking to firm-level pacts or local governments to provide welfare benefits, it is still the state where the key political struggles are being waged by organized labor to improve their livelihoods and ensure that labor rights and standards are observed by firms or local authorities. Thus, it is hardly surprising that even where states are attempting to dismantle national regulatory frameworks that previously hindered labor market flexibility, they are also being sought after by both unions and business to facilitate social dialogue and throw its support behind national agreements to cope with the difficult employment issues related to labor market flexibilization.

From the perspective of transnational actors that have become increasingly more numerous and active across TLIs, too, states remain the only authoritative actor with the capacity to ensure that contracts and social pacts are honored by the negotiating parties.[35] Even where provincial or municipal governments have increasingly set out to conclude direct arrangements with foreign investors, the national state remains the only actor capable of acting as an intermediary wherever these arrangements may be violated since neither local governments nor global corporations have the resources or legal means to enforce their own interpretation of particular clauses.[36] In any case, given the possibility

---

[35] During the late 1970s, in an important book that parted ways with conventional dependency theory, Peter Evans emphasized the significance of the state in managing the relationship between multinational and local capital; see his *Dependent Development: The Alliance of Multinational, State and Local Capital in Brazil* (Princeton: Princeton University Press, 1979). While Evans' evidence and analysis are no longer current, the basic logic of his argument can be adapted to highlight the state's function in managing relations between global and local actors.

[36] An interesting example in this regard are the subnational states of Brazil and India that are now competing to directly conclude agreements with foreign investors and international financial institutions, but with the central government still being the ultimate guarantor of financial arrangements negotiated by states with foreign actors.

that political instability or social unrest in particular regions may threaten the interests of the transnational corporations, it is only too likely that the latter will not conclude agreements with local actors without the confidence that national governments will be prepared to step in to protect their interests as necessary. Moreover, the state represents a cheap and effective means for overcoming principal-agent problems encountered by global corporations in their relations with local subsidiaries embedded in diverse communities with their own particular sets of social relations. This is a particularly important matter where growing underemployment has spurred the growth of informal labor markets that have their own particular norms, networks, and dynamics at the local level.[37] Informal hiring networks may allow for efficient recruitment at the local level, but where this results in the hiring of staff and workers sharing preexisting social ties, it can pose difficulties in terms of maintaining formal regulations, authority structures, and work organization. Since transnational firms are not in the business of projecting coercive power to enforce rules and regulations, they must necessarily rely on the state to intervene in the process of ensuring that local subsidiaries adhere to company protocols where these might involve disrupting the interests of other actors in the surrounding community. To be sure, the capacity of states in reining in subnational actors will vary across TLIs, but this variation reveals the importance of state structures in tracing the effects of global economic actors in particular cases.

Thus, while TLIs at present may be accommodating flexible employment and production practices favored by business, while global corporations may be crossing national boundaries with increasing frequency, and while informal economies may be growing in significance, none of these trends points to the irreversible or inevitable reduction of state capacity vis-à-vis other industrial relations actors. In fact, the negotiations and competition among economic actors — business and labor, global corporations and local facilities — reflect continuities in three key functions that the state has always performed in TLIs: as the most relevant actor in devising the laws and institutions that constitute national

---

[37] "Underemployment" refers to employment that fails to produce incomes that would allow workers to meet minimum standards of living and usually far exceeds the number of unemployed persons. In 1994, for example, 120 million people were officially registered as unemployed worldwide, while an estimated 700 million people were underemployed. See Ankie Hoogvelt, *Globalization and the Postcolonial World* (Baltimore: Johns Hopkins University Press, 1997), 112–3, 139–40; Jeremy Rifkin, *The End of Work, The Decline of the Global Labor Force and the Dawn of the Post-Market Era* (New York: Putnam's, 1995), esp. chap. 12. On the expansion of the informal economy, see Bryan Roberts, "Informal Economy and Family Strategies," *International Journal of Urban and Regional Research* 18 (March 1994): 6–23.

industrial relations, as the ultimate guarantor of whatever contracts and social pacts are negotiated at whatever level, and as the chief mediator in the rationalization of relations between transnational firms and local subsidiaries enmeshed in informal labor markets. Some states are more strongly affected by international economic forces or domestic political unrest, but there has always been great variation in the capacity of states to mediate external influences depending on their resources, structures, and degree of autonomy. In the end, no matter how flexible collective bargaining arrangements, labor markets, and production become, firms and workers are both reliant upon the laws, institutions, and enforcement mechanisms that operate in a given territory, and only the state can provide these by virtue of its claimed monopoly on the legal means of coercion upon that territory.

THE "GLOBALIZATION" OF INDUSTRIAL RELATIONS OR DIVERGENT TRANSITIONS?

Certainly, there is some value in "globalization" as a concept in characterizing the common pressures and dilemmas generated by intensifying transnational flows of capital and technology for economic and political actors who were previously shielded, at least partly, from the effects of the international economy. These new pressures and dilemmas are real, and they are narrowing the options available for state elites who have come to view economic liberalization as an unavoidable means to improving their competitiveness and status in the present international economic order. As part of this process, it is hardly surprising that TLIs have concomitantly taken on the project of restructuring industrial relations with an eye to promoting lower production costs, higher productivity, technological innovation, industrial peace, and labor market flexibility.

These common objectives and imperatives, however, are not producing a *convergence* in patterns of industrial relations across TLIs, certainly not any more so than was previously produced by the pressures and dynamics of late industrialization. Postsocialist transitions have involved a far more dramatic shift in the roles of states in industrial relations than is the case in other TLIs, with unions no longer serving as "transmission belts" and with private employers in the picture for the first time. But even the force of these similar, and highly consequential, changes has not produced any sort of convergence across postsocialist settings, save perhaps in the equally pivotal role of states in restructuring industrial relations. In China and Vietnam, the transition has been so gradual that the old trade union federations, along with their existing structures, functions, and organizational resources, continue to be largely under the control of the state apparatus; and, although union density has declined with the expansion of the private sector, the level still remains very high by international standards in part because firms are promoting unions as a means to preempt industrial conflict.[38] By contrast, in several Eastern European states—notably Poland, Hungary, and the Czech Republic—liberalization proceeded relatively quickly and was accompanied by quasi-corporatist arrangements engineered by state elites able to pressure newly independent (and still fragmented) employers' associations and trade unions to conclude new social pacts.[39] In Russia, too, the state has been the focal point of the effort to create a new national system of industrial relations; but in contrast to Eastern Europe, efforts at building centralized institutions for collective bargaining—in the form of the Russian Trilateral Commission (RTK)—became irrelevant as the sharp divisions between proregime and antiregime groups among both labor and business left the Russian state in a position to ignore the claims of both while engineering a new labor code intended to increase the authority and flexibility of managers.[40] Thus, although the common legacy of socialism may point to some common imperatives in regard to the establishment of new labor market policies and collective bargaining systems, the particular ideas and interests embraced by state elites, the institutional environment in which new laws and pacts are being established, and the pace of market reforms in each country have combined to produce quite different outcomes thus far.

In other TLIs, too, predictions of a convergence upon more decentralized forms of collective bargaining and reduced state intervention in labor markets are being shown to be premature in light of the quite different trends in evidence worldwide. In Ireland, as in Eastern Europe, the state has made a commitment to forge new national social pacts across sectors, successfully establishing a Programme for National Recovery (PNR) that involves a national incomes policy linking high economic growth to moderate wage increases and job creation.[41] In Latin America, it would be a mistake to make too much of current evidence of decentralized collective bargaining in view of the fact that national elites previously shunned central bargaining in favor of national legisla-

---

[38] Chan and Norlund, "Vietnamese and Chinese Labour Regimes."

[39] See Ost, "Illusory Corporatism"; Elena Iankova, "The Transformative Corporatism of Eastern Europe," *East European Politics and Societies* 12 (Spring 1998): 222–64.

[40] For a detailed discussion of the failure of tripartism, see Walter Connor, *Tattered Banners: Labor, Conflict, and Corporatism in Postcommunist Russia* (Boulder: Westview, 1996). On the labor code, see Chen and Sil, "Post-Communist Transitions."

[41] See Eileen M. Doherty, "Globalization, Social Partnership and Industrial Relations in Ireland," in Candland and Sil, eds., *The Politics of Labor*.

tion to regulate labor markets as part of a protectionist development
strategy; in fact, as state elites now attempt to revise labor legislation to
boost the competitiveness of domestic industry, they are also simultaneously attempting to engineer new centralized agreements as a substitute
for governmental intervention. To date, the most successful case in this
regard has been Argentina, where the state not only introduced new
legislation in 1991 requiring that new enterprise-level pacts be officially
approved at the sectoral level but also managed to conclude a 1994
agreement with the General Confederation of Labor (CGT) and centralized employees' associations on steps to preserve social consensus in the
process of introducing more flexible contracts.[42] In India, the state and
national courts have consistently supported business interests against
organized labor, and union density has certainly diminished, but the
continued linkages between competing trade union federations and
competing national political parties has given organized labor sufficient
clout to delay changes in labor legislation that might lead to mass dis-
missals among the small segment of the workforce that is organized.
This has had the consequence of spurring businesses to engage in new
hiring practices to dilute union influence at their workplaces while the
central government has increased labor flexibility by being lax in enforcing existing labor laws.[43] By contrast, in Korea, where national
trade union federations remain relatively ineffective following years of
state repression, the new leaders were able to conduct national-level
negotiations in 1998 to enable the chaebols to lay off workers in exchange for a strengthening of the national social safety net (e.g., the
unemployment insurance fund) and an expanded set of labor rights and
standards.[44]

Such trends, while not examined systematically or in great detail here,
do suggest the need to take seriously the possibility of significant and
persistent differences in what state elites are willing and able to do in
restructuring national systems of industrial relations in light of their
particular interests, circumstances, and institutional inheritances. In
many cases, efforts to deregulate labor markets by restricting the scope
of national labor legislation have been accompanied by corresponding
efforts to promote centralized agreements among peak business and labor organizations. In other cases, efforts to establish more decentralized
forms of collective bargaining have been accompanied by simultaneous
efforts to establish more extensive national legislation, some incorporat-

[42] ILO, *Negotiating Flexibility*, 82–83.
[43] Ibid., 87.
[44] Ibid., 85–86.

ing more numerous welfare provisions and others according more flexibility to employers. And, where it has proven politically difficult to adopt major reforms, "flexibilization" has taken the form of states refraining from uniformly implementing preexisting laws thought to be responsible for labor market rigidities.

Plausible factors accounting for this range of variation include the preexisting institutional arrangements, the variable capacities of states, and specific features of national economies and national political competition. The quite different institutional inheritances in different national contexts, alongside the different meanings or values attached to particular employment practices, suggest that both state and nonstate actors will prioritize and address the challenges associated with global economic forces in quite different ways. In a few cases, it is indeed possible that states will find their capacities eroded and will be forced to discourage centralized bargaining and dismantle national labor market regulations in favor of more decentralized negotiations and enterprise-level pacts. But, as noted above, patterns of change in several TLIs do reflect sufficient variation to suggest that even states with high levels of institutional capacity can opt for quite different approaches in their common efforts to promote flexibilization in employment contracts, labor markets, and production practices. This fact, combined with the likelihood that national elites will act upon different combinations of interests, ideological commitments, or social pressures, suggests that common pressures can produce a quite diverse range of national initiatives, each intended to attend to whatever issue appears to be most politically salient in a given national context—be it employment security, wage levels, social safety nets, or labor rights. As long as states retain some degree of autonomy, the transformation of industrial relations will reflect complex strategies for coping with nationally specific institutional legacies and nationally specific sets of priorities.

CONCLUSION: THE CHANGING, BUT CONTINUING, ROLE OF THE STATE

The above discussion suggests that the role of states in mediating industrial relations—while adapted to new realities involving more competitive pressures, more complex networks of nonstate actors, and more advanced technologies of production—is likely to extend well into the future, producing not convergence but continuing variations across national industrial relations systems. Globalization, while a real phenomenon with real consequences for the manner in which states act, has yet to irreversibly erode the *relative* power of states vis-à-vis other actors in the construction of diverse systems of national industrial relations. Business may be generally favored by state reformers, but "business" itself incorporates quite varied interests depending on sectors and past ties to the state or foreign economic actors. Organized labor may enjoy more autonomy in democratized settings, but it is also more fragmented, with some unions more nervous than others about the implications of new labor institutions and the expanding informal sector. More generally, any attempt at creating standard laws, institutions, or practices related to labor relations cannot but make the state the focal point of the competing actors' strategies. Even corporations consider themselves to be "global" ultimately have plants and offices in particular nations, and as such they must adapt their practices to the particular laws and regulations of those nations while seeking the benefits and protection provided by the state apparatus.[45] While transnational bodies may debate linkages between trading practices and international labor standards, unless such bodies are granted the authority and means to enforce legislation within national boundaries, ultimately it is only with the cooperation and intervention of states that such standards are actually monitored and enforced.

In a broader theoretical context, these observations also serve to highlight some of the fundamental continuities in the relationships between states and their changing international environments. Despite the intensification of global capital flows and the proliferation of global networks, the present behavior of TLIs can be understood in quite familiar terms: states that accept the international order as it is have sought to improve their position within it, frequently relying upon the latest methods and practices of more "advanced" powers in an effort to catch up and perhaps avoid the "growing pains" experienced by the latter.[46] That is, the common attempts by states to engineer the "flexibilization" of industrial relations can be understood as constrained by the imperatives of competing within the international order as they always have. Cer

---

[45] In fact, even in Western Europe — where the density of transnational economic interdependence and the legitimacy of supranational regulatory frameworks is perhaps greater than in any other region — employers exhibit a strong interest in existing national industrial relations systems so that they can secure a stable and predictable environment for production activities. See, e.g., Thelen and Kume, "The Effects of Globalization"; Kathleen Thelen, "Why German Employers Cannot Bring Themselves to Dismantle the German Model," in Torben Iversen, Jonas Pontusson, and David Soskice, eds., *Unions, Employers, and Central Banks* (New York: Cambridge University Press, 1999), 138–69; Anders Kjellberg, "Sweden: Restoring the Model?" in Anthony Ferner and Richard Hyman, eds., *Changing Industrial Relations in Europe* (Oxford: Blackwell, 1998), 74–117.

[46] See the insightful treatment of "borrowing" in Thorstein Veblen's classic study, *Imperial Germany and the Industrial Revolution* (New York: Viking, 1954).

tainly, some states will be more able than others in mediating the impact of domestic social forces and global economic forces, and others will find their capacity tested or partly eroded; but this is not a terribly novel fact given that international economic pressures have always been more influenced by the activities of relatively strong states and have always tested the capacity of relatively weak states. As state theorists have been arguing for two decades, state capacity, structure, and autonomy are *variables*, and these variables are worth examining precisely because they matter in terms of states' abilities to preserve orderly social relations across the territories they claim to control within a given environment.[47]

What the trends associated with globalization represent are the latest series of changes in the international environment within which state actors are having to make calculations about how best to achieve their objectives; if this calculation leads some states to support global corporations and neoliberal economic policies for the time being, this decision cannot be conflated with the irreversible erosion of state capacity in general. As Campbell's chapter in this volume shows, while many states may be experimenting with neoliberal programs, a number have also reversed course to correct for unanticipated political fallout; and, as Duina's chapter suggests, even the member states of the European Union, while subjecting themselves to a more expansive set of supranational laws, not only retain the capacity to refuse to implement these laws if they so choose but can more than compensate for some loss of legislative autonomy in some domains by asserting their authority more vigorously in others. Thus, despite the obvious intensification in the extent and scope of transnational economic and social processes, these changes do not justify conflating the decision of many state actors to adopt a "courtesan role" (n. 13) in the global economy with the irreversible erosion of state capacity. In the particular case of industrial relations, it is very much an open question as to whether state elites are emulating the kind of production and labor market flexibility seen in advanced industrial economies because they view this kind of flexibility as a concomitant of a borderless world; a historical perspective suggests that it is more likely that states are simply doing what they have always done: adapt seemingly effective models to independently enhance social stability, industrial prowess, and international status.

---

[47] This is amply evident in the various types of state embeddedness articulated in Evans, *Embedded Autonomy*. More generally, see the conceptualization of the state in J. P. Nettl, "The State as Conceptual Variable," *World Politics* 20 (1968): 559–92; Eric Nordlinger, "Taking the State Seriously," in Samuel Huntington and Myron Weiner, eds., *Understanding Political Development* (Ithaca: Cornell University Press, 1987); Stephen Krasner, "Economic Interdependence and Independent Statehood," in Robert Jackson and Alan James, eds., *States in a Changing World* (Oxford: Clarendon, 1993).

Finally, the discussion above suggests that it would be theoretically shortsighted — on the part of both proponents and critics of strong views of a globalization-induced convergence — to overlook the attributes that have traditionally served to define and distinguish the state from other collectivities and institutions as a concept in comparative analysis. Of particular relevance is the state's claimed right to bring coercion to bear in enforcing publicly negotiated agreements, be they constitutions, laws, or contracts. As Weber put it long ago: "The claim of the modern state to monopolize the use of force is as essential to it as its character of compulsory jurisdiction and of continuous organization."[48] The claim itself is a universal, indeed essential, element of politics that dates back to ancient empires, city-states, and nomadic tribes; in fact, the modern state may be viewed as simply the most recent and familiar manifestation of the more general transhistorical category covering all forms of political organization (from empires to villages) that have historically laid claim to the right to use force to ensure compliance with publicly negotiated understandings and agreements. While this does suggest the possibility of alternative units taking over this right at some point in the future, there is no indication at present of any other type of political organization challenging the nation-state for the right to press this claim. In the domestic arena, while other actors undoubtedly employ violence in pressuring the state or informally achieving their goals (for example, in the case of violent workers' protest or organized crime), this only reflects quite familiar variations in the autonomy and capacity of states in relation to the populations and territories they claim to govern. Certainly, new global networks — in the form of transnational corporations, ethnic diasporas, or nongovernmental organizations — have proliferated rapidly in the past few decades and have had an impact on the environment within which states seek to exercise influence, but such networks are too segmented, each focusing on issue-specific transnational ties, to supplant the nation-state as the ultimate guarantor of contracts or laws over a given domain.[49] Given that public order and predictable exchange relations at any level remain dependent upon the existence of laws and contracts, and of the *means to enforce them*, it is highly significant that the latter task remains the prerogative of the nation-state, at least formally, and continues to distinguish it from the myriad other actors that have some stake in the global economy.

[48] Max Weber, *The Theory of Social and Economic Organization* (New York: Free Press, 1947), 156.

[49] On this point, see Michael Mann, "Has Globalization Ended the Rise and Rise of the Nation-State?" in T. V. Paul and John A. Hall, eds., *International Order and the Future of World Politics* (New York: Cambridge University Press, 1999), 237–61.

In sum, what is called for in theoretical terms is a more nuanced treatment of order and change that systematically differentiates between (1) changes in the international environment that require states to reassess their national institutions and policies; (2) changes in the objectives of state actors, reflecting in part their relations with various societal actors and in part their attitude toward the international order and the most powerful actors in it; and (3) changes in those fundamental capacities that are a part of the very definition of a state, capacities such as the ability to legally employ the means of violence in order to enforce binding rules within a given territory. Conflating these three fundamentally different types of change, each cast at a different level of generality, would be a grievous theoretical error that will prevent us from recognizing just how state capacities, interests, and functions have, and have not, changed as a result of the specific empirical trends associated with globalization.

Part 4

STATE CAPACITY

CHAPTER 11

The State after State Socialism:
Poland in Comparative Perspective

GRZEGORZ EKIERT

EVEN A CURSORY look at the growing literature on contemporary Eastern European politics reveals a considerable change in thinking about the state and its role in post-1989 transformations. Initially, inherited East European states were considered to be a problem. Decisive measures were contemplated to limit their power, size, and presence in political and economic domains. Recently, state weakness and policy failures have been identified as the main causes of stalled and unsuccessful reforms as well as various pathologies of transformations: disintegration of central authority structures, official corruption and organized crime, explosion of social inequalities, revenue decline, contraction of public services, and so forth. In short, a more powerful and active state is increasingly seen as a necessary solution to the challenges of postcommunist transformations. This change of the analytical and normative optics reveals an interesting irony: communism left behind not a powerful bureaucratic Leviathan but a weak and inefficient state. Consequently, the road to democracy and capitalism in Eastern Europe leads through a massive state-building process. After the first decade of transformations it has become clear that the failure to restructure and strengthen the state apparatus poses serious risks to the entire process of transformations.

In this chapter, I shall focus on the pattern and sequencing of state reforms in Poland. During the first decade following 1989, the Polish state experienced one of the most comprehensive processes of institutional transformations in the region. At the same time, Poland emerged as a leader of market reforms, recorded the dynamic economic growth, attracted a huge share of the direct foreign investment coming to the region, registered significant improvement in living standards of its citizens, and became one of the leading candidates to join the European Union. Is there a relationship between the extent of state reforms and successful economic transformations? Why was the Polish state able to introduce such an extensive package of institutional reforms? What factors favor comprehensive state reforms in the postcommunist environment? These are some of the questions I shall address below.

THE STATE AND TRANSITIONS TO MARKETS AND DEMOCRACY

While political parties, elections, and vibrant civil societies are indispensable for modern democracy, the state has a critical role in shaping, fostering, and protecting democratic regimes. According to Juan Linz and Alfred Stepan, "modern democracy . . . needs the effective capacity to command, regulate, and extract. For this it needs a functioning state and a state bureaucracy."[1] Similarly, the effective state is indispensable in initiating and implementing fundamental economic, political, and social reforms. As Peter Evans emphasizes, "the state remains central to the process of structural change."[2] At the same time, many observers of policy reforms around the world noted that reformers and their advisors were not sufficiently concerned about the importance and consequences of state restructuring. Adam Przeworski criticized the dominant reform strategies in Eastern Europe for their lack of attention to the state. He argued that "the principal mistake of neoliberal prescriptions is that they underestimate the role of state institutions in organizing both the public and private life of groups and individuals. If democracy is to be sustained, the state must guarantee territorial integrity and physical security, it must maintain the conditions necessary for an effective exercise of citizenship, it must mobilize public savings, coordinate resource allocation, and correct income distribution. And if state institutions are to be capable of performing these tasks, they must be reorganized, rather than simply reduced."[3] Robert Kaufman made a similar point: "Through Eastern Europe and Latin America, a central challenge for the consolidation of both democracy and market reforms has been the construction of state bureaucracies capable of implementing economic policies, providing social services, and maintaining public order."[4] Even the World Bank, which for years preached the circumscribed role of the state, rediscovered the importance of the effective state administration: "An effective state is vital for the provision of the goods and

[1] Juan Linz and Alfred Stepan, *Problems of Democratic Transition and Consolidation* (Baltimore: Johns Hopkins University Press, 1996), 11.

[2] Peter Evans, "The State as Problem and Solution: Predation, Embedded Autonomy, and Adjustment," in Stephen Haggard and Robert Kaufman, eds., *The Politics of Economic Adjustment* (Princeton: Princeton University Press 1992), 140.

[3] Adam Przeworski et al., *Sustainable Democracy* (Cambridge: Cambridge University Press, 1995), 12.

[4] Robert Kaufman, "The Politics of State Reform: A Review of Theoretical Approaches," *Estudio/Working Paper* 1997/98, Instituto Juan March (June 1997): 1.

services — and the rules and institutions — that allow markets to flourish and people to lead healthier, happier lives. Without it, sustainable development, economic and social, is impossible."[5]

Such concerns and the renewed appreciation of the importance of the state and its capacity generated a set of general recommendations designed to strengthen the state institutions and enhance the state's capabilities in dealing with challenges of major political and economic transformations. According to Kaufman, efforts at strengthening the state should focus on the following sets of policies:

1. The centralization and political insulation of control over macroeconomic policy, particularly spending and monetary decisions. . . .

2. The decentralization and/or privatization of bureaucracies charged with the delivery of social services — on the assumption that local authorities will be more responsive to constituent demands and that competition among providers will enhance the efficiency of services.

3. The delegation of regulatory functions to independent agencies charged with monitoring service providers. . . .

4. The creation of a more capable cadre of senior civil servants . . . recruited according to meritocratic criteria, provided with considerable discretion . . . , and evaluated in terms of performance standards.[6]

While these and similar recommendations were generated to respond to the governability crisis affecting mostly developing countries, their applicability to postcommunist countries proved to be highly relevant.

Given the centrality of the state in regime transformations and market reforms, it is surprising that until recently reforms of the state have attracted little attention among students of democratization and East European politics.[7] This omission has its roots in the initial conceptualization of the main dilemmas or challenges facing East European societies after the fall of communism. In his influential essay Ralph Dahrendorf set the theoretical agenda for studying the postcommunist transformations, emphasizing the centrality of three parallel developments: establishment of a democratic political regime, creation of a market economy, and reconstitution of civil society.[8] His concerns with the cost of economic transformations and difficulties in restoring viable civil society pushed the issue of state transformations to the background: state restructuring

---

[5] *World Development Report 1997: The State in a Changing World* (New York: Oxford University Press, 1997), 1.

[6] Kaufman, "The Politics of State Reform," 1–2.

[7] See Arista M. Cirtautas, "The Post-Leninist State: A Conceptual and Empirical Examination," *Communist and Post-Communist Studies* 28 (1995): 379–92.

[8] Ralph Dahrendorf, *Reflections on the Revolution in Europe* (New York: Random House, 1990).

was conflated in part with democratization and in part with market reforms. Similar views, underestimating the critical role of the state reforms, were apparent in the debates on the nature of simultaneous transitions.[9]

Such understanding of the principal dilemmas facing East European reformers was based on the mistaken assumptions about the strength and institutional capacity of communist states and on a generalized liberal mistrust of the state. The dominant theoretical approaches in the field of East European studies accepted the notion of a strong, institutionally comprehensive, and capable communist state.[10] It was commonly believed that new democracies in the region inherited such a state. Moreover, in debates on reform strategies, the neoliberal ideas gained the upper hand:[11] the state was construed as a predatory institution eager to interfere in and distort both emerging democratic politics and markets.[12] From such a point of view, the main challenge of transition was to find ways in which the state and its predatory impulses could be constrained by market forces, civil society, and representative institutions.

This understanding of transition dilemmas obscured the fourth fundamental dimension of postcommunist transformations—the state restructuring and building process—that interacts in many critical ways with the formation of the democratic regime, market economy, and new civil society. To illuminate these relations, it is analytically useful and necessary to distinguish between regime and state transformations.[13] This distinction implies that while rapid regime change can fundamen-

---

[9] For the debate on the multidimensional nature of postcommunist transformations, see Claus Offe, "Capitalism by Democratic Design? Democratic Theory Facing the Triple Transition in East Central Europe." *Social Research* 58 (1991): 865–92; Piotr Sztompka, "Dilemmas of the Great Transformation." *Sisyphus* 2 (1992): 9–27; Valerie Bunce, "Comparing East and South," *Journal of Democracy* 6 (July 1995): 87–100; Leslie Armijo, Thomas Biersteker, and Abraham Lowenthal, "The Problem of Simultaneous Transitions," in Larry Diamond and Marc E. Plattner, eds., *Economic Reform and Democracy* (Baltimore: Johns Hopkins University Press, 1995), 226–40.

[10] See Cirtautas, "The Post-Leninist State," 381–84.

[11] See Alice H. Amsden, Jacek Kochanowicz, and Lance Taylor, *The Market Meets Its Match* (Cambridge: Harvard University Press, 1994), 161–70.

[12] See, for example, Andrei Shleifer and Robert Vishny, eds., *The Grabbing Hand: Government Pathologies and Their Cures* (Cambridge: Harvard University Press, 1998).

[13] Robert Fishman analyzed this distinction in the context of democratization in his paper "Rethinking State and Regime: Southern Europe's Transition to Democracy," *World Politics* 42 (April 1990): 422–40, arguing that "a regime determines who has access to political power, and how those who are in power deal with those who are not. . . . Regimes are more permanent forms of political organization than specific governments, but they are typically less permanent than the state. The state, by contrast, is a (normally) more permanent structure of domination and coordination including a coercive apparatus and the means to administer a society and extract resources from it" (428).

tally alter the core political relations, state institutions and modes of action display much greater permanence and institutional continuity. It also highlights inherent tensions between the state and regime transformations. For these reasons a historical institutional approach adopted in this chapter is the most effective strategy in reconstructing temporal trajectories and patterns of state transformations, identifying critical junctures, and explaining outcomes. Moreover, it is also essential to reconstruct not only short-term temporal sequences but also longer historical processes that shape position and capacity of specific states as well as routine strategies the state actors employ to solve dilemmas they face.

Throughout the twentieth century, Eastern European countries were characterized by highly etatist policies by virtue of being late developers and nation-state builders. In fact, as Joseph Rothschild argued, the state-driven socioeconomic development was "a thread of continuity from the interwar period into . . . East Central Europe" under communist rule.[14] At the same time, East European states were traditionally characterized by weak administrative and political institutions, paucity of formal-rational procedures, clientelism, and considerable legitimation deficit. The imposition of the communist rule significantly enhanced despotic as well as infrastructural power of the state.[15] At the same time, however, the weakness of the formal-rational procedures and legitimation deficit persisted. Moreover, the institutions of the party-state were based on interlocking dual hierarchies: functional domains of state activities were coordinated and supervised by the parallel state and party administrative bureaucracies, and the communist party apparatus was the sole locus of authority at all levels of the state organization.

During the five decades of communist rule, East European party-states experienced a complex institutional evolution. In this process not only their repressive policies and capacity markedly declined, but their infrastructural power eroded as well. As David Stark and Laszlo Bruszt noted, by 1989 "weak states faced weak societies. Instead of powerful party-states, this view sees cumbersome but weak bureaucracies, ineffective in achieving the goals of economic growth and social integration, headed by demoralized leaders whose belief in their own ideologies had withered apace with the exhaustion of their political and economic programs."[16]

[14] Joseph Rothschild, *Return to Diversity* (New York: Oxford University Press, 1993), 21.

[15] The distinction between despotic and infrastructural powers of the state was introduced by Michael Mann, "The Autonomous Power of the State: Its Origins, Mechanisms, and Results," in John A. Hall, ed., *States in History* (New York: Blackwell, 1986), 109–36.

[16] David Stark and Laszlo Bruszt, *Postsocialist Pathways* (Cambridge: Cambridge University Press, 1998), 16.

East European states were profoundly affected by the collapse of communist regimes. The rapid disintegration of administrative structures of communist parties in post-1989 Eastern Europe left behind small and organizationally weak states. The disappearance of the party side of the party-state created an institutional void that diminished capacity of these states in many fundamental ways. Swift democratization and the escalating economic crisis exacerbated uncertainties and contradictory pressures on the state apparatus and weakened or fragmented the structures of domination. Political and economic openings exposed these states to global economic forces and political constraints of global politics. At the same time, in contrast to other institutional domains of postcommunist societies, states faced a distinct disadvantage: the recombination of resources, actors, and institutions that characterized much of the developments in the economic domain and within civil society was not an available option for transforming the state.[17] The party side of the party-state disappeared swiftly and thoroughly and could not be legitimately incorporated as one of the constitutive elements of the new democratic state structures.

In many postcommunist countries the rapid and radical devolution of state power took place. It led to the collapse and dismemberment of communist federative states (Czechoslovakia, Soviet Union, Yugoslavia).[18] Political corruption combined with growing autonomy of local and regional structures evoked images of "feudalization" or "soft," fragmented, and administratively weak states of the Third World.[19] Commentators pointed to many specific problems faced by these states, such as the absence of rule of law and low accountability of public officials,[20] fiscal crisis,[21] "state dessertation,"[22] and diminishing state autonomy resulting

[17] For the analysis of recombination strategies in the economic domain, see ibid., and in the civil society domain, see Grzegorz Ekiert and Jan Kubik, *Rebellious Civil Society: Popular Protest and Democratic Consolidation in Poland* (Ann Arbor: University of Michigan Press, 1999).

[18] See Valerie Bunce, *Subversive Institutions: The Design and the Destruction of Socialism and the State* (Cambridge: Cambridge University Press, 1999).

[19] See Jadwiga Staniszkis, *The Dynamics of the Breakthrough in Eastern Europe* (Berkeley: University of California Press, 1991), 171–75; Katherine Verdery, *What Was Socialism, and What Comes Next* (Princeton: Princeton University Press, 1996), 204–28; Kathryn Stoner-Weiss, "Central Weakness and Provincial Autonomy: Observations on the Devolution Process in Russia," *Post-Soviet Affairs* 15 (1999): 87–106. For the debates on the nature of African states, see, for example, Arthur Goldsmith, "Africa's Overgrown State Reconsidered," *World Politics* 51 (1999): 520–46.

[20] Stephen Holmes, "Cultural Legacies or State Collapse? Probing the Postcommunist Dilemma," in Michael Mandelbaum, ed., *Postcommunism: Four Perspectives* (Washington, DC: Council for Foreign Relations 1995), 22–76; "What Russia Teaches Us Now," *The American Prospect* 8 (July–August 1997): 30–39.

[21] John Campbell, "The Fiscal Crisis of Post-Communist States," *Telos* 93 (1992): 89–110.

[22] Guy Standing uses the term to describe deteriorating public services and salaries of

from the capture of state agencies and policies by strategically located elites, firms, and organizations.[23] In short, the relatively weak state of late communism lost not only a great deal of its despotic but also a substantial amount of its infrastructural power as a result of the democratic transition and market reforms. Paradoxically, these considerably weakened states were entrusted with the gigantic task of designing and implementing policies aimed at fundamental transformation and restructuring of political, economic, and social orders of their societies.

The experiences of the first decade of postcommunism generate a fascinating set of questions for students of states:

1. What is the extent of continuity and breakdown in patterns of organization and activities of postcommunist states?

2. How have political struggles over state activities, boundaries, and structures affected newly democratized East European regimes?

3. Are new states expanding or contracting in their institutional organization, size, role in the economy and society, and capabilities?

4. Are new states able and willing to secure individual rights and liberties, provide essential collective goods, and maintain a favorable environment for the promotion of a market economy and democratic participation?

5. Who comprises new state elites and what factors shape and constrain their preferences and policy choices?

6. Are new states transparent, responsive to democratic control and social interests, as well as procedurally fair in their policy making?

7. What factors explain differences and diverging trajectories of state reforms and, more specifically, what is the impact of the EU enlargement prospects on the extent of state transformations?

These questions strike at the heart of what Philippe Schmitter identified as "the most significant issue for contemporary political science: How can democracy be consolidated in the aftermath of the transition from authoritarian rule."[24]

A dearth of serious empirical studies makes it impossible to offer sys-

---

public officials, which eroded the capacity of public administration ("Labor Market Governance in Eastern Europe," *European Journal of Industrial Relations* 3 (1997): 133–59. See also Mario Nuti and Richard Portes, "Central Europe: The Way Forward," in Richard Portes, ed., *Economic Transformations in Central Europe: A Progress Report* (London: CEPR, 1993), 1–20.

[23] See, for example, Joel Hellman, Geraint Jones, and Daniel Kaufmann, "Seize the State, Seize the Day: An Empirical Analysis of State Capture and Corruption in Transition," paper presented at the Annual Bank Conference on Development Economics, Washington, DC, April 18–20, 2000.

[24] Philippe Schmitter, "Interest Systems and the Consolidation of Democracy," in Gary Marks and Larry Diamond, eds., *Reexamining Democracy* (Newbury Park: Sage, 1992), 157.

tematic assessment of the role of the state in postcommunist transitions across the region. It would be also premature to develop comprehensive policy recommendations at this point.[25] We also still struggle with the lack of credible comparative data and difficulties in measuring various dimensions of state activities. Facing such difficulties, this chapter will provide only limited and preliminary answers to the above questions, relying on the experiences of Poland during the last decade.

Poland provides a good starting point for a more comprehensive investigation of the state reforms and their impact on economic and social policies. Engulfed in the devastating economic and social crisis in the end of the 1980s, Poland emerged as one of the most successful reformers and the fastest growing economy in the region by the mid-1990s. During the same time, political, social, and economic disparities among ex-communist countries increased considerably, making the former Soviet bloc one of the most diversified regions of the world (see tables 11.1 and 11.2). During this period, Poland not only succeeded in building a democratic regime and a market economy, but the Polish state underwent fundamental transformations that were more extensive than in any other postcommunist country. It is the contention of this chapter that the scope and direction of state transformation contributed to the overall success of Polish reforms. I shall argue that efforts to recast the state administrative structures and policies were a critical part of the successful transition from state socialism in Poland and provided foundations for the rapid economic growth, rising living standards, and closer integration with Western political, military, and economic structures in recent years.

THE TRANSFORMATION OF THE POLISH STATE

The diverging trajectories and initial outcomes of postcommunist transformation across Central and Eastern Europe may be explained by several factors often construed in terms of competing accounts. Historical legacies and initial conditions, design, timing and sequencing of reforms, quality of new elites and their policies, institutional choices, and the extent of external support provide important clues for the range of outcomes emerging in the region. The causal relations among these factors and their strength, however, are not obvious or easy to determine. More-

[25] Devesh Kapur identifies similar weaknesses in the recent World Bank Development Report pointing to insufficient empirical evidence and absence of specific policy recommendations for strengthening institutional capacities of the state. See "The State in a Changing World: A Critique of the 1997 World Development Report," *Working Paper Series* no. 98-2, Weatherhead Center for International Affairs, Harvard University.

TABLE 11.1

Progress of Political and Economic Transformations in Selected Postcommunist Countries

	Index of Transition Progress[a]	Economic Freedom Index[b]	Country Risk Index[c]	Press Freedom Index[d]	Political Freedom Index[e]	Corruption Perception Index[f]
Czech Republic	36.0	2.20 (27)	60.19 (44)	20 (F)	3 (F)	4.3 (42)
Estonia	35.0	2.05 (14)	54.34 (55)	20 (F)	3 (F)	5.7 (27)
Hungary	38.0	2.55 (42)	61.83 (42)	30 (F)	3 (F)	5.2 (32)
Poland	36.5	2.75 (54)	61.67 (43)	19 (F)	3 (F)	4.1 (43)
Slovenia	34.0	2.90 (63)	71.28 (32)	27 (F)	3 (F)	5.5 (28)
Bulgaria	30.5	3.30 (95)	39.75 (84)	30 (F)	5 (F)	3.5 (52)
Latvia	32.0	2.65 (46)	52.08 (59)	24 (F)	3 (F)	3.4 (57)
Lithuania	32.5	2.55 (42)	50.10 (61)	20 (F)	3 (F)	4.1 (43)
Romania	29.5	3.65 (124)	33.80 (107)	44 (PF)	4 (F)	2.9 (68)
Slovakia	33.5	2.85 (59)	48.44 (66)	30 (F)	3 (F)	3.5 (52)
Albania	25.0	3.50 (110)	28.18 (146)	56 (PF)	9 (PF)	2.3 (84)*
Belarus	16.0	4.25 (146)	29.11 (140)	80 (NF)	12 (NF)	4.1 (43)
Croatia	32.5	3.45 (106)	47.08 (70)	63 (NF)	8 (PF)	3.7 (51)
Ukraine	26.0	3.85 (133)	29.96 (134)	39 (PF)	7 (PF)	2.6 (75)

[a]*Source*: European Bank for Reconstruction and Development, *Transition Report 2000* (London: November 2000), 14, 34, and 36. Economic transition indicators are combined with legal transition indicators.

[b]*Source*: Gerald O'Driscoll Jr., Kim R. Holmes, and Melanie Kirkpatrick, *2001 Index of Economic Freedom* (Washington, DC: Heritage Foundation 2001). Lowest score 5.0, highest score 1.25. The index is composed of factors including political risk, trade policy, taxation, government intervention in the economy, monetary policy, wage and price control, property rights, capital flows and foreign investment, banking regulation, and black market.

[c]*Source*: *Euromoney*, March 2000. Highest possible score 100.

[d]*Source*: Leonard R. Sussman, ed., *Press Freedom Survey 2000*, Freedom House 2000. Countries scoring 0–30 on 100-point scale are regarded as having a free press; countries scoring 31–60 are partly free.

[e]*Source*: *Freedom in the World. The Annual Survey of Political Rights and Liberties 1999–2000*, Freedom House 2000. Highest possible score 2, lowest possible score 14.

[f]*Source*: *Transparency International*, 2000 Corruption Perception Index, www.transparency.de. This index is constructed as a compilation of a number surveys conducted in each country and ranges between 10 (highly clean) and 0 (highly corrupt). The score for Albania is from 1999 index.

over, their impact may decrease or increase in different stages of transition and differ across the region, and they may interact in many complex ways. There is still much research to be done to entangle particular patterns of reforms and to generate the sufficient evidence necessary to understand specific cases of postcommunist transformations. New theoretical and empirical efforts are essential to provide convincing cross-regional comparative accounts.

The reform process in Poland has several distinct features in comparison with other postcommunist countries. The Polish transition began in

TABLE 11.2
Selected Economic Indicators, 1989–1999

	Years of GDP Decline	GDP Fall after Recovery	GDP Growth, 1989–94	GDP Growth, 1995–99	GDP Growth, 1989–99	1999 GDP (1989 = 100)	GDP per Capita, 1999	Unemployment, 1999
Czech Republic	6	Yes	−2.0	1.5	−0.4	95	$5,189	9.4
Estonia	6	Yes	−6.2	4.5	−1.3	77	$3,564	12.3
Hungary	4	No	−2.6	3.4	0.1	99	$4,853	9.1
Poland	2	No	−1.1	5.8	2.0	122	$3,987	13.0
Slovenia	4	No	−2.1	4.0	0.7	109	$10,020	7.5
Bulgaria	6	Yes	−4.6	−1.6	−3.2	67	$1,513	16.0
Latvia	4	Yes	−8.3	3.0	−3.2	60	$2,582	14.4
Lithuania	5	Yes	−9.4	3.2	−3.7	62	$2,880	14.1
Romania	7	Yes	−4.6	−0.8	−2.9	76	$1,517	11.5
Slovakia	4	No	−3.5	4.0	0.6	100	$3,650	19.2
Albania	4	Yes	−2.9	6.3	1.3	96	$1,102	18.0
Belarus	6	No	−4.3	3.1	−1.0	80	$777	2.1
Croatia	6	Yes	−7.3	4.3	−2.0	78	$4,467	12.6
Ukraine	10	No recovery	−10.3	−5.5	−8.1	36	$619	4.3

Note: GDP data from EBRD, Transition Report 2000, November 2000.

1980 with the emergence of the Solidarity movement and was characterized by rapid mass mobilization and open political struggle between the newly constituted independent organizations and the entrenched forces of the party-state. This early effort of democratization was aborted by the imposition of martial law and the delegalization of the Solidarity trade union. Its legacies, however, shaped Polish politics through the 1980s.[26] By the end of the decade, democratization was back on the agenda, this time leading to the orderly transfer of power to new political elites. But this long process of deconstruction of the Polish party-state left a visible imprint on the consolidation phase taking place after 1989.

As a result of the "round table" negotiations that began in Warsaw on February 6, 1989, Poland became the first country in the Soviet bloc to initiate a peaceful transfer of political power. The semidemocratic elections in June 1989 led to the political triumph of the relegalized Solidarity movement, the first noncommunist government in the region was in office by the end of the summer, and the Communist Party dismantled itself by January 1990. The transfer of power was followed by comprehensive transformations of the national political institutions and local administration and radical economic reforms. The new political elites that emerged from the Solidarity movement set Poland on the course toward liberal democracy and a market economy.

The transformation policies, however, had to be forged and implemented amid the deepening economic crisis, regional political chaos, as well as disintegrating regional economic and political institutions. These external adversities combined with radical macroeconomic stabilization measures contributed to a sharp contraction of the economy, decline in real incomes, dramatic rise in unemployment, new social inequalities, and growing insecurity. Few people anticipated such harsh realities, and public opinion polls registered considerable disappointment with government policies. Professional and social groups threatened by the changing economic environment, especially in heavy industry and agriculture, responded with strikes and protests. In Poland mass protest actions were more common than in any other postcommunist country[27] and contributed to both political instability and a relatively high level of accountability for reform measures and policy decisions implemented by the ruling elites.

At the same time, the political consensus concerning the extent, speed,

---

[26] See Grzegorz Ekiert, *The State against Society* (Princeton: Princeton University Press, 1997).

[27] See Grzegorz Ekiert and Jan Kubik, "Contentious Politics in New Democracies," *World Politics* 50 (1998): 547–81.

and sequencing of institutional reforms, which initially unified the new elites, unraveled. The post-Solidarity political bloc, united for the 1989 elections and initially constituting a single caucus in the parliament, split into several fiercely competing parties with contrasting programs and political agendas. Consequently, during the first postcommunist decade, Poland experienced a turbulent political evolution. It had four parliamentary, three local, and two presidential elections, as well as ten consecutive prime ministers and eight governments. Not long after its political triumph in 1989, the Solidarity-based political movement disintegrated, and descendant political parties were often unable to form effective electoral coalitions. Ironically, the ex-communist parties were returned to power as a result of the 1993 elections and for the next four years were in charge of guiding the transformation process. In the following elections in 1997, the coalition of parties built around Solidarity was able again to wrest political power away from ex-communist parties and revitalize the reform agenda.

To summarize, the Polish case stands out among all postcommunist transitions due to at least five unique features. They include:

1. Pioneerism and tradition of political struggles. The unraveling of state socialism began in Poland in 1980 with the rise of Solidarity, or arguably even earlier, during the rebellions of 1956, 1968, 1970, and 1976. The symbolic, intellectual, and institutional aspects of this revolution were far more pronounced and articulate than in other countries of the region, and massive oppositional resources were generated. Moreover, the institutional evolution of the Polish party-state was greatly accelerated, resulting in, among other things, autonomization of the state administration and redefinition of the relationship between the party and state bureaucracies.

2. Formation and disintegration of the massive political movement. Both the rise of Solidarity in 1980 and its revival and disintegration in 1989–91 had a decisive formative impact on the shape of Polish postcommunist politics.

3. Administrative reform. Poland carried out the earliest and most comprehensive administrative reform in East Central Europe. As a result, in the first stages of transition the state was significantly decentralized, and local communities were burdened/blessed with a number of administrative prerogatives and responsibilities. In several subsequent steps, the central state administration and state finances were thoroughly reformed, and the new layer of self-government was added. The reform of the major state services (pensions, health, education) followed.

4. Political fragmentation and instability. Poland experienced more political conflicts and more intense political competition than other countries in the region. As a result, the country experienced frequent government turn-

over and a large number of elections. The highly competitive and unstable political life together with free media contributed to a higher degree of accountability, more political control over policies, restraint of rent-seeking behavior, and less corruption.

5. Early and radical economic reform. Poland's first democratic government implemented radical macroeconomic measures, known as "shock therapy," early in the transition process. Moreover, the reform momentum was maintained through the entire period, despite changes of government and ruling coalitions.

The combination of these five features heavily influenced the Polish political and economic transformations. Massive political mobilization and the initial consensus about the need and direction of reforms created a strong momentum for comprehensive institutional transformations. The reactivation of local elites (through Citizens' Committees) and the decentralizing administrative reform led to the decoupling of national and local/regional politics. This, in turn, shielded local social, political, and—most importantly—economic processes from the volatility of central politics.[28] Vice versa, state policies were at least partially insulated from local challenges. Moreover, the intense political competition at all levels of the political organization prevented the stabilization of semireformed institutions and the entrenchment of the early winners of economic reforms.[29] Such a situation helped to maintain the momentum for further reforms. Finally, the concentration of the most costly economic measures during the initial period of transition helped to preempt and forestall the opposition to reforms, made them irreversible, and created conditions for the fast recovery, solid economic performance, and growing legitimacy of the new political and social order.[30]

At the first glance, the transformation of the Polish state can be perceived as a chaotic process driven exclusively by unexpected exigencies and the short-term political calculations of elite politicians. In their comprehensive evaluation of the Polish administrative reform, Andrzej Kidyba and Andrzej Wrobel argue that

[28] See Jan Kubik, "Decentralization and Cultural Revival in Post-communist Transformations," *Communist and Post-Communist Studies* 27 (1994): 331–55.

[29] This situation contrasts with the developments in some other countries, especially Russia, where short-term economic winners were able to create a "partial reform equilibrium" with "concentrated rents for themselves, while imposing high cost on the rest of society" (Joel Hellman, "Winners Take All: The Politics of Partial Reform in Postcommunist Transitions," *World Politics* 50 [1998]: 204–5).

[30] For comparative data on public opinion, see, for example, Richard Rose and Christian Haerpfer, "New Democracies Barometer V," *Studies in Public Policy* no. 306 (Glasgow: Center for the Study of Public Policy, University of Strathclyde, 1998), 17, 25.

the reform of public administration in Poland lacks a coherent and national program to be implemented gradually. Subsequent governments, in their attempts to realize temporary political goals or provide ad hoc solutions to problems which arise unexpectedly, have tended rather to support their own, frequently short term visions rather than considering long term implications. Consequently, the system of administration tends to expand to incorporate new institutions whose raison d'être is dubious at best or whose existence is calculated for a short period only. It is no wonder that under such adverse conditions internal relations within the administration suffer, the organization lacks clarity, effectiveness wanes and all sorts of barriers and limitations multiply.[31]

While such views mirror the prevailing popular perceptions, casting of the reform process in terms of chaos, particularism, and inefficiency may be highly misleading, especially when one compares Poland's experiences with those of other postcommunist countries. The uncertainties and turmoil of the state transformation process reflect, above all, the political and institutional complexity of such massive state reforms and their social impact. Any significant change in even highly inefficient state policies or institutions disrupts everyday routines and expectations, has weighty distributional consequences, and directly affects wide segments of the population and many powerful social actors. Consequently, opposition to reforms can be easily mobilized and ensuing political struggles contribute a sense of profound instability. In addition, the perception of chaos is magnified by intense political conflicts and struggles among political elites that characterize democratic competition as well as the process of designing, enacting, and implementation of the specific reform measures.

In contrast to those who emphasize chaos, political expediency, and inefficiency, the process of institutional reforms in Poland can be seen as remarkably determined, motivated by a grand design, and generally consistent. Although it has been slow and convoluted, it was based on the considerable consensus among main political actors, regarding the ultimate direction and goals of reforms. It was guided by a set of well-defined objectives that were initially elaborated during the roundtable negotiations in 1989: state decentralization and self-government for local communities, small and efficient central state administration, fiscal discipline, reduced role of the state in the economy, generous welfare policies, as well as transparent and efficient regulatory institutions. These general objectives remained unchanged through the subsequent

---

[31] Andrzej Kidyba and Andrzej Wrobel, *Public Administration in Poland: Its Structure and Powers*, Economic and Social Policy Series, no. 34 (Warszawa: Friedrich-Ebert-Foundation Poland, 1994), 7.

debates and were reflected in reform proposals and measures implemented by the consecutive governments. There were, however, intense
controversies regarding particular reform designs and their likely impact
on various social and professional groups. Political conflicts and debates
centered not on objectives but on institutional strategies and proposals
for specific social policy changes. Conflicts were particularly intense because they were firmly rooted in competing political visions and programs
and much less in particularistic interests of elite politicians. Nowhere did
the dominant neoliberal vision clash with traditional social-democratic
sentiments and ideas so intensely as in the domain of social policy and
state obligations vis-à-vis various social and professional groups.

Due to the highly contested nature of each proposed reform measure,
the specific government proposals were carefully designed, widely con-
sulted, and quite efficiently implemented. This highly partisan and de-
manding policy-making environment had beneficial, although often unanticipated, impact on specific reform measures in the long run. What
were frequently criticized as unnecessary obstructions and irresponsible
delays in introducing necessary measures and attributed to the pettiness
or ideological zeal of politicians resulted in a better reform design and
more control over their outcomes. The history of the long-stalled mass
privatization program provides a good example of such a situation. Because of delays caused by intense political conflicts, Poland was able to
avoid most of the problems that plagued hastily implemented Czech
and Russian mass privatization schemes.

It is not only the policy design and the contentious policy-making
environment that characterized the state reform process. The transformation of the Polish state followed a particular sequence of reformist
measures. It started with the amendments to the communist constitution that changed fundamentally the system of government, and with
the reform of local administration. The creation of the local self-government was the first legislative initiative of the newly established upper
chamber of the Polish Parliament (Senat). The reform, implemented in
March 1990, created 2,483 democratically constituted territorial units
(*gminy*). In the spirit of the principle of subsidiarity, the act empowered
local communities to deal with local issues.[32] The local self-government

[32] See Renata Wrobel, *Cztery Lata Reformy* (Warszawa: Presspublica, 1994); Hellmut
Wollman, "Institution Building and Decentralization in Formerly Socialist Countries: The
Cases of Poland, Hungary, and East Germany," *Environment and Planning* 15 (1997):
463–80; Joanna Regulska, "Local Government Reform," in Richard F. Staar, ed., *Transi-
tion to Democracy in Poland* (New York: St. Martin's Press, 1998), 113–32; Lena Ko-
larska-Bobinska, ed., *Druga fala polskich reform, 1989–1998* (Warszawa: Instytut Spraw
Publicznych, 1999); Kolarska-Bobinska, ed., *Cztery reformy. Od koncepcji do realizacji*
(Warszawa: Instytut Spraw Publicznych, 2000).

was granted considerable powers and resources and took over many tasks performed previously by the state administration (maintenance of infrastructure, primary education, health services, administration of public property, partial responsibility for maintenance of law and order, etc.). During the same year, 254 regional offices (*urzedy rejonowe*) designed as auxiliary organs of the state administration were established to increase efficiency of the state apparatus and to facilitate the relationship between self-governed *gminas* and the state.

The reform of the local government was followed by the reform of the state finances and its extractive capabilities. It included the introduction of the new tax system (personal income tax was introduced in 1992 and the VAT in 1993) and the reform of tax collection mechanisms. The implementation of the new tax system was well prepared and successful. It ensured the uninterrupted flow of revenues and a relatively high level of tax compliance. The 1997 OECD survey stated that "maintaining fiscal revenues has been a major challenge in all countries in transition. In Poland, tax revenues, non-tax revenues and social security contributions have been comparatively well maintained."[33] Fiscal stability was a critically important issue for securing the progress of transformations by allowing the maintenance and expansion of, among other things, safety nets and large social programs. As Theda Skocpol argues, the "state's means of raising and deploying financial resources" is the most important factor in explaining the state's "capacity to create or strengthen state organizations, to employ personnel, to coopt political support, to subsidize economic enterprises, and to fund social programs."[34] In fact, the postcommunist welfare state became more extensive: the share of social expenditures in GDP increased from 17 percent in 1989 to 32 percent in 1995.[35]

The first post-1989 governments made serious efforts to design and facilitate organizational and institutional changes within the state administration, although the governmental instability and ensuing political debates as well as the complexity of reforms greatly slowed down the pace of transformations envisioned at the beginning of transition.

[33] OECD Economic Surveys: Poland 1997 (Paris: OECD Publications, 1997), 39.

[34] Theda Skocpol, "Bringing the State Back In: Strategies of Analysis in Current Research," in Peter Evans, Dietrich Rueschemeyer, and Theda Skocpol, eds., *Bringing the State Back In* (New York: Cambridge University Press, 1995), 17. See also Jose Antonio Cheibub, "Political Regimes and the Extractive Capacity of Governments: Taxation in Democracies and Dictatorships," *World Politics* 50 (1998): 349–73; John L. Campbell, "The State and Fiscal Sociology," *Annual Review of Sociology* 19 (1993): 163–85.

[35] See, for example, Tomasz Inglot, "Historical Legacies, Institutions and the Politics of Social Policy in Hungary and Poland, 1989–1999," in Grzegorz Ekiert and Stephen Hanson, eds., *Capitalism and Democracy in Central and Eastern Europe: Assessing the Legacy of Communist Rule* (New York: Cambridge University Press, 2003).

Although the noncommunist reformers lost power to ex-communists, the PSL-SLD governments (1993–97) continued the program of transformations, focusing their attention on the reform of the central administration.

The legislation enacted in 1996 commenced the process of fundamental changes in the structure and operation of the government and state administration. It laid foundations for the creation of a strong government and rationalization of its organizational structures. It also increased the prerogatives of the prime minister, facilitated more efficient management of state assets, and established the professional civil service. The main intention of the reform was to focus the activities of government ministers on policy and regulatory issues and relieve/prevent them from micromanaging the economy and provision of state services. The act strengthened ministries responsible for macroeconomic regulation (especially the Ministry of Finance), created better management of public property, and improved the quality and stability of civil service. The transformation of the national-level administration was completed in 1997 by additional legal regulations and especially by the Act on the Polish National Bank, extending the power and autonomy of the central bank. As a result, Poland maintained remarkable financial and currency stability and was able to control inflation, and its central bank emerged as a powerful national actor.[36]

The territorial reform of 1998 constituted another critical element in the process of state transformations. It created the second tier of the local self-government by establishing 365 new, self-governing territorial units (*powiaty*). At the same time, the reform reduced the number of state-administered regions from 49 to 16 in order to create large and economically viable regions and decrease the state direct involvement in local affairs. The regional offices created in 1990 were abolished, and state administrative functions were consolidated. This reform left nearly 50 percent of the state budget in the hands of local communities, transferred important social tasks to the local self-government, and streamlined the structure and prerogatives of the state administration.

The next stage of state transformations comprised the most difficult and controversial reforms: the pension system, health care, and education. The question of how to redesign these critical services and programs has been hotly debated since 1989, and consecutive governments developed various policy proposals.[37] The detailed reform projects were completed in 1998 and a political consensus was reached about their

[36] See Wojciech Maliszewski, "Central Bank Independence in Transition Economies," *The Economics of Transition* 8 (2000): 749–89.

[37] For the detailed evaluation, see Stanisława Golinowska, *Political spoleczna. Koncepcje-instytucje-koszty* (Warszawa: Poltext, 2000).

design, merits, and necessity. The Solidarity-led government, which succeeded ex-communists in 1997, moved the projects through the Parliament and vigorously pushed ahead with implementation. In 1999 Poland introduced ambitious and comprehensive pension reforms. The existing pay-as-you-go system was transformed into the three-pillar system based on individual retirement accounts.[38] Two mandatory sources were created: (1) the state-run social security component (first pillar), managed by the legally autonomous public organization, the Social Insurance Institution (ZUS) (which also covers disability, sickness, and accident payments), and (2) the fully capitalized component managed by strictly regulated private pension funds (second pillar). The ZUS collects contributions for both pillars. These two components were supplemented by the third pillar — voluntary private insurance. The system is designed to achieve long-term financial sustainability and an increase in future benefits, which depend on the amount paid by individual contributors. It also guarantees a minimum pension. As part of the reform, a system of state-regulated but privately managed national investment funds was established in 1998, creating twenty-one new financial institutions.

Also in 1999 the health system reform was introduced. The responsibilities for funding and delivering health services were decentralized. The reform established sixteen territorially based Health Care Funds and a special one for the military and police employees. The funds pay medical benefits to all insured under their jurisdiction and sign contracts with doctors and hospitals for the delivery of all medical services. All employees pay mandatory premiums collected by the ZUS and transferred directly to the funds. Under the reform the insured person is able to choose his or her doctor and the health care institution in which he or she wants to be treated. The new system was designed to introduce competition in the health sector and, at the same time, to establish more rigorous control of health expenditures and reduce waste and mismanagement.

The reform of the education system was launched in1999 as well. It introduced a number of fundamental changes, initially mostly at the primary and secondary education level. The cycle of instruction was redesigned, curricula changed, and even more responsibility for financing and running schools was delegated to the local self-government.

All three reforms were quite efficiently implemented, despite considerable opposition from various professional groups in affected sectors and

---

[38] See Katherina Muller, *The Political Economy of Pension Reform in Central Eastern Europe* (Chaltenham: Edward Elgar, 1999); Hans-Jurgen Wagener, "The Welfare State in Transition Economies and Accession to the EU," *West European Politics* 25 (2002).

opposition parties. The decade-long delay in reforming these major spheres of state activities reflects well-known difficulties and dilemmas common to both developed and transition countries. As Robert Kaufman argued, "the administrative difficulties in creating or strengthening elite macroeconomic agencies are generally less severe than those of reforming larger, service-providing segments of the state apparatus."[39]

This brief overview suggests that the Polish state experienced extensive institutional transformations during the first decade following the collapse of state socialism. Despite intense political conflicts over the content and implementation of reforms that produced the appearance of administrative ineffectiveness and institutional chaos, the Polish state developed better capacity to respond to challenges of simultaneous transitions than many of its postcommunist neighbors. It is also better organized and more effective, and it seems to possess more "infrastructural power" than its communist predecessor ever had. Interestingly, the logic of state transformation in Poland corresponds well with the policy recommendations advocated by the World Bank and other international financial organizations. In the remainder of this chapter, I will briefly describe the direction of state transformation in Poland as measured against the agenda of state reform, stressing the need for centralization and insulation of control over macroeconomic policy, decentralization and privatization of social services, delegation of regulatory functions to independent agencies, and creation of more capable civil service.

CENTRALIZATION AND POLITICAL INSULATION OF CONTROL OVER MACROECONOMIC POLICY

Compared to the period before 1989, the autonomy and relative capacity of the Polish state have been enhanced, despite the substantial devolution of its power. First of all, after 1989, when many expected to see the huge, bureaucratic "communist Leviathan" cut down and limited, the new postcommunist state in Poland actually grew in terms of employment and the number of specialized central state agencies (see table 11.3). The Polish state became much bigger during the analyzed period. Employment in public administration more than doubled, increasing from 69,319 in 1989 to 171,246 in 1998. In 1999 46,000 employees were added, provoking a public debate about the excessive expansion of the state apparatus.[40] Interestingly, the growth of employment in the state administration outraced significantly the growth of

---

[39] Kaufman, "The Politics of State Reform," 9.
[40] See the interview with Witold Kiezun in *Gazeta Wyborcza*, October 30, 2000.

TABLE 11.3

Employment in State Administration and Local Self-Government, 1989–1998

	1988	1989	1990	1991	1992	1993	1994	1995	1996	1997	1998
Central state's agencies	32	35	37	39	40	43	44	—	—		55[a]
State administration	71,135	69,319	75,229	93,344	104,739	115,374	133,330	141,494	156,856	163,487	171,246
Local self-government	96,716	92,260	83,583	77,551	90,110	108,333	135,022	139,295	133,369	142,114	138,227

Sources: *Rocznik Statystyczny* (Warszawa: GUS, 1989–1999). For 1987–89 local state administration includes those employed in 49 provincial offices (*urzędy wojewódzkie*). Since 1990 it includes those employed in 49 provincial offices and in 254 newly created regional offices (*urzędy rejonowe*). On January 1, 1999, the number of provincial offices was reduced to 16 and an additional level of local self-government was introduced comprising 308 new territorial units. Data do not include employees of the Ministry of Internal Affairs (employment increased from 145,014 in 1990 to 181,494 in 1993, to 187,102 in 1996, and 184,700 in 1998), Ministry of National Defense (civilian employment and the size of the armed forces decreased from 363,400 in 1990 to 314,400 in 1993 and 289,968 in 1996), and Ministry of Justice (with employment of 39,739 in 1993), with the exception of employees of the ministerial office.

[a]The number of central state agencies in the end of 1999.

TABLE 11.4
Employment in the Public Sector in Poland, 1990–1998

	1990	1993	1995	1996	1997	1998
Public-sector employment	8,941.9		5,613.9	5,394.9	4,823.9	4,621.1
Percent of all employed	54.9%		38.1%	35.9%	31.2%	29.2%
Armed forces	363.5	314.4	309.0	290.0	287.5	283.6
Internal security	145.0	181.5	185.0	187.1	188.7	184.7

Source: Rocznik Statystyczny (Warszawa: GUS, 1998), 126, (1999), 130.

employment in the local self-government, despite the fact that considerable responsibilities were shifted to the local self-government.

The growth of state employment can be attributed to the efforts to reorganize the old while building new spheres of the state administration in order to respond to new domestic and international challenges and regulatory needs engendered by the emergence of markets as well as the requirements of the EU accession process. In fact, the overall size of the public sector (including state-owned enterprises) decreased approximately by half as a result of privatization policies. There was also a significant reduction in the size of the armed forces, as illustrated in table 11.4. Ironically, by the end of the decade, employment in the internal security apparatus was much higher than it had been under the old regime. As a result of this expansion, the Polish state is much bigger than the state in other postcommunist countries, especially those where the reform process is stalled or reversed. Tito Boeri demonstrates that employment in the state sector (excluding state enterprises) increased during the transition period in the more successful Central European countries, while it declined in the less successful countries of the former Soviet Union.[41] Similarly, when one looks at government spending as a percentage of GDP (one of the routine measures of state size), on average government expenditures declined only from 46.6 to 43.9 percent in successful reformers in Central Europe (Visegrad countries), while they fell from 50.8 to 33.1 percent in the countries of the former Soviet Union.[42] Moreover, as the OECD data in table 11.5 show, general government employment has already reached the level of some West European welfare states. This significant expansion of the state size in terms

[41] Tito Boeri, Structural Change, Welfare Systems, and Labor Relocation: Lessons from the Transition of Formerly Planned Economies (Oxford: Oxford University Press, 2000).

[42] Nauro F. Campos and Fabrizio Coricelli, "Growth in Transition: What We Know, What We Don't and What We Should," CEPR Discussion Paper, no. 3246 (March 2002): 23, 67.

TABLE 11.5

General Government Employment as a Percentage of Total Employment

	1995	1997	1998
Czech Republic	5.4	5.8	5.8
Hungary	7.3	7.2	—
Poland	18.0	18.4	—
Belgium	19.2	18.7	18.4
Denmark	30.3	30.2	30.0
France	24.9	24.9	24.5
Germany	13.2	12.9	12.6
Ireland	13.2	12.2	11.2
Italy	18.0	17.5	—
Spain	15.5	15.6	15.1
Sweden	32.1	31.5	—

Source: Analytical Databank, OECD.

of employment and a high level of state spending provoked intense debate on the economic effects, desirability, and limits of state growth. Many critics argued that Poland cannot sustain such a sizable state in the long run without hurting economic freedoms, competitiveness, and country's economic performance.

Second, the new state became quite effectively insulated from old organized interests and, therefore, more autonomous. According to David Bartlett, it experienced the shift of "power within the state administration away from the branch ministries, which had served as the main venue for particularistic bargaining under communism, and toward agencies of macroeconomic regulation."[43] In Poland, the Ministry of Finance became the locus of governmental power, and the minister of finance was elevated to the rank of the deputy prime minister. This shift of power away from spending ministries and the breakdown of old networks and linkages between the state and organized social actors provide important clues for understanding the capacity of the Polish government to introduce and sustain radical economic and social reforms.

The autonomy and power of ministries responsible for macroeconomic regulation were enhanced through consecutive reforms of the governmental administration and by the creation of the independent central bank. Policymakers also benefited from the window of opportunity provided by the radical breakdown of the old and the slow emergence of

[43] David Bartlett, "Democracy, Institutional Change, and Stabilization Policy in Hungary," Europe-Asia Studies 48 (1996): 48.

new domestic interest groups.[44] The 1996–97 reform of the central administration also strengthened the power of the prime minister, ensured better coordination of the government activities, and separated policy making and regulatory functions from everyday administrative tasks. The creation of sixteen large regions in 1998 and the delegation of many tasks previously held by the central administration to new regional offices streamlined state activities even further. Moreover, in 1996, following several years of preparation and debates, the legislation creating the professional civil service was introduced. It established rules and procedures in accordance with international standards. The reform intended to depoliticize the state administration and created conditions in which high-ranking state employees were shielded from the impact of transient government changes. Positions within the state administration subjected to political turnover were clearly defined and limited to the highest posts in the government (ministers, deputy ministers, general directors) and regional administration. The law also introduced tenure positions, public competition for higher managerial posts, and professional training programs.

Third, the extractive capacity of the Polish state has been greatly expanded through reform of the tax system completed by 1994. In terms of design, tax reforms followed existing European models. Their implementation was successful, and collection mechanisms have been working reasonable well. According to the OECD survey, "the Polish authorities took a very cautious and thorough approach to introducing the VAT, which has paid off handsomely . . . VAT receipts grew from month to month and quickly exceeded the revenues collected from the old turnover tax. . . . enforcement has been vigorous and as a consequence there are no problems with tax arrears."[45] As a result, financial stability was achieved and budget deficits have been under control. Sustainable streams of revenues allowed an increase in spending in some critical areas (infrastructure, internal security) as well as securing necessary funding for emergency spending and restructuring of the most troublesome sectors of Polish industry (armament, steel, coal mining) and agriculture.

Finally, the Polish state was able to push for the radical reform of large social services, laying foundations for a modern welfare system. The 1999 pension reform was the boldest and most comprehensive in comparison with other postcommunist countries at that time. Fundamental reforms of the health services and education followed earlier

[44] For the elaboration of this point, see Leszek Balcerowicz, *Socialism, Capitalism and Transformation* (New York: Central European University Press, 1995).

[45] *OECD Economic Surveys: Poland 1994* (Paris: OECD Publications, 1994), 173.

measures aimed at decentralization and commercialization of social services. For example, the legislation adopted in 1991 allowed the establishment of private schools at all levels of education. As a result, by the
end of the decade, 26 percent of all college students were trained in over
one hundred new private universities and colleges. In short, through the
twin process of privatization and fiscal as well as administrative decentralization, the foundations for more efficient and sustainable social policies were established. Moreover, substantial progress has been made in
privatizing state-owned enterprises and banks as well as in restructuring
the deeply distorted and notoriously troubled heavy industry sectors,
such as coal mining and steel industries.

In sum, since 1989 the inefficient and small state inherited from the
old regime has been greatly transformed. The state administration has
become larger, better organized, professionalized, and in many ways
more efficient. The state apparatus has been increasingly focused on
policy making and regulatory functions. Moreover, state finances were
rationalized and public spending and monetary policies have been relatively sound. Additional resources have been devoted to the maintenance of law and order and infrastructure. It can be argued that the
state reforms created relatively stable institutional foundations to facilitate economic growth and foreign investment. They contributed to rising living standards and alleviation of many social problems. They also
made possible the progress of the EU accession process and integration
with Western political and economic organizations.

DECENTRALIZATION AND PRIVATIZATION

Two parallel processes contributed to the significant decentralization of
state functions and ways in which the delivery of social services was
transformed. First, two waves of local government reforms created two
tiers of self-governed territorial units. This allowed many tasks performed previously by the state administration to be delegated to local
authorities on the assumption that they are better equipped to identify
spending priorities and oversee efficient use of funds. Encouraged by the
results of the first wave of decentralization in the 1990s, the 1998 legislation, creating the second tier of local self-government, increased the
responsibilities and amount of public funds controlled by local self-governments. In 1997, during the debates on the second round of territorial
reforms, the internal report of the Polish government stated that

> the results (especially economic ones) achieved by local self-government
> during the first six years following the reform proved beyond any doubt
> that the strategy of decentralization was correct. Despite the difficult insti-

tutional, political and economic environment, gminas maintained fiscal balance, and registered 1.8% surplus in their budgets. Local officials were very careful in taking new credits and were able to avoid the debt trap. Moreover, gminas were eager to invest (20% of their income was invested in various infrastructural projects) contributing significantly to overcoming the recession and stimulating subsequent economic growth. Activities of the local self-government had also a profound impact on stabilization and regulation of property rights.[46]

Second, the process of privatization reduced substantially the direct state involvement in the economy. Poland's multitrack privatization process benefited from the involvement of local self-governments to whose jurisdiction the substantial amount of state property was transferred.[47] While small-scale privatization was quickly and efficiently implemented, the acrimonious political debate about blueprints for mass privatization postponed its implementation for several years. The delay allowed the Ministry of Privatization to develop a more effective and economically viable program, expanded the scope of more efficient capital privatization, and opened more opportunities for direct foreign investment. As a result, privatization was more gradual and decentralized and has been taking place in a better prepared and regulated environment than in many other countries. Moreover, growing stabilization of the economic situation, better macroeconomic results, and increasing international perception that Poland's transformations are on the right track brought a steady stream of foreign investment. By 1998 Poland had become one of the biggest recipients of foreign direct investment in the region.[48]

REGULATORY OVERSIGHT AND THE DELEGATION OF REGULATORY FUNCTIONS TO INDEPENDENT AGENCIES

In general, external controls over the state's administration in postcommunist countries were expanded as a result of the revived parliamentary, judicial, and media oversight. The new states relinquished some of their power both upward to the international agencies and organizations (World Bank, IMF, etc.) and downward to local self-governments. The constraints imposed by international lending institutions were especially effective in reducing the state's capacity to pursue inflationary policies and to freely implement major policy changes. In addition, Po-

---

[46] Ministerstwo Spraw Wewnetrznych i Administracji, *Panstwo sprawne, przyjazne, bezpieczne* (Warszawa, 1997), 7.

[47] See John Earle et al., *Small Privatization* (Budapest: CEU Press, 1994), 205–17.

[48] See EBRD, *Transition Report 2000* (London: EBRD, 2000), 74, 79–91.

land's institutional choices, such as granting independent status to the central bank, introducing the VAT, or pursuing fiscal and administrative decentralization, facilitated bureaucratic self-restraint and fiscal discipline. Moreover, successive governments paid special attention to developing regulatory capacities and frameworks. In many instances this insistence on efficient regulations delayed the implementation of reform measures. The development of capital markets can serve here as a good example. According to the OECD,

> the general approach pursued by the authorities has been first to assure that regulatory safeguards meeting international standards were in place. . . . This may have slowed the development of markets somewhat, but it was felt that it would assure against the risks inherent in the unregulated development of security markets. In line with this strategy, the powers of the Security Commission were further enhanced in December 1993 with a preemptive widening of the scope for penalizing stock exchange offenses.[49] Other regulatory bodies were created as well to oversee specific policy areas.

The highly competitive and politicized environment that magnified the political oversight and accountability of politicians and state personnel provided an important impulse for heightened concerns about regulatory efficiency and transparency. Unintended consequences or problems caused by specific policies were frequently used as powerful political weapons by the parliamentary and extra-parliamentary opposition. In addition, the reform measures were hotly contested by mighty trade unions, professional organizations, and other interest groups, as well as being scrutinized by the media. These multiple points of critique and opposition forced each government to prepare, revise, and consult on countless projects before any degree of consensus was reached and final measures could be accepted by the Parliament. To defend policy proposals, the government always commissioned in-depth policy analyses exploring their potential consequences from both domestic and foreign experts and consultants. Moreover, the prospect for EU accession facilitated the adoption of many specific institutional solutions that became accepted as European standards. As a result, in contrast to many other postcommunist states, Poland has developed a relatively efficient regulatory framework, increased accountability of state officials by creating independent regulatory agencies, and put in place relatively effective institutional mechanisms of enforcing laws. This, in turn, reduced the levels of corruption, increased tax compliance, and provided a relatively stable, predictive, and secure environment for business activ-

---

[49] OECD *Economic Surveys: Poland 1994*, 175.

ities.[50] In 1998 Britain's Economist Intelligence Unit gave Poland the highest grade among all postcommunist countries in a ranking of business environments. Other assessments of the economic and political situation in the region also acknowledged significant improvements in many areas and consistently placed Poland at the top of their rankings (see table 11.1).

CONCLUSIONS

Despite some common misconceptions about the strength and capacity of communist party-states, in the wake of the state socialism collapse, East European states were small, weak, and ineffective. In Mann's terms, they had considerable "despotic power" and weak "infrastructural power," that is, the capacity to "penetrate civil society and to implement logistically political decisions throughout the realm."[51] Through the late 1970s and 1980s the communist states presided over the longest peaceful economic decline in the twentieth century and gradually lost their control and institutional grip on their societies. In 1989 much of their "despotic power" was gone with the inauguration of democracy and rule of law, and their "infrastructural power" eroded even further as a result of the regionwide economic depression and institutional chaos of multiple transitions. The rebuilding of state institutions became one of the most critical tasks facing new political elites. The fall of state socialism opened up the opportunity for institutional reconfiguration and redefinition of state powers and functions. Yet, despite an initial flurry of official declarations, debates, and partial reforms, the institutionalization of the new state architecture and practices faced real problems. Institutional and legal reforms were slow in coming and often have not been sufficiently deep to reshape the inherited state apparatus and alter the behavior of state functionaries. In fact, partial reforms increased the vulnerability of state institutions to corruption and multiplied their weaknesses.[52]

The range of initial outcomes of state transformations varies signifi-

---

[50] It is important to emphasize that after the initial surge in crime rates in the early 1990s, they stabilized in the mid-1990s and even started to decline in certain categories after 1995. See *Rocznik Statystyczny 1997* (Warszawa: GUS, 1999), 65–67.

[51] Michael Mann, "The Autonomous Power of the State: Its Origins, Mechanisms and Results," *Archives Europeennes de Sociologie* 25 (1984): 188–89.

[52] Interestingly, the index of governance created on the basis of the enterprise survey conducted in the region has a U-shape, with higher values for the least and the most reformed countries. Similarly, the extent of state capture studied by the EBRD analysts show that partially reformed countries are most likely to be affected. See *Transitions Report 1999*, 115–21.

cantly across the region. Some communist countries experienced the spectacular state collapse and dismemberment. In others, especially in the successor states of the former Soviet Union, state reforms were blocked or mishandled and the state apparatus was captured by powerful interest groups. This led to rapid pathologization of the political and economic life (official corruption, organized crime, stripping of state assets, etc.), which in turn led to financial instability, collapse of services, and a serious governability crisis.[53] In contrast to the post-Soviet cases, the process of state reconfiguration was more successful in countries of East Central Europe. Although the transformation process has been uneven and its outcomes are still uncertain, countries such as Czech Republic, Hungary, or Poland have been able to reshape the institutional architecture of the state and enhance its capacity. This may explain, in part, the progress these countries have made in consolidating their democracy and building a market economy.

Observers and students of democratic transitions have become convinced that efforts to create an effective state are the indispensable element of the successful political and economic transformations. In its 1996 report the World Bank emphasized that "getting the government's own house in order—achieving tighter control on expenditure, better budget management, and tax administration, while reforming fiscal relations between levels of government—is a high priority for advanced and lagging reformers alike."[54] And, in fact, the experiences of the last decade increasingly show that the democratic future and economic prosperity of postcommunist countries hinge to a large degree on their ability to build the efficient, accountable, and democratic state.

The analysis presented in this chapter reveals a largely unexpected picture of state reform in Poland. In contrast to many other countries in the region, Poland's ruling elites were relatively successful in rebuilding the state and public administration during the first decade of postcommunist transformations. Through a highly contentious process, marked by fierce political debates, countless reform proposals, and both deep structural and piecemeal changes, Poland has constructed a stronger, more capable and efficient state. The new state is characterized by a high degree of accountability, as well as the ability to regulate emerging markets and prevent excessive rent seeking and corruption.[55] The re-

---

[53] See, for example, Stephen Holmes, "What Russia Teaches Us Now: How Weak States Threaten Freedom," *The American Prospect*, no. 33 (July–August 1997); Hellman, "Winners Take All"; and Valerie Sperling, ed., *Building the Russian State* (Boulder: Westview Press, 2000).

[54] *From Plan to Market: World Development Report 1996* (Oxford: Oxford University Press, 1996), 110.

[55] See "Corruption in Poland: Review of Priority Areas and Proposals for Action," *Report by the World Bank* (Warsaw: World Bank, October 11, 1999).

formed state developed relatively effective extractive capacity and is able to provide essential public goods, maintain or even expand the indispensable safety nets, and deliver social services. In fact, Poland is on its way to achieving the goal of creating an "efficient, friendly, and secure state," outlined several years ago in the government reform proposal. It can be argued that the robust economic growth and rapidly rising living standards can be, to a large degree, attributed to this success in rebuilding the central state administration, expanding the local self-government, and reforming entitlement programs.

How one can explain the success of Polish reforms? Several factors may account for this outcome. First, Poland entered the postcommunist period with a wide-ranging consensus among all significant political actors regarding the need for fundamental structural reforms. Nowhere in the region were communist institutions and policies more discredited and delegitimized than in Poland. The depth of the economic crisis provided additional urgency and encouraged politicians to seek innovative solutions to problems they had to confront. Moreover, this consensus was based on the shared acceptance of neoliberal ideas among new political elites. These ideas were embraced not only by a large group of politicians who were well-educated, experienced in opposition activities against the old regime, and Western oriented, but also by the majority of the former ruling elite. They had broad popular support as well. Neoliberal views, according to observers, were "very visible in the media, especially in the press, which, at least in Poland, has had a very liberal, pro-market bent." Paradoxically, they were also influential among the actors traditionally hostile to liberalism: "Solidarity was probably the only trade union in the world that, for a short period of time at least, supported radical market reform."[56] In addition, the scope and boldness of the economic reforms introduced by the first post-1989 government gave additional impetus to other fundamental reform projects.

Second, Poland's postcommunist politics has been characterized by robust political competition. It produced a higher degree of accountability, more political control over policies, and restraint in rent-seeking behavior, and it kept the issue of reforms at the center of political agenda. In fact, the EBRD research shows that countries with more competitive and fragmented (run by multiparty governments) systems achieved greater progress in economic reforms. The Polish case suggests that the same regularity applies to state reforms as well.[57] Moreover, the nature of the emerging party competition secured the continuation of reform policies, despite frequent changes of ruling coalitions. The Polish party system has strong centripetal tendencies, extremist political views

---

[56] Amsden, Kochanowicz, and Taylor, *The Market*, 168.
[57] See *Transition Report 1999*, 104 and 112.

on both sides of the political spectrum are marginalized, and main competing parties embraced relatively similar reform agendas. In addition, the pluralist and competitive nature of Poland's civil society (with its politically divided and organizationally fragmented labor movement) prevented the emergence of powerful interest groups able to capture the state and block the reforms.

Third, the prospects for EU enlargement created a set of powerful incentives to reform various aspects of public administration and state practices in order to conform as close as possible to the West European standards in the effort to fulfill the pre-accession obligations and secure earlier admission to the European Union.

Finally, the timing and sequencing of reforms created a virtuous dynamics. The sequence of reform measures — decentralization, enhancement of extractive capabilities, reform of the central administration, second phase of decentralization, reform of public services — seems to be optimal for sustaining the reform momentum and securing implementation of successive reform measures. This factor lends credibility to the path dependency ideas emphasizing the importance of sequencing and earlier events in the process of institutional change.[58]

The transformation of the Polish state is still underway. It will take several more years for all elements of the reform to be in place and for their outcomes to become apparent. The process, however, is well advanced, and Poland is likely to have a fully reformed state sooner than many of its postcommunist neighbors.

---

[58] See, for example, Paul Pierson, "Increasing Returns, Path Dependence, and the Study of Politics," *American Political Science Review* 94 (2000): 251–67.

CHAPTER 12

Rotten from Within:
Decentralized Predation and Incapacitated State

MINXIN PEI

As a CRITICAL characteristic of political systems, weak state capacity is widely observed in the developing world. The concept of state capacity promises such analytical utility that it has been used repeatedly, as an explanatory variable, to probe the causes that promote — and stifle — economic development in developing countries.[1] At the same time, state capacity has itself become a dependent variable. Some scholars have attempted to explore the factors that generate and increase state capacity. This study, however, concerns itself with the erosion of state capacity in countries experiencing regime and/or economic transitions.

Regime and economic transitions have produced massive political, social, and economic dislocations — some temporary and others long-lasting — in many parts of the world. Among the dislocations observed, the erosion of state capacity is arguably a defining characteristic of transition, as the examples of the former Soviet Union, Eastern Europe, China, and other countries in the developing world demonstrate. Moreover, compared with countries where the state, as an authoritative administrative organization, has simply collapsed and political anarchy has prevailed, countries that have seen their state capacity decline perhaps ought to consider themselves fortunate.[2] The decline of state capacity per se is not necessarily a curse — or a blessing — for the countries where such a development has occurred. In some cases, the decline of the state may be viewed as largely a positive political and economic development if it occurs in a country where the ancient regime has used

---

[1] The argument that state capacity is a decisive factor in economic development has been made in numerous works. See Chalmers Johnson, *MITI and the Japanese Miracle: The Growth of Industrial Policy, 1925–1975* (Stanford: Stanford University Press, 1982); Stephan Haggard, *Pathways from the Periphery: The Politics of Growth in the Newly Industrialized Countries* (Ithaca: Cornell University Press, 1990); Robert Wade, *Governing the Market: Economic Theory and the Role of Government in East Asian Industrialization* (Princeton: Princeton University Press, 1990).

[2] For an early discussion on failed states, see Gerald Helman and Steven Ratner, "Saving Failed States," *Foreign Policy* 89 (Winter 1992–93): 3–20.

the apparatus of the state to suppress individual freedom and productive economic activities. The decline of state capacity is likely to increase both democracy and economic growth in these countries (as in the more successful transition countries in Eastern Europe and Latin America). In most cases, however, the erosion of state capacity is a more troubling trend, especially when such erosion is accompanied not by corresponding expansion in democracy or economic growth, but by decreases in the economic well-being of the population, social order, and equality.

The decline of state capacity in transition countries has rekindled interest in the theoretical issues related to this topic. In this chapter, I attempt to apply the concept of state predation to an analysis of the decline of state capacity. Contrary to the "weakness of social control" thesis offered by the theorists of state-society relations, the focus of this study is on the changing character of state predation and its direct effects on declining state capacity. Unlike the "weakness of social control" thesis, which measures state strength vis-à-vis societal strength, this chapter probes the capacity of the state to control its own agents as the most important factor in explaining declining state capacity in transition countries. The central argument of this chapter is that it is not the increase of state predation, but the emergence of decentralized state predation, that has been largely responsible for declining state capacity in transition countries.

The chapter is organized as follows. The first section reviews the literature on state predation and explores the relationship between state predation and state capacity. The second section discusses the effects of regime transition on state predation and state capacity and develops a theory of decentralized state predation. The third section applies this framework to China's transition experience.

STATE PREDATION AND STATE CAPACITY

State Predation

The idea of a predatory state—a state that expropriates wealth from society in the form of taxes or equivalents to sustain itself in power—has been around for a long time.[3] This concept has recently gained currency as the rise of institutionalist literature refocuses our attention on

---

[3] For the most systematic treatment of the concept of predatory state, see Douglass North, *Structure and Change in Economic History* (New York: Norton, 1981), 20–32.

the relationship between political institutions and economic performance.[4] In particular, the revival of institutionalism has again elevated the role of the state in economic development.[5]

To be sure, the renewed interest in the state this time is different, as is the role envisioned for the state in economic development. Unlike the idea of the "developmental state," which, as popularized by scholars of East Asia two decades ago, has a direct role in correcting market failures, the new role of the state is said to be that of a provider and enforcer of institutions and institutional rules and norms.[6] This distinction is significant because the perspectives on the state behind it are fundamentally different. In the theory of the developmental state, the state is perceived as a "helping hand," which preemptively corrects market failure and enables the private sector to grow. In contrast, institutionalists view the state as a force for both good and evil. As North eloquently puts it, "The existence of a state is essential for economic growth; the state, however, is the source of man-made economic decline."[7] Although the state may be a "helping hand" that specifies and protects efficient property rights, it can also be a "grabbing hand" that expropriates the wealth of its people.[8]

For political scientists studying developing countries, the grabbing-hand perspective resonates with great appeal because the theory of the predatory state (the essence of which is captured by the grabbing hand metaphor) provides a persuasive explanation for the weakness of the state and the overall poor performance of government. To be sure, in the conventional measures of state strength, the extractive (predatory) capacity itself is considered an indicator of the power of the state. The greater such capacity, the stronger the state is said to be.

However, from the predatory state perspective, the state's extractive capacity can undermine the state itself if left unchecked. The harm inflicted on the state by its own predation originates from two sources: centralized and decentralized predation.

---

[4] See Douglass North, *Institutions, Institutional Change and Economic Performance* (New York: Cambridge University Press, 1990); Thrainn Eggertsson, *Economic Behavior and Institutions* (Cambridge: Cambridge University Press, 1990).

[5] The best example is World Bank, *World Development Report 1997: The State in a Changing World* (Washington, DC: World Bank, 1997).

[6] On the developmental state in East Asia, see Johnson, *MITI and the Japanese Miracle*; Wade, *Governing the Market*.

[7] North, *Structure and Change*, 20.

[8] For a discussion on the state as a "grabbing hand," see Andrei Shleifer and Robert W. Vishny, *The Grabbing Hand: Government Pathologies and Their Cures* (Cambridge: Harvard University Press, 1998).

CENTRALIZED PREDATION

The first-generation theory of the predatory state, which does not make a distinction between the principal and the agents of the state, focuses exclusively on the aggregate level of state predation and treats predation as the political imperative of the ruler (either in its individual form or in its collective embodiment). There are several key underlying assumptions in principal predation. First, state predation is considered universal: rulers are monopolists of both violence and public goods. Predation (in the form of taxes) is simply the price private producers of wealth pay for such monopolistic services. Second, the most important factor that limits the level of a ruler's predation is self-interest. To use Olson's colorful analogy, self-interested rulers behave like "stationary bandits" who are unlikely to risk future revenue streams by looting the current stock of wealth of their subjects. They will raise the level of taxation only up to the level that maximizes their tax revenues.[9] Third, rulers are supposed to have an "encompassing interest" that is akin to the national interest.

But centralized predation can get out of control, endangering both the long-term economic welfare of the ruler and the capacity of the state. Several factors can cause centralized predation to reach the point where short-term gains for the ruler will come only at the cost of potential long-term revenues. First, the ruler's "encompassing interest" may, as often happens, diverge fundamentally from that of the state. For example, the ruler's personal greed may become insatiable. The ruler and close cronies may loot wealth, not to provide public goods, but to line their own pockets, thus creating a kleptocracy.[10] The ruler's "encompassing interest" may also become too ambitious for the nation's good. Desire to acquire a larger territory (hence tax base) or international prestige may motivate the ruler to extract excessively from society to build a strong military.[11] Second, the ruler's monopolistic position never remains secure. There is always a possibility that a domestic or foreign rival can seize the monopoly.[12] This structural insecurity affects the ruler's time horizon and the rate of discount on future revenues.[13] A ruler with a short time horizon is likely to apply deep discount rates to

[9] Both North and Olson made this point. See North, *Structure and Change*, 21–24; Mancur Olson, "Dictatorship, Democracy, and Development," *American Political Science Review* 87 (1993): 567–76.

[10] Susan Rose-Ackerman, *Corruption and Government: Causes, Consequences, and Reform* (Cambridge: Cambridge University Press, 1999), 114–21.

[11] Olson, "Dictatorship, Democracy, and Development."

[12] Eggertsson, *Economic Behavior and Institutions*, 323.

[13] Margaret Levi, *Of Rule and Revenue* (Berkeley: University of California Press, 1988).

future revenues and behave like a "roving bandit" who prefers to confiscate all the current wealth even though the future tax revenue from the same stock of wealth will be significantly larger. Finally, the absence of a third-party enforcer makes the ruler's commitment to self-restrained predation incredible. Temptations for the ruler to break promises and increase predation always exist. History has shown that rulers have honored their promises frequently in the breach.[14]

DECENTRALIZED PREDATION

The second-generation theory of the predatory state emphasizes predation by agents, rather than by the principal. Although agency costs were identified as a constraint on the ruler's ability to maintain a desired level of extraction, the effects of such costs on state predation have not been explored until recently.[15] Scholars who focus on the role of agents in state predation see decentralized predation as more harmful to the interest of the state. Shleifer and Vishny demonstrate that centralized corruption (a form of monopolist predation) generates higher aggregate revenue for the state (because the state keeps its rate of extraction at the optimal level) than decentralized corruption (a form of predation by state agents acting as "independent monopolists"), which not only raises the overall level of theft (i.e., making corruption more widespread) but reduces the *aggregate amount* of income for the state. Since predatory agents simultaneously compete with other predatory agents for the same source of revenue, they have the incentive to steal everything, behaving essentially like Olson's "roving bandits."[16] The welfare loss from decentralized predation is much greater than centralized predation. Decentralized predation, moreover, has emerged as a more prevalent problem today as regime transition in many countries has restructured some of the key institutions governing principal-agent relations in these countries (more on the effects of transition on decentralized predation below).

A distinction needs to be made between predation and corruption. Generally speaking, predation refers to an act of a state. Although it is carried out through the agents of the state, the primary purpose of predation is to sustain the ruler (also the collective entity called the state). In a strictly technical sense, predation by the state is legal, as most tax and other revenues mandated by the state are levied according to some

---

[14] Olson, "Dictatorship, Democracy, and Development."

[15] North, for example, saw agency costs as a serious constraint on the ruler's ability to take full advantage of the monopolist position. See Eggertsson, *Economic Behavior and Institutions*, 324.

[16] Andrei Shleifer and Robert Vishny, "Corruption," *The Quarterly Journal of Economics* 58 (1993): 599–617.

form of legal procedures. In theory, predation and corruption should
not have any direct relationship because these two phenomena are influenced by entirely different factors. As suggested, the degree of predation
is determined by the rulers' time horizon, discount rates applied to future revenues, and agency costs. The degree of corruption is primarily
influenced by the rulers' ability to monitor and discipline agents and by
the level of state intervention in the economy. Conceivably, corruption
needs not to exist in a predatory state in which agents are effectively
monitored and disciplined (such as in Singapore).

In contrast to predation, corruption is an act by an agent of the state.
The primary purpose of state agents in engaging in corrupt acts is to
enrich themselves, not the state, although a corrupt act invariably involves the use (abuse) of a public office occupied by the agent in question. Moreover, even in the most corrupt political systems, corruption —
as opposed to legalized state predation — is considered illegal, and its
perpetrators face real and substantial risks.

However, the theoretical distinction between predation and corruption can be hopelessly blurred in reality because of the agency problem.
A fully disciplinary predatory state does not exist in practice. The agency
problem turns into a leakage problem if agents divert revenues collected
in the name of the state into their private pockets — one of the most
prevalent symptoms of corruption. In theory, the degree of corruption
in a predatory state heavily depends on the degree of centralization. In a
more centralized predatory state in which agents are more tightly monitored, there should be less corruption (leakage). In more decentralized
predatory state in which agents are less effectively monitored, there
should be more corruption (leakage).

State Capacity

Although there is a broad consensus on the concept of state capacity,
there are disagreements as to the factors that determine such capacity.[17]
In the state-society perspective on state capacity, the determinant of
state capacity is the relative balance of strength between the state and
society. States that are weaker relative to the societies they govern are
said to lack the capacity to dominate their societies.[18] Moreover, weak

---

[17] According to Migdal, there are four main state capacities: those of penetration, regu-
lation, extraction, and appropriation. Joel Migdal, *Strong Societies and Weak States:
State-Society Relations and State Capabilities in the Third World* (Princeton: Princeton
University Press, 1988), 4.

[18] See Migdal, *Strong Societies and Weak States.*

states that allow parochial societal interests to influence policy are said to lack "state autonomy." Scholars who narrowly focus on the internal characteristics of the state as determinants of its capacity, however, believe that state capacity is mainly a product of the organizational qualities of the state (such qualities may include bureaucratic norms, procedures, recruitment, and socialization).[19]

The perspective of the predatory state sheds additional light on understanding the determinants of state capacity. At the first glance, it may seem inconsistent or even tautological to apply a concept, which in itself is related to a critical aspect (i.e., extraction) of state capacity, to an analysis of state capacity. However, such inconsistency and tautology may be more apparent than real because an analytical focus on state predation leads us to examine a critical determinant of state capacity — the state's capacity to control itself.

Obviously, predation — whether centralized or decentralized — has a direct impact on state capacity. If predation is centralized and used mainly to provide public goods (including the fixed costs of regime maintenance), it may likely contribute to state capacity. On the other hand, if predation is centralized but its proceeds are spent by the top rulers for personal consumption, purchase of political support, or transfer to overseas bank accounts, it definitely weakens state capacity by diverting resources away from the provision of public goods.

The case that decentralized predation undermines state capacity is much stronger. Since agents do not identify with the "encompassing interest" of the supreme ruler, decentralized predation can only result in the transfer of the state's tax revenues to the private pockets of state agents, depriving the state of the resources needed to maintain its capacity. Empirical studies based on evidence from the former Soviet bloc show that the impact of decentralized predation on public finance can be substantial. Indeed, once decentralized predation reaches a certain level, the aggregate amount of state revenues falls considerably because private entrepreneurs will respond by moving most of their business activities underground and avoid taxation altogether.[20] Studies of the effects of decentralized predation (or corruption) on government and economic performance have demonstrated that the state's capacity to

[19] See Max Weber, "Bureaucracy," in H. Gerth and C.W. Mills, eds., *From Max Weber: Essays in Sociology* (New York: Oxford University Press, 1946), 196–244; Theda Skocpol, *States and Social Revolution* (New York: Cambridge University Press, 1979); Johnson, *MITI and the Japanese Miracle.*

[20] Simon Johnson, Daniel Kaufmann, and Andrei Shleifer, "The Unofficial Economy in Transition," *Brookings Papers on Economic Activity* 2 (1997): 159–221.

provide public goods (including enforcement of property rights) is the most adversely affected by corruption.[21]

In addition, decentralized predation can undermine state capacity in other indirect ways. Decentralized predation compromises other aspects of government functions (such as law enforcement and regulation of socioeconomic activities) as state agents sell their services to private customers and/or steal revenues that ought to be remitted to the state. Predation by state agents has a corrosive effect on the behavioral norms of state agencies. Decentralized predation, which requires that agents conceal information from superiors, reduces the amount and quality of information transmitted to superior decision-makers. Bad decision making due to a deficit of reliable information then becomes a systemic feature of the state. Decentralized predation is likely to encourage local state agents to collude with criminal elements as state agents may allow such elements to operate in their jurisdictions with immunity in exchange for a portion of the proceeds from their criminal activities. State agents also need the assistance of such criminals to hide their loot. In the worst cases, the state may break down into countless local mafia fiefdoms, causing the fragmentation of political authority.[22]

TRANSITION AND STATE PREDATION

Regime transition—which changes the defining institutional arrangements of a political system—unavoidably involves a restructuring of the mechanisms through which the agents of the state are controlled and incentivized. This restructuring of principal-agent relations is likely to increase, at least in the short-term, the discretion and autonomy of agents while reducing the effectiveness of control by the principal. This is largely because restructuring of governing institutions typically involves redistribution of power and rerouting of information flows. Such restructuring may also create temporary vacuums of power, which normally would favor agents. Strictly speaking, regime transition does not necessarily require decentralization. However, the regime transitions in the late twentieth century—whether democratic transitions or market transitions—were mostly decentralizing transitions. Moreover, in theory

---

[21] Paolo Mauro found that corruption tends to hurt government expenditure on education the hardest. See Paolo Mauro, "Corruption and the Composition of Government Expenditure," *Journal of Public Economics* 69 (1998): 263–79. Mauro also found that corruption lowers investment and reduces growth. See Paolo Mauro, "Corruption and Growth," *The Quarterly Journal of Economics* 110 (1995): 681–712.

[22] For an account of the criminalization of the state apparatus, see Stephen Handelman, *Comrade Criminal: Russia's New Mafiya* (New Haven: Yale University Press, 1995).

decentralization of state power does not need to lead to an increase in decentralized predation as long as such decentralization is accompanied by decentralization of monitoring and control of state agents. If decentralization of power is not followed by measures to monitor the compliance of state agents, the risks of decentralized predation will rise. On the other hand, if the power of monitoring state agents is also decentralized, or delegated to nonstate actors such as the media and civic groups, decentralized predation may be reduced or contained. Indeed, comparative studies of the transition experience in the former Soviet bloc countries show that the degree of good governance is positively related to the degree of democratization and civil liberties.[23]

The increase of decentralized predation during transition has been amply documented in the works by scholars of transition in Eastern Europe and the former Soviet Union. Joel Hellman's study of reform in the former Soviet bloc countries suggested that the ruling elite was able to capture the state and reap all the benefits of partial economic reforms.[24] Michael McFaul and Federico Varese found that members of the Communist ruling elite in the former Soviet Union were able to use their institutional privileges and exploit the loopholes in the property rights regimes to steal public assets in the privatization process.[25] In an insightful analysis of the collapse of the former Soviet Union, Steven Solnick showed that transition that decentralizes authority tends to cause increasing theft of state assets.[26]

Theoretically, the type of posttransition state predation observed by country specialists and journalists is qualitatively different from that during the pretransition era. In pretransition communist countries, state predation was centralized. Two characteristics define centralized predation under communist rule. First, the aggregate amount of revenues generated was large (reflected in the government revenue as a share of GDP). Second, a significant amount of the revenues was used to provide public goods (mainly national defense, health and education spending). Consequently, countries ruled by communist regimes en-

[23] See Joel Hellman et al., "Measuring Governance, Corruption, and State Capture," *World Bank Policy Research Working Paper 2312* (Washington, DC: World Bank, 2000); Ase Grodeland, Tatyana Koshechkina, and William Miller, "Foolish to Give and Yet More Foolish Not to Take — In-depth Interviews with Post-Communist Citizens on Their Everyday Use of Bribes and Contacts," *Europe-Asia Studies* 50 (1998): 651–77.

[24] Joel Hellman, "Winners Take All: The Politics of Partial Reform in Postcommunist Transitions," *World Politics* 50 (1998): 203–34.

[25] Michael McFaul, "State Power, Institutional Change, and the Politics of Privatization in Russia," *World Politics* 47 (1995): 210–43; Federico Varese, "The Transition to the Market and Corruption in Post-socialist Russia," *Political Studies* 45 (1997): 579–96.

[26] Steven Solnick, "The Breakdown of Hierarchies in the Soviet Union and China: A Neo-institutional Perspective," *World Politics* 48 (1996): 209–38.

joyed a higher level of human development relative to their economic development, especially in the literacy rate, infant mortality rate, and life expectancy.[27]

By contrast, posttransition state predation is decentralized and manifests itself in various forms of official corruption. Decentralized state predation reduces the aggregate amount of state revenue as agents divert public money into private pockets; it also causes a fall in the provision of public goods, as state agents convert public resources into private consumption. Although the phenomenon of decentralized state predation in posttransition countries has received enormous attention, there is little understanding as to the causes that led to the transformation of centralized predation into decentralized predation.

We believe that the key to understanding the emergence of decentralized predation is the ideological and institutional constraints on state agents' opportunist behavior. Phrased differently, centralized predation becomes decentralized when the state, as the principal, has lost effective control over its agents. Of course, different types of regime transition generate different dynamics that affect principal-agent relations. In communist states that saw a quick collapse of the ancient regime, state agents were greatly advantaged by even the temporary decline of the authority of the principal. In those societies, the agents' theft of the assets of the state was completed within a relatively short period of time. However, the patterns of posttransition agent predation diverged dramatically in those postcommunist states that experienced the dual transition. As Hellman's work shows, new regimes with a higher degree of democracy and more complete market reforms tend to restrain such predation, while new regimes with less democracy and partial economic reforms are beset by increased levels of agent predation.[28]

By comparison, agent predation followed a different dynamic in postcommunist systems that saw market liberalization but no political transition (such as China and Vietnam). In these societies, the political authority of the principal (the state) remains unchallenged. However, the decentralization of decision making, which is needed to reincentivize state agents, led to a restructuring of the contracts between the state and its agents that proved to be extremely advantageous to the latter. Therefore, the key to understanding the rise of agent—or decentralized—predation is to examine both the preexisting institutional conditions and transition-related institutional changes that have structured and restructured principal-agent relations. Specifically, changes in the

---

[27] See the United Nations, *Human Development Report 1994* (New York: Oxford University Press, 1994).

[28] Hellman, "Winners Take All."

following four institutional factors are responsible for the transformation of state predation in postcommunist societies.

DEGREE OF CENTRALIZATION AND CLARITY OF PROPERTY RIGHTS

In theory, the degree of centralization and clarity of property rights is negatively correlated with decentralized predation—in countries with high level of centralization and clarity of property rights, the level of fiscal leakage from the state through agent theft or misappropriation tends to be low. Under the prereform communist system, despite the lack of clarity of property rights, the high degree of centralization of such rights was the decisive institutional factor that limited agent predation (i.e., private use of official power for personal gains). In practice, the centralization of property rights meant that agents retain little discretion in many routine management issues. Although state ownership created no real owners, the high degree of centralization of state ownership also prevented large-scale theft of the state's property. Of course, the mono–property rights regime in the manufacturing and much of the service sector and the high degree of centralization of property rights led to extremely inefficient economic behavior, mostly because the old system provided little incentives for agents to improve the financial performance of the state's assets.[29] There was, however, an advantage of the old system: its highly centralized property rights regime prevented massive theft of state wealth by the agents. The decentralization of property rights during the transition phase in most state-socialist systems was originally designed to increase the incentives of the agents so that the state's assets could become more productive. In some countries, the decentralization of property rights also involved, as in China, the transfer of formal ownership of state assets from the central government to local governments. Such decentralization granted the state's managerial agents a wide array of discretion in operating state-owned enterprises (SOEs), especially regarding investment and compensation. Although there is no evidence showing that decentralization of property rights alone contributed to efficiency gains, the combination of lack of clarity of property rights and decentralization of such rights has led to widespread asset-stripping and other forms of theft by state agents.[30] In postcommunist societies, the theft of state assets has become a large-scale problem not only due to decentralized property rights, but also because of the proliferation of property ownership forms, especially hybrid ownership forms.

[29] See Janos Kornai, *The Political Economy of State Socialism* (Princeton: Princeton University Press, 1990).

[30] For a study of asset-stripping by state agents in China, see X. L. Ding, "The Illicit Asset Stripping of Chinese State Firms," *The China Journal* 43 (2000): 1–28.

The emergence of hybrid ownership forms created "institutional depositories" to which stolen state assets could be transferred.

MONITORING OF AGENTS

Given the institutional changes entailed in regime transition, the old system of monitoring state agents is likely to break down. Rule changes are frequent and confusing during transition, resulting in poor coordination among various state agencies monitoring agent behavior (such as the secret police, tax authorities, auditors, and financial controllers). The breakdown of monitoring becomes even more likely if those state agents in charge of monitoring other state agents detect the latter's theft but decide to divide up the spoils through a collusive arrangement with the thieving agents, instead of reporting their malfeasance to the principal. (This certainly seems to be the case in China and Russia, where one of the most corrupt government bureaucracies is the anticorruption agency). Transition frequently entails changes in political values and erodes the political authority of principals. Agents face negligible risks in defying the authority of principals. Erosion of principal's authority makes effective monitoring of agents ineffective. The monitoring of agents has also become more difficult under reform because of the multiplication of transaction channels. As Ding observed, interfirm transactions almost did not exist under the old system, in which ministries directly controlled SOEs' sales and purchase processes. As a result, monitoring agents' business deals was easier under the old system. In the transition era, the advent of marketization replaced the firm-ministry-firm transactions chain with the more efficient firm-to-firm transactions chain. Consequently, the number of transactions exploded, making effective government monitoring nearly impossible.[31]

EXIT OPTION AND ROVING BANDITRY

Large-scale theft of state assets was made less likely under the old communist system by the absence of exit options from the state sector for nearly all agents. Regime transition has opened numerous exits for these agents. Such exit options include ownership stakes and managerial positions in the new private or semiprivate firms and overseas investment opportunities.[32] These exits effectively allowed these "stationary bandits" under the old system to become "roving bandits" because they can

---

[31] Ibid.

[32] X. L. Ding's investigation shows that Chinese managers have diverted a significant amount of state wealth into private overseas holdings. See Ding, "Informal Privatization through Internationalization: The Rise of Nomenklatura Capitalism in China's Offshore Businesses," *British Journal of Political Science* 30 (2000): 121–46.

steal and then store their loot safely elsewhere. The time horizon of state agents with lucrative exit options is likely to be short, thus increasing the level of intensity with which such agents steal the state's assets.

EROSION OF INSTITUTIONAL NORMS

Institutionalists like North have long recognized the role of institutional norms in constraining agent opportunism and the free rider problem.[33] As a concept, institutional norms is vague and difficult to define. In practice, institutional norms may derive much of their legitimacy and appeal from the prevailing ideology of the political system. In the case of communist systems, it may be controversial to claim that the communist ideology had any appeal. One can legitimately point to the widespread cynicism among the ruling elite of the ancient regime. It is nevertheless conceivable that even residual ideological appeals of communism, socialism, or nationalism might have played a role in constraining the predatory behavior of the agents under the old regime. During transition, the total bankruptcy of the communist ideology meant that state agents were under no effective constraints imposed by institutional norms.

DECENTRALIZED PREDATION AND EROSION OF STATE CAPACITY IN CHINA

Since China's transition to a market economy began in 1979, massive changes have occurred in its political system, economy, and society. Judging by aggregate economic data, China's economic reform under a Leninist party seems to be an unqualified success. The size of China's GDP quadrupled in twenty years; its linkage with the world economy has broadened and deepened to an unprecedented degree; more than two hundred million people were lifted out of abject poverty.[34] This increase in China's comprehensive national power, however, is accompanied by a decline in the capacity of the Chinese state.

The Decline of State Capacity in China

The erosion of the capacity of the Chinese state can be measured in several dimensions—such as its capacity to extract revenues and to pro-

---

[33] North, *Structure and Change in Economic History*, 45–58.

[34] For an authoritative estimate of China's economic growth and developmental achievement since 1979, see World Bank, *China 2020* (Washington, DC: World Bank, 1997).

TABLE 12.1
Government Revenues, 1979–1996

Year	Budget Revenue (billion yuan)	Percent of GDP	Off-Budget Revenue (billion yuan)	Percent of GDP	Total Revenue as Percent of GDP
1979	114.6	29.54	45.2	11.6	41.14
1985	200.4	22.25	153	17.0	39.25
1990	293.7	15.79	270	14.52	30.31
1992	348.3	13.07	385.4	14.46	27.53
1993	434.8	12.58	143	4.14	16.72
1994	521.8	11.18	186	3.99	15.17
1996	740.7	11.08	389.3	5.82	16.9

Source: Statistical Yearbook of China, various years.

vide public goods. The decline of the fiscal revenues of the Chinese government is the most pronounced evidence of the erosion of state capacity.[35] Official data on government revenues, presented here in table 12.1, indicate a dramatic decline (more than 55 percent) over a seventeen-year period. The Chinese revenue-to-GDP ratio of 16 percent is about half of the average for developing countries.[36] To be sure, many factors contributed to the fall in the government's revenues (the most important among which were the poor financial performance of state-owned enterprises and the state's failure to extract revenue from emerging private firms).[37] Behind the dramatic fiscal decline, however, there is a more complex reality—a reality that only reconfirms the linkage between decentralized predation and the declining extractive capacity of the state.

A careful analysis of the aggregate fiscal revenues of the Chinese government reveals that the actual aggregate decline is not as dramatic as presented in table 12.1. The data in the table exclude a considerable portion of off-off-budget revenues collected by local governments and various government agencies but not recorded as on-budget government revenues. Most of the off-off-budget revenues are collected in the form

[35] For a well-known and influential study of the fiscal decline of the Chinese state, see Wang Shaoguang and Hu Angang, Zhongguo guojia nengli baogao (A report on the capacity of the Chinese state) (Shengyang: Liaoning renmin chubanshe, 1993). Also see Nicholas Lardy, "When Will China's Financial System Meet China's Needs?" Center for Research on Economic Development and Policy Reform Working Paper 55 (Stanford: Stanford University, 2000).

[36] Le-Yin Zhang, "Chinese Central-Provincial Fiscal Relationships, Budgetary Decline and the Impact of the 1994 Fiscal Reform: An Evaluation," The China Quarterly 157 (1999): 115–41.

[37] Zhang, "Chinese Central-Provincial Fiscal Relationships."

of special-purposes local levies (housing funds, health insurance funds, unemployment insurance funds, and special infrastructure capital funds). Estimates provided by the central government's tax authorities suggest that unauthorized levies collected by provincial/local governments and other government agencies amounted to about 10 percent of GDP in the late 1990s — an amount almost equal to the total tax revenues collected by the central government.[38] Research by Chinese economists independently confirmed similar magnitude of off-off-budget revenues collected by local authorities.[39] On the surface, the redistribution of revenues among the different levels of the Chinese state may not seem to warrant serious concerns about the erosion of state capacity. However, the massive leakage of fiscal revenue out of the central treasury to local treasuries, as happened in China, should not be treated merely as an accounting change. Firstly, because off-off-budget revenues are collected and disposed at the discretion of local government officials (state agents), there is practically no transparency in the collection and spending processes. Such revenues are thus easily abused — both in the form of excessive collection and diversion to illicit purposes and even private pockets. Some of the most egregious cases of corruption reported in China all involved the use of off-off-budget revenues.[40]

Second, local revenue-collectors behave like independent monopolists and have incentives to maximize short-term revenues for the local treasuries, even though such practice leads to lower aggregate government revenues. Indeed, widespread decentralized predation in China seems to have squeezed the predation by the central state, as shown by the steady decline of the revenues collected by the central government. It has also led to a decline of about 25 percent of aggregate government revenue.[41]

Third, contrary to popular beliefs, rising local revenues at the expense of revenues for the central government have actually failed to improve local public finance. In fact, because a considerable (though hard-to-

---

[38] State General Administration of Taxation, "Guanyu wuoguo feigaishui wenti de yanjiu" (A study on the issue of converting fees into taxes in China), *Jingji yanjiu cancao* 86–87 (September 1998): 8.

[39] Zhang, "Chinese Central-Provincial Fiscal Relationships."

[40] The best example is the largest corruption scandal in Beijing's history. The executive vice-mayor, who alone controlled the capital's off-off-budget accounts, was accused of diverting several billion *yuan* of the city government's funds into various illegal schemes and the pockets of numerous mistresses. He committed suicide in the spring of 1995 after he was tipped of his impending arrest.

[41] This estimate is arrived at by comparing the official figure for total aggregate revenue in 1979, which was about 40 percent of GDP, with the estimated total aggregate revenue in the late 1990s (which included budge revenues, off-budget revenues, and off-off-budget revenues), which was about 30 percent of GDP. See State General Administration of Taxation, "Guanyu wuoguo feigaishui wenti de yanjiu," 8.

TABLE 12.2
China's Budget Expenditures, 1976–1995 (Percent)

	1976–1980	1981–1985	1986–1990	1991–1995
Administration	5.3	7.8	11.8	13.7
Agricultural Infra-				
structure, R & D	4.6	2.2	2.0	2.0
Educational Capital				
Expenditures	0.59	1.18	1.16	1.06
Educational Aid to				
Poor Areas	na	0.06	0.07	0.02
Poverty Relief	1.96	1.64	1.70	1.71

Source: *Statistical Yearbook of China*, various years.

measure) portion of the off-off-budget revenues collected by the local governments has been wasted and stolen, local public finance has deteriorated significantly across China. A Ministry of Finance study of local public finance in seven provinces conducted in the mid-1990s reported that between half to three-quarters of county governments surveyed reported large fiscal deficits and had difficulty meeting government payrolls and performing routine functions of administration.[42]

In addition to the deteriorating capacity of revenue extraction, the Chinese state has become less able to provide public goods, such as health, education, environmental protection, and law and order. On the expenditure side, the decline of public goods provision is registered in the decreasing or stagnant spending (table 12.2). The official data on public expenditures from 1976 to 1995 show a dramatic decline in agricultural infrastructure and research and development, and stagnant outlays in education and poverty relief. Government auditors have found that poverty relief funds were routinely stolen by corrupt officials (one audit of the 48.8 billion yuan earmarked for poverty relief in the 1997–99 period uncovered theft of 4.3 billion yuan, almost 10 percent of the total).[43] At the same, however, administrative outlays have increased greatly. The data in table 12.2 show that, on a relative basis, administrative expenditures more than doubled over a fifteen-year period while public goods expenditures declined or stagnated.

Another way of measuring the declining capacity to provide public goods is to measure China's improvement in human development. According to the United Nations Development Program, China's human

[42] Ministry of Finance, "Xianji caizheng weiji jiqi duiche" (The fiscal crisis of county governments and solutions), *Caizheng yanjiu* 5 (1996), 55–59.

[43] Xinhua News Agency dispatch, quoted in *New World Times* (U.S.), July 21, 2000, 4.

TABLE 12.3
Rising Crime Rate

Year	Criminal Cases Filed with Police	Cases Solved	Case Solution Rate (%)
1982	748,476	579,320	77.4
1984	514,367	395,548	76.9
1986	547,115	433,315	79.2
1988	827,597	626,491	75.7
1990	2,216,997	1,263,688	57.1
1992	1,582,659	1,079,517	68.2
1994	1,660,737	1,298,005	78.2
1996	1,600,716	1,279,091	79.9
1998	1,986,068	1,264,635	63.7

Source: Zhongguo falu nianjian, various years.

development index rose 0.227 from 1960 to 1980, a period that saw both economic disasters (the Great Leap Famine of 1958–61) and political turmoil (the Cultural Revolution of 1966–76). In the period of 1980–98, during which China's GDP per capita income more than quadrupled (from 138 to 727 in 1995 U.S. dollars), its human development index rose only 0.231 (a smaller increase than achieved by Indonesia in the same period). If one factors in economic growth rate, the improvement in human development index, which is perhaps the most reliable tool to gauge a state's effectiveness in providing public goods (especially health and education), has actually slowed down dramatically during the reform period. The prereform China, which was able to use strong, albeit coercive, state power to mobilize resources, achieved the same magnitude of improvement in human development with an increase of GDP per capita of 80 percent.[44]

The erosion of state capacity may also be measured by the rising crime rate and the falling rate of crime resolution. On the surface, official data on crime rates show a relatively reassuring picture (table 12.3) Although the crime rate nearly tripled from the early 1980s to the end of the 1990s, the Chinese law enforcement authorities reported a resolution rate ranging from 57 to 80 percent. However, it is widely known that such sensitive official statistics are often doctored to project a public image of an effective government. In practice, Chinese police have been found to underreport crime statistics while exaggerating crime res-

[44] United Nations Development Program, *Human Development Report 1998* (New York: Oxford University Press, 1998), 141; United Nations Development Program, *Human Development Report 2000*, at www.undp.org.

olution rate. An examination of public opinion polling data shows a different picture. Rising lawlessness has indeed become a top concern for the Chinese public. According to the surveys conducted by an independent and highly respected private polling firm, Horizon, crime was ranked as the number one issue in 1995 and 1996 in sampled Chinese urban areas. In 1997 and 1998 it was ranked as one of the top five concerns.[45]

Declining state capacity inevitably reduces the government's ability to provide environmental protection—another key public good. There is mounting evidence in China that its environment has been severely degraded in recent years. Of course, an important cause of China's environmental degradation is the country's rapid economic growth and unique energy supply/consumption profile (with low-grade coal supplying two-thirds of the energy needs). However, by international standards, the Chinese government is an ineffective provider of environmental protection. According to authoritative sources, environmental degradation has reached alarming levels in China, threatening not just the well-being of the current population, but making China's future development unsustainable. The following statistics illustrate the degree of environmental degradation in China:

- Land—Half of China's land is affected by soil erosion. Acid rain affects 40 percent of the country. Up to 93 percent of China's forest area is threatened.[46]
- Water—A huge quantity of water pollutants—11.7 million pounds per day in 1997—is discharged into Chinese rivers. This figure is twice the 5.5 million pounds discharged by the United States each day and thrice the amount discharged by India. Only 77 percent of industrial wastewater received some treatment in 1995. Nearly half of industrial wastewater discharged failed to meet the government's standards.[47] In 1999 the Ministry of Water Resources reported that 46 percent of China's 700 major rivers were polluted.[48] As a result of severe pollution of China's water supplies, only 67 percent of the population have access to safe drinking water (significantly below India's 81 percent). According to the Washington-based World Resources Institute, 700 million people in China (56 percent of the population) drink water that does not meet government

[45] Ru Xing, *Shehui lanpishu 1999* (1999 social blue book) (Beijing: Shehui wenxian chubanshe, 2000), 103.

[46] Robert Benewick and Stephanie Donald, *The State of China Atlas* (New York: Penguin Books, 1999), 84–89.

[47] The World Resources Institute, *World Resources, 1998–99: A Guide to the Global Environment* (New York: Oxford University Press, 1998), 121.

[48] Dispatch from Xinhua News Agency, August 2, 2000.

standards. Water shortage affects many parts of China. More than half of China's 640 cities have inadequate water supplies.[49]

- Air — Tests conducted in 88 cities in 1995 showed that more than half of them had SO2 levels exceeding the World Health Organization guidelines; 85 of them exceeded the WHO's guideline on TSP.[50]

- Measurable costs of pollution — The World Bank estimated that air and water pollution cost China nearly 8 percent of GDP (or U.S. $54 billion) a year.[51] Air pollution alone is directly responsible for 178,000 premature deaths in urban areas. If there is no improvement in China's air quality, 600,000 urban Chinese are expected to die of premature deaths due to pollution, and 5.5 million would have chronic bronchitis by 2020.[52]

Decentralization of Predation: Evidence

Measuring decentralized state predation poses a serious methodological challenge because many predatory activities in this category are both illegal and hidden. In this study we adopt a two-pronged approach. First, we attempt to measure the size of the predatory state at subnational levels. Second, we examine illegal predatory activities commonly characterized as corruption to estimate the level and scope of decentralized predation.

Aggregate national data unambiguously show that the Chinese state, when measured in the number of officials and employees in government agencies (excluding teachers and those working in nonprofit government institutions such as hospitals), has grown rapidly in the reform era. From 1953 to 1978 the average annual growth rate of officials and employees in government agencies was 1.8 percent. From 1979 to 1990 the rate was 6.7 percent — more than three times higher. The rapid growth in personnel forced the government to increase its administrative expenditures correspondingly. From 1979 to 1990 annual growth in the government's administrative expenditures averaged 10.4 percent (compared to 4.0 percent for 1953–78). The 10.4 percent annual increase in administrative costs is more than three times the 3 percent annual rate of growth of budgetary revenues for 1979–90.[53]

[49] Ibid.

[50] World Resources Institute, *World Resources, 1998–99*, 117.

[51] World Bank, *Clear Water, Blue Skies: China's Environment in the New Century* (Washington: The World Bank, 1997), 23.

[52] Benewick and Donald, *The State of China Atlas*, 84–89.

[53] Central Government's Office of Personnel Management, *Zhongguo xingzheng gaige daxushi* (General trends of administrative reform in China) (Beijing: Jingji kexue chubanshe, 1993), 236.

Growth of personnel in subnational governments accounts for most of the rapid increase in the size of the Chinese state. This fact is consistent with our decentralization of predation thesis: the expansion of the size of the subnational state is more likely to cause decentralized predation as the number of agents multiply. Official data indicate that while the number of officials employed in the Chinese national bureaucracy hardly expanded, the number of officials working for subnational governments exploded and greatly exceeded the legal limit set by the central government. Take the data for 1990, for example. The number of officials and employees in all subnational governments and party bureaucracies was 3.66 million, about 600,000 over the legal limit. Of these 600,000 "excess" officials and state employees, only 30,000 were working for provincial governments. The remaining "excess" officials and state employees — 570,000 — were agents employed in various subnational government bureaucracies.[54] The presence of more than half a million "excess" officials in various agencies of local governments is an important cause of decentralized predation — these officials must extract from society in order to support themselves. This, indeed, appears to be the case with the government agency — the local branches of the State Administration of Industry and Commerce — that wields enormous power over the private sector through its regulatory authority. Data for 1990 show that there were 44,000 excess officials and employees in the agency's local branches (about 25 percent higher than the legal limit).[55] The government's price-inspection agency also reported a similar proportion of "excess" employees. Because these two agencies function, in reality, as decentralized predators on the private sector, the local state must employ "excess" officials in order to extract more wealth from private entrepreneurs.

Another approach to studying decentralized predation is to look at the use of revenues illegally collected by subnational political authorities (as much as 10 percent of GDP).[56] Because there is no way of knowing the portion of such revenues stolen by subnational government agents, researchers may be forced to rely on various data on official corruption in China, even though, as I have explained, state predation and corruption are conceptually distinct. Analytically, one may treat corruption as a proxy of decentralized state predation because the likelihood of official corruption rises significantly in a political system featuring a high level of decentralized state predation.

---

[54] Ibid., 246–47.

[55] Ibid.

[56] State General Administration of Taxation, "Guanyu wuoguo feigaishui wenti de yanjiu," 8.

TABLE 12.4
Corruption Cases Filed and Investigated by the Prosecutor's Office

Year	Embezzlement	Bribery	Illegal Use of Public Funds	Total
1990	59,012	35,674	15,540	110,226
1991	53,835	27,275	15,762	96,872
1992	46,826	19,651	15,926	82,403
1993	49,294	20,475	22,367	92,136
1994	51,923	27,696	22,493	102,112
1995	51,340	30,080	20,618	102,038
1996	50,306	31,623	18,454	100,383
1997	47,797	27,152	18,101	93,050
1998	46,219	23,046	14,977	84,242

Source: Zhongguo falu nianjian, various years.

Among scholars who study corruption in China, there is a general consensus that the level and scope of corruption has increased dramatically since economic transition began in 1979.[57] Indeed, public opinion surveys conducted by various sources consistently show that, in the 1990s, official corruption had become one of the top three issues regarded as "of great concern" by the Chinese public.[58] But reliable estimates of the level and scope of corruption have not been attempted. In this study, we attempt to gauge the level and scope of corruption by scrutinizing published official statistics.

For obvious reasons of maintaining regime legitimacy, the Chinese government does not release reliable data on official corruption. Nevertheless, one can gain some information from the data that are openly available in China. The Chinese government publishes annual statistics on corruption cases prosecuted in the courts (tables 12.4–12.5). The data in table 12.4, which may be interpreted as illustrating the scope of corruption (i.e., the number of officials prosecuted), show that, despite public perception of runaway corruption, the number of corruption

[57] See Yan Sun, "Reform, State, and Corruption: Is Corruption Less Destructive in China than in Russia?" Comparative Politics 32 (1999): 1–20; Zengke He, "Corruption and Anti-corruption in Reform China," Communist and Post-Communist Studies 33 (2000): 243–70; Ting Gong, "Forms and Characteristics of China's Corruption in the 1990s: Change with Continuity," Communist and Post-Communist Studies 30 (1997): 277–88; Xiaobo Lu, Cadres and Corruption: The Organizational Involution of the Chinese Communist Party (Stanford: Stanford University Press, 2000).

[58] The surveys were conducted in urban areas from 1995 to 1999. Corruption was ranked as the third most important issue from 1995 to 1997; it rose to be the second most important issue in 1998; it became the most important issue in 1999. Ru Xing, Shehui lanpishu 1999, 87, 103.

TABLE 12.5

Number of Corruption Cases Involving Large Sums of Money and
High-Ranking Officials Investigated by the Prosecutor's Office

Year	Percent of Large-Sum Corruption Cases[a]	Percent of Cases Involving High-Ranking Officials[b]	Number of High-Ranking Officials Implicated
1990	22.7	1.7	1,386
1991	24.8	1.3	1,015
1992	40.6	1	652
1993	39.6	1.6	1,037
1994	47.5	2.6	1,768
1995	50.7	3.2	2,285
1996	57.1	3.6	2,461
1997	68.3	3.8	2,222
1998	31.7	4.9	1,674

Source: Zhongguo falu nianjian, various years.

[a]Cases involving large sums of money, called da an, are defined as those in which the sums of embezzlement and bribes exceeded 10,000 yuan; this sum was raised to 50,000 yuan in 1998.

[b]Cases involving high-ranking officials, called yao an, are defined as those in which government officials at or above the county level (xian) or department level (chu) are implicated.

cases prosecuted in Chinese courts remained relatively constant in the 1990s (averaging 90,000 a year). Neither was there any large fluctuation even in the types of corruption-related crimes that were prosecuted.

However, even such sanitized data show the rising level of corruption, as measured by the amount of money involved in prosecuted cases. As shown in table 12.5, the share of corruption cases characterized as "large" (involving large sums of money) tripled from 1990 to 1997. This is reliable evidence that the level of corruption, as measured by the money involved, has risen at least twofold in eight years (after adjusting for inflation). The numbers in table 12.5 also show that the scope of corruption (i.e., the type of officials involved) may have expanded greatly. Compared with the early 1990s, when high-ranking officials were implicated in only 1 percent of all cases, share of prosecuted corruption cases involving high-ranking officials rose fivefold in a mere eight years. The effects of corruption perpetrated by high-ranking officials are far more insidious than that by low-ranking officials. Obviously, because high-ranking officials serve as agents monitoring the behavior of less senior agents, corrupt high-ranking officials can hardly be relied upon to perform this function effectively. Worse still, their venal habits are likely to inspire their subordinates to engage in similar corrupt activities, thus multiplying the effects of corruption.

TABLE 12.6

Number of Party Members and Government Officials Investigated and Punished,
October 1992–June 1997

	Cases Filed	Cases Closed[a]	CCP Members Disciplined or Punished and Expelled[b]	CCP Members Both Expelled and Punished by Law[c]	High-Ranking Officials Disciplined or Punished[d]
Number	731,000	670,100	669,300	37,492	22,046
Annual average	153,895	141,074	140,905	7,893	4,641

Source: Report of the Central Disciplinary Committee to the CCP 15th Party Congress, *Legal Daily*, September 24, 1997, 1.

[a]Case closing rate is 91.7 percent.

[b]Some 121,500 were expelled, averaging 25,579 a year.

[c]The rate of legal prosecution of all disciplined or punished members is 5.6 percent.

[d]Punished officials accounted for only 3.3 percent of all punished members; only 6,812 of them, or 31 percent, were prosecuted.

Analysis of the data on corruption provided by another official, and perhaps more authoritative, source, the Disciplinary Commission of the Central Committee of the Chinese Communist Party, reveals several noteworthy features of corruption in China. Although China's top anticorruption agency does not publish detailed accounts of its work, the work report given by its chairman in 1997 offers a comprehensive picture of the extent of corruption inside the Communist Party (table 12.6). The most striking observation one may make is that China's top anticorruption agency has applied unusual leniency in dealing with party members whose malfeasance has been investigated and proven. On the surface, the committee appears to be highly effective, closing about 90 percent of the cases filed each year and meting out some sort of punishment to almost all the party members whose misdeeds it investigated and established. A closer look at the types of punishment administered by the committee makes it clear that the committee treats corrupt party members with surprising leniency. First, the majority (about 82 percent) received no more than symbolic reprimand. Only a small number — 18 percent of those punished — were expelled from the party in the six-year period covered by the report. The likelihood of criminal prosecution is low. The overall prosecution rate is extremely low — just 5.6 percent of all party members found guilty of corruption (averaging about 8,000 a year) were subject to prosecution. The data in table 12.4 indicate that the number of cases involving bribery, embezzlement, and illegal use of public funds averaged about 95,000 per year from 1992 to 1997. This suggests that fewer than 1 in 10 of the individuals prosecuted on corruption charges in Chinese courts was a party member.

The overwhelming majority of those convicted of corruption-related charges appear to be non-party members.

Despite this overall level of leniency of treatment, the anticorruption agency appears to have taken a harsher stand toward high-ranking officials (those with county- or departmental-level positions and above). The overall prosecution rate for high-ranking officials who were disciplined and punished was 31 percent—more than five times that for all party members.[59]

Explaining Decentralization of Predation

Earlier in the chapter I identified four factors that either cause or contribute to decentralized predation during regime or economic transition: (1) decentralization of property rights; (2) declining monitoring capability; (3) new exit options; and (4) erosion of ideology and institutional norms. These factors are also the underlying causes of the emergence of decentralized predation in China.

DECENTRALIZATION OF PROPERTY RIGHTS

A salient feature of China's economic reform is the decentralization of control rights (i.e., the rights over the cash flow from operations of state-owned assets) from the national authorities to provincial/local authorities. Intended as an incentive to improve the efficiency and output of these assets that were managed by local authorities, the decentralization of control rights fundamentally changed the system of property rights in China. To be sure, the process of the decentralization of control rights was gradual. In 1984 the central government decided that the control rights of state-owned enterprises (SOEs) were to be delegated from the ministries and provincial authorities to major industrial cities where these SOEs were located. Such control rights included, most critically, the rights to determine wages, benefits, and bonuses, as well as the use of capital, thus making local governments and SOE managers effective owners of these assets who would gain all the benefits of ownership but assume none of the liabilities. The central government, however, retained its control rights over large SOEs in critical sectors (such

[59] There are two plausible explanations for this surprising finding. First, the higher prosecution rate for senior officials signals the party's conscious strategy to punish senior agents more severely in order to warn *other senior agents*, given the critical position such agents occupy in the chain of command. Second, senior officials who were punished were likely those who had weak political protection. They were like a self-selecting group: their weak political protection made them more likely targets of anticorruption probes; once their misdeeds were established, their punishment is likely to be more severe due to weak political protection.

as power generation, telecom, petrochemical industries, machine tools, and coal production). Within a decade, the central government exercised effective control rights over only 5.4 percent of all SOEs (although these large SOEs generated 34.8 percent of China's industrial output).[60] Decentralization of control rights contributed to decentralized predation through several channels. It created more opportunities for local officials and SOE managers to appropriate the rents created by local monopolies and other political intervention. Indirectly, the presence of these assets with decentralized control rights would attract local predators, such as various government regulators and tax collectors, who used to be kept away by the political power of the central government. Because SOE managers now in control of these assets were politically less powerful than these local state agents, the latter could demand various illicit payments from the SOEs without fear of political retribution, thus joining in the looting of public wealth (since the liabilities of SOEs were ultimately assumed by Chinese taxpayers).

Another important trend accompanying the decentralization of control rights of state properties was the decentralization of the state's regulatory power over licensing, investment, and capital markets. Local officials now in control of such regulatory authority thus were granted enormous power to sell rents and pocket the proceeds. Strictly speaking, rents created by market distortions should be considered a form of predation (taxation) on society at large because purchasers of such rents (private entrepreneurs or foreign investors) eventually recover their rent payments through higher prices or inferior services and products.

DECLINING MONITORING CAPABILITY

Decentralized predation occurs when the principal (the state) suffers a decline in its capability to monitor its agents. In the Chinese case, a considerable decline in the state's monitoring capability seems to be another critical cause of the emergence of decentralized predation. Several factors contributed to this decline. First, a conscious policy of administrative decentralization implemented in the early 1980s moved a significant amount of appointive and monitoring power over government officials from the central government to local governments. This change was probably responsible for an absolute decline of the state's monitoring capacity. One study showed that the central government directly monitored only seven thousand officials after this decentralization.[61] The spillover effects of the decentralization of administrative monitor

---

[60] *Jingji yanjiu cankao* (Economic research and reference), July 24, 1998, 9.

[61] Yasheng Huang, "Administrative Monitoring in China," *The China Quarterly* 143 (1995): 828.

ing were profound. Granted new administrative powers by the central government but unchecked at the local level, regional political bosses were able to establish fiefdoms and gain monopolistic power. Published press reports show that such power was routinely abused, ranging from local bosses selling government offices to the rise of local mafia connected with such local bosses. Ironically, political decentralization has failed to enhance the legitimate political authority of local government officials (who in turn act as principals). On the contrary, their legal authority often declines even as their power to use illegal instruments of power increases. Press reports indicate that local government officials are often stymied in implementing government policies and enforcing laws because they face strong opposition from junior officials in control of micro fiefdoms. In one extreme case, the mayor of a medium-sized city announced that he would seek a special budget of 15 million yuan to "buy out" the power of fourteen local bureaucracies (i.e., independent monopolists) that had been living off various administrative fees and obstructing the mayor's efforts to reform local state-owned enterprises.[62]

Second, simultaneous with the declining monitoring capacity of the state is the end of mass revolutionary terror that was the hallmark of the Maoist era. In prereform China, state agents were subject to monitoring by ordinary citizens who were given unusual power by the Maoist revolutionary regime. Ordinarily, such power was exercised through various forms of open or secret denunciations that exposed misdeeds by government officials. More importantly, the Maoist regime launched periodic mass political campaigns during which citizens were encouraged to expose official corruption. Third, despite market-friendly economic policies, the post-Mao regime maintained a policy of political repression that primarily targeted the liberal intelligentsia and the media. The persecution of journalists and liberals silenced the media and degraded the media's function of policing the behavior of government agents.

EXIT OPTIONS

Availability of exit options affects state agents' calculation regarding self-dealing. Everything else being equal, the availability of such options may likely reduce the time horizon of agents, increase their discount rates on future predatory revenues, and motivate them to intensify the level of predation. Evidence from China confirms this logic. Whereas the closed system in Maoist China left few exit options available for state agents, the post-Mao economic opening multiplied exit options for them. Unencumbered by any conflict-of-interests laws, government offi-

---

[62] *Nanfang zhoumuo* (Southern weekend), August 10, 2000.

cials are allowed to serve on boards of private firms while in office and to form private firms after leaving office. New investment laws and financial autonomy allowed state-owned enterprises and local governments to make sizable investments in foreign countries, thus giving them foreign legal entities to conduct private business deals and hide illicit funds. Liberalized travel and immigration restrictions allowed children of senior officials to study and emigrate abroad. In many cases, government officials' overseas relatives and children formed offshore companies or managed nominally state-owned foreign subsidiaries that become depositories of their ill-gotten wealth. The explosion of foreign trade and investment transactions has created easy and smooth channels through which wealth plundered within China can be converted into hard currency and transferred abroad. Studies by Chinese economists estimate that capital flight — a proxy for the transfer of illicit funds from China to offshore accounts — averaged $37 billion at the end of the 1990s, representing almost 4 percent of Chinese GDP.[63]

In the Chinese case, moreover, there are two institutional features of the cadre management system that influence the time horizon of government officials. The first is the mandatory retirement of almost all government officials (except ministers and provincial governors) at the age of sixty. Originally implemented to inject fresh blood into the Communist Party and the state bureaucracy, this term-limit system drastically reduces the period during which officials may hope to collect the rents from their positions (mainly because it takes many years for an individual to work his or her way up inside the rigid official hierarchy). The second is the practice of rotation of cadres that began in 1990. As a measure to prevent the entrenchment of local political bosses, the regime frequently rotates county, prefecture, and provincial officials. The unintended effect of this institutional practice is to turn these officials, literally, into "roving bandits." As a result, such "involuntary exit" motivates Chinese officials to accelerate their schedule of rent collection. In practice, this acceleration is translated into higher taxes, fees, and bribes.

DECLINING IDEOLOGICAL AND INSTITUTIONAL NORMS

Many scholars have observed the declining appeal of the communist ideology in post-Mao China.[64] The causes of the erosion of ideology are easy to identify. Indeed, post-Mao political demobilization and pro-

---

[63] *Financial Times*, July 9, 2000, 1.

[64] See X. L. Ding, *Decline of Communism in China* (New York: Cambridge University Press, 1994); Yan Sun, *The Chinese Debate over Socialism* (Princeton: Princeton University Press, 1997); Andrew Nathan, *China's Transition* (New York: Columbia University Press, 1997), 174–97.

market economic reforms necessitated replacing the Communist ideology with economic incentives as the main source of motivation. Experience in other communist societies suggests that official ideologies must
be personalized by charismatic leaders in order to have real appeal to
the masses. As in China, the death of such charismatic leaders means
the end of the personalized ideology. Erosion of ideological appeal then
becomes inevitable in spite of the ruling parties' efforts to resurrect or
reinvent it. The lack of reliable surveys on political values (a politically
sensitive subject for the government) makes it difficult to assess the
magnitude of ideological erosion and its impact on political behavior in
China. Nevertheless, there is mounting evidence that the old-style communist ideology has lost its attractiveness to both the ruling elites and
ordinary citizens. A survey of more than seven thousand midlevel Communist Party officials conducted in the late 1990s revealed that half of
the respondents thought "communism is too far from reality."[65] The
fact that the ruling Communist Party launched innumerable "rectifica-
tion" campaigns to reinvigorate the party ideologically in the reform era
is, in itself, hard evidence of erosion of ideological values. Internal surveys conducted among a small number of officials also indicate that
they believed a renewed emphasis on ideology and morality could counter
the effects of the general moral decline.[66] Surveys conducted among Chinese youth show a similar decline of communist ideology and a corresponding rise of individualist and materialist values. When a group of
youth was asked in the mid-1990s whether "matters of the collective
are more important than those of an individual," 20 percent disagreed
and 33 percent said "don't know." Twenty-eight percent of the same
group rejected the claim that ideals were more important than money.
When asked whether one "one should seize the day to enjoy life," 31
percent said yes, and 27 percent said "don't know." Forty-two percent
of the respondents thought "human beings are born selfish."[67] Public
attitude toward bribery also seemed relatively tolerant. In a 1994 survey, respondents were asked, "if paying a bribe can solve an urgent

[65] *Zhongguo dangzheng ganbu luntan* (Chinese cadres' tribune) 1 (2000): 32.

[66] In a survey of 220 senior Communist Party officials being trained at the Central Party
School in Beijing in December 1997, Chinese researchers found that these officials identified ideological methods — including exemplary behavior by officials, moral and ethical
education — as the most effective measures for improving social norms. The same group of
officials also believed that intensive ideological and ethical education of government officials was one of the two most effective methods against corruption (the other one being
the establishment of checks and balances within the government). Lu Xueyi, ed., *Shehui
lanpishu 1998* (Social blue book 1998) (Beijing: Zhongguo shehui kexue chubanshe,
1999), 142–43.

[67] Lu Xueyi, ed., *Shehui lanpishu 1995–96* (Social blue book, 1995–96) (Beijing:
Zhongguo shehui kexue chubanshe, 1996), 240.

problem of yours, would you pay?" Nineteen percent said "definitely yes"; 35 percent said they would pay "depending on circumstances, 35%"; 22 percent replied "don't know"; and only 25 percent said "no."[68]

The direct relationship between declining ideological and institutional norms, on the one hand, and the rising level of decentralized predation in China is difficult to prove conclusively without further research and reliable empirical data. In this study, I offer this line of argument mainly to suggest a plausible link between them.

CONCLUSION

Strong state capacity is one of the basic political requirements for countries in economic and political transition. In many countries, states fail and governability declines when the state's capacity erodes during such transition process. Ironically, as this study attempts to demonstrate, state capacity tends to be the most scarce when it is most needed. For countries in transition, the greatest threat to state capacity comes from within the state. As my theoretical exploration and empirical case study suggest, state capacity suffers when various transition-related factors enable state agents to gain effective control of property rights of public assets, establish independent political/economic monopolies with little accountability, have easy exit options, and feel no ideological constraints. States that fail to control their agents risk falling into the trap of decentralized predation that eventually saps the vigor of the state apparatus. An important finding of this study is that decentralized predation is not inevitable during transition. It occurs in political systems in which decentralization of power has occurred without accompanying measures of decentralized empowerment. If the process of transition and institutional restructuring makes it difficult, if not possible, for the central political authorities to monitor and police their agents, they must politically empower societal groups and civic institutions that can counter a decentralized predatory state. The fact that, among transition countries, those that have successfully avoided the trap of decentralized predation were also the more successful in developing and consolidating democratic institutions and the rule of law suggests that to rebuild state capacity, one must first empower society.

[68] *Chinese Youth Daily*, January 21, 1995, 1.

What States Can Do Now

G. JOHN IKENBERRY

THIS VOLUME poses the question: what can states do now? This is a question that has both theoretical and real-world significance. Scholars have long been interested in determining the character and salience of states in the modern world. At the most basic level, this question concerns the logic and relative importance of the states and societies in shaping politics and policy across time and space. Other scholars are interested in the divergent character of states — party, administrative, and legal institutions — and the implications of these differences for the way a country engages in politics and confronts socioeconomic challenges. Still other scholars look more specifically at states as organizational entities — as purposive actors — and explore their capacities to operate within both their domestic society and the international system. What unifies this scholarly enterprise is a conviction that world political development, industrial society, and modernity itself have been and continue to be shaped in systematic ways by the interplay of state and society. To answer the question — what can states do now? — is to probe the importance of the basic institutional sinews of politics and to understand the changing ability of states to grapple with the deep problems of socioeconomic order and change.[1]

---

[1] This conclusion — and the chapters in the book — argue that it is useful to think of the state as an organizational entity that is at least partially separate from the larger society of which it is a part. While the society encompasses the wider territorial entity, the state is the political organization that asserts rulership of the society. It is the administrative, legal, and political institutions that together monopolize legitimate force and territorial sovereignty within its borders. This is the view associated with the writings of the German sociologist Max Weber: states are compulsory associations claiming control over territories and the people within them. "Administrative, legal, extractive, and coercive organizations are the core of the state," Theda Skocpol argues. "These organizations are variably structured in different countries, and they may be embedded in some sort of constitutional-representative system of parliamentary decision making and electoral contests for key executive and legislative posts." Theda Skpopol, "Bringing the State Back In: Strategies of Analysis in Current Research," in Peter Evans, Dietrich Rueschemeyer, and Theda Skocpol, eds., *Bringing the State Back In* (New York: Cambridge University Press, 1985), 7.

These theoretical challenges unfold in the real world where the environment in which states operate is constantly changing. The contemporary debate about the state is given urgency by dramatic shifts in the international system: the collapse of communism, the rise of market states in the developing world, the geopolitical dominance of the United States, and — in the background — the gathering forces of economic globalization. In the poor and underdeveloped parts of the world, societies are struggling to build even rudimentary states. The search is for law and order itself and legitimate institutions of government. In the former communist world the challenge is to reform and reengineer the state. Reformers seek to overturn the corrupt vestiges of state socialism and construct accountable institutions. In the advanced capitalist world there are serious questions about the viability of sovereign territorial states in an era of open markets and mobile capital. In the age-old contest between state and market, market seems to be winning. In the meantime, Western Europe — the birthplace of the modern, territorial state — is now the locale for an ongoing experiment aimed at transcending the state. But even in Western Europe, a full abolition of the state — its sovereignty, democratic authority, and national appeal — is strongly resisted. To ask the question — what can states do now? — is to seek very practical solutions to these contemporary challenges.

This book has examined these questions. The authors do not all speak with the same theoretical voice. Yet they do share the view that answers to the question — what can states do now? — will be found only through close scrutiny of the political relations between states and societies within specific, well-defined settings. Beyond this, the chapters, taken together, support three general findings.

First, states continue to be critical organizational vehicles for modern political order. General claims that states are, as such, withering away or turning into simple market agents cannot be sustained.[2] State capacities are not everywhere dwindling. As in the past, state capacities continue to evolve, declining in some areas and rising in others. There are no rival political formations — local, regional, transnational, or global — that have the full multidimensional capacities of the state. No rival political formations have come close to attracting the loyalties or normative legitimacy of the state. In many parts of the world, as Jeff Herbst's and several other chapters show, the pressing problems of everyday life

[2] For major arguments about the decline or retreat of the state, see Martin Van Creveld, *The Rise and Decline of the State* (New York: Cambridge University Press, 1999); Susan Strange, *The Retreat of the State: The Diffusion of Power in the World Economy* (New York: Cambridge University Press, 1996). For a critique, see Linda Weiss, *The Myth of the Powerless State* (Ithaca: Cornell University Press, 1998).

are generating pressures for "more state," not "less state." There is also a growing demand for the "perfecting" of the state—reducing corruption, extending the rule of law, regulating new technologies and market externalities.

This broad claim is all the more persuasive if the issue of state capacity is seen in historical perspective. States have always been political organizations with contested powers and capacities. It takes a very ahistorical or idealist image of the sovereign, territorial state to argue otherwise. Stephen Krasner has shown that state sovereignty has been compromised and transgressed throughout history and not just today.[3] The absolutist states of Europe were dependent on international banking groups to support their wars. States have continuously evolved as they have interacted with transnational capitalist society. In early modern Europe, interstate competition, technological change, and the increasing size of states and scale of war fueled the transformation in the relationship between state and society. In the years between 1400 and 1700, rulers mostly contracted with mercenary troops and relied heavily on capitalists within their region for loans and the collection of taxes. After 1700 and into the present era, states created mass armies and navies, with soldiers drawn increasingly from their own population, the military establishments became formally part of the state, and the administrative organs of the state became directly responsible for the fiscal management of the national territory. As Charles Tilly and others have shown, states have been in a continuous process of bargaining with and adjusting to mobile capitalists, and the most advanced countries have over the centuries tended to develop increasingly sophisticated extractive tools to keep pace with the expanding scale and scope of markets.[4]

This argument about the dynamic and enduring capacities of states is less controversial today than it might have been just a few years ago when the forces of economic globalization seemed to be so unrelenting. But by the late 1990s—perhaps beginning with the 1997–98 Asian financial crisis—global economic turmoil had led to widespread rethinking of unfettered open markets and given states new legitimacy to regulate trade and capital flows in the pursuit of economic stability. States are not simply agents of international capital or stripped down facilitators of economic openness. Overall, it is less convincing today than only a few years ago to argue that modern territorial states are incompatible with the great march of modernization. The terrorist events of Septem-

---

[3] Stephen D. Krasner, *Sovereignty: Organized Hypocrisy* (Princeton: Princeton University Press, 1999).

[4] Charles Tilly, *Coercion, Capital, and European States: AD 990–1990* (Cambridge, MA: Basil Blackwell, 1990).

ber 2001 also reinforce the notion that states are utterly necessary to
the provisioning of security. T. V. Paul underscored this claim in his
chapter: the state's most enduring role has been the guardian of society's
physical well-being, and there is little evidence that societal demands for
security are diminishing. The destabilizing dynamics of global capitalism and the rising threats of transnational terrorism may require new
forms of international cooperation, but it will not be a substitute for
well-run states that can enforce rules and organize protection.

The second general claim that emerges from these chapters is that
what it takes to be a strong, effective state has evolved. Capable states
today are not likely to be heavy-handed bureaucratic or authoritarian
entities. The first half of the twentieth century belonged to strong states
that could mobilize their societies for industrialization and war. Indeed,
as various moments in the interwar era, authoritarian and state socialist
regimes had a distinct advantage over decentralized, liberal-constitu-
tional states. But over the longer term, these advantages disappeared —
and disappeared with world-transforming consequences. States need to
be flexible and work efficiently with societal groups. Implicit in this
conclusion is a paradoxical claim: states that institutionally restrain the
coercive power of government — through normative consensus and legal-constitutional rules — actually unleash the ability of government
leaders to work with and through society to mobilize resources and
solve problems. The capacities of the state ultimately come from the
strength of the normative and legal order in which it operates. Societal
groups are more likely to work with rather than resist the exertions of
the state. The power of the state emerges from its ability to harness the
social capital and resources of the people it rules.

This argument is implicit in the distinction that Michael Mann made
some years ago between the "despotic" and "infrastructural" powers of
the state.[5] The despotic powers of the state are great when it can act
coercively without legal-constitutional restraint. The infrastructural
powers of the state refer to the ability of the state to penetrate society
and organize social relations. This shifts the discussion of what it means
to be a strong state. The French absolutist state in the eighteenth century was not nearly as powerful as its constitutional British rival. Its
arbitrary powers were considerable, but it lacked the ability to penetrate society and draw on the assets of groups and classes. It was not
able, for example, to tax the aristocracy, and international lenders were
much more reluctant to extend credit to France than to the British government. This gave Britain a considerable advantage in its military

---

[5] See Michael Mann, "The Autonomous Power of the State: Its Origins, Mechanisms
and Results," in John A. Hall, ed., *States in History* (Oxford: Basil Blackwell, 1986).

struggles with France during this era.[6] Likewise, during the twentieth century, democratic-constitutional America and Britain had an advantage over their fascist and state socialist rivals because they were able to mobilize for war more efficiently.[7]

Third, the chapters in this volume argued, indirectly at least, for an analytic approach to understanding the changing character of states. They argued that it is useful to disaggregate the state's functions and relationships. States are multipurpose entities that operate in many realms. Their capacities can be manifest in a variety of ways. One disaggregating step is to distinguish between various dimensions of state power and authority. In this regard, Stephen Krasner identified four types of state sovereignty. Domestic sovereignty refers to the authority of the state within the country itself. The state may be more or less capable and authoritative in its relations with society. Interdependence sovereignty refers to the ability of state authorities to control transborder flows of goods, capital, people, and so forth. International legal sovereignty refers to the status of a state under international law. Is a state recognized as a sovereign state that can enter into international agreements and treaties with representatives who are entitled to diplomatic immunity? Finally, Westphalian sovereignty refers to exclusion of external actors in the de facto operation of the domestic political system. States that are subject to manipulation by outsiders, such as the International Money Fund or a regional great power, may be legally sovereign but lack Westphalian state capacity.[8]

This formulation allows for more precise specifications of what states can and cannot do. Many poor, developing countries tend to be weak in terms of domestic, interdependence, and Westphalian state capacity. They are sovereign states only in the legal sense. The major Western states in the international system tend to be stronger in terms of domestic and Westphalian sovereignty but also highly interdependent. Indeed, as John Campbell noted, it is precisely because the advanced industrial countries have developed effective state capacities to manage their domestic socioeconomic orders that they are willing to open their borders to high levels of international economic flows. Moreover, in the small European states, as Peter Katzenstein has argued, the necessity — but also vulnerability — of being integrated into regional and global markets actually strengthens the state's position in its dealings with labor and

[6] Douglas North and Barry Weingast, "Constitutions and Commitment: Evolution of Institutions Governing Public Choice in 17th Century England," *Journal of Economic History* 49 (1989): 803–32.

[7] David Lake, "Powerful Pacifists: Democratic States and War," *American Political Science Review* 86 (1992): 24–37.

[8] Krasner, *Sovereignty*, chap. 1.

industrial groupings.[9] More generally, in disaggregating the components of state capacity, it is possible to gain a more global perspective on the state. The world is full of compromised and failed states, but the larger legal-normative structure of the state system continues to reinforce the primacy of states as the dominant political form. In other words, in posing the question — what can states do now? — it is useful also to ask: what can rival-alternative political forms do?

This book is an exercise in disaggregating and examining components or aspects of state capacity. Insights have been offered by looking at different types of states, different regional manifestations of the state, and different functional settings. It is useful to look more closely at several of these dimensions.

NORMATIVE BASES OF THE STATE

It is remarkable how varied the social and normative bases of state power have been across historical epochs. The evolution in state types — from the princely state to the dynastic state to the territorial state to the nation-state — is a grand transformation in the character of state power and the sources of state authority. The rise of nationalism and the nation-state in the late eighteenth century entailed a fundamental reworking of the state's relationship to the society in which it was situated. As John Hall argued in the introduction, the tying of states to nations — indeed the invention of "the nation" — radically expanded the power and reach of the state, even as it made the state more dependent on the consent and loyalties of society. The rise of nation-states altered the bases of state legitimacy. State leaders were driven to establish their legitimacy on the basis of their ability to manage the country efficiently and to wrap themselves in the normative appeal of the nation.[10] This normative transformation that accompanied the rise of modern states underscores the importance yet shifting character of political identity to the legitimacy of the state itself.

The chapters by Bernard Yack and Brendan O'Leary explored the complexities of nationalism as a source of state legitimacy. Yack argued that nationalism is an integral component of the liberal democratic state. Liberal democracy is a form of political order built on commitment to majority rule and limited government. Yack maintained that the critical link between liberal democracy and nationalism is popular sov-

---

[9] Peter Katzenstein, *Small States in World Markets* (Ithaca: Cornell University Press, 1985).

[10] For a recent discussion of the changing bases of state legitimacy, see Philip Bobbitt, *The Shield of Achilles: War, Peace, and the Course of History* (New York: Knopf, 2002),

ereignty. The notion of a defined community that is the repository of rights and sovereign authority gives voice to nationalist politics. The implications of this argument are several. One is simply that it is illusory to think that liberal ideals and institutions can serve to tame nationalist tendencies. If Yack is correct, it will be difficult if not impossible to cut the link between liberal forms of politics and the sources of nationalism. Another implication is that there will be a growing tension between liberal democracy and the globalization of the world system that has been promoted by liberal democratic states. If globalization undermines notions of nationalism and the bases of popular sovereignty, the underpinnings of liberal democracy itself are threatened. But it is also possible that nationalism can act as a sort of break on the globalist pursuits of liberal democratic states. This issue ultimately comes down to the question: is popular sovereignty and the nationalist politics that it promotes of greater political weight than the forces of global economic and political integration?

Brendan O'Leary argued that political orders built around heterogeneous ethnic groups put a premium on the proper construction of governing political institutions. Multiethnic states function either through the federal rule of a dominant ethnic group — a Staatsvolk — or through the operation of consociational arrangements. Ethnic divisions put at risk the nation-state, but they also provide a powerful incentive for the designing and building of state institutions. The federal option may be available to the United Kingdom because it has the English to serve as the dominant group that keeps the system together and ensures stable rule. But the European Union does not have a Staatsvolk, and so its only basis for political order is a consociational arrangement that protects the rights of the smaller European states and specifies the rules of power sharing. In effect, both Yack and O'Leary made arguments that show the limits of governance structures above the nation-state — whether at the regional, transnational, or global level. For Yack, liberal democracy is animated by and reinforces national identity. O'Leary sees limits on the ability of dominant states to centralize political authority above ethnic or national-based units without anchoring its political architecture in power sharing between weak and strong states or other political groupings.

Anatoly Khazanov argued that Russia is still in the process of building a national identity that fits with its postcommunist state. The democratic movement in Russia has struggled to articulate a persuasive civic nationalism that replaces the older imperial Russian identity and competitor ethno-national identities associated with Slavic and Asian parts of the former Soviet Union. Khazanov makes a convincing case that to build a new democratic state it is necessary to construct a new national identity, a task fraught with difficulty, situated as Russia is at the core of a failed multiethnic empire. This entails more than introducing notions of citizenship and democratic rights. A new narrative of Russian civic nationalism — a national political culture — is needed. Yet Khazanov is skeptical that there is "ideological space" in Russia for a national political identity other than ethnic nationalism, which will inevitably include authoritarian and anti-Western strands. While it is possible to have nationalist and liberal movements coincide in the West — as Barnard Yack would acknowledge — in Russia the dominant elements of nationalism tend to work against democratic ideals and institutions.

What emerges from these chapters is a powerful message: nationalist political identity is a critical aspect of society that shapes and constrains the state. Liberal democratic states are built on and encourage nationalist politics. Likewise, the emergence of nationalism, at least in the West, has strengthened states by building dynamic ties among society, political institutions, and rulers. But the specific character of nationalism — its ethnic, racial, or parochial content — can also cripple the state by creating unresolvable internal political conflict between groups or limiting the ability of democratic institutions to function. The absence of an enlightened national ideology in Russia places a severe limit on the ability of democratic institutions to effectively operate. In a very real sense, states rise or fall on the basis of the political identity of the territory and nation that they command.

A world of open markets may work to the advantage of states with particular types of national identities — particularly states with civic-oriented rather than ethnic-oriented identities. Civic nationalism is group identity that is composed of commitments to the nation's political creed. Race, religion, gender, language, or ethnicity are not relevant in defining a citizen's rights and inclusion within the polity. Shared belief in the country's principles and values embedded in the rule of law is the organizing basis for political order, and citizens are understood to be equal and rights-bearing individuals. Ethnic nationalism, in contrast, maintains that individuals' rights and participation within the polity are inherited, based on ethnic or racial ties.[11] Khazanov rightly points out that few if any states possess purely civic national identity — national identities might best be seen as existing on a continuum between civic and ethnic ideologies.

The advantages for states that have incorporated a civic national identity — such as the United States — are several. First, ethnic and reli-

---

[11] This distinction is made by Hans Kohn, *Prelude to Nation-State: The French and German Experience, 1789–1815* (Princeton: Van Nostrand, 1967). See also Anthony D. Smith, *The Ethnic Origins of Nations* (Oxford: Basil Blackwell, 1986).

gious identities and disputes are pushed downward into civil society and partially removed from the political arena. If global economic and political integration renders ethnic and religious identities within countries more insecure and conflict-prone, the most stable polities will be those that keep those conflicts semiprivatized within society. Moreover, if groups of countries — in the West but also beyond — are organized around civic nationalism, this will be a source of cohesion and cooperation. Throughout the industrial democratic world, major elements of political identity are based on sets of abstract and juridical rights and responsibilities that coexist with private ethnic and religious associations. Political order — domestic and international — is strengthened when there exists a substantial sense of community and shared identity. Civic nationalism, rooted in shared commitment to democracy and the rule of law, provides a widely embraced identity across most of the advanced industrial world and part of the glue that holds this stable and secure transregional world together. Finally, countries with civic identity have advantages in the ability to absorb and integrate immigrants within a stable yet diverse political system.[12] This integrative capacity should grow in importance. The mature industrial democracies are all experiencing a decline in their birth rates and a gradual population aging. Immigration is increasingly a necessary aspect of economic growth. A country's willingness and ability to accept immigrants — putting it on the receiving end of the brain drain — gives it an edge in knowledge and service industries. In particular, the United States, incorporating, indeed even celebrating, a civic national identity, has pioneered a new form of multicultural and multiethnic political order that appears to be stable and increasingly functional with the demands of globalization.

THE STATE AND NATIONAL SECURITY

States exist within a competitive system of states, and this has powerful and enduring impacts on their character and actions. The sovereign state was born out of war. The earliest capabilities of states — taxing and administrative organizations — were designed to generate resources to wage wars and resist conquest by other states. Beginning with Westphalia in 1648, the great postwar peace settlements have provided the occasions to codify the sovereign and territorial rights of states. Many of the great innovations of the modern state — bureaus for industrial planning and economic management, research and development agen-

---

[12] For a discussion of America's advantages in absorbing high-tech trained immigrants compared to Japan and Europe, see David Ignatius, "Europe's 'Diversity Envy,'" *The Washington Post*, June 24, 2001.

cies, and sprawling military complexes — are the result of the great wars and geopolitical conflicts that marked the twentieth century.[13] Charles Tilly captured this basic historical reality when he famously remarked that "war makes states and states make war."

Scholars of *realpolitik* offer insights about how the anarchy of international relations impacts what states do. Because there is no overarching structure of authority in world politics, such as a single global empire or world government, states are left to their own devices. This is the fundamental legal definition of state sovereignty: no authority exists above states that can act authoritatively to dictate the policies of states. States have the final word and the ultimate veto. A deep insecurity among states is the immediate implication of anarchy. A state can never be completely sure that other states will not act against it. War is never completely out of the question, even among countries that are currently quite friendly and cooperative. As a result, the capacity of the state to act strategically and mobilize societal resources will matter a great deal in alleviating these insecurities.[14] There are no absolute or simple deductions from anarchy, but the general structure of competitive interstate relations does appear to create incentives for states to promote national economic gains, protect national autonomy, and be responsive to the relative power consequences of international political and economic relationships.[15]

Over the centuries, what differentiated states from other social and political actors most fundamentally — reflecting its claim to the monopoly of the use of violence within its domain — has been its role in providing security.[16] If this function were to erode either because other actors arrogated the security role or because security itself was less essential, the very character of the modern state would be called into question. It is therefore necessary to inquire into the status of states as providers of security in the contemporary world.

T. V. Paul made the case that the circumstances that have reinforced the primacy of states over the long haul — insecurity in world politics — have not fundamentally changed. It is true that among the traditional great powers, war has been nonexistent for over fifty years. Nuclear

[13] See Daniel Deudney and G. John Ikenberry, "After the Long War," *Foreign Policy*, no. 94 (Spring 1994): 21–35.

[14] For the classic statement of the problem of anarchy, see Kenneth Waltz, *Theory of International Politics* (New York: Wiley, 1979).

[15] For a good survey of the political economy implications of realist theory, see Jonathan Kirshner, "The Political Economy of Realism," in Ethan Kapstein and Michael Mastanduno, eds., *Unipolar Politics: Realism and State Strategies after the Cold War* (New York: Columbia University Press, 1998).

[16] See G. Poggi, *The Development of the Modern State* (London: Hutchinson, 1978).

weapons and decades of Cold War stalemate among the superpowers explain a great deal of this great power peace. So too does the fact that most of the great powers are now mature market democracies that are bereft of territorial ambition and have an expanding array of shared economic interests.[17] But even if direct security threats are missing in the advanced industrial world, more diffuse insecurities still exist. Governments still spend money on defense and maintain large standing armies. Geopolitical competition from outside the West—for example, from a rising China or an unsettled Russia—is a latent worry that continues to drive the security actions of states. Outside the West, particularly in the Middle East and South Asia, the security environment looks decidedly worrisome, and it is difficult to argue that the insecurities of international anarchy have changed at all.

Although the advanced democracies do not worry about great power war and territorial invasion, insecurity has taken on wider dimensions. As Paul noted, these mature states still compete over economic and technological gains. Since the end of World War II, insecurity within these countries has expanded to include economic insecurity; it is the deep societal worries about job loss and economic instability that loom largest, and these are insecurities for which the state has claimed responsibility. Indeed, during the same postwar decades in which traditional worries of invasion and war have declined, the state's legitimacy—and the political standing of the incumbents who occupy it—has increasingly come to hinge on the provision of economic security. Moreover, economic security is measured not simply in terms of employment and steady economic growth. It is also defined in relative terms—in the ability of states to keep up with the economic and technological gains of other societies. Thus states must be actively involved in fostering investment and technological investment. American and European competition over advanced aviation technologies and markets reflects a deeper competition by major states to remain at the cutting edge of industrial modernization. In the contemporary era, it is possible to argue that the security function of states has expanded, not contracted, and this is due not to the persistence of old geopolitical threats but to the profound expansion of the collective societal definitions of security and the state's security protection role.

The terrorist events of September 11, 2001, suggest another changing aspect of the state's national security role. For the first time in its modern existence, the United States found itself directly under violent attack. The threat of catastrophic terrorist attack is a new reality for the

---

[17] For a discussion of the long era of great power peace, see Robert Jervis, "War in an Era of Leading Power Peace," *Political Science Quarterly* 98 (March 2002).

United States and the rest of the world. A small group of determined individuals not directly connected to other states may well be able to acquire biological, chemical, and nuclear weapons that can kill thousands or even millions of innocent civilians. The American political reaction to the attacks on the World Trade Center and Pentagon reveals a great deal about the modern state. The manner in which the United States mobilized itself and deployed military forces abroad shows the dramatic — if normally politically latent — capacity of the state to act in the name of national security. Administration officials have been able to pass sweeping homeland defense measures that expand the scope of the state's domestic law enforcement and surveillance role. Likewise, the rise of transnational terrorism has returned the sovereign territorial state to the center of world politics. Globalization and the new technologies that facilitate transnational society have suddenly shown their dark and dangerous side. The importance of the territorial nation-state has been reaffirmed. After all, if all governments were accountable and capable of enforcing the rule of law within their sovereign territory, terrorists would find it difficult to operate. An emerging doctrine seems to be emerging in the Bush administration: governments will be held responsible for what goes on inside their borders. A state's domestic sovereignty — to use Krasner's terms — must be made complete or that state will risk losing its Westphalian sovereignty through external military intervention by the United States. In the age of catastrophic terrorism, the world will never be completely safe until it is completely filled with sovereign states that have effectively established political control and the rule of law within their national territory. If this vision is correct, the world is just entering, and not leaving, the era of the territorial state.

The chapter by Jeff Herbst underscored the structural challenge that faces most of Africa in its search for viable territorial states. This part of the world is not contemplating postmodern political forms but rather looking for the first steps in state building. Herbst argued that the catalyst for state building in the West — interstate war — is not present in Africa. Wars on this continent tend to be inside territorial units and offer all the misery and social disarray that European wars generated in the past, but none of the positive state-building impacts. At the same time, the legal-diplomatic norms of state sovereignty extended by the international community do provide stability in formal political boundaries. As a result, political struggle between competing tribal groups do not result in the redrawing of territorial borders, a winnowing process that was at the heart of state building in Europe. If the Western pathway to political development is not available to Africa, neither is an alternative pathway visible. Herbst argued that the crafting of national political identities and national state building ideologies are necessary. But they are not likely to emerge anytime soon.

STATES AND ECONOMIC GLOBALIZATION

The most dramatic challenge to the modern nation-state would seem to be globalization. The globalization of the world economy is one of the most powerful and salient features of our age. Trade, investment, capital, services, ideas, and people are all increasingly in movement on a global scale. Few areas of the world today are outside the reach of this modernizing and expanding world economy. Rapid advances in transportation and communication technology have reduced the barriers posed by geography and distance. Governments around the world have facilitated economic globalization by embracing policies of openness and liberalization. The result is not just increasing interdependence between countries and regions, but the emergence of a complex and highly integrated system of trade, production, and finance.

There is a vigorous debate among scholars about the sources and implications of globalization. Many liberals stress the deep forces of industrialization and modernization that have and continue to alter politics, the state, and international relations. Others focus more narrowly on the effects of rising economic interdependence and see a profound impact on the ability or willingness of states to wage war. Norman Angell is remembered for arguing before World War I that war between Germany and Britain — each the second best customer of the other — was not likely because it would not pay.[18] Others stress what Albert Hirschman calls the doux-commerce thesis: that "the expansion of the market would restrain the arbitrary actions and excessive power plays of the sovereign, both in domestic and international politics."[19] The most prominent argument in the globalization debate, popularized by journalists such as Thomas Friedman, is that states are losing their capacity to shape economic outcomes, both at home and abroad.[20]

Others argue that growing economic interdependence is not fundamentally altering the state or world politics. States continue to operate within an anarchic system and will continue to respond to the incentives and constraints that anarchy imposes. States will protect their security

[18] Norman Angell, *The Great Illusion: A Study of the Relation of Military Power to National Advantage* (New York: G. P. Putnam's, Sons, 1910).

[19] Hirschman, "Rival Views of Market Society," in *Rival Views of Market Society and Other Recent Essays* (New York: Viking, 1986), 107.

[20] Thomas Friedman, *The Lexus and the Olive Tree: Understanding Globalization* (New York: Farrar, Straus, Giroux, 1999).

and autonomy within the global economy, seeking the gains of economic exchange but resisting the political vulnerabilities and security risks of economic dependence. Ultimately, as Kenneth Waltz argues, economic interdependence has "weak effects" in world politics; it is more a dependent variable than an independent variable in the relations among states.[21] Some states in the world economy — weak states — have lost their ability to control economic outcomes, but strong states have not lost their ability to manage and control external economic relations.

Other realists stress hegemony rather than anarchy and see open markets as an outgrowth of larger-order building projects by leading states. Robert Gilpin argues that open markets mirror the ongoing dynamic of rise and decline of leading states. Markets do not spring to life automatically but rather occupy the space created by the world's dominant state and its partners. The subsequent flow of trade, investment, and technology gradually redistributes power and wealth; states rise and fall; and the markets open and close accordingly. At the core of Gilpin's work is the proposition that markets are in their essence neither autonomous nor self-regulating. An open world economy, marked by free trade, currency convertibility, and capital mobility, can be secured only by the power and steady hand of a powerful leading state.[22]

John Campbell challenged the thesis that globalization is undermining or weakening the state. He argued that the extent of globalization has been exaggerated along with its effects. State autonomy and capacity have not been eroded nearly to the extent claimed in the globalization thesis. The world has witnessed a steady postwar rise in trade and foreign direct investment, but national economies — overwhelmingly more integrated at home than abroad — are still where the bulk of economic activity takes place. Nor has globalization had the radical impacts posited in popular accounts. Global capital mobility has not undermined the capacity of states to tax businesses, nor has government spending been constrained by a "race to the bottom" in the advanced industrial countries. The last decades have not simply been an era of relentless deregulation. Capital markets have been deregulated, but in other areas, such as bankruptcy policy, there has been reregulation. In some countries, such as Japan in the area of telecommunications, the initial experiment in deregulation has been reversed. Campbell's basic message is that globalization is not irreversible. States act in some do-

[21] Waltz, "Structural Realism after the Cold War," *International Security* 25 (Summer 2000).

[22] See Robert Gilpin, *U.S. Power and the Multinational Corporation* (New York: Basic Books, 1975); Gilpin, *The Challenge of Global Capitalism: The World Economy and Its Discontents* (Princeton: Princeton University Press, 2000).

mains to open markets, but their capacities to regulate markets through domestic measures or international agreements has not disappeared. This argument is strengthened by another observation by Campbell — namely, that there has been less convergence in national policies and institutions than globalization theorists expected. States can block and redirect pressures to adopt neoliberal policies for long periods of time or they can build new capacities to influence markets even as they lose other capacities.

Christopher Hood made similar arguments in the area of state taxation. The ability to tax is the sine qua non of state power. It is as vital to the primacy of states and their monopoly on the use of force. The question is whether the rise of open international capital flows is eroding the capacity of states to tax. After all, if capital is able to move abroad, the state would seem to lose its ability to extract revenues. Hood found little empirical evidence that this problem has become serious. States are still able to tax and spend in the way they have become accustomed. Indeed, the extractive capacities of the advanced industrial states have actually increased, measured in terms of taxation as a proportion of the GNP. Some major states outside the West, such as China and Russia, have experienced a decline in the ability of the state to tax, but as Min-xin Pei noted in his chapter, this has been a problem associated more with corruption and organized crime than with globalization. Likewise, Hood noted that even if international capital mobility were to pose problems for the ability of states to extract revenue by traditional means, states can develop new capacities, such as leasing state assets, shifting tax burden to domestic industries, and imposing new taxes of the Internet economy.

Rudra Sil noted that recent claims about the worldwide impact of globalization are similar to the "universalist" expectations of modernization theory. In particular, today's intensifying global competition and technological innovation are seen as pressures pushing countries toward convergent market-based practices. Sil probed this thesis as it relates to collective bargaining between national employers associations, trade union federations, and labor ministries in transitional late-industrializing countries such as India, Russia, Egypt, and Brazil. Sil found that the state remains central to collective bargaining and societal wage settlements. There is no ready substitute for state elites and political leadership in these bargaining situations. Moreover, distinct national institutional structures, which reflect variations in development strategies and ideologies, the mechanisms of governance, and particular historical experience, persist and together produce great diversity in national patterns of industrial relations. Sil argued that globalization pressures actually reinforce the state's pivotal role in the structuring of industrial relations even when, in some instances, collective bargaining is being decentralized and labor markets are being deregulated. Transitional late-developing countries may be pursuing policies that are more favorable to business interests and global corporations may be more active in the domestic economy, but Sil found no irreversible erosion in state capacity in its relations with social and business actors.

Global economic integration is a salient feature of our age, and it does have impacts on what states can and cannot do. But globalization is not simply an autonomous secular process emerging from the unfolding logic of capitalism and technological innovation. States have made active choices to open market and integrate economies. In some areas, such as agriculture, the advanced states have shown their determination to prevent open markets and trade, much to the dismay of trade economists and others. States are also making choices to reregulate markets in some areas and taking steps to shape the terms of globalization. In the aftermath of the 1997–98 Asian financial crisis, some developing countries, such as Malaysia, have imposed regulations on the inflow and outflow of "hot" capital. Disputes among mainstream economists about the virtues of unregulated capital flows serve to strengthen the hands of government officials who seek to reestablish governance in this area.[23]

Finally, states have responded to the pressures and instabilities of globalization through various sorts of international agreements. States seek to strengthen their ability to provide greater measures of domestic social and economic security by strengthening interstate governance mechanisms. States give up some formal sovereignty in the process, but in so doing they attempt to get in return some new real capacity to deliver on domestic promises. It is a political gambit of sorts for building new state capacity.

The classic case of this approach is the postwar economic settlement at Bretton Woods and its compromise of "embedded liberalism." Britain and the United States were both looking for ways to preserve an open world economy while also allowing postwar governments sufficient discretion to manage the domestic economy. The old options of either a nineteenth-century-style free trade system or a closed and managed-style national capitalism were both unacceptable, except to right-wing and left-wing ideologues. The "embedded liberal" settlement involved building a managed trade and monetary order that underpinned a relatively open system of trade and payments. However, this order

[23] See Dani Rodrick, "Trading in Illusions," *Foreign Policy* (March/April 2001): 54–62; Joseph E. Stiglitz, *Globalization and Its Discontents* (New York: Norton, 2002).

also had rules and institutions that allowed governments to protect and stabilize their domestic economies.[24]

A similar gambit is being pursued within the European Union, where national governments are attempting to increase their capacities to accomplish goals by giving up a substantial measure of sovereignty. The pooling of sovereignty within the EU may actually create more (not less) real control by states over trade and the ability to deliver on promises of economic security. Obviously, there is no simple inverse relationship between the relinquishment of sovereignty and new state capabilities, nor are all these gambits successful. But what is clear is that, perhaps paradoxically, the building of international and supranational organizations is often driven by states attempting to enhance (not relinquish) their powers.

Recent efforts to create regional trade associations, such as NAFTA, also show states attempting to use international agreements as a tool to pursue domestic economic goals. Outside Europe, the proliferation of regional trade groupings is not driven by a supranational vision. The attempted creation of regional trade associations is a by-product of insecure governments' quest for new tools to stimulate employment and a stable regional political community. To some degree, they reflect a waning in the effectiveness of more conventional macroeconomic tools, such as fiscal and monetary policy.

STATE AUTONOMY

State autonomy refers to the organizational independence of states and the ability of state officials to plan and act according to their own agendas. States with little or no autonomy are simply instruments of societal or transnational groups and interests. States with substantial autonomy have an institutional standing to resist societal pressures and develop and implement their own goals. High levels of state autonomy are not necessarily a good thing. State socialist and authoritarian regimes, after all, are highly autonomous. State autonomy is an aspect of Michael Mann's argument about "despotic" power. Likewise, states that are undergoing transitions to democracy are in the process of shedding state autonomy. But countries that have autonomous states — in the sense that they have stable political rules, legal-rational authority, corruption-free institutions, and competent bureaucracy — do tend to be

---

[24] John G. Ruggie, "International Regimes, Transactions and Change: Embedded Liberalism in the Post-war Economic Order," *International Organization* 36 (1982): 379–417; G. John Ikenberry, "A World Economy Restored: Expert Agreement and the Anglo-American Postwar Settlement," *International Organization* 46 (1992): 289–321.

successful and widely admired. When people within societies are searching for ways to promote economic development and put their country
back on a path of social advancement, they frequently are looking for
these aspects of state autonomy.

Global and regional economic integration would appear to be a long-
term threat to state autonomy. As we have seen, this is implicit in the
popular versions of the globalization thesis. Countries moving from
communist or state-socialist regimes to democratic-market systems also
place the state's organizational capacities in jeopardy. The inability of
states in parts of the developing world to mobilize their societies for
economic growth and modernization is rooted in the failure of the
states to establish themselves as effective bureaucratic and legal-rational
organizations. Several chapters in this book have explored the sources
and changing character of state autonomy.

Francesco Duina examined the autonomy of national legislatures in
Western Europe and South American where common markets and regional integration threaten to undermine state authority. The legal system of common markets deprive national legislatures of control over
trade policy and the ability to regulate the flow of goods across national
borders. The building of supranational economies would seem to doom
the capacities of national political authorities — including parliaments —
to govern. Duina, however, finds that national legislatures may lose
some levers into the economy but they retain many others, including
authority over services, labor, and capital, even though these areas are
also integral aspects of the emerging common market. National governments also retain undisputed control in areas such as culture and education. Common markets do entail a diffusion of political authority, but it
is not a straightforward process. The opening of economic borders actually activates national legislatures to expand their authority in social
and cultural spheres impacted by the expanding common market. Indeed, perhaps paradoxically, national political authorities enjoy an
increased sense of legitimacy as market integration rises, due to the
protective, stabilizing, and democratic accountability functions that national governments continue to offer. Duina found that a sort of division of labor tends to be emerging in the European Union — and to a
much lesser extent in South America — between supranational and national levels. The intrusions of the European Union and Mercosur are
highly varied across socioeconomic policy areas. Legislatures do undergo a transformation in what they do. But the implementation of
common market remains in their hands. The result is a complex and
evolving pattern of national and supranational governance in which legislatures continue to claim formal and symbolic authority.

Grzegorz Ekiert and Minxin Pei showed the different trajectories of state autonomy in Poland and China. In Poland, the postcommunist regime has succeeded in carrying out governmental reforms and establishing the state as a capable agent of political and economic modernization. Ekiert showed that the key to postcommunist transformation of Poland was the reorganization of the state itself. The sequencing of reforms mattered. The early success of political reform — and the strengthening of the administrative system of government — set the stage for effective market reform. The development of a credible state with legal-rational political authority kept the Polish government from falling into the downward spiral experienced in other postcommunist politics — what Ekiert calls the "pathologies of transformation" — namely, the decline in government authority, official corruption and organized crime, exploding social inequalities, revenue decline, and eroding social services. Political mobilization and the initial consensus about the need and direction of reforms created momentum for far-reaching governmental transformation. The result was a strong government with rationalized organizational structures. The power of the prime minister was strengthened, a professional public service was established, and the government acquired greater competence in the management of state assets.

Minxin Pei described the very different experience of China, where the state is growing weaker and more predatory. The decentralization of government authority in China is unleashing wide-spread and institutionalized political corruption. Local and regional political authorities have been able to use the transition process to gain control of property rights of public assets and establish independent political and economic monopolies. The absence of countervailing ideological controls or effective mechanisms for accountability means that there are no serious checks on the decentralized predatory actions of the state. China lacks what Poland has developed — namely, a capable yet accountable state that operates according to the rule of law to promote an efficient national economy. Political reform in China has been associated with decentralization of state powers, but it has not been accompanied by the development of mechanisms of accountability.

The accounts of changing state capacities in Poland and China underscore the more general insight found throughout this book: that effective, successful states in today's world tend to be strong but not unconstrained. States need to be flexible but also work within efficient, rule-based political frameworks. States need to be strong without being coercive. States that institutionally restrain the coercive powers of government — either because of a normative consensus on the rules of the game or through legal-constitutional rules — actually empower the state to work effectively with society. Ultimately, the capacities of states come from the strength of the normative and legal-institutional order in which they operate.

MODERNIZATION AND THE STATE

Today's Western democratic states were beneficiaries of the postwar economic boom that lifted the fortunes of the advanced industrial world. In a larger sense, they were also the beneficiaries of modernization itself. For two hundred years, the modernization of industrial societies went together with the building of capable and legitimate states. The nation-state itself was the most effective vehicle for economic and social advance.[25] This book has asked the question: are states still the predominant political form in which societies modernize and advance? The authors have found new challenges to the centrality and capabilities of states, but they have not identified new political forms that offer systematic and global alternatives to states. The relationship between the nation-state and modernity is perhaps more ambiguous today than in earlier decades and centuries, but if the relationship is awkward, they still are tied together.

In the past, Western states grew in importance as they redefined their roles and obligations and thereby consolidated the relationship among citizen, civil society, and the state. Since the eighteenth century, the development of citizenship and the expansion of the state went together. Western countries tackled the civil, political, and social aspects of citizenship in order, and in successive centuries.[26] In each great struggle a more profound set of connections was forged among the individual, society, and the evolving Western state.

The growing "fit" among citizenship, civil society, and the state that emerged in the West beginning in the eighteenth century was often more conflictual than smooth. On the European continent, states emerged before civil society. Driven mostly by war, states suddenly became important — taxing, conscripting, and encouraging loyalty. As Michael Mann puts it, "states were becoming cages, trapping subjects within their

[25] For an examination of the link between "progress" and the state, see Gianfranco Poggi, "The Modern State and the Idea of Progress," in Gabriel A. Almond, Marvin Chodrow, and Roy Harvey Pearce, eds., *Progress and Its Discontents* (Berkeley: University of California Press, 1982), 337–60.

[26] T. H. Marshall, *Class, Citizenship, and Social Development* (New York: Doubleday, 1949). See also Reinhard Bendix, *Nation-Building and Citizenship: Studies of Our Changing Social Order* (New York: John Wiley and Sons, 1964); Albert Hirschman, *The Rhetoric of Reaction: Perversity, Futility, and Jeopardy* (Cambridge, MA: Belcap Press, 1991).

bars."[27] Partly in response, civil society was itself constructed — manifest in political citizenship, nationalist ideology, and a nascent civic culture. But, increasingly, robust civic societies also provided the territorial and social base for the building of more capable states. Strong states — that is, those capable of extracting resources, commanding loyalty, and pursuing coherent goals — are not built on weak or poorly organized civil societies. The opposite is more often the case. Although seemingly at odds, the great struggles to build citizenship, civil society, and states actually reinforced each other, and together they gave shape to modern nation-states.

The rise of Western capitalism and industrialism also served to strengthen the state. Expanding economies went together with expanding national governments. Since its early moments, industrialization was dependent on the building of the legal, bureaucratic, and regulatory capacities of national governments. In the early phases of commercial capitalism, states actively set about building national markets — establishing regulatory standards, labor practices, and taxing regimes. At later stages, states became more directly involved (often as partners with capitalists) in stimulating new industries and technologies. At each stage, states also took advantage of their political sovereignty to regulate foreign trade and investment, placing themselves at the center of economic development. Along the way, the vulnerabilities of industrial capitalism also generated pressures by workers, capitalists, and others for new social services and protections. Just as states had become more tightly coupled with citizenship and civil society, so too did they become tightly coupled with industrial capitalism.[28] Even though capitalist society was, from the beginning, fundamentally transnational, states remained the vehicle of economic modernization.

Sometime in the last few decades, this close relationship between political and economic advancement and state building has been seen by some to have ended, or at least to have become more problematic. As Edward Mortimer has argued, sometime in the postwar era "modernity became global."[29] In Western Europe, where modernization is tied to European integration, and elsewhere around the world, the citizen's relationship to the state and the state's grip on society have loosened.

This volume has explored the various dimensions of the evolving ca-

---

[27] Michael Mann, "Nation-States in Europe and Other Continents: Diversifying, Developing, Not Dying," *Daedalus* 122 (1993): 117.

[28] Andrew Shonfield, *Modern Capitalism: The Changing Balance of Public and Private Power* (London: Oxford University Press, 1965).

[29] Edward Mortimer, "Identity to Cling on To," *The Financial Times*, April 4, 1994, 16. On the globalizing of modernity, see Anthony Giddens, *The Consequences of Modernity* (Stanford: Stanford University Press, 1990), 63–65.

pacities of the state. Faced with the swirling pressures of globalization and shifting societal loyalties, states have themselves evolved and adapted. States have shed some state roles and expectations; they have discovered new roles and responsibilities, and they have built international coalitions and agreements that reinforce the capacities of states. States have removed themselves from some economic spheres, but they have also found new roles in areas such as environmental protection and the guardian of national cultural values. The emerging agenda in international trade and economic talks — the so-called Doha trade round launched in 2001 — will grapple with state responsibilities to protect labor and environmental standards. Despite the rapidity of contemporary global economic and technological change, states and nation-states remain stubbornly anchored within the global political order. No great alternatives to states have arrived on the scene. Moreover, states are not prisoners of a fixed genetic code, rendering them incapable of adapting to sharp shifts in the environment. The modern Western state looks as different from its eighteenth-century forerunner as the modern multinational corporation does from the British East India Company, founded on the last day of the sixteenth century. Modernity and the state remain tied together.

Contributors

T. V. PAUL is James McGill Professor of International Relations in the Department of Political Science at McGill University. He is the author of _India in the Word Order: Searching for Major Power Status_ (with B. Nayar, Cambridge, 2002), _Power versus Prudence: Why Nations Forgo Nuclear Weapons_ (McGill-Queen's, 2000), and _Asymmetric Conflicts: War Initiation by Weaker Powers_ (Cambridge, 1994), and co-editor and contributor to _International Order and the Future of World Politics_ (with John A. Hall, Cambridge, 1999) and _The Absolute Weapon Revisited: Nuclear Arms and the Emerging International Order_ (with Richard J. Harknett and James J. Wirtz, Michigan, 1998).

G. JOHN IKENBERRY is Peter F. Krogh Professor of Geopolitics and Global Justice at Georgetown University. He previously taught at Princeton and the University of Pennsylvania. He has also served on the staff of the State Department's Policy Planning Bureau and been Senior Associate at the Carnegie Endowment for International Peace. He is the author of _After Victory: Institutions, Strategic Restraint, and the Rebuilding of Power after Major War_ (Princeton, 2001), which won the APSA book award for best book in the area of History and International Relations (the Paul Schroeder/Robert Jervis Award). He is the co-author of _State Power and World Markets_ (Norton, 2002), editor of _America Unrivaled: The Future of the Balance of Power_ (Cornell, 2002), and co-editor of _American Democracy Promotion_ (Oxford, 2000).

JOHN A. HALL is James McGill Professor of Sociology at McGill University. After reading Modern History at Oxford, he took his Ph.D. at the London School of Economics (LSE). He has taught at Southampton, LSE, and Harvard before joining McGill in 1991. His books include _Powers and Liberties_ (California, 1986), _Liberalism_ (North Carolina, 1989), _Coercion and Consent_ (Blackwell, 1994), _International Orders_ (Blackwell, 1996), _The State of the Nation: Ernest Gellner and the Theory of Nationalism_ (Cambridge, 1998), _International Order and the Future of World Politics_ (Cambridge, 1999), and with Charles Lindholm, _Is America Breaking Apart?_ (Princeton, 1999).

ABOUT THE CONTRIBUTORS

PETER BALDWIN is Professor of History at the University of California, Los Angeles. He is the author of _The Politics of Social Solidarity: Class_

Bases of the European Welfare State, 1875–1975 (Cambridge, 1990) and *Contagion and the State in Europe, 1830–1930* (Cambridge, 1999). He has a book forthcoming on the AIDS epidemic as a public health issue in historical and comparative terms.

JOHN L. CAMPBELL is Professor and Chair in the Department of Sociology, Dartmouth College, and Adjunct Professor of Political Science in the Institute of Political Science, University of Copenhagen, Denmark. His previous works include *Collapse of an Industry: Nuclear Power and the Contradictions of U.S. Policy* (Cornell, 1988), *Governance of the American Economy* (Cambridge, 1991), and *The Rise of Neoliberalism and Institutional Analysis* (Princeton, 2001). He is currently writing a book about the problems with institutional analysis in political science and sociology.

FRANCESCO DUINA is Assistant Professor in the Department of Sociology at Bates College in Lewiston, Maine, and has also taught at Harvard University. He is the author of *Harmonizing Europe: Nations States within the Common Market* (SUNY, 1999). His recent articles and essays have appeared in the *European Law Journal, Review of International Political Economy, Current Politics and Economics of Europe, Journal of European Public Policy*, and *Polity*.

GRZEGORZ EKIERT is Professor of Government and Chair of the Committee on Degrees in Social Studies at Harvard University. He is the author of *The State against Society* (Princeton, 1996), co-author (with Jan Kubik) of *Rebellious Civil Society: Popular Protest and Democratic Consolidation in Poland, 1989–1993* (Michigan, 1999) and co-editor (with Stephen Hanson) of *Capitalism and Democracy in Central and Eastern Europe* (Cambridge, 2003).

JEFFREY HERBST is a Professor of Politics and International Affairs and Chair of the Department of Politics at Princeton University. He has also taught at the University of Zimbabwe, the University of Ghana, Legon, the University of Cape Town, and the University of the Western Cape. He is the author of *States and Power in Africa: Comparative Lessons in Authority and Control* (Princeton, 2000) and several other books and articles.

CHRISTOPHER HOOD is Gladstone Professor of Government and Fellow of All Souls College, Oxford. He has held professorial positions at the University of Sydney and the London School of Economics and continues to work part-time at the LSE's Centre for Analysis of Risk and Regulation. His publications include *Explaining Economic Policy Reversals* (Open University, 1994), *The Art of the State* (Clarendon, 1998), and *Regulation Inside Government: Waste-Watchers, Quality Police and Sleaze-Busters* (with Colin Scott and others, Oxford, 1999).

ANATOLY KHAZANOV is Ernest Gellner Professor of Anthropology at the University of Wisconsin-Madison. He is the author of several books and articles on Russia and other postcommunist states, including *After the USSR: Ethnicity, Nationalism, and Politics in the Commonwealth of Independent States* (Wisconsin, 1995) and *Nomads and the Outside World* (Cambridge, 1984). His current research interests include nationalism, nation-state, and transition from totalitarian/authoritarian rule.

BRENDAN O'LEARY is Director of the Solomon Asch Center for the Study of Ethnopolitical Conflict and Stanley I. Sheerr Chair in the Social Sciences at the University of Pennsylvania. He was previously Professor of Political Science and chair of the Government Department at the London School of Economics. His books include *The Asiatic Mode of Production* (Basil Blackwell, 1989), *Right-Sizing the State: The Politics of Moving Borders* (with Ian. S. Lustick and Thomas Callaghy, Oxford, 2001), *Theories of the State* (with Patrick Dunleavy, Macmillan, 1987), and with John McGarry, *Policing Northern Ireland: Proposals for a New Start* (Blackstaff, 1999), *The Politics of Antagonism: Understanding Northern Ireland* (Athlone, 1996), *Explaining Northern Ireland: Broken Images* (Basil Blackwell, 1995), and *The Future of Northern Ireland* (Oxford, 1991).

MINXIN PEI is Senior Associate and Co-Director of the China Program at the Carnegie Endowment for International Peace. He is the author of *From Reform to Revolution: The Demise of Communism in China and the Soviet Union* (Harvard, 1994). His articles on China have appeared in *The China Quarterly, Modern China, Foreign Affairs, Foreign Policy*, and *Journal of Democracy*. His research covers democratization in East Asia and the politics of economic reform in China. He is completing a book titled *China's Trapped Transition: The Limits of Developmental Autocracy*.

RUDRA SIL is Associate Professor of Political Science at the University of Pennsylvania. He is author of *Managing Modernity: Work, Community, and Authority in Late-Industrializing Japan and Russia* (Michigan, 2002). He has also co-edited *The Politics of Labor in a Global Age: Continuity and Change in Late-Industrializing and Post-Socialist Economies* (Oxford, 2001) and *Beyond Boundaries? Disciplines, Paradigms, and Theoretical Integration in International Studies* (SUNY, 2000).

BERNARD YACK is the Lerman-Neubauer Chair of Democracy and Politics at Brandeis University. He is the author of numerous books, including *The Longing for Total Revolution* (Princeton, 1992), *The Problems of a Political Animal* (California, 1993), and *The Fetishism of Modernities* (Notre Dame, 1997). He is also the co-editor (with Judith Shklar) of *Liberalism without Illusion* (Chicago, 1996). He is currently completing a book entitled *Nation and Individual: Contingency, Choice and Community in Modern Political Life.*

Index